IRON KNIGHTS

The U.S. 66th Armored Regiment in World War II

Gordon A. Blaker

STACKPOLE
BOOKS

Dedicated to the officers, noncommissioned officers, and men
of the 66th Armored Regiment

Copyright © 1999 by Gordon A. Blaker

Published in paperback in 2008 by
STACKPOLE BOOKS
5067 Ritter Road
Mechanicsburg, PA 17055
www.stackpolebooks.com

Cover design by Tracy Patterson

Printed in the United States of America

10 9 8 7 6 5 4 3 2 1

ISBN 0-8117-3470-6 (Stackpole paperback)
ISBN 978-0-8117-3470-7 (Stackpole paperback)

The Library of Congress has cataloged the hardcover edition as follows:

Blaker, Gordon A., 1955–
    Iron Knights : the United States 66th Armored Regiment.
       p. cm.
    Includes bibliographic references and index.
    ISBN 1-57249-122-1 (alk. paper)
    1. United States. Army. Armored Regiment, 66th—History. 2. World War, 1939–1945—Regimental histories—United States. 3. World War, 1939–1945—Personal narratives, American. 4. World War, 1914–1918—Regimental histories—United States.
D769.3055 66th.B58 1999
940.54'1273—dc21
                                99-10002

Contents

Illustrations

Maps

Foreword

This book portrays the mechanics used by the 66th Armored Regiment in satisfying its basic and necessary obligation of closing with and destroying the enemy. From its baptism of fire in the mud of Flanders Fields in World War I to the triumphant march into the capital of Hitler's defeated Reich in 1945, this is the story of the Iron Knights of the 66th Armored Regiment. The arms of the 66th proudly bear the heraldic symbol of the eldest son denoting the regiment's preeminent status as the U.S. Army's senior armored regiment.

Story days, glory days, gory days, they are all here. And boring sections like countless noncombat road marches? These marches were not so boring after all. The message is: you must learn how to be there at the right place at the right time. The 66th exemplified their unit motto of *Semper in Hostes* (Always into the enemy) by taking advantage of those opportunities to engage and defeat the enemy.

The book skeleton is fact from file—facts from numerous written accounts such as official army records and after-action reports. And more facts from more files (research done in various libraries with this unit's historical documents). The evidence is that Gordon Blaker used them all. The meat: anecdotes by soldiers who were there. Gordon Blaker uses both written accounts from and personal interviews with numerous veterans of the 66th from commanders to tank drivers. The letters and diaries of the soldiers of 66th, both those who made it from "Benning to Berlin" as well as those of our comrades who paid the ultimate price, bring the story to life. Impossible to assemble all the personal memories. The samples used are vivid and meaningful.

The book is a good stone in the pyramid of the History of Combat; "Iron Knights" is a fine story.

Semper In Hostes, Iron Knights!

Captain James M. Burt, Congressional Medal of Honor
Commander, B Company, 66th Armored Regiment
April 1997

Preface

William Rape, a platoon sergeant in Company H, 66th Armored Regiment, poignantly remembered his unit's first day of fighting in the hedgerows of Normandy:

> We went down to Carentan about D plus 8 to rescue the 101st Airborne Division, who were cut off by the Germans. Those paratroopers were very grateful when we got there. We gave them food, ammunition, and anything we had that they wanted. I hope I never see anything like that again. When it was over we drove up the road a ways. The road had a high bank on either side. The German soldiers were marching in columns on both sides of the road. We caught them with artillery and machine gun fire. I had never seen as many dead in all my life. Some were leaning on the bank and looked like they were still alive. I saw the 29th Infantry boys go over and take their guns and shake them to see if they were alive. Trees were blown down, and many cows and horses were killed. I remember pulling out into a field, stopping, and getting out of my tank and sitting on a log. I said aloud, "I believe everything and everybody but us is dead."

Tech. Sgt. William Rape, 17 June 1944

The purpose in writing this history of the 66th Armored Regiment is to provide the first narrative account of the United States Army's most senior and distinguished tank regiment. The overall approach of this history is to juxtapose the accounts of the soldiers with the historical narrative drawn from the official reports and journals of the regiment. Many veterans from mechanics and tank drivers to company commanders and staff officers have provided interesting personal accounts of life in the regiment. These accounts have provided the important human dimension to the regiment's history. From these soldiers' words came a sense for the excitement, fear, and devotion these men felt in peace and war.

The history of the 66th Armored Regiment is a microcosm of the history of the U.S. armored force. It is the oldest tank regiment in the U.S. Army as indicated by the heraldic symbol for the eldest son displayed on the shield of the regimental crest. The regiment has played a vital role in the development of American armor from the beginnings in World War I through the present.

The direct ancestor of the 66th Armored was the first American heavy tank unit formed in World War I and the only one to see action during the war. The 301st Tank Battalion, as the 66th Armored Regiment's ancestor, was designated in September 1918, and fought its first battle at the formidable Hindenburg Line. This battle, in which the 301st suffered heavy casualties, taught the new American tankers valuable lessons which they were able to use in subsequent actions in the autumn of 1918. The 301st Tank Battalion had helped prove the value of the tank in combat and contributed to the defeat of Germany on the Western Front.

After the war the 301st was the larger of the two tank units to survive the military reductions that followed "The War to End All Wars." Converted to a light tank unit in the 1920s, it trained on a shoestring budget through the Inter-War Years. During this period the army leadership struggled with the problem of how tanks should be used and who should control them. After enduring several redesignations, the unit was designated the 66th Infantry Regiment (Light Tanks) in 1932. During the late 1930s the 66th served as a test for new ideas in the employment of tanks.

All doubts about the usefulness of the tank and its importance on the battlefield ended in September 1939 when German tanks crushed Poland using Blitzkrieg tactics built around a fast moving armored force. As the only fully formed and active tank regiment in the army in 1939, the 66th took the lead in developing and testing new tactics, weapons, and equipment. Under the bold leadership of George S. Patton the regiment trained hard for the war that Patton and many other professional soldiers were certain would soon touch the United States. The 66th played a leading role in the great army maneuvers of 1941, which served as a test of the army's tactics, leadership, and equipment, especially the tank. The newly created 2nd Armored Division, with the 66th Armored Regiment's light tanks, showed that there were few places a tank could not go to crush the opposition in record time.

The regiment entered the war by landing on the shores of North Africa in Operation Torch, where a part of the regiment fought its first action against a Vichy French tank force four times its size. After a period of amphibious training, the 66th Armor landed in Sicily and fought from the beach north to Palermo. After the Sicilian campaign the regiment moved to England to prepare for the invasion of Normandy.

The 66th, having gained battlefield experience in the Mediterranean theater, landed on Omaha Beach in the second week of June 1944. In Normandy the regiment was heavily involved in some of the bloodiest hedgerow fighting before the St. Lo breakout. While fighting in the encircle-ment of the ancient German capital of Aachen, Capt. James M. Burt, a tank company commander in the regiment, earned the Medal of Honor. During the Battle of the Bulge the regiment marched seventy miles one night to attack the north flank of the German salient. After the Battle of the Bulge the 66th returned to Germany and fought across the North German plain against often fanatical resistance, ending the war on the Elbe River.

My thanks to the hardworking and always helpful staff of the follow-ing institutions: The National Archives, Washington D.C. and Suitland, Maryland Branch; the Patton Museum of Armor and Cavalry and the U.S. Army Armor School Library, Fort Knox, Kentucky; the U.S. Army Mili-tary History Institute and the Army War College Library, Carlisle Barracks, Pennsylvania; the Army Center of Military History, Washington D.C.; and the Second Armored Division Museum, Fort Hood, Texas.

My respect and thanks to the following veterans of the 66th for con-tributing their letters, diaries, memories, and photographs: Edmund Bedat, Chaplain Luke Bolin, Lt. Fred Brems, Ralph Brill, Sgt. Patrick Burke, Capt. James Burt, George Campbell, Maj. Curtis Clark, Capt. Donald Critchfield, T/5 Edward Cuthbert, Lt. Foster Davis, Chief John Derden, 1st Sgt. Tho-mas Domarecki, Don Evans, Sgt. Jack Fabian, Peter Facelli, Sgt. Arden Gatzke, John Gedney, Lt. John Getsinger, Cpl. Kenneth Grogan, S.Sgt. Herbert Gwinn, Lt. Col. Lindsay Herkness, Jr., Sgt. David Hetherington, Vince Hooper, M.Sgt. Bernard Hylinski, Sgt. Ben Kulig, George Lincoln, Sgt. Harry Martin, Lt. Lennie Mathews, Sgt. John Mayo, Capt. Coulter Montgomery, Cpl. Louis Morett, Lt. William Page, Maj. Norris Perkins, Henry Raab, S.Sgt. Bill Rape, Capt. John Roller, Lt. Lamar Russell, Lt. Lewis Sasser, Lt. Finis Smith, T/5 Frank Stanley, Cpl. Randall Steady, Maj. Cameron Warren, Henry Williams. This is their story.

Thanks also to the ladies of the regiment who contributed to the story. Mrs. Amzi R. Quillian, Mrs. Sally Q. Gates, Mrs. Celeste Sasser Springer, Mrs. Luke Bolin, Mrs. John Roller, Ms. Pat Collins, Ms. Mary Lynn Pete, Mrs. Beverly Warren-Leigh.

A special thanks is owed to the following veterans who helped and contributed a wealth of material and assistance: Dr. Norris H. Perkins, who collected the memories of fourteen members of his company and provided me with constant support and encouragement; Capt. James Burt, recipient of the Medal of Honor, for writing the foreword and being a generous contributor of his memories; the late Cameron G. Warren whose support and faith in my work has made this book possible.

Thanks to my proofreaders: Sheri Edvalson, Tamara Miles, and my wife, Karen. Thanks to my map-makers: Mark Thomson and Stacy Booth. Thanks to my photographers: Dr. Norris Perkins and Danna Johnson. Special thanks to Dr. Mary Lou Ruud and Dr. Jane Dysart for their guidance and endurance.

The greatest debt of gratitude I owe to my friend and fellow tanker (retired) Mark Thomson who single-handedly entered the entire first draft into the computer while also proofreading and providing armor-wise comments on the manuscript. Once again, Mark, I could not have done it without you.

My wife, Karen, has given up much to help me in writing this book, and I deeply appreciate it.

Overall, the history of the 66th Armored Regiment is the history of the American armored force. No other American tank unit has existed as long and as continuously as the 66th Armor. The history, development, and tactics of the U.S. armored force are reflected in the history of the 66th Armor. The 66th's history lies in the story it tells about the American soldiers who served in the regiment. The soldiers' letters and diaries and the accounts of the veterans can provide a sense of what it was like to serve in the tank unit that was always on the cutting edge of the American armored force.

"Always Into the Enemy"

Introduction to American Military Organization

The purpose of this section is to provide those readers unfamiliar with military organizations with the basic knowledge necessary to understand armored (tank) units.

The rank structure of the United States Army is very similar to that of almost every army in the world. This structure, as it evolved through history from its beginning in the Roman Army, is divided between officers and enlisted men. Officers generally enter the army with a college education from West Point or a civilian college or university. The officers are responsible for leading and commanding the men of their units in peace and war. They generally plan the training and movements of the unit. Officers are expected to serve as an example to their subordinates at all times. American army officers have a long tradition of leading their men personally and sharing the hardships.

The enlisted ranks are made up of two groups: the noncommissioned officers and the enlisted men or troops. The noncommissioned officers (NCO) are the professional soldiers who form the backbone of the army. The NCOs handle the daily training and duties of the enlisted men. In an armor unit, the NCOs hold the two senior positions on a tank crew: those of tank commander and gunner. The more senior ranking NCOs also occupy key positions in each unit from platoon through army. The NCOs generally train and tutor new officers as they learn the skills necessary to lead their units. All officers, from lieutenant through general are usually wise to listen to the advice and counsel of their experienced NCOs.

The lower enlisted men, also known as troops or soldiers, are the primary fighters and workers of the army. These men are the newest members of the army with up to four years in service. Many of them are not professional soldiers and will return to civilian life after serving their enlistment period of three to six years.

The organization of the units in the United States Army underwent several changes during the period 1918–1945. The following section is generalized to provide a basic knowledge. The details of organizational changes will be addressed as they occurred in the text.

The most basic element of an armor unit is the tank crew, in World War II generally five men. The senior man on the tank is the tank commander (TC), normally an NCO in the rank of sergeant or staff sergeant. He is responsible for the training, safety, welfare, and performance of his crew and the tank. The next man is the gunner, normally an NCO with the rank of sergeant or corporal. The gunner is responsible for the aiming and firing of the tank main gun and coaxial machine gun (mounted next to the main gun) at targets directed by the TC. The driver, bow machine gunner, main gun loader, and (on the M3 Lee) the radio operator round out the crew; all of these men are enlisted soldiers.

The next level of organization is the platoon, which consists of five tanks and is led by a lieutenant, who also commands one of the tanks (in armor units, all commanders up through battalion also command the tanks on which they fight). A platoon sergeant, who also commands one of the tanks, assists the platoon leader. He is the senior NCO, normally a technical sergeant.

Three platoons and a headquarters section make up the tank company. Commanded by a captain, with a lieutenant as an executive officer (second in command), and assisted by a first sergeant, the company is really the basic armor element. There are two tanks in the company headquarters section, one of which is used by the company commander. The other tank normally carried the field artillery forward observer attached from the supporting artillery battalion (he directs the supporting artillery fires). Other parts of the headquarters section provide support in the form of maintenance, supply, and food (termed mess). There were approximately 100 men in a World War II tank company. The field artillery equivalent to the company is a battery, and in the cavalry, a troop.

The tank battalion is generally the lowest echelon capable of independent operations. The battalion consists of three tank companies and a large headquarters company and is commanded by a lieutenant colonel. The strength of the battalion runs to about 39 officers and 700 enlisted men, and mans 59 tanks and 180 other vehicles. The commander is assisted by a major serving as the executive officer and a staff that works in the functions of personnel, intelligence, operations, and logistics (modeled after the French system, these positions are S1 through S4, respectively), with additional specialists in maintenance and communications, all in turn supported by teams of specialists. The S1 (also referred to as the adjutant) is usually a captain, and he controls all the personnel functions for the battalion, including orders, transfers, promotions, correspondence, and awards, to name a few. The S2 section is also led by a captain and handles all matters related to intelligence gathering and analysis. The S3 is the senior staff member, usually a senior captain or major, who is responsible for planning the battalion's operations and training, as well as helping the commander control the battalion's activities in peace and war. The S4 section, led by a captain, handles all of the logistics for the battalion, covering a wide range from ammunition and fuel, to food, water, repair parts, and any other supplies needed. The staff is but one part of the headquarters company. The bulk of the company consists of specialty platoons: maintenance, communications, reconnaissance, mortar, and others.

The armored regiment, commanded by a colonel, was composed of three tank battalions and a number of specialized companies, to include reconnaissance, machine gun, and maintenance. The approximate strength was 130 officers and 2,200 enlisted men. The brigade was of similar strength and organization but made up of battalions from different branches, usually a mix of armor and infantry.

A division usually consisted of three regiments, supporting artillery (four battalions, referred to as the Division Artillery or Divarty), and a number of specialized battalions. The division commander was a major general (two stars) assisted by two brigadier generals, one of whom was the assistant division commander and the other the artillery commander. The corps was a flexible structure that could have from two to five divisions, with the number varying over time, and several specialized battalions and brigades (tank destroyer for example). Corps were commanded by major generals for the most part during World War II.

ARMY ORGANIZATIONAL CHART

Rank	Abbre-viation	Years in Service	General Position
Officer			
General	Gen.	28–40	Theater Commander
Lieutenant General	Lt. Gen.	26–40	Army Commander
Major General	Maj. Gen.	24–35	Corps/Division Commander
Brigadier General	Brig. Gen.	24–30	Assistant Division Commander
Colonel	Col.	18–26	Regimental Commander

(continued)

Rank	Abbre-viation	Years in Service	General Position
Lieutenant Colonel	Lt. Col.	10–20	Battalion Commander
Major	Maj.	8–15	Battalion Executive Officer/S3
Captain	Capt.	3–10	Company Commander/Bn Staff
First Lieutenant	1st Lt.	1–4	Company Executive Officer
Second Lieutenant	2nd Lt.	0–2	Platoon Leader
Enlisted			
First Sergeant	1st Sgt.	10–24+	Company First Sergeant
Master Sergeant	M.Sgt.	10–24+	Battalion Staff NCO
Technical Sergeant	T.Sgt.	8–15	Platoon Sergeant
Staff Sergeant	S.Sgt.	6–12	Tank Commander
Sergeant	Sgt.	3–9	Tank Gunner/Commander
Corporal	Cpl.	2–5	Tank Gunner
Private First Class	Pfc.	1–3	Tank Crewman
Private	Pvt.	0–1	Tank Crewman

PART I

The Beginnings
1918–38

CHAPTER 1

Join the Tank Corps!

Dawn broke over the Western Front trenches near Flers on 15 September 1915 just like most other autumn mornings in France with a light ground fog. Attacks often began at dawn and the British Somme offensive was now three months old. The German infantry were on full alert but nothing could have prepared them for the gigantic steel monsters that crawled slowly towards them that morning. The British army was using tanks for the first time in an effort to break the stalemate of trench warfare. Faced with something new and terrifying, the German infantry fled and the tanks reached their objective. A new age of warfare had begun and American soldiers would soon learn about the tank first hand.

The lineage of the 66th Armored Regiment began when its ancestor, the 1st Separate Battalion, Heavy Tank Service, 65th Engineers, was formed in February 1918.[1] Since April 1917 when the United States entered World War I, the United States had been struggling to create a new and much larger army. The United States Army soon realized it needed to follow the other warring powers by creating a tank force.

The tank was born of the need to break the stalemate of trench warfare. A vehicle was needed that would cross wide trenches, crush barbed wire entanglements, and destroy machine gun nests. The tank was a combination of the track-laying tractor that could cross or crush almost anything and the successful armored cars in use since the beginning of the war. The very traditional British army intially rejected the concept of the tank. After rejection by the army, First Lord of the Admiralty, Winston S. Churchill, directed development of the first British tank by the Royal Navy in 1915.

The reason many parts of the tank have naval names to this day is a result of this early sponsorship of the "land ships."

By January 1916 the first British Mark I tank, known as "His Majesty's Landship Centipede," or more commonly, "Mother," underwent trials.[2] This first tank weighed about twenty-eight tons and moved along at just over three miles per hour. Measuring approximately thirty-two feet in length, fourteen feet in width, and eight feet high, it was an impressive sight. The first tanks and all the later World War I British versions were made in two basic types. The "male" type was fitted with a six-pound cannon in each of its side sponsons. The "female" carried machine guns instead.

This new and very secret weapon was shipped to the Western Front labeled as a "tank" because, covered by a tarpaulin, its size and shape resembled a giant water container. The first tanks entered battle at Flers-Courcelette during the Somme offensive in September 1916. Although few of the nearly fifty tanks reached their objective, those that did proved their worth.[3] Equipped with two cannon and four machine guns, these monsters were able to cross an eleven-foot trench and crush through yards of barbed wire. The race to build more and better tanks followed.

In February 1918 the U.S. Army began recruiting soldiers for the formation of the first tank units. "High quality men were sought for this new and fascinating branch of the army."[4] Men were recruited from army camps around the country. The first heavy tank battalion was formed at Camp Meade, Maryland. By the last week of February enough volunteers had arrived to organize four companies. The first three companies, A, B, and C, became the 1st Separate Battalion.[5]

The recruiting poster of the Tank Corps portrayed a fierce black panther lunging forward with bared teeth and claws beneath the motto "Treat 'Em Rough."[6] In the background heavy tanks were fighting on a battlefield of trenches and barbed wire. The bottom of the poster read "Join the Tank Corps."[7]

The volunteers from every branch of the army spent most of their first month undergoing what seemed like endless drill and inspections. The schedule was lightened somewhat by drill competitions and baseball games. On 16 March the unit was redesignated as the 1st Heavy Tank Battalion, Tank Service.[8] Awakened by reveille at 0445 hours on 20 March the battalion had a full physical examination, an inspection, and a march with full field packs.[9] This long day was the battalion's final exam before departing Camp Meade.

The battalion marched out of Camp Meade on the morning of 23 March and boarded a train. After a brief rest stop in Philadelphia, the men spent the night in the old day coaches of the train halted in the Jersey City rail yard. After arrival and a very brief stay at Camp Merritt, New York, the battalion boarded a ferry on the Hudson River at Hoboken and was carried to the largest ship in New York Harbor, the White Star Liner, *Olympic*. The massive vessel was crowded with thousands of soldiers who were trying to navigate around the ship's interior with the assistance of small cards bearing instructions similar to this:

Keep this card No. 75
Your Quarters are on Deck F
    Compartment E
You will occupy
    ONE BERTH
You will mess in Compartment X
At mess No. 31 – 2nd Sitting[10]

At 1030 on 28 March 1918 all soldiers were ordered below, so as not to give German spies any information as the *Olympic* set sail. When the men were allowed back on the deck, the Statue of Liberty was already lost over the horizon. That first afternoon the soldiers watched the British crew prepare their six-inch guns for action against the dreaded German U-boats. As darkness fell, all portholes were covered, lights were masked, and the soldiers ordered below as the convoy blacked out.[11]

On Friday, 5 April, the *Olympic* arrived safely in the harbor of Brest, France. As the new American tankers watched, all the other American troops disembarked. The next afternoon, with only the 800 men of the battalion left as passengers, the *Olympic* departed France. That night while en route to Southampton, England, the men experienced a real U-boat alarm when a nearby freighter was torpedoed.[12]

The battalion disembarked late in the morning on Monday, 8 April, and marched three miles to a temporary rest camp in the beautiful countryside near Southampton. On their first evening in England the battalion was treated to a band concert at the American YMCA. The next morning the tankers marched back to Southampton and boarded a train for the town of Wareham in Dorset. All the residents of Wareham turned out to give the Americans a rousing welcome. A local band led the battalion through the town, and the village schoolmaster led the children in giving the Americans three cheers.[13]

On 9 April 1918 the battalion arrived at Camp Worgret where they were billeted in six rows of one-story barracks. The British beds consisted of three long boards stretched across two small trestles topped with a straw-filled sack. These were quite a surprise to the Americans, but the adventurous Yanks were delighted to discover that they shared the camp with the Women's Army Auxiliary Corps, known as "Waacs."[14]

After a full day of rest and exploring the local pubs, the men began their training on 11 April. They were under the leadership of the white-sweatered instructors of the British Army Physical Training Corps. After being issued rifles and bayonets, neither of which were a part of a tank soldier's equipment, the men began learning bayonet drill. Other training included semaphore signaling, British army drill and marching, and physical training ("P. T.").[15]

In late April the battalion was redesignated for the second and third time since February. On 16 April the unit became the 41st Heavy Battalion, Tank Corps. Shortly thereafter the unit designation was again changed, this time to the one it would retain throughout the war, 301st Tank Battalion.[16]

On 7 May 1918 the Americans began their first tank training. The three companies of the battalion rotated from Camp Worgret through the different courses of training at Sanford, Lulworth, and the main tank training camp at Bovington. At Bovington the British Tank Corps had created a training area to look just like the Western Front, with trenches, craters, and shattered trees.[17]

The U.S. tankers were very impressed by the competence of their British instructors and the thoroughness of the course.[18] The maintenance courses covered all aspects of the tank, its engine and track. The instructors patiently and thoroughly explained all the workings of the heavy tank, assisted by detailed charts and models. The classroom instruction was followed by days of hands-on work in the heat, grease, and grime of the huge vehicles.

The tank on which the battalion was trained was the Mark IV. This tank, introduced in the summer of 1917, was an improvement over the previous Marks. It had thicker armor (12mm) and many other modifications that added to the efficiency of the crew. The tank crew on these vehicles consisted of eight men. The tank commander, generally an officer, sat beside the driver in the front turret. Two gearsmen were located near the rear of the tank and had to change the gears and use the brakes to help the driver steer the tank. All four crewmen were required to drive the tank. Two other men manned the six-pound cannon in the front of each sponson, and the last two men fired the machine guns mounted in the rear of the sponsons. Two additional machine guns were on board, one located in the front turret and the other in the rear compartment.

The Mark IV weighed 28 tons, but, driven by a Daimler six-cylinder engine that produced only 100 horsepower, it was underpowered.[19] Still, the tank moved along at almost four miles per hour. Despite its faults, the Mark IV was the first tank produced in large numbers (1,100).[20]

After several frustrating months of training the men were on real tanks:

we were happy, for what was there more to be desired than a place on the driver's seat, and the thrill of pulling a monster out a deep trench, nose pointing to the sky with the engine's deafening roar, the acrid never-to-be-forgotten smell of exploded gas, scorching grease, and hot steel, the quick shutting down of the throttle, the gentle swing to earth, and then the triumphant roaring answer of the engine to the opening of the throttle and the more-the-merry clanking of the track plates.[21]

The camps at which the battalion trained varied considerably in the quality of their accommodations. Wareham with its wooden barracks was comfortable. At the other end of the spectrum, however, was Sanford, which consisted of a small group of tents at an abandoned pottery.[22] Eleven miles away at Lulworth Camp the men could visit the beach or the fine hotels and restaurants of the seaside village. Memorial Day weekend passes allowed the men trips to London, Poole, and Bournemouth.[23]

Brig. Gen. Samuel D. Rockenbach, a cavalry officer, was appointed the first chief of the U.S. Tank Corps in December 1917. In the early summer, Rockenbach made a deal with the British for the 301st to receive British heavy tanks. This was necessary because production problems were delaying the arrival of the new Anglo-American tank until the fall. The British agreed to outfit the 301st in exchange for the battalion to be attached to British forces in France.[24]

At Lulworth, and later Hyde Heath, the Americans trained in gunnery with the tanks' six-pound cannon. After firing from a stationary tank the men took turns firing the gun while the tanks were moving. Throughout the summer the 301st Tank Battalion prepared for the day when they would join the British and French tankers on the battlefield.[25]

When Brigadier General Rockenbach inspected the 301st Tank Battalion, he expressed his views about the nonsense of tankers carrying rifles and bayonets. This opinion came much to the delight of the soldiers. A week later Brigadier General Glasgow, commander of the British tank training, also inspected the battalion. These visits gave an indication that the battalion was soon to leave for France.

On 23 August 1918 the 68 officers and 768 enlisted men of the battalion left Camp Worgret, now called Headquarters 301st Center, Tank Corps American Expeditionary Force (A.E.F.) and boarded a train for Southampton en route for France.[26] Upon departure the men wore the olive drab (O. D.) wool uniform, overseas cap, shoes, and wrapped puttees (leggings).

Individual equipment consisted of a helmet, pistol with belt and holster, gas mask, first aid pouch, and full infantry pack. The soldiers also carried a small amount of additional clothing, such as an overcoat and two pairs of socks, in "squad rolls."[27] Each company headquarters brought along a small field desk, typewriter, medical case, a crate of office supplies, and 300 pounds of cooking utensils.[28]

The battalion arrived at Le Havre on the morning of 23 August. After a brief stay in some dirty cattle sheds-turned-barracks, the 301st packed into railroad box cars for an overnight trip to the village of Bermicourt. On 30 August a group of officers and noncommissioned officers left for a visit to the front line near Arras. Very early the next morning two sergeants from Company C were killed by German artillery fire while advancing with a British tank unit. The next, happier, event was the issue of the battalion's own tanks. The men eagerly set to work preparing their tanks for action, realizing that their lives could easily depend upon the mechanical condition of their tanks.[29]

The tanks the 301st received were new Mark Vs and Mark V Stars. The Mark V improved on the Mark IV that had been used in training by enabling the driver to control the vehicle without assistance. The Mark V Star was six feet longer than the standard Mark V, allowing it to cross trenches that were up to thirteen feet wide and to carry extra troops and supplies. The more powerful 150 horsepower engine of the Mark V was offset, however, by the Star's thirty-three ton weight. Both the Mark V and the Star were made in three versions. The male mounted a six-pound gun in the front of each side sponson. In the female edition the six pounders were replaced by machine guns. The composite, or hermaphrodite, had a six pounder on one side and a machine gun on the other.

The battalion received forty-one tanks and issued them as shown in the chart below.[30]

	Mark V Star Male	Mark V Star Female	Mark V Star Composite	Mark V Male	Mark V Female	Mark V Composite	Total
Co. A	9	2	4				15
Co. B	7	2		3	1	3	16
Co. C				7		9	16

After a few days of mechanical work and cleaning, the tankers were met with their first challenge. They had to load the tanks onto rail cars, probably the only task for which they had not been trained. The time and labor spent in loading the huge vehicles on the flatcars was an indicator to the men of the large amount of work involved with being in the tank battalion.

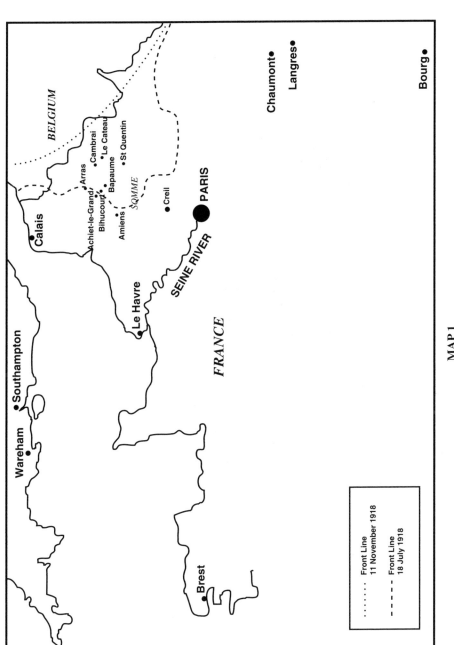

MAP 1
France 1918

Wareham
Southampton
Calais
Belgium
Arras
Achiet-le-Grand
Bihucourt
Bapaume
Amiens
Cambrai
Le Cateau
St Quentin
SOMME
Creil
Le Havre
PARIS
SEINE RIVER
FRANCE
Brest
Chaumont
Langres
Bourg

Front Line
11 November 1918

Front Line
18 July 1918

BRITISH
MARK-V-STAR
TANK
MODEL – – – 1918
WEIGHT – – 32 TONS
SPEED – – 4 M-P-H
CREW – – 8 MEN
GUNS – – 2-6 PDRS
4-MGS

Mark V (Male) tank used by the 301st Tank Battalion.

Norris H. Perkins

Once loaded, the train traveled through Arras during a heavy German shelling, giving the battalion their baptism of fire. On the morning of 7 September the battalion detrained at the Achiet-le-Grand railhead and moved to the small village of Bihucourt.[31]

The village had been totally destroyed, so the 301st moved into the recently vacated dugouts built by New Zealand soldiers. The Americans quickly adapted to life below ground, making the rat-infested, soggy dugouts as comfortable as possible. Discarded petrol cans were valued because they could serve a wide variety of functions, from cooking pots and wash pans to shelves and pillows.[32]

On Sunday, 8 September, the battalion's brigade commander, a British general, inspected the unit and promised to treat them as his own. For the next two weeks the men worked on putting their tanks into prime condition. Many of the vehicles had suffered damage from the train ride through the German bombardment on the trip to Bihucourt. They oiled, checked, and sighted the guns. Ammunition was tested and loaded aboard the tanks. In addition the men carefully installed and checked the compasses, an invaluable accessory on the shrouded battlefield.[33]

During this time the men had many new war experiences. They saw a captured German A7V tank and dead German soldiers for the first time. They experienced a night air raid, during which one of the German planes was shot down in flames. The Americans' dislike of "The Hun" grew as they saw evidence of German desecration of an old French cemetery and a soldiers' monument in Bapaume.[34]

On the morning of 19 September the battalion commander and company commanders of the 301st held a conference. The commander of their parent unit, the 4th Tank Brigade, outlined the Allied plan for an attack on the Hindenburg Line, a strong German defensive belt established earlier that year.[35] For this attack the 301st would be under the command of the 4th Brigade which was to be attached to the U.S. 27th Division, a part of the American II Corps assigned to the British 4th Army.[36] The 4th Tank Brigade consisted of the 301st, two British tank battalions (1st and 4th), and the British 4th Tank Supply Company.[37]

Unfortunately for the 301st and the 27th Division, their assigned sector was one of the most strongly defended positions of the Hindenburg Line. The American sector was opposite the seven-kilometer long St. Quentin Canal Tunnel. This interesting tunnel had been built between 1802 and 1810 and carried the canal underground through the French countryside.[38] It was the place where the tanks could attack the German lines without crossing the canal, an attack the Germans expected and prepared for.

The battalion moved on four trains from Achiet le Grand to Equancourt on 21 and 22 September. Each of the four trains arrived after dark to prevent German observation.[39] The battalion then moved about two miles to a wooded valley near Manancourt where the men spent the rest of the night camouflaging their tanks. Most of the tankers slept under their tanks or beneath tarpaulins hung from the side of the tank. They occupied their days repairing items damaged during the last trip and making further preparations for battle.[40]

At a planning conference on 23 September, the commander of the 301st was ordered to coordinate at once with the 27th. The following evening the commanders of the 27th Division and the 301st initiated their planning and coordination. One tank company would support each infantry regiment in the attack by crushing the barbed wire and knocking out the German machine-gun nests. The unit commanders met to coordinate link-up of their units, signals to be used, and how the two units could support each other during the attack. The tank companies were allotted to the infantry regiments of the division with Company A (fifteen tanks) to the 107th Infantry and Company C (fifteen tanks) to the 108th Infantry. Ten tanks of Company B were assigned to the 105th Infantry Regiment. The seven remaining tanks of the 301st were allotted to the reserve force of the Australian Corps.[41]

On 25 September the 27th Division headquarters hosted a conference attended by all the officers of the 301st down to the section leader (five tanks). From that conference until the attack date (Z day) the tank officers met daily with their infantry counterparts.[42] The battle plan was for the 107th Infantry supported by Company C's tanks to advance on the left side of the division sector. The 108th Infantry supported by Company A would advance on the right in the 27th Division sector. Both infantry regiments would advance with two infantry battalions abreast, followed by one battalion in reserve. One section of five tanks would lead each infantry battalion. The 105th Infantry, as the division reserve with the ten Company B tanks, followed the 107th Infantry utilizing the same formation as the lead regiments.[43]

CHAPTER 2

Into the Breach:
The Hindenburg Line Attack

On the nights of 27/28 and 28/29 September the battalion moved first to Villers-Vancon and then to the start line of the attack. On the afternoon of the twenty-eighth (Y Day) at Villers-Vancon, the tanks were refueled and lubricated. The second night's approach march proved to be very difficult. The tanks moved out at 2200 hours to cover the 8,500 yards forward to the start line. The last part of the route from the "lying up place" to the start line, a distance of 3,000 yards, had been marked by the reconnaissance parties of the battalion. One sergeant was killed and two officers wounded in the marking of the routes. The battle plan also included aircraft flying in the area to mask the noise of the approaching tank engines. Only one plane was heard that night, but the artillery fire apparently was successful in masking the tank noise. The approach march was made under an artillery barrage of high explosive and gas.[1]

In spite of all the coordination with the infantry regiments prior to the attack, a major problem arose between Company C and the 107th Infantry. Because a preliminary infantry attack on 28 September had failed, the regiments of the 27th Division were 1,000 yards short of the start line. All units had been instructed to adjust their start time to ensure that they crossed the start line at the Z hour of 0700. The commander of the 107th decided not to adjust his unit's start time. As a result Company C went into the attack without infantry. The 107th Infantry lagged far behind and never caught up with Company C or the units on either flank.[2]

As the tanks of Company A crossed forward of the British front line en route to the start line, two were destroyed by British mines. These mines

13

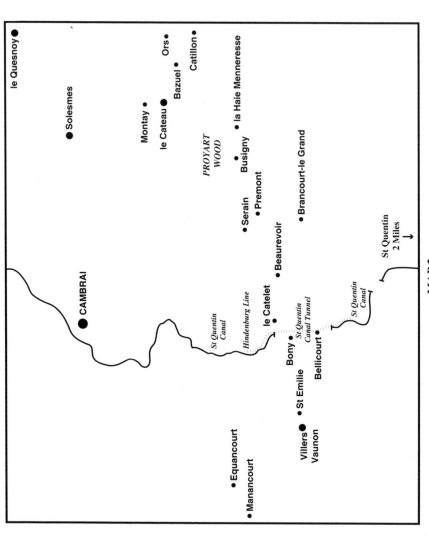

MAP 2
The Somme
August–November 1918

had been emplaced that spring and forgotten until Company A had the misfortune of finding them. Companies A and C crossed the start line on time and just behind a rolling artillery barrage. This barrage moved barely ahead of the friendly forces at a rate of 100 yards every four minutes. For the first hour of the attack the artillery support worked well, and the smoke blew toward the German lines. But at 0800 the wind changed and the Americans found themselves in a dense cloud of their own. Visibility quickly went to zero, with drivers unable to see the tracks of their own tanks. Many tanks fell into unseen trenches and sunken roads and most lost contact with each other and the infantry. With all visible references lost, the tank commanders relied on their compasses and continued forward.[3]

It was during this first battle that the tankers discovered that the inside of a heavy tank was a hellish place. Temperatures inside the poorly ventilated steel box were usually at least 90 degrees and in the summer rose to well over 100 degrees. The crew was deafened by the tank's exposed engine and other moving parts, and the darkness inside was relieved only by the small amount of light coming through the vision slots and gun ports. Whenever enemy machine gun fire hit the tanks the impact of the bullets would throw off fragments of the interior of the tank armor. These deadly fragments were called splash or spall. Hand signals between crewmen were difficult to see in the smoke-filled interior. In addition, the ride was very rough, and only two of the crew could see when the tank was about to hit or fall into something.

Whenever the tanks were not shrouded in smoke they were under intense German fire.[4] Nearly half the tanks lost during the attack were destroyed by German artillery fired directly at them over open sights.[5] A direct hit by a 77mm or greater artillery round was frequently catastrophic to both tank and crew. Aside from the artillery, the Germans fired armor-piercing bullets from massive antitank rifles. These single-shot weapons did not usually pierce the tank's armor but could wound one of the crewmen or damage a vulnerable part of the tank.

Sgt. Carl Rosenhagen was a crewman on a Company C hermaphrodite tank commanded by Lieutenant Dunning. He described the events he experienced when his tank came upon a group of nearly twenty German machine guns on the right side of their tank:

> the whole inside of the tank seemed on fire from the sparks of the armor-piercing bullets...It was so intense one gunner laid back away from his gun, and I jumped down and took his place. Pvt. Adams...looked up from the gun he was on, and his face was a mass of blood.[6]

Quickly realizing some heavier firepower was needed, Sergeant Rosenhagen signaled the driver to turn towards the machine gun nest. When the tank turned, the driver was badly hit by some of the machine gun fire directed at his vision slot. The driver yelled for help, but Rosenhagen urged him on: "For God's sake, Barney, keep on driving until we get through this mess."[7] The driver hung on long enough to bring the tank around so that the six-pound gun in the left sponson could be brought to bear. Firing caseshot at less than fifty yards the gun crew quickly silenced the machine guns.[8]

The 301st went into battle that morning with forty tanks. By the time the battalion reached the German lines only about eight tanks were still moving forward; only one tank reached the next phase line, the St. Quentin canal tunnel. Fortunately most of the tanks that had mechanical problems or had only been damaged by enemy fire were able to limp back toward the lines.[9]

The tank commanded by Lieutenant Dunning of Company C was the one tank to advance to the canal tunnel. It had turned around and was headed back to friendly lines when it was finally hit. Sergeant Rosenhagen described the destruction of his tank at approximately 1200 hours that day:

> A shell hit us on the right rear and tore a hole in our back end, busting our main water line running up to the motor. In no time, steam filled the tank so bad, I don't know how any of the rear crew lived through it; as we had our front windows gasping for air. We came to the bottom of a ridge 10 or 15 feet high and tried to climb it, but the motor conked and knocked so bad and would not pull anything even in the lowest gear. I shoved the gear in reverse and backed onto the level. There were two terrific explosions outside the tank, and then a shell hit us on top. ... and the whole tank seemed to be on fire. I climbed thru Lt. Dunning's seat, the only way I could get out, and came along the motor, by the six (6) pounder, over the transmission; when I saw the lower door open on the right side and I slid out. In the smoke and fog I could see two (2) of our boys running away, and I hollered to them and they came back. Lt. Dunning got his face burned getting through and out of the tank. I was lucky, as I kept my head buried in my arms...The four (4) of us ran for some small trenches we could see ahead, and while in there; the largest German I had ever seen made a running jump over us in the trench. I don't know whether he was a runner carrying a message, or if he had started to go to Berlin.[10]

This began an ordeal for Lieutenant Dunning's crew that was to last through dawn of the following day. Miles behind German lines, the crew began working their way back to friendly positions. They narrowly missed being captured by the Germans or killed by Allied artillery barrages. Rosenhagen used the Big Dipper to guide them back to their lines during the night. Often crawling, the men were nearly stepped on by German soldiers more than once. Dawn found them trapped by the machine gun fire from both sides a short distance in front of the British lines. A short time later British soldiers rescued them. Later, in the hospital, Rosenhagen slept for thirty hours.[11]

The battalion's debut had been a bloody one. Three officers, including Capt. Kit Varney, the commander of Company A, and seventeen men had been killed. Sixty-three were severely wounded and another twenty-three slightly so; seven men were missing. But while the attack in the 27th Division sector failed, the 30th Division had breached the Hindenburg Line and held their new positions.[12] This attack was the beginning of the end for the German army which would remain in retreat until the end of the war.

The 301st's report attributed their failure to several problems. First was insufficient counterbattery artillery fire that resulted in the destruction of many of the battalion's tanks by direct German artillery fire. Second was the 107th Infantry's failure to advance with Company C, leaving both forces without mutual support. Third, the infantry, in several areas, failed to "mop up" or clear enemy dugouts and trenches, leaving the Germans able to attack advancing units from the rear. In addition the wind change turned the smoke barrage into a serious handicap which had resulted in the ditching of many tanks. Also, the tanks had failed in some cases to cooperate with the infantry which resulted in the separation of the two forces. Lastly, the failure to establish one definite start line for all units contributed to the lack of mutual support.[13]

Maj. Ralph I. Sasse, the battalion tactical officer, concluded his report with lessons and suggestions. The importance of smoke in daylight attacks was proven. He suggested that the tanks be equipped with their own smoke-producing device. "The object of the Tanks is to get the Infantry to its Objective," Sasse stated.[14] Some tank commanders had moved too quickly, losing contact with their infantry; therefore the infantry was not in position to clear buildings and dugouts. Sasse emphasized the importance of tanks and infantry training together before the battle. The Mark V Star was found to be underpowered and mechanically less reliable than the basic Mark V. The training in gas masks both day and night was seen as a key training need.[15] Interestingly enough, these lessons are still very applicable today.

Although the 301st Tank Battalion's debut was unsuccessful, they won the respect and admiration of the units with which they served.[16] Considering the German concentration of weapons in that sector, it is very doubtful that the attack would have succeeded even if everything had gone as planned. Because the 27th Division attack sector was in the only part of the Hindenburg Line not protected by the St. Quentin Canal, the Germans had gone to great lengths to fortify this obvious avenue of approach.

The next week was spent recovering and salvaging the damaged, ditched, and destroyed tanks. The 301st encamped along the Cambrai-St. Quentin railroad between Villers-Faucon and St. Emilie. The battalion's dead were recovered and buried in the cemetery at Bony, which serves to this day as an American military cemetery of the Great War. Meanwhile, the successful attack of the 30th Division on the 27th's right was furthered by Australian troops who widened the salient.

Planning for the battalion's next attack began with the 30th Division on the evening of 5 October. That same night the battalion's remaining twenty-two tanks moved a distance of nine kilometers to the area near Bellicourt. Following a postponement of Z Day, the officers of the 301st met with their infantry counterparts on 7 October. The companies' reconnaissance officers collaborated under the direction of the battalion reconnaissance officer to plan the approach march routes. The attack was now set for Sunday, 8 October, and its plan called for the 301st to lead the 117th and 118th Infantry Regiments behind a rolling barrage. British Whippet light tanks of the 6th Tank Battalion would join the 301st.[17]

The battalion began its approach march for the attack at 1900 hours on 7 October. The march, conducted in extreme darkness over numerous trenches and sunken roads for 9,000 yards, was remembered as one of the hardest marches the battalion ever made. At zero hour minus three, the tanks were refueled while the section leaders and reconnaissance officers scouted forward. During the last 30 minutes of the march, German artillery shelled the tanks and German aircraft bombed them. Twenty of the battalion's twenty-three tanks made it to the start line; three tanks were down with mechanical problems.[18]

The 301st went into battle with a burning desire for revenge against the Germans. At zero hour, 0510, the battalion crossed the start line and moved forward across excellent terrain. The tanks cleared numerous German machine gun nests from behind a railroad embankment, opening the way for the infantry. Without the tanks, the attack would have failed at that point and resulted in the loss of hundreds of infantrymen. One tank crew overran and captured a German artillery battery that the tank crew had managed to approach from the rear. Many of the tanks reached the final objective. Cooperation and communication between the infantry and the tanks were excellent; both branches expressed great satisfaction with the performance of the other. The battalion saw two men killed and three officers and thirteen men wounded. The attack was a complete success, and the American tankers were satisfied that they had vindicated their previous losses.[19]

Major Sasse included many interesting suggestions in the battalion's battle report. The report recommended that half of the ammunition for the six-pound gun be case shot, which was most effective in destroying enemy machine gun nests and troops. Reported problems with the machine gun belts were attributed to insufficient training. In addition, soldiers had made several good suggestions to improve the effectiveness of the tank crew during combat. Some of their input included: When the tank commander was seated beside the driver in the front, a crewman should stand behind him to relay instructions to the rest of the crew. Also, the compass should be mounted forward by the driver and commander and fitted with a light for night operations. Some sort of protection was needed against bullet splashes as well, especially in the side sponsons. Ampoules of ammonia, which were used to counteract the effects of mustard gas, should be provided in larger quantities. Finally, tank commanders should be given every opportunity to study the area they would be crossing both personally and via maps and aerial photographs.[20]

After about a week of rest and repairing tanks, the 301st returned to battle. The battalion left Serain, their camp for that week, on the afternoon of 15 October and moved to the shelter of a railroad embankment near Busigny. After a day of rest and maintenance the battalion moved forward with twenty-five tanks at midnight to be in position for the attack that was to begin at 0510 hours on 17 October. On the west side of Proyart Wood the battalion refueled and then moved to the start line in two columns. Company A, under Captain Ralli, supported the 27th Division and moved north of La Haie Menneresse. Companies B and C, under the command of Captain Clark, supported the 30th Division by moving south around the village. During the night's march, five tanks did not reach the start line because of mechanical problems.[21]

Leading the infantrymen forward from the start line, the 301st gave valuable assistance to the infantry in reaching and crossing the small Selle River, 500 yards forward. Upon reaching the river the infantry crossed as the tanks sought shallow fording sites. All but two tanks easily found their way across the stream. Dense fog limited the effectiveness of the tanks, but some of them were able to support the infantry quite well in spite of the reduced visibility. Also, several tanks ran out of ammunition during the attack. Although twenty tanks crossed the start line and engaged the enemy, only three made it all the way to the objective, 2,500 yards away.[22]

By the end of the day seventeen tanks had made it back to the battalion rally point near Proyart Wood. A direct hit had knocked out one tank, and one had burned. Two tanks were still ditched, one in the river and the other in a pond. Of the seventeen tanks that returned to the rally point, none was fit for further service without major repairs. The battalion lost one officer and one soldier killed that day, and eight soldiers had been wounded.[23]

Although the poor visibility and mechanical problems had plagued the battalion, the tanks still played a vital part in reducing the German defenses for the infantry. The number of mechanical problems was probably indicative of the ever-increasing amount of wear and tear on the thirty-ton machines. The battalion report of lessons learned, written by the battalion commander, Maj. R. B. Harrison, like Sasse's earlier report, emphasized the tankers' duty to support the infantry in every possible way. A second point made was that it was the duty of every tank crew to fight as long as their tank was able, regardless of how confused the situation.[24]

Following the 17 October attack the battalion encamped at Busigny and worked to repair as many tanks as possible. Because of the losses in both tanks and men, the remainder were organized into a provisional company. The evening of 20 October saw the commander of the 301st receive notice to take part in a night attack on 22/23 October. The twelve remaining tanks of the 301st left Busigny on the afternoon of 21 October and moved to the "lying up" point. The provisional company organized as three sections to support an attack of the 6th Division towards the northeast and between the towns of Bazuel and Catillon. Zero hour was 0120 on 23 October. This night attack, made without any preparatory artillery barrage, caught the Germans by surprise.[25]

Each of the three tank sections of the 301st supported an infantry brigade, with three tanks forward and one in reserve. Experiencing initial success, most of the tanks continued to provide support to the infantry until mid-afternoon on the twenty-third. In most places opposition was slight because of the element of surprise and a growing sense of defeat amongst the German forces. The armies were now fighting across ground that had been German territory for the past four years.[26]

Sergeant Rosenhagen, back in action with Company C, took an opportunity to record some of his night battle experiences:

We ran into a very deep fog not long after we passed the end of the tape that had been laid to guide us to our correct positions. We ran into a terrific shrapnel fire, and the Germans [sic] timing was very good; shells exploding 50 to 75 feet over the top of the tanks. One of the crew was wounded by the shrapnel. We went thru heavy phosgene gas concentrations, which made some of the crew very sick, vomiting and retching. The Germans were also throwing Chlorine Gas shells which were very deadly. About 8 or 9:00 o'clock that morning we came back a little way to let out sick crew members, and picked up replacements for them.

We went back, mopping machine gun nests. We also found a battery of German field pieces behind an elevated railroad track. They were trying to knock us out, but they were not able to.[27]

This attack proved once again the value of the compass when visibility was minimal. But the battalion's report criticized the piecemeal assignment of tank sections to several infantry units. The participation of some infantry and artillery units impressed the officers of the 301st as being somewhat weak.[28] In spite of the problems, however, the 301st had conducted a successful night attack over unfamiliar ground.

Following the night attack the battalion withdrew to the vicinity of Serain where it received replacements and reorganized. On 6 November the battalion moved northeast to Montay on the Selle River. In nearby Le Cateau the men were able to buy fairly recent newspapers and other sorely missed luxuries. They also saw increasing signs of German collapse around Montay.[29]

On 11 November, while the battalion was en route from Montay to the area to the northeast of Le Quesnoy, the Americans passed grinning British soldiers marching the other way. Finally one of the British soldiers said, "You're going the wrong way, Yank; the guerre's finis."[30] The war was over, and now all the 301st had to do was find a way home. That night there was no celebration as weary soldiers merely found a place to lie down and sleep. They moved on to Le Quesnoy the next day. This wonderful town had been so far behind the lines that it was undamaged. For the first time in months, the Americans stayed in buildings, often in feather beds, as the grateful French townspeople pampered them.[31]

After only a week or so the battalion marched back to Solesmes and boarded a train that carried them across the ravaged battlefield of the Somme. The battalion moved to Magnicourt, remembered by the men as a muddy, wet, and windy, God-forsaken hole.[32] The men were billeted in drafty, wet barns, and as a result, there was a great increase in the sick rate as the weather worsened. Brigadier General Rockenbach, who inspected the battalion there, praised them for their service in the war. The biggest event for the men, however, was a sit down Thanksgiving dinner in a mess hall that the men "had built for the occasion in the backyard of a farmhouse."[33] The dinner was remembered as excellent, and the evening was topped off by entertainment from a little French girl who sang folk songs for the men. The grateful soldiers rewarded her with a large amount of candy. At the end of the month the battalion was issued badly needed new clothing.[34]

In December 1918 the battalion began to return to a peacetime military routine, beginning with guard duty and inspections. In mid-December the battalion marched to much better accommodations in Saulty, 28 kilometers away. There they resumed classes and training of the same type they had received in England. These activities kept the less-than-enthusiastic men busy. For Christmas the officers of the battalion sponsored a Christmas party for the local children. A Christmas dinner was served, and the men produced a play for their entertainment. In turn they received one of the best Christmas presents possible—a large delivery of mail.[35]

At the beginning of 1919, the battalion began a more rigorous training schedule, and rumors of an anxiously awaited move to a port abounded. Every morning began with physical training led by the battalion commander, Major Sasse; the full training days might be finished with a movie at the YMCA. Finally, on 13 February the battalion boarded a train for a three-day journey south through Amiens, Creil, Chaumont, and Langres before detraining at Brennes. The battalion was billeted in a cold and wet plateau camp near Bourg. During their brief stay they were deloused for the first time, to the delight of all. Soon the battalion boarded another train of boxcars and continued the journey, finally arriving in Marseilles on 21 February. The soldiers enjoyed the warmth and comfort of the Mediterranean port as they awaited orders to sail. Finally, the battalion departed France on 28 February aboard the liner *President Wilson* and an old transport, the *Europa*.[36]

After a ten-day voyage the ships arrived in New York, and the men moved to Camp Mills. After the camps in England and France, Camp Mills with real barracks, American food, canteens, and movie theaters seemed pleasant. On 21 March the 301st arrived back at Camp Meade, Maryland. There the men resumed a peacetime routine that the war-weary and homesick veterans found distasteful, to say the least. Finally, during the last week in April, all those wanting to be discharged were demobilized and allowed to return home.[37]

The 301st Tank Battalion was the only heavy tank unit to see action in the war. During its short time in battle the battalion acquitted itself quite well under difficult circumstances. Many lessons had been learned on the tactical use of heavy tanks to support infantry attacks. The fighting spirit of the American tankers gave much needed strength to the weary British forces on the Somme front. The 301st and the other new American forces were vital in bringing World War I to a victorious close.

CHAPTER 3

Lean Times:
The Inter-War Years

In June 1921 the Tank Corps was completely reorganized and all units redesignated. The official document for the reorganization was Circular 165 of the War Department dated 22 June 1921. This circular was in turn a supplement to the General Instructions of Circular No. 400, War Department, 1920.[1] But the several redesignations of the 301st Tank Battalion only involved renaming the unit, not changing the organization itself.

The redesignation and reorganization of 1921 split the 301st Tank Battalion into various new organizations. Headquarters and Headquarters Company of the 301st joined with their counterparts of the 303rd to form the Headquarters and Headquarters Company of the new 17th Tank Battalion. Company A became Company B of the new 15th Tank Battalion. Company B was redesignated as Company B of the 17th Tank Battalion. Company C was expanded by a transfer of selected men and equipment to become Companies A, B, and C of the new 16th Tank Battalion.[2]

The lineage of the 66th Armored Regiment is traced from Company C, 301st Tank Battalion through the 16th Tank Battalion. The 16th Tank Battalion remained at Fort George G. Meade (Camp Meade) through the 1920s. The record during this period of the unit's history is scant at best. One of the few remaining documents is a letter from Maj. Sereno E. Brett, the battalion commander. The letter is a request for army authorization for the battalion's silk battle streamers. Army battle streamers, colored differently for each war, are labeled with the name of a battle or campaign in which a unit participated. The 16th Tank Battalion lineage was traced back to two tank battalions that had fought in the World War. The 16th Battalion was allowed the battle streamers earned by the 301st in the Somme offensive. The 345th Tank Battalion had earned the Meuse-Argonne and St. Mihiel offensive battle streamers. The streamers were carried by the 16th because the Headquarters and Headquarters Company of the 345th had been redesignated as the same unit of the 16th Tank Battalion.[3]

In 1929, the army redesignated and reorganized its tank battalions into two regiments. The change in organization was directed by a letter from the Commanding General, III Corps Area, entitled "Redesignation of Infantry (Tank) Units."[4] The letter, dated 13 August 1929, was pursuant to the authority of Circular 165 of the War Department, dated 22 June 1921, that was in turn supplementary to the general instructions in Circular 400, War Department, 1920.[5]

The 16th Tank Battalion was redesignated as the 1st Battalion of the 1st Tank Regiment and was comprised of three companies of light tanks. The 15th became the 2nd Battalion of the regiment and consisted of two companies of light tanks and one of heavy tanks.[6] The 2nd Battalion of the 2nd Tank Regiment (Heavy) was formed from the 17th Tank Battalion. The 2nd Regiment, which had no active headquarters, was comprised of only one battalion which was attached to the 1st Tank Regiment.[7] When the 1st Tank Regiment was created in August 1929 it was commanded by Lt. Col. Channing E. Delaplane. Maj. J. A. McGrath commanded the 1st Battalion, assisted by a staff of five officers (three captains and two first lieutenants).[8]

On 21 April 1932 the 1st Battalion, with Company I of the 3rd Battalion attached, participated in the graduation of the Tank School class at Fort Meade. The unit conducted a mounted pass in review before Col. H. L. Cooper, who was both the regimental commander and the post commander of Fort Meade, with all sixty light tanks of the regiment present at Fort Meade. The leading platoon of Company C was the first in the army to be equipped with radios. The radio represented a major improvement in armor tactics, because it allowed the platoon leader or company commander to control his unit in poor visibility and rough terrain where hand signals were useless. This impressive pass in review was the first of its kind for the 1st Tank Regiment and the first for the tank units at Fort Meade since 1923.[9]

On 21 June 1932 the Headquarters, III Corps Area, ordered a tank platoon to Fort Myer, Virginia to train the 3rd Cavalry Regiment on riot control tactics. Led by 1st Lt. Robert Childs, the 1st Platoon, Company B, 1st Battalion, 1st Tank Regiment consisted of five M1917 light tanks, four equipped with only machine guns and one mounting a 37mm cannon. The platoon had twenty-four enlisted men to man the tanks. Six tank transporter trucks and a Chevrolet light repair truck provided the transportation and maintenance support for the platoon.[10]

After preparations, the platoon left Fort George G. Meade, Maryland, at 0900 hours on 21 June. As the platoon left Fort Meade one of the tank transporters ran off the road and overturned. After checking the injuries and damage, Lieutenant Childs led the rest of the platoon to Fort Myer, arriving there at midnight. A replacement truck was sent to join the platoon later that night.[11]

The next day the 1st Platoon began drilling with designated elements of the 2nd Squadron, 3rd Cavalry and the 3rd Battalion, 12th Infantry. Together the officers and NCOs of these units commenced work to determine the most effective combined-arms formations for riot control. After drilling and practicing various riot control formations and maneuvers, they determined the best formation to be one tank working with a squad of infantry or mounted cavalry.[12]

In the late spring of 1932, the units became involved when thousands of World War veterans converged on Washington, D.C. to persuade Congress and President Hoover to approve immediate payment of the "Bonus." This Adjusted Compensation Certificate had been passed by Congress in 1924. The "Bonus" provided for the payment of $1.00 and $1.25 for every day of service in the armed forces in the United States and overseas, respectively. The drawback to this substantial payment was that it was a twenty-year endowment that was not to be paid until 1945 or upon the veteran's death. By spring of 1932 a large number of unemployed veterans and many congressmen believed the "Bonus" should be paid immediately.

The "Bonus Expeditionary Force" (BEF) was led by Walter Waters, an unemployed cannery manager from Oregon. When he arrived in Washington in late May 1932, the BEF consisted of nearly 15,000 men. Within a month the BEF numbered over 50,000 in twenty-seven camps around the capital. Members of the American Communist Party occasionally tried to stir up trouble amongst the strongly patriotic veterans but usually met with no success. In mid-June the Patman bill, which would have authorized early payment of the "Bonus," was defeated in the Senate. Congress was then able to get most of the Bonus marchers out of the capital by giving them money for train fare home. But by late July some 5,000 to 10,000 veterans still remained in shacks, tents, and condemned government buildings around the city. It was in one of these condemned buildings that a group of veterans attacked two policemen. One of the policemen shot and killed two veterans in the scuffle, and numerous policemen and veterans were seriously injured in the several riots that followed.[13]

The District commissioners asked President Hoover for federal troops to restore order. Hoover reluctantly agreed and gave Secretary of War Patrick Hurley specific orders on the use of troops. The president wanted unarmed soldiers to clear the downtown area of veterans and escort them to their camps. The secretary relayed the orders to Army Chief of Staff Douglas MacArthur, who brashly decided to ignore Hoover's orders about how the soldiers were to be used.[14] MacArthur's disobedience and the brutal handling of the "Bonus Army" was to be the final blow in President Hoover's rapidly declining popularity.

On 28 July the Fort Myers' units were alerted to move to the capital. On that date the situation with the BEF had gotten out of hand. At 1430 hours orders were received for the platoon to move at once to the south side of the Ellipse in the capital. The units linked at the Ellipse and received their instructions.[15]

At 1600 hours the detachment moved up Pennsylvania Avenue to 7th Street where the tanks were unloaded from the transporters. The detachment deployed across the width of the avenue initially, with a cavalry troop leading with drawn sabers.[16] A second cavalry troop was next in the column with the infantry battalion bringing up the rear of the detachment.[17] The detachment cleared Pennsylvania Avenue down to 3rd Street directly in front of the Capitol reflecting pool, stopping there for the infantry battalion to clear the Bonus camp on the south side of the avenue. The soldiers drove out the camp's occupants with tear gas grenades before entering the camp and destroying it. The cavalry troops and the tank platoon moved south on 3rd Street while infantry swept through the east end of the Mall. When the tanks and cavalry reached the intersection of 3rd and C Street, one cavalry platoon and one tank were detached to keep the crowds of curious onlookers from entering the area. The main force then moved west on C Street to 12th Street to a large Bonus camp, which was located between C and D Streets at 12th Street.[18] Lieutenant Childs' report states that this was where many of the alleged communists, who were believed to have caused most of the trouble, were located.[19] After the soldiers cleared the camp of its remaining occupants, the tanks were loaded onto the tank transporters. The platoon then moved to 13th and D Streets where the rest of the force was assembling. There the force ate dinner before beginning a move on the largest Bonus camp. This camp was located on the Anacostia Flats along the south bank of the Anacostia River. The tank platoon moved to the bridge linking the capital area with Anacostia to the south. While the infantry and cavalry moved toward the Bonus camp, the tank platoon unloaded and set up a blockade across the bridge to prevent anyone from crossing toward the city center.[20]

At approximately 2200 hours, General MacArthur ignored President Hoover's directive and ordered the troops to move against the Anacostia Flats Bonus camp. Preceded by tear gas, the infantry and cavalry moved into the camp and began destroying it. As the troops began torching the camp, the veterans, in a last act of defiance, set fire to their own shacks. Within one hour the entire camp was engulfed in flames.[21] Together with the Headquarters Troop of the 3rd Cavalry, the tank platoon remained in position on the bridge throughout the night until relieved at 1500 hours the next day by the 1st Battalion, 12th Infantry.

After being relieved of their bridge blockade mission, the tank platoon, with several other units, moved up Pennsylvania Avenue to the Capitol in order to clear another Bonus camp behind the Library of Congress. This camp had already been abandoned, so the tanks moved to the intersection of 4th Street and Missouri Avenue. They soon received orders to return to Fort Myers at 1830 hours.[22]

The soldiers who participated in this sad episode were praised by Col. H. N. Cootes, the commander of the 3rd Cavalry, for their discipline and self-restraint. The soldiers had never fired their weapons in the face of the occasionally heavy pelting by bricks and cobblestones.[23]

Although General MacArthur had disobeyed the president's orders, President Hoover took full responsibility for the brutal eviction of the Bonus marchers. The Battle of Anacostia Flats, as it came to be known, marked the end of both the Bonus Expeditionary Force and Herbert Hoover's good reputation.[24] Following the foray into Washington D.C., the platoon returned to its home station of Fort Meade.

In August 1932 one platoon from the 1st Battalion had traveled to Cumberland, Maryland, to participate in a military demonstration for the Cumberland Fair. The platoon, comprised of two 37mm gun light tanks and three machine gun tanks, was supported by six tank carrier trucks, a 1/4-ton cargo truck, and a passenger car. With two officers and twenty-four enlisted men, the platoon left Fort Meade at 0500 hours on 22 August and arrived at Cumberland Fairgrounds at 1040 hours the next day. On the evenings of 25 and 26 August the tank platoon fought mock battles with Company G, 1st Maryland Infantry (Machine Gun). The battles, performed with the deafening sounds of blank ammunition and smells of burnt cordite, drew the largest crowds the community had ever seen. The platoon and the event received much commendation and publicity, and was judged an apparent success in the regimental report. The platoon returned to Fort Meade on 27 August.[25]

The units of the regiment conducted a great deal of road marching in 1932, reporting 4,969 miles traveled by tanks and 28,985 miles by the wheeled vehicles. Road marches are a vital part of a tank unit's training. The three basic things a tank unit must be proficient at are moving, shooting, and communicating. A tank unit must be capable of arriving at a specific point some distance away in good order and be ready for combat. Military road marching, which at first glance may appear to be simple, requires careful and repetitive training. A successful march requires that all the tanks and other vehicles maintain a designated speed, normally twenty-five miles per hour, and an interval between vehicles of normally 100 yards. The factor that makes maintaining speed and interval difficult is known as the accordion effect. This is caused when a column of vehicles starts, stops, makes turns, or climbs a hill. The lead vehicle starts and soon reaches the designated speed of the march. The second vehicle, waiting for the first to move, must go just a little bit faster to catch up with the lead vehicle. The effect becomes greater the farther back a vehicle is in the column. The twentieth vehicle in the column may have to go nearly twice the designated speed of the first vehicle to catch up with the rest of the column within a few miles. This problem also occurs when the vehicles have to slow to make a turn. After the turn, vehicles usually go too fast to close the gaps caused by the lead vehicle returning to the designated speed. The problem is made even more difficult because military road marches are almost always conducted under radio silence. The careful training of all tank and vehicle crews is necessary to prevent a road march from becoming chaotic. The key factor in maintaining speed and interval during road marches is making all changes in speed gradually. During road marches, maintenance and rest halts are normally made every three to four hours. The tracks of tanks are hundreds of moving parts that are subject to great stress during a road march, especially on hard surface roads. Fatigue on the marches, especially during maneuvers, is a problem for which the halts are intended to provide some measure of relief. Because considerable discipline and training is required to conduct successful road marches, they are a frequent part of tank unit training.

The report for these units does not give any indication when the marches were done or the march distances. It was noted that during 1932 no tank firing was conducted.[26] Two of the most vital elements of tank unit training are road marches and tank gunnery. In 1932 road marches had been thoroughly done while the equally important area of tank gunnery had been totally neglected. This uneven training was almost certainly due to a lack of ammunition or at least a lack of funding to pay for both ammunition and the fuel required for road marches.

The 2nd Battalion, with attachments of Company F, 2nd Tank Regiment; Company A, 7th Engineer Battalion; and the 72nd Ordnance Company conducted their annual practice march from Fort Benning, Georgia, to Jacksonville, Florida, and back. The march column departed Fort Benning on the afternoon of 20 September 1932 and marched for four days. Moving as far as 102 miles a day, the column normally marched from 0600 until 1500 hours daily. From 25 September through 28 September the 1st Battalion and attachments performed unspecified "usual camp duties" at Camp Foster near Jacksonville.[27] On 29 September the unit began their return march to Fort Benning, arriving there on 2 October.[28]

Company G of the 3rd Battalion conducted its annual practice march from 6 to 11 September 1932. The company traveled along a 375-mile route through New Hampshire. The other company of the battalion also conducted their annual practice march in New Hampshire, marching 373 miles between 19 and 24 September, along a slightly different route than Company G.[29]

On 12 September the units of the regiment at Fort Meade and Fort Benning celebrated Organization Day by company ceremonies and a holiday. A unit organization day is the date that is commemorated annually as the date the unit was first raised or some other significant date in the unit's history. The date chosen for the 1st Tank Regiment, and subsequently the 66th Infantry (Light Tanks), was 12 September. On that date in 1918 the first American tanks received their baptism of fire in the St. Mihiel Salient.[30] The two companies of the 3rd Battalion at Fort Devens observed a joint organization day with the other units on the post on 7 October.[31] In October 1932 the regiment was again redesignated. This redesignation gave the regiment the numerical designation that they retain to the present day. Per War Department letter AG 320.2 Inf. dated October 25, 1932, Subject: Designation of Infantry Units Equipped with Tanks, the 1st Tank Regiment became the 66th Infantry (Light Tanks) Regiment.[32]

In October 1932 the regiment was located at several different posts in the eastern United States. The headquarters, 1st Battalion, and Company I, consisting of 34 officers and 486 enlisted men, were located at Fort George G. Meade, Maryland. The regimental band of one warrant officer and twenty-eight men moved in September from Fort Meade to Fort Hayes, Ohio. The 2nd Battalion was at Fort Benning, Georgia and comprised of 21 officers and 360 soldiers. The 3rd Battalion, consisting only of Companies G and H, garrisoned at Fort Devens, Massachusetts, with 10 officers and 197 enlisted men. The total strength of the regiment at the end of 1932 was 61 officers, 1 warrant officer, and 1,124 enlisted men.[33]

The regimental commander, Col. H. L. Cooper, and the executive officer, Lt. Col. R. W. Kingman, were assisted by a staff of two majors and eight captains. The Service Company, commanded by Capt. S. J. Raymond, came under the regimental headquarters and performed the maintenance and transportation services for the regiment. Maj. D. T. Greene commanded the 1st Battalion, which consisted of Companies A, B, and C. Maj. A. F. Kingman commanded the 2nd Battalion (Companies D, E, and F). The 3rd Battalion at Fort Devens was commanded by Maj. F. R. Waltz.[34]

The busiest and probably most important day of the year in many army units was Armistice Day. There was a significant demand for units to march in the Armistice Day parades that were held in nearly every community in the country. A detachment of two officers and thirteen enlisted men of Company C of the 1st Battalion participated in the celebration held by the Dorcester Post No. 91 of the American Legion in Cambridge, Maryland. Three light tanks carried on their Standard Class B tank carriers and other support vehicles participated in the parade. The detachment also fought in a mock night battle with Company C of the 1st Maryland Infantry (Machine Gun).[35] One platoon of Company I, which was attached to the 1st Battalion and led by Lt. R. R. Winslow, participated in the Armistice Day parade in Baltimore. The platoon had five tanks on tank carriers, one additional carrier, one Chevrolet $1/4$-ton truck, one passenger car, and a motorcycle in the parade.[36]

The year 1933 began with the normal military routines but ended with the regiment heavily involved in President Roosevelt's effort to help the country out of the Great Depression. From January through March, the regiment conducted regular winter training, which consisted of schools for all personnel.[37] The schools for officers concentrated on military tactics, while the soldiers attended schools covering a vast array of subjects from land navigation and vehicle maintenance to communications.

But not all of the regiment's time was spent in training. On 3 January the units of the regiment began construction of a swimming pool at Fort Meade. In the regiment's barracks quadrangle, the soldiers began excavating a large hole in the ground measuring over 100 feet long, 45 feet wide, and 14 feet deep. Under the direction of Capt. S. J. Raymond, the Service Company commander, the first concrete was poured. The project was done with money donated by the companies and volunteer troop labor of the regiment together with the detachment of the Quartermaster Corps. On Sunday, 21 May, the opening ceremony was held for the 66th Infantry (Light

Tanks) swimming pool, which featured a twenty-foot-high, two-level diving platform. Following music from a borrowed band, the regimental commander, Colonel Cooper, gave his opening remarks. After acceptance of the new pool by Regimental Sgt. Maj. C. J. Hartt, five men from each company made the initial plunge into the pool from the diving platform. Swimming races, a diving competition, and a wrestling match comprised the rest of the morning's activities. At noon the regiment had a special dinner to mark the occasion.[38]

Newly elected Pres. Franklin Delano Roosevelt's efforts to bring the country out of the Great Depression had a direct impact on the 66th Infantry Regiment (Light Tanks) in April 1933. The entire regiment ceased their military training to help build the Civilian Conservation Corps (CCC). The officers and men of the regiment were needed to lead and train the huge number of men joining the CCC. Until the CCC was fully formed and organized, the soldiers provided a framework upon which the CCC could build. The regiment's CCC duties continued until mid-December 1933 when most of the officers and men returned to military duty. Because of the CCC duties and a curtailment of ammunition allowances, the annual tank marksmanship course was not conducted in 1933.[39]

Throughout the year small detachments from the regiment were sent out to various locations to participate in public relations events. Typical of these missions was a detachment of three tanks and three tank carriers from Company I which traveled to the Pimlico Race Track in Baltimore on Saturday, 10 June 1933. The occasion was a military tournament hosted by the 110th Field Artillery of the Maryland National Guard. After an exhibition during the afternoon, the tanks participated in a mock night battle for a crowd of thousands.[40]

Lt. R. D. Graves led his platoon of Company A to Hagerstown, Maryland, on 25 August for the State Convention of the American Legion. Company I sent two tanks and their carriers to march in the National Recovery Act (NRA) parade sponsored by the Tank Corps Post No. 19 of the American Legion in Washington, D.C. Occasionally, during the rest of the year, small detachments from the regiment participated in town parades, mock battles, and county fairs. The regiment observed its Organization Day in September and Armistice Day in November with appropriate ceremonies. The strength of the regiment when the year ended was 61 officers and 1,141 enlisted men.[41]

At the 2nd Battalion, 66th Infantry's (Light Tanks) Christmas Party in December 1933, the battalion commander, Lt. Col. John H. Stutesman, began one of those special traditions found in most of the tank units. The origin of most of these military unit traditions has been lost with the passage of time. Fortunately, this special tradition of the regiment has been faithfully recorded and passed down through the years. At the officers' Christmas Party at his quarters on Fort Benning, Lieutenant Colonel Stutesman announced the establishment of the Order of the Little Red Tank of the Anti-Machine Gun League, Tank Chapter No. 1. The Order was created as a society to which only "Tankers" could belong. Lieutenant Colonel Stutesman displayed common sense in also allowing the higher commanders of "Tankers" to join the order. The special insignia of the order was a small red toy tank in the image of the Renault used by the Americans in the World War. "The red color of the insignia is heraldic of the bravery of these tankers gone before, and symbolic of the terror which tanks, on the field of battle, strike into the hearts of the foes of our country, and of the principles for which our country stands."[42] The Latin motto chosen for the order was "Sursom Conda," literally translated as "Let your tails be lifted."[43] Lieutenant Colonel Stutesman, the first Grand Master of the Order and originator of the motto, translated it more loosely as "Keep your tails up."[44]

The new year, 1934, began with the 66th Infantry (Light Tanks) Regiment receiving an important letter on "Tentative Motorization Program" dated January 12, 1934.[45] This letter designated the number of each type of army motor vehicle to be assigned to the regiment. These new vehicles would allow the regiment to transport all of its soldiers and equipment for the first time. The regiment was to receive 151 new vehicles of the following types:[46]

Five-passenger sedan	1
Motorcycles with side cars	42
Eight-passenger reconnaissance trucks	23
$1/2$ ton pick-up trucks	41
$1^1/_2$ ton trucks	27
$2^1/_2$ ton trucks	17

From February through June, the 2nd Battalion stationed at Fort Benning provided officers and men, tanks and trucks to support the training of students at the Infantry School. This support included participation in field exercises, tactical problems, and demonstrations of the light tank capability.[47]

The elements of the regiment garrisoned at Fort Meade became the stars of a newsreel in the spring of 1934. The Metrotone Moving Picture Corporation filmed the light tanks supporting an infantry assault for a newsreel to be released on Army Day, 6 April. Most noteworthy was the communications test that the regiment conducted during the filming. The tanks were directed by radio from the 1st Battalion commander's truck located away from the field. The test was successful in demonstrating that the tanks could be directed in a maneuver by radio commands given from a radio located outside the immediate area.[48]

During April and May the 1st Battalion participated in a wide range of activities from parades and reviews to maneuvers and tactical problems. On the ceremonial side, a platoon from the 1st Battalion led by Capt. Jean Edens marched in the Army Day parade on 6 April. On 4 May all the soldiers of the regiment at Fort Meade participated in the ceremony marking the laying of the cornerstone for the new Post Chapel. In the arena of military training and tests, the regiment participated in several significant events. In early April a detachment from Company I demonstrated for the Officers' School at Fort Meade the use of light tanks to dispense chemical agents. The slow speed of the old tanks and changing wind direction could have made this a risky procedure at any time. Later the some month, Company I demonstrated how to entrain and detrain a company of tanks from railroad flatcars for the Officers' School. Selected noncommissioned officers, such as those holding positions as tank platoon leaders in the absence of officers, also attended these demonstrations. From 9 to 11 May the 1st Battalion, Company I, and Service Company conducted a small field exercise. The units moved on different routes to a bivouac site on the Patuxent River at Old Forge Bridge. During the day of 10 May the units prepared for a night road march to an attack position and to reconnoiter the routes to be used. A heavy rain in the early evening turned the roads into a mire but failed to delay the tanks from arriving at the attack position on time. At 0500 hours on 11 May the exercise began; it was completed by 0900, after which the units returned to their barracks.[49]

At Fort Benning, the 2nd Battalion embarked on its annual practice march from 19 June to 2 July. The 12 officers and 216 men of the battalion were joined by over 120 officers and men of Company F, 67th Infantry (Medium Tanks), the 29th Infantry School Detachment, and detachments from the Chemical Warfare Service and the Medical and Ordnance Departments. The convoy road marched between 80 and 123 miles daily under the hot southern sun. The 762-mile march included stops at Jacksonville, Florida, and Savannah, Georgia. The column was comprised of fifty-five vehicles of thirteen different types, from motorcycles and passenger cars to tank carriers and machine gun buses. The only tanks that actually marched on their own tracks in the convoy were three Christie tanks. These tanks demonstrated their capabilities at the convoy stops in Jacksonville and Savannah. Communication between the sections of the convoy as they marched in the eight-mile-long string of vehicles was difficult. The first tank radio sets did not function very well because of their limited range and a problem with their unshielded radio motors. Telephone and telegraph systems were used for longer range communications that were beyond radio capabilities.[50]

In June, at Fort Meade, the regiment began preparations for its summer training of National Guard soldiers by training and qualifying their instructors. By the end of the month a group of officers and NCOs became qualified instructors in pistol and machine gun marksmanship, and another group was trained in running the weapons ranges. During July and August the regiment supported summer training camps for the Virginia National Guard and the Infantry School of Fire. Another detachment of soldiers supported the Civilian Conservation Corps Reconditioning Camp at Holabird Quartermaster Depot in Baltimore.[51]

The 2nd Battalion at Fort Benning supported the United States Military Academy summer training for the cadets. On 6 August the West Point cadets were able to drive and ride in the tanks and witness a firepower demonstration of the light tank.[52]

In August and September 1934, the two companies of the 3rd Battalion at Fort Devens conducted their annual practice road march and tank marksmanship. On 13 August Company G and the battalion Headquarters Company departed Fort Devens for the 220-mile march to the firing ranges at Fort Ethan Allen, Vermont. The companies traveled through East Westmoreland, New Hampshire, and Hartford and Montpelier, Vermont, before arriving at Fort Ethan Allen on 16 August. At the post artillery range the tanks fired the preliminary and record target practice for the tanks' 37mm cannons and machine guns.[53]

Company H left Fort Devens a few weeks later and followed the same road march route and schedule as the other elements of the 3rd Battalion. After completion of their gunnery practice, the 3rd Battalion (-)[54] entrained at Fort Ethan Allen for the return trip by rail. Traveling on two separate trains the battalion arrived back at Fort Devens on 14 September.[55]

The regiment celebrated Organization Day at Fort Meade on 11 September 1934 with a regimental field meet and a baseball game with the 34th Infantry. The next day the 1st Battalion organized a full war strength tank company as detailed by the Army Table of Organization No. 10, dated 10 April 1933. At that time, the company personnel strength consisted of six officers and 139 enlisted men. The vehicles assigned to the company were the following:[56]

Passenger car	1
Motorcycles	4
Light tanks	15
Light tank carriers	15
Class B cargo trucks	13
Kitchen truck	1
Light repair truck	1
Gasoline truck	1
Water cart	1

The new company trained in field maneuvers, road marching, reconnaissance, and bivouacking in preparation for the III Corps Area maneuvers.[57]

After their brief training period, the new company left Fort Meade on 28 September for a 77-mile road march to Fort Hoyle, Maryland. At Fort Hoyle the 66th's war strength company was attached to the 16th Infantry Brigade for the III Corps Area concentration (maneuvers). From 1 through 5 October this company participated in daily road marches of between 18 and 21 miles, returning to Fort Meade on 5 October. This company participated in various phases of the Corps Area maneuvers from 8 to 12 October. Following these exercises the personnel and vehicles of the company returned to their original companies of the 1st Battalion.[58]

The units of the regiment garrisoned at Fort Meade fired their preliminary and record target practice from 13 October to 14 November 1934. The tank companies fired tank marksmanship (37mm cannon and machine guns) while the Service Company completed pistol marksmanship qualification. On 23 November the four tank companies at Fort Meade competed for the Greene Tank Marksmanship Trophy. Company A won for the second year in a row with a score of 437 of a possible 500 points.[59]

The month of December 1934 found the troops preparing all of the M1917 6-ton tanks, the tank carriers, and the Class B trucks for storage. This was directed by a letter, dated 17 October 1934. The regiment, which finished the task by 31 December, was finally retiring the tanks that they had used since returning from the World War sixteen years earlier.[60]

As 1935 began, the elements of the 66th at Fort Meade found themselves tankers without tanks. On 11 March the regimental commander, Col. J. P. McAdams, wrote a letter to the army adjutant general outlining the problem of training a tank regiment without tanks. The letter requested that two of the twelve .50 caliber machine guns requisitioned by the regiment for use on the new T-2 light tank be provided as soon as they were ready for delivery by the manufacturer. The plan involved using the two machine guns for instructional weapons in the regiment's gunnery school. Colonel

McAdams pointed out that the regiment's training was handicapped considerably because it was confined to theoretical instruction on the T-2 tank and its armament.[61]

Aside from waiting for the new tanks, eventually receiving them, and beginning the process of learning about them, the regiment was able to do little else other than some practice road marches with their wheeled vehicles. The 3rd Battalion (-)[62] conducted their annual practice march from Fort Devens to Fort Meade and back. Traveling between 179 and 258 miles daily, the battalion covered the distance one-way in three days. The road march crossed three mountain ranges and totaled 1,043 miles.[63]

Company H of the 3rd Battalion furnished a supply detachment of one officer and thirty-three men to the 1st Army maneuvers that took place near Watertown, New York, from 2 July through 6 September. Between 6 August and 4 September the Headquarters Company of the 1st Battalion furnished the headquarters detachment for III Corps during the 1st Army maneuvers.[64]

The units of the regiment at Fort Meade conducted their annual practice road march to Virginia Beach, Virginia, in mid-September. The units moved 271 miles to Virginia Beach in two days, then spent ten days training before returning home in a one-day march.[65]

By the beginning of 1936 all the units of the regiment at Fort Meade had received their new light tanks. The 2nd and 3rd Battalions were to receive their new tanks within the year. Unfortunately, the new tanks were of several different types, creating problems that were to get worse over the coming year. The more types of tanks and tank engines a unit had, the more difficult maintenance, spare parts resupply, and training became.

On 21 March 1936 Company D of the 2nd Battalion received the last of their eighteen new light tanks. This one company now had as many as four different models: the T2 prototype; the M2, the M2A1, and the M2A2. Company E was next to receive their new tanks.[66]

At Fort Benning the 2nd Battalion was required to devote an ever increasing amount of men and vehicles to support the Infantry School. The school required tanks, trucks, and soldiers to move, instruct, and train their students. These school-support details, as they are known, often come with little or no notice, crippling a unit's training when a large number of soldiers and/or vehicles are required for school support. Any shortcomings have grave consequences for the tasked unit's officers. These details also have an adverse effect on a unit's planned training. The details ranged widely in the number of men and vehicles, the purpose, and the duration. From 20 to 24 January, twenty-seven soldiers were provided to the Infantry School as assistant instructors in Tank Weapons. Convoy instruction from 22

Returning to earth. A M2A2 light tank crests a hill at speed. Fort Devens, Massachusetts, 1937.

Bernard Hylinski

Tanks of 3rd Battalion on maneuvers. A M2A3 with its distinctive octagon turrets and longer track-base is on the left. The M2A2 with its round turret is at the right. Fort Devens, Massachusetts, 1939.

Bernard Hylinski

3rd Battalion formation of M2A2s and M2A3 light tanks at Fort Devens, Massachusetts, 1939.
Bernard Hylinski

through 30 January used twenty $1^1/_2$-ton cargo trucks, four $^1/_2$-ton trucks, four reconnaissance cars, and two motorcycles with sidecars.[67]

Beginning in April, many of the taskings from the Infantry School were for an entire light tank company consisting of sixteen tanks. The company taskings were normally for demonstrations and tactical problems for the students at the Infantry School.[68] These demonstrations included "Tanks in Attack," "Motorized Pursuit Problem," and "Attacking in Support of an Infantry Brigade."[69]

The 2nd Battalion conducted a road march from 3 through 6 May for the primary purpose of testing the maintenance and "roadability" of the new M2 light tank. The battalion marched through Thomasville, Georgia, to Carabelle, Florida, covering the 237 miles in two days. After bivouacking at Carabelle the column returned 230 miles through Dothan, Alabama, to Fort Benning. In addition to the 13 officers and 203 enlisted men of the 2nd Battalion, the column included 12 officers and 122 men from Company F, 67th Infantry (Medium Tanks), representative units from the Medical Corps and the Ordnance Corps, and a group of observers. The vehicle list included seventeen M2 light tanks from Company D, 2nd Battalion, five T3 prototype medium tanks from Company F, 67th Infantry, and fifty-eight wheeled vehicles ranging from motorcycles to $2^1/_2$-ton cargo trucks. The only maintenance problems noted were three broken fan belts on Dodge $2^1/_2$-ton cargo trucks. The new tanks had done well on their reliability test. Unfortunately the same cannot be said of the radio sets the tanks carried.

Radio communication was only possible between the march serials when they were stopped.[70]

Between 17 and 20 June the 2nd Battalion participated in the Corps Area maneuvers at Fort Benning. For the maneuvers the 2nd Battalion was reorganized into a composite battalion: the Headquarters and Headquarters Company of the 2nd Battalion joined with Company D, brought up to new provisional Table of Organization & Equipment (TO&E) strength, and Company F, 67th Infantry (Medium Tanks) at normal strength. The composite battalion of 17 officers and 308 enlisted men participated in the day and night maneuvers from 18 June until 0900 hours on the twentieth.[71]

A wheeled transport column from the 2nd Battalion carried a group of 118 recruits the 318 miles from Fort Benning to Fort Screven, Georgia, on 1 August. The convoy of 52 vehicles then moved to Savannah, where they picked up 6 officers and 301 cadets from West Point and carried them back to Fort Benning for a period of instruction at the Infantry School.[72]

The 3rd Battalion, still consisting only of Companies G and H, left Fort Devens for a 220-mile move to Fort Ethan Allen near West Bolton, Vermont. In Vermont, the 9 officers and 216 men of the battalion participated in the 18th Brigade maneuvers. On 29 August the battalion returned to Fort Devens in a heavy rainstorm.[73]

The units of the regiment at Fort Meade conducted the first leg of their annual practice march 175 miles to Bethany Beach, Delaware. Eleven officers and 376 men traveled in 86 wheeled vehicles; no tanks participated in the road march. But on 18 September 1936, the regimental commander decided to have the units return to Fort Meade early. A hurricane moving up the Atlantic coast had quickly become so violent that he decided an immediate departure was necessary to prevent equipment and vehicles of the regiment from being destroyed.[74]

On 5 October 1936 the quota of eighteen new M2A2 light tanks for Company E and three tanks for the Headquarters Company, 2nd Battalion, was filled. The battalion soon put the new tanks to use during a demonstration of a tank battalion and a division tank company supporting an infantry brigade in an attack. The demonstration was done for the chief of infantry (a major general in charge of the infantry branch at the War Department) on 15 October 1936.[75]

The 3rd Battalion (-), commanded by Lt. Col. William L. Roberts, conducted their annual practice road march from 23 to 25 October. Leaving Fort Devens at 2300 hours on 23 October, the battalion moved 196 miles in the dark, fog, and rain to arrive at West Point at 0900 the next morning. After a day of rest and maintenance the battalion returned to Fort Devens on 25 October.[76]

In the fall of 1936 the Tables of Organization (TO) authorization for tank units was changed. This document dated 22 October 1936 increased the authorized personnel strength of the battalions from 329 to 431 enlisted men and from 20 to 27 officers.[77] A follow-up document, dated the same day, increased the tank company strength from 93 to 112 enlisted men and from 5 to 6 officers.[78] The officer strength of the battalion headquarters company rose from five to nine officers and the number of enlisted men went up to ninety-five from the earlier number of fifty men. The regimental service company was deactivated by the authority of a War Department letter from the Adjutant General's Office dated 4 November 1936, Subject: Service Company, 66th Infantry. The new authorization of the headquarters' company of the 1st and 2nd Battalions absorbed the personnel from the Service Company.[79]

In 1937 the 66th Infantry (Light Tanks) gradually received the increase in personnel strength authorized in the fall of 1936. At the beginning of 1937 the regiment had a total strength of 50 officers and 1,224 enlisted men. By the end of the year, 64 officers and 1,492 enlisted men were assigned.[80]

The 2nd Battalion at Fort Benning conducted their annual practice road march from 26 through 30 April 1937. Company F, 67th Armor (Medium Tanks) and the 15th Ordnance Company were attached to the battalion for the march. This road march, in addition to the normal purpose of training the battalion, also served as a strategic model test for the Infantry Board and to instruct Tank Course students of the Infantry School.[81] The Infantry Board was interested in determining if a tank battalion could road march several hundred miles and then go straight into an attack against an enemy force.

Lt. Amzi Rudolph Quillian graduated from West Point in 1937 and was assigned to 2nd Battalion, 66th Infantry (Light Tanks) at Fort Benning. He was born and raised in North Georgia and attended the North Georgia Military Academy prior to his appointment to West Point. Known as "Rudy" he was known as a fine leader who also had a lot of compassion. He was a "West Pointer" who was admired by the many reserve officers who would soon fill the regiment.[82]

The column departed Fort Benning on 26 April and traveled 116 miles to Fort McPherson, Georgia. The next day's march of 104 miles to Fort McClellan, Alabama, was done as a tactical problem. The battalion put out reconnaissance elements to its front and flanks to observe for enemy forces. The march ended with a tank battalion attack on an assumed (imaginary) enemy at Fort McClellan.[83]

Unit photograph of Company B, 66th Infantry (Light Tanks) at Fort Meade, April 1937. Note the age of some of NCOs.

The units returned to Fort Benning via Fort Oglethorpe, Georgia, along a 379-mile route. The return march was also conducted as a tactical problem. The planned attack on an assumed enemy at Fort Benning was canceled because reconnaissance elements reported that heavy rains had made the unpaved roads very soft and muddy. The effect of running more than fifty tanks over these dirt roads would have left them with deep ruts for years. The decision was made to move the units back to Fort Benning in a nontactical manner over paved roads.[84]

The 1st Battalion, plus Company I, made their annual practice road march from Fort Meade to the National Guard reservation at Indiantown Gap, Pennsylvania. Nineteen officers and 376 enlisted men from the 66th participated, along with one officer and six enlisted men from the Medical Corps, and seventy-three men from the 30th Ordnance Company. The following vehicles were driven on the march:[85]

Light tanks	38
$1/2$-ton trucks	18
$1^1/2$-ton trucks	27
$2^1/2$-ton trucks	6
Reconnaissance cars	10
Gasoline tankers	3
Passenger car	1
Ambulance	1

The designated uniform for the march was field caps, woolen shirts, cotton breeches, mounted leggings, and service shoes. This was a garrison or everyday peacetime uniform as opposed to a combat uniform. The new Tables of Basic Allowances designated what each man was allowed to bring with him. This document allowed an officer one trunk locker (thirty-six inches long, twenty-four inches wide, and eighteen inches high) and one bedding roll. It also allowed one barracks bag for each enlisted man.[86]

For the road march the regiment and its attachments were organized into five serials or march units. The first four serials consisted basically of one tank company each, with the headquarters elements and attachments comprising the last march unit. The first serial departed Fort Meade at 0500 hours on 17 September for the 132-mile trip. The convoy traveled through Baltimore to Westchester, Maryland, then to Gettysburg and finally Harrisburg, Pennsylvania. At Gettysburg, the serials halted for thirty minutes for refueling and maintenance checks. In Baltimore a horse belonging to the Western Maryland Dairy became frightened by the noise of the tanks. The unfortunate animal bolted in front of a Company C tank and was hit by the tank's track. Seriously injured, the horse had to be destroyed.[87]

Mechanical problems during the road march were very minor. The maintenance section repaired oil leaks on two tanks en route. Another two tanks threw the guide rollers off their tracks and had to be repaired. One motorcycle and one $2^1/_2$-ton truck also required attention along the march. One of the two tanks with the guide roller problem was the last vehicle to arrive at Indiantown Gap at 1900 hours.[88]

Between 18 September and 1 October the regiment participated in regimental, brigade, and Corps Area maneuvers at the Indiantown Gap. On 2 October the regiment, its attachments, and an element of the 34th Infantry made a road march to return to Fort Meade. The only mechanical problems were with two tanks that required bogey wheel replacement.[89]

Company D of the 2nd Battalion made their second annual practice road march when they joined the 29th Infantry (Reinforced) for their annual march. The units departed Fort Benning via Maxwell Field, Alabama, on 1 and 2 October.[90]

On 1 September 1938 the Headquarters and Headquarters Company and Maintenance Company of the 66th Infantry (Light Tanks) Regiment were inactivated. War Department Circular 16 designated the regiment as a tactical unit that exists only in wartime or when needed to supervise and coordinate the tactical operations or its subordinate tank battalions. This circular also designated the battalion as both an administrative and a tactical headquarters. The new designation of the battalion, combined with the

A M2A3 with its twin turrets and a M2A4 of 3rd Battalion at Fort Devens, 1938.
Bernard Hylinski

M2A3 light tank of 3rd Battalion. The tank had twin turrets giving it the nickname "Mae West." The larger commander's turret on the left mounted a .50 caliber machine gun and the smaller turret a .30 caliber machine gun. Fort Devens, Massachusetts, 1939.

Bernard Hylinski

fact that three battalions of the regiment were located at three different posts, dictated the elimination of the regimental headquarters. A new TO No. 7-81, dated 17 March 1938, inactivated the regimental Maintenance Company.[91]

The inactivation of the regimental headquarters turned out to be rather short-lived. Almost exactly one year later the War Department reversed its decision to inactivate the regimental headquarters elements of the 66th Infantry because of the planned concentration of all three battalions of the regiment at Fort Benning, Georgia. When the decision to reactivate the headquarters was announced, the chief of infantry objected. Col. L. R. Fredendall, executive officer to the chief of infantry, stated that all new soldiers being assigned to tank units should be assigned to the new medium tank companies being created in the 67th Infantry (Medium Tanks). The 67th was in the process of expanding from one battalion and a separate company (Company F) to two full battalions. Fredendall's letter, dated 29 September 1939, expressed concern that the men necessary to man one medium tank company, which was being activated in July 1940, had not been provided.[92]

Brig. Gen. F. M. Andrews, the War Department assistant chief of staff, wrote a memorandum to the chief of staff on 12 October 1939 deciding the issue. The regiment's maintenance company would remain inactive because the company duplicated functions of the battalion maintenance company. The Regimental Maintenance Company was to be activated only upon mobilization of the Armed Forces.[93]

The War Department did not reverse its decision to activate the regimental headquarters and headquarters company. It provided the following reason:

> Because of the probable concentration of the battalions of the 66th Infantry for training in the near future, it appears advisable to activate this unit, both that it may exercise its legitimate functions, and that the necessity for this unit can be definitely determined.[94]

After an absence of only one year, the three battalions of the 66th once again had a regimental commander and staff.

PART II

War Clouds
1939–41

CHAPTER 4

The Rebirth of American Armor

When Adolf Hitler began his first moves to acquire portions of other countries' territory in 1936, it attracted the attention of many senior U.S. Army officers. These men had fought the German army only eighteen years earlier and now began to fear that they might have to repeat the experience. The officers remembered the American army's difficult struggle to build a large modern army in a very short time in 1917–1918. Most of the officers remembered with some bitterness the rapid demobilization of the army and the years of neglect that followed the end of the World War. These veteran officers, now all colonels and generals, were determined to do everything within their power to prevent being unprepared again. As Hitler's armies marched into a growing number of neighboring countries, the American officers became more concerned and made increasingly serious efforts to update the army in every area from training to tanks.

Following the impressive performance of the German Panzer divisions during the brief campaign in Poland, the American military leadership began to show an increased interest in the neglected American tank units. In December 1939 the War Department ordered the immediate concentration of all infantry tank units at Fort Benning, Georgia. The 66th Infantry (Light Tanks) was reunited as a regiment upon the arrival of the 1st Battalion and Company I from Fort Meade and the 3rd Battalion (-) from Fort Devens. This concentration of tank units from around the country to Fort Benning was completed on 10 January 1940.[1]

Once all the tank units were assembled, they were organized into a provisional tank brigade. Within this brigade were elements of three emerging tank regiments: the 66th, 67th, and 68th. The medium tank unit, the 67th, consisted only of a headquarters company and two tank companies. The 68th was in the process of trying to organize two battalions from a variety of separate tank companies and platoons that had arrived from all over the country. The 66th, with the only regimental headquarters and headquarters company, was utilized as the provisional brigade headquarters. Brig. Gen. Bruce Magruder was appointed the commanding general, and Col. Alvin C. Gillem, the commander of the 66th, became the executive officer. The regimental staff of the 66th was to support six tank battalions instead of the normal three of a regiment. The brigade quickly realized the maintenance and logistical problems created by the lack of the regimental maintenance and service companies. These two companies had been disbanded in 1938 when the army inactivated the regimental headquarters. The brigade headquarters was in the unenviable position of having to support twice the number of vehicles and men with none of the necessary assets. For logistical support the Headquarters company set up a small detail under the logistics officer (referred to as the S-4) to fill the void left by the absence of the Service Company. During one three-day maneuver this detail distributed 39,000 gallons of gasoline and field rations for 2,200 men in seven different locations, often making round trips of 120 miles.[2]

M2 half-track of the 2nd Armored Division's 78th Field Artillery towing a field piece. Note the insignia on the hood and the water-cooled machine gun. Fort Benning, 1940.

Norris H. Perkins

Lacking a training directive from the War Department, the tank bri-gade created its own in the first months of 1940. The brigade headquarters later found that the War Department never planned to provide a training directive to the brigade for fear of hindering the tankers' training efforts. The problems of training the tank brigade were compounded by the great diversity of the tank platoons, companies, and battalions assembled at Fort Benning. Because of local commander interests, training facilities, and equipment, the level of training of the tank units varied greatly, allowing no common starting point for training.[3]

In January 1940 the provisional tank brigade, led by the 66th, deter-mined that only ten weeks were available for the brigade to conduct tank training prior to engaging in the first combined arms maneuvers. They spent the first four weeks in a combination of basic training and tank-cannon and machine-gun firing. The units fired the weapons courses as the ranges were available, and the firing was conducted concurrently with basic training on the ranges. Whenever a crew was not actually firing they trained in map reading, reconnaissance, maintenance, and the use of field expedient re-pairs. The basic training also included tank driving, communications, cam-ouflage, and gas (chemical) instruction.[4]

Beginning in March, the battalions of the 66th and the other tank units of the brigade began combined arms training with the 1st Infantry Division. These combined exercises were to familiarize all the different unit command-ers with the problems of operating with other branches. The first week of this training focused on an infantry battalion with a company of light tanks from the 66th attached. Other training periods teamed various size infantry and tank units with each other in various tactical situations. In late March and early April the units conducted large-scale exercises with several battalions of tanks working with the 1st Infantry Division in preparation for the corps maneuvers.[5]

The officers of the provisional tank brigade gained important skills in the reconnaissance of terrain. All the terrain, bridges, roads, and other fea-tures of Fort Benning were quickly recorded on the post map and used to enhance the efficiency of the tank units during the exercises. This training was later to prove exceptionally helpful in the Louisiana Maneuvers. By consolidating the terrain information gained during their reconnaissance missions, all officers of the brigade were able to learn a new piece of ter-rain very quickly.[6]

As a result of the mutually beneficial training with the 1st Infantry Division, the brigade attempted to attach tank battalions to the 5th and 6th Divisions for training. But because of the distance between the units and the limited time available, only one battalion of the 66th was available to

Rail loading M2A3 of C Company en route to Louisiana Maneuvers. April 1940.
Bernard Hylinski

travel to Fort McClellan, Alabama, where the two divisions were stationed, for two weeks of training.[7]

To help in spreading the knowledge gained from the combined training period, the provisional tank brigade prepared a brief manual entitled "Tank Employment in Support of Foot Infantry."[8] This brief guide was written to assist the infantry officers at all levels on how best to work with or fight against tanks. Colonel Gillem, commander of the 66th, commented, "no opportunity should be omitted to combine the training of combat units which, though essentially different in composition and equipment, are tactically effective when used together."[9]

Following the combined training period, the provisional tank brigade staff prepared a survey of the brigade's present and future training needs. This survey was to assist the IV Corps commander and his staff in planning for the further training and employment of the brigade.[10]

The survey began by addressing some of the personnel problems in the brigade. When the tank units concentrated at Fort Benning in January, many of the units were short of the authorized number of officers. This officer shortage worsened when twenty-six officers (twenty percent) from the brigade were detached for duties around Fort Benning unrelated to tanks. This not only weakened the tank units but also caused twenty-six tank officers to miss valuable training. A second personnel problem was that the brigade, unlike infantry units, did not have any reserve officers serving their one-month training tours.[11]

The problem of spare parts for the maintenance of the brigade's tanks was serious. The 66th had three different types of light tanks powered by seven different types of engines, both gasoline and diesel. Six different generators, five different starters, and three types of voltage regulators were in use on the tanks. Imagine the difficulty of getting the correct spare part to fix a tank broken down sixty miles away during a night maneuver. Fortunately, the tanks proved to be very reliable and mechanical breakdowns were few.[12]

The brigade instituted several types of reports to keep track of the condition and availability of all of its vehicles. The officers gained valuable experience in planning and executing all road movements. Some of the road marches the brigade conducted included 1,500 vehicles traveling 350 miles. The lessons learned about refueling, march control, and vehicle and march serial intervals were to prove invaluable in the coming months.[13]

The relatively new area of radio communications was still experiencing growing pains. Initially there were some provisions in the brigade for the maintenance and repair of the tank radio sets. Many repairs, however, could be made only at the Brooklyn, New York, Signal Depot and took up to eight months to be completed. To remedy the situation, brigade headquarters was successful in getting a small detachment of signal men assigned to service the radios.[14]

Many other men also were vital to the smooth functioning of the brigade. The attached medical personnel were in the process of determining how to treat and remove casualties from inside a tank. Military police were crucial for maintaining a constant flow of traffic in congested areas, such as road intersections, during maneuvers and road marches. Also, the close relationship between engineers and tankers was well established during the combined training; habitual training between the two branches was considered necessary so that each understood the needs of the other.[15]

For clothing and equipment, the tank officers determined what was required based on their experience. The field uniform most useful to tankers was a pair of coveralls that allowed a soldier to move around in the tank without becoming caught on objects in the confined space. Coveralls were relatively cool in the summer and could be made warm in the winter by adding clothing underneath. Leather jackets or windbreakers with tight fitting cuffs and waistband were needed for use outside the tank. Face masks and goggles were necessary for protection from the dust, especially for the driver in the last tank in a column traveling at high speed on a dusty road.[16]

In April and May of 1940, the 66th and the rest of the provisional tank brigade took part in the Louisiana Maneuvers. These maneuvers were part of the country's effort to build up a strong military because of concern over the ominous events in Europe and the Far East. The 3rd Army maneuvers conducted at corps level were the largest ever conducted by the army in peacetime. The maneuvers were planned by the 3rd Army commander, Maj. Gen. Stanley D. Embick, and directed by Gen. George C. Marshall, the army chief of staff. The provisional tank brigade was attached to the IV Corps, which had four of the old square infantry divisions (with four infantry regiments each), for the first phase of the exercise. This first phase pitted the provisional tank brigade from the Infantry Branch against their rivals from the cavalry, the 7th Cavalry Brigade (Mechanized).[17]

Lt. Col. Bradford G. Chynoweth, an officer assigned to the 66th, drove the Buick, which he had used in England with its right drive, to the maneuvers. En route he was pulled over by a police motorcycle patrol. Chynoweth recalled:

> A burly policeman came to my window, got out his book and said: "Smart guy, eh?" I asked what he meant. He said, "Driving your car from the wrong side, that's what I meant!" I looked down and he suddenly noticed my wheel. He took off his hat, his chin dropped, and he said, "I'll be dawged! I never saw anything like that!" They all drove off looking sheepish.[18]

The first phase of the maneuvers showed strongly the importance of terrain reconnaissance and engineer support to the success of the tanks. Engineers were invaluable to tank units faced with the numerous rivers and swampy areas of Louisiana. But even when the terrain was firm enough to support tanks, sudden weather changes could drastically change that situation. During one key action the brigade was forced to launch a breakthrough attack across a previously suitable area that had just been drenched by a heavy downpour. In spite of the drastic change in the condition of the ground, the controlling headquarters insisted that the brigade conduct the attack as planned. The results were disastrous. Only some twenty percent of the tanks were able to make it through the quagmire and reach the objective. Colonel Gillem, in his conference for the officers, commented:

> The impression gained by many present was that the tanks were impotent, faulty in design, and of questionable military value. This conclusion is erroneous and, if that faulty commitment of tanks is properly evaluated, the price paid, which was limited to injured feelings on the part of tank personnel, was indeed a bargain. For from that failure, which cost no lives and deprived us of no tanks, a valuable lesson can

be drawn; That lesson is——a commander charged with the responsibility of committing tanks over adverse terrain must be willing to pay the price for faulty commitment.[19]

Effective communications also faltered during this phase. The cross country speed and mobility of the tanks during attacks often resulted in the tanks outstripping their communications. When the tanks were out of communication range, the headquarters would lose control of their combat elements. Control was often reestablished by aircraft from the Army Air Corps.[20]

During the first phase, tanks often were not committed against the enemy until the infantry had encountered the full force of the enemy resistance. Then, just as often, the infantry commanders committed their tank forces piecemeal in less strength than was required to be successful. The survey recommended that tanks be committed to battle as soon as they were needed and normally in not less than battalion strength.[21]

Overall, the Louisiana Maneuvers were conducted with an extensive list of rules that hampered the tankers. On 20 April Lieutenant Colonel Chynoweth wrote a letter to Col. E. L. Gruber, the chief controller of the maneuvers, expressing some of his frustrations:

Dear Colonel Gruber,

It seems likely that you do not know that tanks, in this maneuver, are not permitted off the roads except in one leased and very unsuitable bivouac area. They must also stop whenever they arrive within 100 yards of an enemy. It is like trying to play football on a bowling alley. I feel certain that you do not understand this situation, as you would not emphasize the fact that tanks were "not concealed", "attacked from the air" in a public critique, if you did know it. The tank units worked hard in preparation for the maneuvers. It is a great disappointment to them to be forced to spend their time halted on roads while airplanes attack them overhead, cavalry rush at them from the side roads, and control officers solemnly point out their failure to take advantage of cover, and even lecture them quite scathingly about being caught in column on the road.

We understand the limitations of this maneuver, and are willing to play the game (absurd a game as it really is for us) for the sake of training of high command and staff. But *PLEASE* don't rub salt in our wounds by making us listen to suggestions that we "didn't take cover" or didn't this or that...

Constructively yours,
B. G. Chynoweth
Lt. Col. 66th Inf.[22]

Despite these numerous problems, during the maneuvers the tank brigade was responsible for several successful counterattacks. The tanks had the advantage of mobility, firepower, and armor while moving over familiar ground. Counterattacks were most effective when supported by artillery fire and aircraft.[23]

In the second phase of the 1940 Louisiana Maneuvers, the Provisional Tank Brigade changed sides and joined the IX Corps, which had three of the new triangular divisions comprised of three infantry regiments each. The Provisional Tank Brigade and the 7th Cavalry Brigade worked together.[24]

One of the objectives of the second phase was "to test the organization and operations of a provisional mechanized force."[25] This force was comprised of elements of both the Provisional Tank Brigade and the 7th Cavalry Brigade. The two brigades were given forty-eight hours to organize the force and move it seventy-five miles into an attack. Brigadier General Magruder and Brig. Gen. Adna R. Chaffee, commander of the 7th Cavalry Brigade, quickly organized the force and planned the operation. The force consisted of two light tank battalions from the 66th, a medium tank company, a motorized infantry regiment, an artillery battalion, a reconnaissance regiment minus their horse squadron, and attachments of engineers and medics. In spite of many of the elements having never worked together and the short lead time, the operation was a great success.[26]

M2A4 tanks of 1st and 2nd Battalions moving out in the early morning at Fort Benning in April 1941.

Norris H. Perkins

The most significant result of the Louisiana Maneuvers was that it determined the future of a separate mechanized force, one independent of both the infantry and the cavalry. General Marshall followed the recommendations of those officers committed to a separate mechanized force. This group of soldiers included Embick, Magruder, Chaffee, Chynoweth, and an old cavalryman who served as an umpire for the exercise, Col. George S. Patton, Jr. The recommendations called for the creation of four armored divisions, one for each field army. Under General Marshall's guidance, Chaffee devised a plan for the creation of the divisions by 15 April 1940. The word "armored" was chosen because the cavalry branch disliked the word "tank" and the infantry did not like the word "mechanized." Neither branch wanted the new force to have a name that had been used by a rival branch.[27]

On 15 July 1940 the War Department activated the Armored Force under the command of Brigadier General Chaffee. Chaffee was also appointed as the commander of the I Armored Corps, consisting of the 1st and 2nd Armored Divisions. At Fort Benning the 2nd Armored Division was formed under the command of Maj. Gen. Charles L. Scott. Upon activation the division had only 99 officers and 2,202 enlisted men.[28] The new division was a mere skeleton of its newly authorized 754 officers, 69 warrant officers, and 13,795 enlisted men (a total of 14,618 personnel).[29]

The division's main force was its 2nd Armored Brigade commanded by newly promoted Brig. Gen. George S. Patton, Jr. The brigade consisted of three armored regiments, two of light tanks and one of medium tanks. The 66th Infantry (Light Tanks) was redesignated as the 66th Armored Regiment (Light) on 15 July. At the time, the 66th was the only armored unit that was close to its authorized strength in men and equipment. The two other regiments, the 67th and 68th, existed primarily on paper. Indeed, only about two companies worth of medium tanks were available at Fort Benning for the 67th.

As an armored regiment, the 66th received a coat of arms worthy of their past. The following is a description of the 66th's arms from the unit's Organization Day program of 1940.

> The insignia of our regiment very clearly symbolizes the complex family tree of the 66th. The Red, Yellow and Blue represent the three arms, Artillery, Cavalry and Infantry from which the members of the Tank Corps were drawn when it was organized in 1917 and 1918. The small shield in the upper right of the main shield is the Coat of Arms of the city of Langres, France where part of this unit was organized. The label, a bar with the three point suspension, indicates that we are the heir-apparent and hence inherit the proud traditions of the Tankers of the

A.E.F. Above this shield crouches the fabulous medieval monster, the Wyvern, whose glance is death. The Wyvern, symbol of the tank, goes through fire, crushes, destroys. The Wyvern's head turns to the right which in heraldic lore means victory. Our motto "Semper in Hostes", means "Always into the enemy". The Regiment is proud of the record of its predecessors in the battles of the World War, where they gained glory on the Somme, at St. Mihiel, and in the Meuse Argonne, and where by unselfish devotion to the duty and extreme sacrifice, they drew from General Pershing the statement that "The high percentage of casualties in Officers and men tells the tale of splendid morale and gallantry in action and of their unselfish devotion to duty".

The other combat units of the division were the 41st Armored Infantry Regiment, the 14th Field Artillery Regiment (Armored), the 78th Field Artillery Regiment (Armored), and the 2nd Reconnaissance Battalion. The support units consisted of a battalion each of Engineers, Ordnance, Quartermaster, and Medical.

The problems involved in organizing and building the new division were immense. Most of the units suffered from a severe lack of equipment and men. The soldiers of the new division were housed mostly in tents spread out along an eight-mile stretch from Harmony Church to Lawson Field at Fort Benning.

The early days of organization and training in the late summer and fall of 1940 tried the ingenuity and patience of the officers and men. They had few precedents for guidance in organizing an armored division, little equipment, and too little time to learn by trial and error.[30]

1st Lt. Herbert S. Long was born in 1913 in San Antonio, Texas. He graduated from St. Mary's University in San Antonio and was commissioned as a second lieutenant in the cavalry. After serving as a cavalry officer he was assigned to the 66th in 1940. He joined the 1st Battalion as a platoon leader.[31] He would become known for his trademark mustache and pipe.

Another officer who arrived in 1940 was 1st Lt. Norris H. Perkins from Milwaukie, Oregon. He joined the U.S. Army following the German invasion of Holland in May. He had been commissioned as a reserve officer in 1935 while earning his degree in architecture at the University of Oregon. He arrived at Fort Benning in September and was initially assigned to Machine Gun Company as a platoon leader.

On 18 September 1940 Major General Scott was assigned as the commander of the I Armored Corps. Upon Major General Scott's departure several weeks later, Brigadier General Patton assumed command of the 2nd Armored Division.[32]

Lt. Norris Perkins of Machine Gun Company at Fort Benning in January 1941. Note the leather jacket with the crest of the 66th painted on the breast.

Norris H. Perkins

Brigadier General Patton was famous for his rules for the appearance of his soldiers. The 2nd Armored Brigade Training Memorandum No. 21 from October 21, 1940, provides an excellent example:

1. Regimental commanders will take appropriate action in connection with the following.

    a. When riding in tanks all crew members will wear helmets with chin straps buckled under chins.

    b. Military garments are designed to be fastened. The wearing of coats, slickers, and windbreakers, as if they were bath robes will be discontinued except when indoors.

    c. Pockets are not hand rests.

    d. Remember that *all* brass showing on the uniform is to be polished, this includes buttons.[33]

Patton was equally concerned with the division's training. On 29 October the 66th was ordered to have one tank company demonstrate an attack. Brigadier General Patton, who was to observe the attack along with all available in the regiment, directed that the following be stressed:

    a. An approach march against the enemy whose attack position is not known.

    b. Action taken on coming under Anti-Tank fire.

    c. Use of covered approaches.

    d. Use of supporting fire either by tanks within the platoon, or platoons in the company, or both.

    e. Action upon the capture of the enemy position.[34]

In November, as part of the army's efforts to inform the interested public about the new armored force, the 66th Armored Regiment hosted a visit of seventeen prominent newspaper correspondents. Colonel Gillem, the regimental commander, and the regimental staff had coordinated the entire program for the three-day visit, from lodging and entertainment to military demonstrations of the tanks and visits to the firing ranges. Later, Colonel Gillem received a letter from Major General Fredendall commending the program that had been carried out for the correspondents.[35]

In early December the entire 2nd Armored Division, still severely under strength, conducted a 600-mile road march to Panama City, Florida. The great column included 101 light tanks of the 66th Armored and 24 medium tanks of the 67th.[36] The division spent three or four days at Panama City before beginning the return march.

Bernard Hylinski joined the army in February 1937 and served with the 66th at Fort Devens before moving with the regiment to Fort Benning. In December 1940 he was serving as a motorcycle scout in Machine Gun Company. The scouts practiced a maneuver in which they attacked at 25–30 miles per hour, then laid their bikes over and went into a firing position with their Thompson sub-machine gun. The men, dressed in their Class A uniforms, were practicing this grueling maneuver for a visit by Secretary of War Stimson on Lawson Field. The practice for the visit had gone on for hours and the men were tired and dirty. General Patton had motorcycle scouts gathered in a circle for a critique. Patton strode in amongst the scouts and said, "I want you to gather around close." As the men moved in around their division commander he looked around at them and remarked, "Boy, I can tell you one thing if looks could kill I'd be a dead Son of a Bitch." Patton then gave his men a big smile and congratulated them on a job well done.[37]

On 6 January 1941 Colonel Gillem conducted a division officers school on the Panama City road march. He began the school by commenting that a much greater amount of time is spent marching to battle than is spent in battle. The first topic discussed was the selection and reconnaissance of the start point or IP of a road march. This is the point where the different serials or march units successively enter the march routes. To avoid stopping the serials or forcing them to be late to reach the IP, a careful reconnaissance from the bivouac to the IP must be made by each unit.[38]

Secretary of War Stimson's visit to Fort Benning in December 1940. General Patton speaks to the audience about the maneuvers they are watching.

Norris H. Perkins

Colonel Gillem discussed some of the factors that affect a road march done in peacetime through the countryside and towns. Serials could be interrupted by everything from trains to farm tractors. Allowances had to be considered also for the heavy army trucks that had more problems in the hills than did the tanks. The use of a brief time lag between serials helped in keeping these factors from affecting more than one serial at a time. Urban areas created other problems. The units had to be trained to reduce the interval between vehicles and speed prior to entering towns and then to resume normal interval and speed upon leaving them.[39]

Reconnaissance elements marked routes in practice for the future when road marches would have to be done on rainy nights over unmarked roads and trails. Command vehicles had to be easily identifiable so that messengers could find them. Maintenance vehicles doing repair work had to be well marked so that approaching vehicles would not confuse them with the previous serial.[40]

Units were required to send out an advance detail to lay out its bivouac and then guide the vehicles into their respective locations. Properly conducted, a unit could move directly into a bivouac without halting on the road or at the entrance. Moving thirty vehicles that have been traveling at twenty-five miles per hour into a confined wooded area at night with no visible lights requires good training. The reconnaissance units that are the first, both into a bivouac and out again, should be in a separate area to allow both the main units and the reconnaissance elements to get some rest.[41]

Colonel Gillem concluded the school by congratulating the officers on a well-executed road march. At some point the success of the whole unit could depend on just one man doing his assigned duty. He reminded the officers to prepare themselves and train their units "so that by improvisation and determination they can overcome" any obstacles.[42] An example improvising included making up for only having one real tank in the company by using trucks with stovepipes mounted to simulate the gun.[43]

It was because of one of the weekly division officer schools that Major General Patton received his most famous nickname. One evening a group of officers were at their quarters waiting to go to the school. Lieutenant Perkins, an officer in the 66th, recalled:

> In these talks, he was trying to get us used to the idea that we were going to war...And he says, "You men, you've got to be prepared for it." And one evening we were looking at our watches and Lieutenant Alfred Kirchner...said, "Well, I guess it's time to hear Old Blood and Guts" and the response was a roar of laughter. Up until then he had been called The Green Hornet for the way he raced around the maneuver area in his tank, wearing a gold helmet. So, from then on, he was Blood and Guts...[44]

In the first three months of 1941 the 2nd Armored Division began to fill as thousands of new recruits arrived. These new soldiers entered three months of basic training at the division replacement center that had been organized by Major General Scott before his departure.[45]

Thomas Domarecki of Mount Carmel, Pennsylvania entered the army in February 1941 with the first group of one-year draftees. He joined at Fort Dix and received his issue of uniforms including a number of articles from World War I. Domarecki and eleven other men were sent to Fort Benning where they joined Company H. There was a regimental inspection every Saturday morning and Domarecki and the others appeared wearing their wrap legging and old model overcoats. General Patton as the inspecting officer appeared in front of twelve from Fort Dix and shouted, "What is this? Get these men the hell outa here and over to main post and get them out-fitted like soldiers."[46]

An officer who joined the 66th in February was Lt. Hugh R. O'Farrell from Athens, Georgia. He was a big Irishman standing six feet, four inches. He graduated from the University of Georgia and began his long and distinguished career with the 66th in Reconnaissance Company.[47] He is remembered by his peers and subordinates in the regiment as a real leader of men and a no "B.S. kind of a guy."[48]

The 3rd Battalion of the 66th, having been garrisoned at Fort Devens, Massachusetts, for many years, was comprised almost entirely of northerners.

Lieutenant Perkins and Lieutenant McConnell of H Company at Fort Benning in April 1941.
Norris H. Perkins

This began to change with the move to Fort Benning and the influx of new recruits. One of these new men was John Mayo, a farmer from Oxford, Florida. In July of 1940 a friend had convinced him to join the army with him. Mayo soon found himself one of two southerners amongst "a bunch of Yankees" in Company H, 3rd Battalion, 66th Armored.[49] The young southerner recalled something the company first sergeant did after the company had received "7 or 8 more southern fellows" from a rural background:

> Sergeant Windword was determined to try to make us farm boys walk straight...one day, he called a meeting in the day room...he had all of his NCOs there, plus all of the new recruits out of the company...he was a man that could get his point over without discriminating against you as an individual...he had all of the PFCs and all of the privates line up against the wall...he started out with our heels, telling us to put our heels together against the wall and our toes pointed at an angle of 45 degrees, and our legs and knees straight without stiffness, our butt against the wall, and let the hands hang naturally, with the thumbs along the seams of the trousers. And the head and eyes straight forward with the head back against the wall.
>
> Well, what he was doing, he was giving us the definition of a soldier at attention...we were standing at attention, and all of a sudden he gave us a command, he says, one step forward, move! So we all stepped

Private Terrebone mans the .30 caliber machine gun on a M2A4 light tank of H Company in the pine forests of Fort Benning. Note the tanker's helmet on the front fender. April 1941.

Norris H. Perkins

out in one step, well, we were all just straight as a board after we took the one step forward...he says, Now god damn it, walk that way, and he turned and walked out of the room...[50]

The division, especially the 66th, was dealt a heavy setback in April 1941 when it was required to furnish a cadre of officers and NCOs for the new 3rd Armored Division being formed at Camp Beauregard, Louisiana. In fact, the 66th, because it was the only "full-size" tank regiment in the army in early 1940, continuously lost its veterans to begin new units through 1940 and 1941.[51]

In early May the entire division with its thousands of new recruits conducted a week of tactical training at Fort Benning. This was Patton's last chance to polish his division's skills before their debut in the 2nd Army maneuvers the next month in Tennessee.[52]

John Mayo, a tank driver in Company H, recalled the interesting manner in which the light tanks of the 66th were guided:

> ...the tank commander was standing in the turret of the tank, the driver would be right down under his feet, so if he wanted the driver to move forward, he would just touch him in the back with his foot. And if he wanted him to turn right, the driver would pull the right lever on the tank until he'd lift his foot off of his right shoulder. And then, if he wanted him to turn left he'd press the left shoulder and you pull the lever until he lifted his foot off the left shoulder, and that's the way they directed you as to how to drive. And then if he wanted you to go faster, he'd tap you on the back of the head. If he wanted you to slow down, he'd tap you on the head. If he wanted you to stop, he would just press his foot on your head lightly, and hold it there until you stopped the tank.[53]

But this method did not always proceed smoothly. Lieutenant Perkins had a terrifying experience with his tank driver one night in a forest at Fort Benning:

> My new driver panicked in the dark and froze on the throttle...I jammed down on the top of his head and I couldn't get him to stop. He was absolutely panic-stricken, frozen on the throttle, but he would turn. We were in a pine forest off a road through the forest and bushes, and I was desperately trying to keep him from hitting a tree. Every time a tree would loom up in the dark, I would press him across the shoulder and get him to turn. We were zigzagging all over the place, crisscrossing the road. Finally, I lost control of him and he ran into a pine tree, about 8 inches in diameter. I instantly looked up (although it was dark I could see the sky) and a shock wave ran up that pine tree like somebody had shaken the end of a rope, and about 15 feet of the dead top of

Field repairs on a M2A4 in the forests of Fort Benning. The engine has been pulled and rests on the ground behind the truck.

Norris H. Perkins

the tree broke off. I ducked and it lit right across the turret. That guy became a good driver later, after we exchanged some unpleasantries about his bone head and my heavy foot.[54]

In mid 1941 the United States Army began conducting large-scale maneuvers in which entire divisions engaged in simulated combat across the American countryside. The units had been engaged in intensive small-unit through division-level training during the previous year, and the large-scale exercises were the next step in the training process. These large-scale maneuvers placed several divisions against each other in mock combat.

The primary purpose of these large-scale maneuvers was to train a division, corps, or field army how to maneuver and fight in a situation simulating war conditions as closely as possible. A secondary purpose was to test and evaluate new tactics, organizations, and equipment in a tactical environment. The best way to determine how a new tank or other vehicle would perform was to put it in the hands of real soldiers during maneuvers. They would drive the new vehicle over all types of terrain for hundreds of miles, quickly bringing any problems with the new vehicle to the surface.

The maneuvers had several purposes in the training process. For the higher ranking officers, those commanding a battalion or larger unit, these exercises gave them the opportunity to command and maneuver their units with the goal of defeating the enemy force and capturing the objective of their mission. These objectives were often a town of military importance, a major road or rail intersection, or a bridge.

The junior officers received vital training in leading their units through unfamiliar territory to reach their mission objective successfully. This often proved difficult since they had to maneuver through natural and man-made obstacles and many enemy ambushes and opposition. These young officers, many of them in the army for less than a year, were responsible for leading their units quickly to the objectives with a minimum of real or simulated losses. Often a young lieutenant or captain was ordered to lead a column over a hundred miles through unfamiliar areas at night. He had to accomplish this night navigation using a hooded flashlight over a map in a rough-riding tank.

The noncommissioned officers (NCOs) performed their normal function of conducting the day-to-day care and training of the soldiers. The maneuvers, which lasted for several weeks, provided the NCOs with a captive audience in a field environment. The senior NCOs often spent time training the junior officers who were supposed to lead them. It was in the senior NCO's best interest to teach his officer everything he could because the unit's survival might later depend on the officer's ability. The smart young officers understood and respected the experience and knowledge of the NCOs and listened to their guidance. The maneuvers trained the soldiers in road marching, driving under all sorts of conditions, and living in the field. The importance of maintaining one's vehicle was sometimes learned the hard way in the exercises.

The maneuvers were made to be as realistic as possible by several means. Almost all weapons were supplied with blank ammunition that provided very convincing smoke and sound. In addition, battle sounds were frequently provided by trucks and aircraft equipped with loudspeakers.

A large organization of controllers managed the maneuvers. Each unit was accompanied by one or more umpires who were officers or NCOs drawn from other like units. (For example, a company umpire was a company commander from a unit not participating in the exercise.) Other umpires were in charge of important crossroads, bridges, ford sites, and other installations. When two units engaged in simulated combat, the umpires decided the outcome based on a large number of factors, such as surprise, number of weapons on each side, and obstacles. The umpires were the primary means of providing feedback to a unit on its performance following the exercise.

Inside view of the driver's compartment of a M2A4 tank.

Norris H. Perkins

Inside view of the gun breech of a M2A4 light tank.

Norris H. Perkins

Student officers at the tank maintenance course at Fort Knox in March 1941. The officers are standing beside a Continental 7-cylinder, air-cooled radial engine of the M2A4 tank.

Norris H. Perkins

CHAPTER 5

Patton's Blitzkrieg:
The Tennessee Maneuvers

In June 1941, the 66th Armored Regiment, as a part of Maj. Gen. George Patton's 2nd Armored Division, participated in the Second Army Maneuvers conducted in the Camp Forrest area of middle Tennessee. Located southeast of Nashville around the towns of Murfreesboro, Shelbyville, and Manchester, the rugged area was considered unsuitable for tanks by most of the military commanders. Many expected the mountains, forests, and several rivers of the area to give the opposing side's infantry a considerable advantage over Patton's tanks.

The 66th Armored Regiment, commanded by Col. William H. H. Morris, entered the maneuvers with a strength of 81 officers and 1,153 enlisted men.[1] The ninety-nine light tanks of the regiment and their crews moved from the Fort Benning area to Cookeville, Tennessee, on the northeastern edge of the maneuver area, by train. Major General Patton, determined to get his division into the maneuvers undetected, had the trains arrive at their destinations and unload under cover of darkness.[2] The wheeled vehicles of the regiment moved along the eastern leg of the division's two primary routes, covering the distance over two nights. Moving at twenty-five miles per hour, the 118 jeeps, trucks, scout cars, and 64 motorcycles of the regiment took twenty-three minutes to pass by a location.[3] During the night of 14 June 1941, the regiment moved out from Fort Benning and followed Route 27 north to a concealed bivouac at Fort Ogelthorpe just south of the Tennessee border. The unit left the bivouac at 2000 the next night, passed through Chattanooga and arrived at their bivouac near Cookeville, Tennessee at 0220 on 16 June.[4]

Recovering a M3 Stuart which turned over when the soft shoulder of the road collapsed. June 1941.

Norris H. Perkins

Formation of A Company commanded by Capt. Dexter Griffin. June 1941.

U.S. Army Military History Institute

3rd Battalion loaded aboard a train for the journey to Tennessee. June 1941. Note the wooden wedges that were used to block the tracks.

Norris H. Perkins

Men of the 66th getting some rest after forty-eight hours of continuous movement.

Norris H. Perkins

The units of the 2nd Armored remained in their concealed bivouacs through the day of 16 June preparing for the coming action, with the exception of the division's reconnaissance units, which began to seek out the opposing maneuver forces.[5] The first exercise, designated C-7, had 2nd Armored Division as a part of the Red force reinforcing the 5th Infantry Division (also a Red unit), that was defending against a strong attack by the Blue VII Corps. The VII Corps, composed of the 27th and the 30th Infantry Divisions, had been pushing east against the 5th Infantry Division between the towns of Shelbyville and Manchester.[6] The 2nd Armored plan called for the division to conduct night marches in five columns around the flanks and rear of the Blue forces, launching their attacks from five different directions as dawn broke on 17 June.[7] The 66th, which had the longest night march of all the Red units, left their bivouac late on the night of 16 June and marched 130 miles in a wide sweep around the northern edge of the maneuver area.[8]

The long night road march proved to be eventful for Captain Lumpkin's Company H. When Sergeant Rape's tank driver was unable to keep up with Captain Lumpkin, as he led the company at fifty-five miles per hour, Sergeant Rape took over as driver. As Sergeant Rape drove the tank up over the high arched center of the Caney River bridge an oncoming vehicle's headlights blinded him.[9] He recalled:

> I touched the right lever and hit the concrete rail, tearing down about 20 feet of it, and turning the tank over in the middle of the bridge. The tank was rocking a little and I thought we were hanging on the edge of the bridge. I said to the guys "Be still, I think we're hanging on the edge". When I surveyed the situation, I saw we were just in the middle of the bridge.[10]

The fortunate crew exited the tank and a wrecker came forward to tow the damaged vehicle away. The concrete bridge rail had sheared off the right front sprocket of the tank, producing a catastrophic amount of damage. Captain Lumpkin, unaware that the accident on the bridge was holding up most of his company, continued along the route at a breakneck speed. Lieutenant Perkins, the executive officer of Company H, who was temporarily in command of the battalion trains, was trying to keep track of where the units were so he could bring the trains forward. He decided to try to catch up with Captain Lumpkin. Finally Lieutenant Perkins came upon a tank whose crew told him they had given up trying to keep up with their speeding commander, who earlier had a mechanic remove the tank's governor so it would not limit his speed. Lieutenant Perkins took off in the pitch dark, his jeep traveling sixty-five miles per hour to catch the company commander.

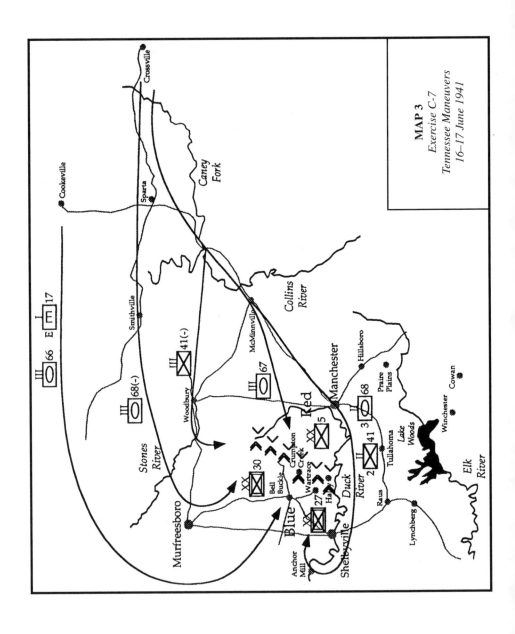

MAP 3
Exercise C-7
Tennessee Maneuvers
16–17 June 1941

Sgt. Bill Rape (on the tank) and the crew of H-3 pose by their tank after the disastrous bridge crash. Note the sheared front spocket and housing.

Norris H. Perkins

After several miles, the lieutenant came upon the tank cruising along at nearly sixty miles per hour.

> My blue lights highlighted this monstrosity traveling down the highway with its red and blue exhaust flames shooting out the twin exhaust ports in the back...and along the top of the tank's track long wavering blue tongues of static electricity were licking along the sides of the tank. It was a sight out of Hades.[11]

Eventually the lieutenant came upon a place in the road wide enough to allow the jeep to pass the tank without being crushed; thus finally ended what became known as "the Wild Ride of Capt. Lumpkin."[12]

At dawn, Exercise C-7 began violently as Patton's armored columns hit the flanks and rear of the Blue forces from several directions at once. Slowed by their longer march, the 66th launched their attack into the rear of the Blue 30th Infantry Division near the little town of Bell Buckle at 0845. The regiment's attack was coordinated with the Red force that had come around the southern flank of the Blue forces and the Army Air Corps 8th Bomb Squadron. Around 1100 the 66th had encountered strong resistance from antitank defense at Bell Buckle. Exercise C-7 was terminated at

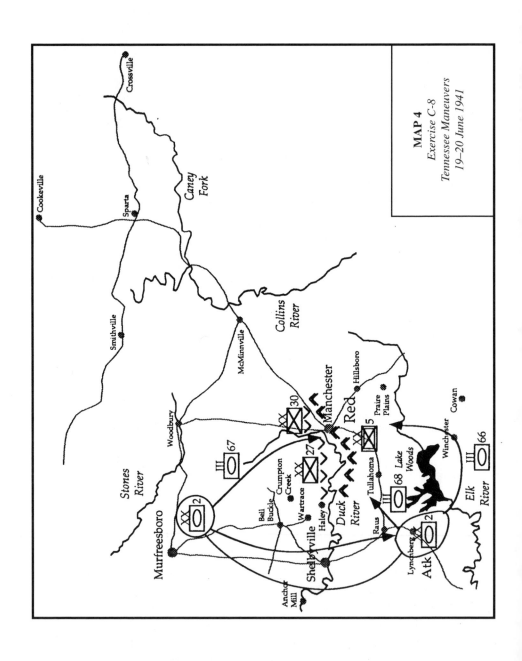

MAP 4
Exercise C-8
Tennessee Maneuvers
19–20 June 1941

M2A4 light tank of G Company.

1941 Dodge T202-VC1 command car with weary crew. June 1941.

Bringing down city hall. The tank that sheared the wall off the Bell Buckle City Hall. June 1941.

Norris H. Perkins

1140 after the Red force had put the Blue forces on the defensive and driven them back in several places.[13]

During the attack on Bell Buckle, a tank of the regiment was involved in one of the most interesting accidents of the Tennessee Maneuvers. One of the tanks was negotiating a long "S" curve in the town when it suddenly encountered a delivery truck in the narrow street. The tank driver swerved up onto the sidewalk to avoid hitting the truck and lost control of the tank. The tank slid along the front of the Bell Buckle City Hall, the tank's brush guard removing an entire course of bricks from the building wall. The entire two-story brick wall then collapsed into the street and buried the tank. Lacking the support of the wall, the 2nd floor of the building sagged, and the furniture slid out, falling onto the brick pile around the tank. The only injury was to the tank commander, who got a minor bruise from a brick that hit his helmet. Later when Major General Patton was asked why the tank couldn't see the Bell Buckle City Hall that it had damaged so badly, he replied, "How can you expect a tank to see that City Hall when Bell Buckle isn't even on the map?"[14]

For the second exercise, the 2nd Armored Division changed sides and joined the Blue forces of VII Corps. Exercise C-8 had the Blue forces attacking the Red defensive positions to the north of the Duck River between

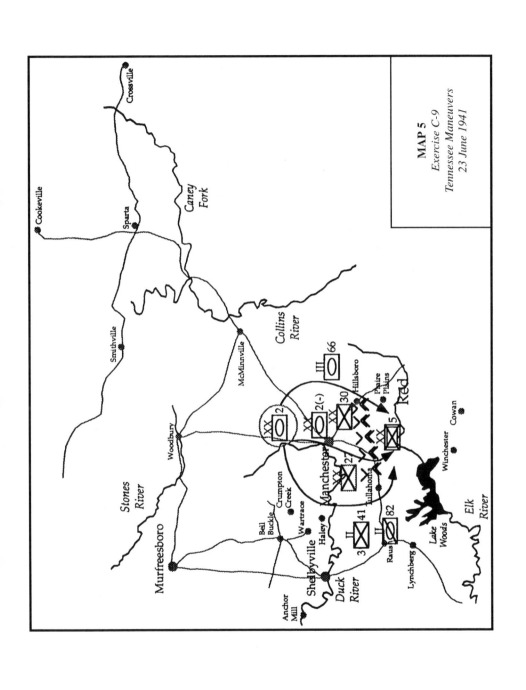

MAP 5
Exercise C-9
Tennessee Maneuvers
23 June 1941

Shelbyville and Manchester. During the first day, 19 June, the Blue force attack made little progress, but the threat of envelopment caused the Red forces to break contact and withdraw south of the Duck River during the night.[15] While the medium tanks of the 67th Armor crossed the Duck River and continued to attack the Red forces, the 2nd Armored Brigade with the light tanks of both the 66th and the 68th Armor moved from their bivouacs south of Murfreesboro around the west side of Shelbyville to an assembly area near Lynchburg before dawn on 20 June. The two light tank regiments were ordered to attack into the rear of the Red 5th Infantry Division at 0700, the 68th via Tullahoma and the 66th via Winchester. The 66th advanced slowly, having to cross the Elk River twice before arriving in the area where they expected to encounter the Red forces. Exercise C-8 was terminated just as the 66th Armor made contact with the Red 5th Infantry Division. After the exercise the 2nd Armored Division regrouped in bivouac areas approximately five miles north of Manchester.[16]

In Exercise C-9 the 2nd Armored remained with the Blue VII Corps, whose mission was to attack the Red forces which were defending a line running west from Hillsboro towards Tullahoma. With no rain for two weeks, the roads had become very dusty, making vehicle intervals of 300 yards or more a necessity during road marches. In these conditions, the 2nd Armored Division did something that really surprised their opponents; they launched a straight forward frontal attack. At this point in the maneuvers Patton's opponents were so concerned about his characteristic flank attacks that they had numbers of their forces guarding their rear areas. The reconnaissance company of the regiment had first established contact with the Red forces at 0630 that morning. The 66th Armored Regiment, reinforced by two battalions of the 41st Infantry Regiment, one battalion of the 78th Field Artillery and a company of the 17th Engineers, moved into an attack position about 0930. At 1000 a courier delivered an order for the attack to begin at 1100. Efforts to contact the 8th Bombardment Squadron to coordinate their supporting attack in front of the 66th met with difficulty, and the attack had to be delayed until 1120. At the appointed time, the 66th and its attached units launched their attack south toward the town of Prairie Plains as the aircraft of the Army Air Corps staged a bombing raid in front of them. The attack went off as planned, meeting only scattered resistance, and the regiment reached the Elk River by 1215.[17] The main effort of the division hit the center of the Red front line at 1330 and quickly brought about the termination of the exercise at 1400.[18]

The final exercise of the Tennessee Maneuvers, C-10, placed the 2nd Armored Division back on to the Red side. The Blue VII Corps was defending a line between the Duck River on the north and the Elk River on

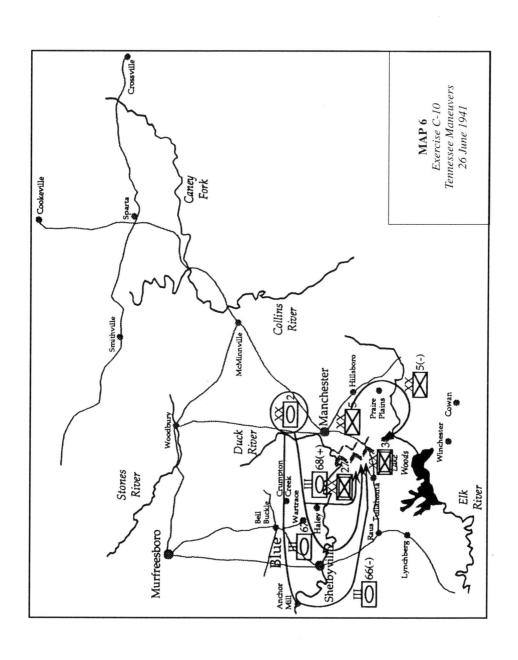

MAP 6
Exercise C-10
Tennessee Maneuvers
26 June 1941

Tankers of H Company cleaning their weapons at the end of the maneuvers. At the left is Daumont Valentine who was later transferred to 1st Armored Division where he was killed in action.

Norris H. Perkins

the south. To protect their flanks the Blue engineers simulated the destruction of every bridge and the mining of every fording site along both rivers.[19] The division left their bivouac about five miles north of Manchester after dark on 25 June and moved into forward assembly areas near Crumpton Creek. After some delay and losses because of the Blue mines, the division's 82nd Reconnaissance Battalion had secured three ford sites on the Duck River by 0700. The entire 2nd Armored Division led by the 82nd Reconnaissance and the 41st Infantry moved around the north flank of the Red forces and crossed the Duck River well behind the Red defensive line between 1000 and noon. The 66th Regiment crossed the river at Anchor Mill, less one battalion, which crossed at Haley under the control of the 68th Armor and pushed rapidly to the vicinity of Raus. The main body of the 66th was just beginning its attack from the west when the exercise was terminated at 1320.[20]

At the end of the maneuvers, three trains, each carrying one of the 66th Armored Regiment's battalions, loaded between 0600 and 0730 on 29 June at Cowan, Tennessee. The tanks detrained at Sand Hill, Georgia the next day and moved back to Fort Benning.[21] The wheeled vehicles of the regiment

M2A4s rail loading at Cowan, Tennessee in preparation for the return to Fort Benning.
Norris H. Perkins

conducted two night road marches along the same routes that they had used to get to Tennessee, staying at Cedartown, Georgia the day of 30 June.[22]

The Tennessee Maneuvers were the first of several large-scale maneuvers that were to provide invaluable training for the soldiers who soon would be thrust into real battle. The Report of Operations from these maneuvers indicates their importance. First, the resupply of units during the maneuvers was performed only at night with the exception of the first exercise (C-7). Repair of the damaged or broken down vehicles among the 2nd Armored Division's 2,400 wheels and tracks was accomplished quickly, no easy feat in field conditions. At the end of the exercise seven vehicles, two of which were tanks, were still under repair or had been evacuated to higher-level maintenance. Second, the division's medical units had efficiently handled the simulated casualties. It was noted, however, that the simulations were insufficient to properly test the division's medical assets, because every soldier used as a simulated casualty is one soldier who is not with his unit learning the tactical lessons of the maneuvers. Even a soldier whose vehicle is broken down is required to help fix it rather than serve as a simulated casualty. There were also actual casualties during the maneuvers: one death (cause not listed) and three officers and thirty men hospitalized.

New M2A4 light tank. First introduced in early 1941, it was the first American tank with a turret with 360-degree traverse and a 37mm gun. The two fixed side machine guns are a remainder of the infantry support role of the tank. Fort Benning, 1941.

Norris H. Perkins

Lt. Joe Moore of H Company with his M2A4 on a rough Tennessee road. June 1941. Note the flexibility of the suspension.

Norris H. Perkins

Third, several other tests were successful. Mission type orders, in which the subordinate is only told what is to be done and allowed to decide how to best accomplish the mission, proved to be superior for tactical orders. Couriers, primarily mounted on motorcycles, were used successfully as backup to radio communications. The new blue (blackout) driving lights proved to be satisfactory. These blue lights, only about one-sixth as detectable as red light, gave adequate illumination for careful driving. Normal march speed of twenty-five miles per hour was possible but difficult to maintain with the new lights.[23]

In addition, the report addressed several areas that required further work. Additional training was needed in the proper use of both ground and aerial reconnaissance. Supply and maintenance vehicles had, on several occasions, hampered the movement of combat elements, an unfortunate side effect of the principle of supporting units well forward and close to the far-ranging tank columns. The report forcefully reminded the tankers that they were not invulnerable. Also, the cavalry-charge method of attacking antitank guns, weapons quite capable of killing tanks, was quickly seen as foolish. Tank crews were instructed to use their mobility to bypass antitank guns so that the tank's superior firepower could be used to wreak havoc on enemy units without antitank protection. Patton, a longtime advocate of combat branches working together in battle, made what came to be known as his "Musicians of Mars (Roman God of War)" talk in the conclusions:

> There was a tendency toward individualism in separate units. The rifleman was intent on shooting, the tanker on charging, the artilleryman on firing, and so on. Battles are not won that way. To obtain harmony in music each instrument must support the others; to obtain harmony in battle each weapon must support the others. Battles are won by team play.[24]

All through the inter-war years the proper use of tanks had been hotly debated. The Tennessee Maneuvers put an end to the debate.

> In view of the fact that each maneuver was terminated from 12 to 24 hours ahead of schedule, and the fact that each maneuver terminated on the same day in which the 2nd Armored Division entered into action, it is obvious that the proper employment of armored forces radically changes all former conceptions of the tempo of battle.[25]

Patton's tanks, moving at between twenty and fifty miles per hour, were able to strike the enemy from several directions at once, so opponents of the 2nd Armored now had to be able to defend their flanks and rear in addition to their front-line. The Report of Operations read in part:

The defender in each case was faced with the threat of attacks from all directions, any one of which was sufficient to disrupt the scheme of defense. Therefore former conceptions of missions such as "driving the enemy back" to a certain line or gaining a series of limited objectives by "pushing" the enemy are and should be changed, by the proper employment of armored divisions, to complete and rapid destruction of the enemy in place.[26]

With the conclusion of the Tennessee maneuvers, the leaders of the armored force had proven that warfare had entered a new era, in which highly mobile armored forces would dominate the battlefield.

CHAPTER 6

Swamps and Snakes:
The Louisiana Maneuvers

2nd Lt. James M. Burt joined the U.S. Army in February 1941. Growing up in the hills of Massachusetts and New Hampshire during the Depression he had worked in a wide variety of jobs including trapper, carpenter's helper, and field hand. He had graduated from Norwich University in 1939 with a reserve officer's commission and had gone to work as a chemist. In July 1941 Burt had completed the Maintenance Course at Fort Knox and was assigned as C Company Maintenance Officer. The crusty company maintenance sergeant was very busy and none too pleased to have a second lieutnanant on his turf. The sergeant finally looked at his new boss and asked, "What did you learn at Knox?" Lieutenant Burt was impatient to report several items of maintenance information, but he paused and then replied "How to play golf." The old sergeant soon grinned a little and the two got along fine after that.[1]

The 66th Armored Regiment, as part of the 2nd Armored Division, participated in the Louisiana Maneuvers held between 9 August and 3 October 1941. These maneuvers were conducted in an area of western Louisiana and eastern Texas generally bounded by Shreveport in the north, Alexandria in the east, Lake Charles in the south, and Nacogdoches, Texas, on the west. The majority of the exercises took place in the more restrictive area between the Sabine River on the west and the Red River on the east. Most of the maneuver area consisted of vast areas of swamp or soft ground, dense forests, and a limited road network. The soldiers often found that although many areas appeared to be firm ground, vehicles or even men would quickly become mired. This maneuver area would make the rugged Tennessee maneuver look easy by comparison. A tank, in spite of its great weight, is better able to traverse soft ground because its track distributes the weight more evenly than does a wheeled vehicle, thus providing better traction than tires. The Louisiana Maneuvers would show the limits to this capability.

The regiment departed Fort Benning on 9–10 August 1941 bound for Louisiana with the rest of the 2nd Armored Division. The tanks, half-tracks, and their crews moved by rail, covering the distance in two days. The wheeled vehicle column of the 66th consisted of 226 vehicles and was comprised mainly of ninety 2$\frac{1}{2}$-ton trucks (the army's primary workhorse) and eighty-seven motorcycles. Traveling along U.S. Highway 80 and U.S. Highway 171, the wheeled vehicles moved into a concealed bivouac near Grand Cove, Louisiana.[2]

One of the officers who arrived just in time for the maneuvers was Lieutenant Cameron J. Warren. He graduated from Montana State University with a degree in Forestry and Engineering and joined the 66th at Fort Benning in July 1941. He remembers his first encounter with General Patton during the 1941 Louisiana Maneuvers:

> I saw him in his field headquarters and in the field. What a sight. All decked out in his tank helmet and two ivory handled pistols. He would ask a front line trooper why he wasn't moving. Whatever the reply, usually that he was planning his attack, Patton would say, "A good plan executed now is much better than a perfect plan executed ten minutes from now. Get your ass moving."[3]

During the Louisiana Maneuvers the army was still short of many items because its rapid growth in 1941 outpaced available supplies and production. Many of the newest units participated in the maneuvers with only a fraction of their authorized weapons and equipment. Some soldiers were carrying wooden weapons, and a tree trunk could be used as an antitank gun. An antitank gun crew could aim and fire their tree trunk at an attacking tank and knock it out, if the umpire was available to rule on the battle.[4]

The scenario for the Louisiana Maneuvers had a Blue force led by VIII Corps defending against a Red force invasion of the Louisiana coast.[5] The Red forces, consisting primarily of the V Corps, had advanced north to the vicinity of Lake Charles.[6] The main strength of the VIII Corps was in its three infantry divisions, the 2nd, 36th, and 45th.[7] For the first exercise the 2nd Armored Division was attached to the Blue VIII Corps. The division's mission for this exercise was simply to "attack the enemy and destroy him wherever found."[8] On the afternoon of 16 August the 66th Armor moved from its initial bivouac near Rosepine to a concealed position near the town of Benson.[9]

Half-track and jeep at the regimental headquarters during a break between exercises.
Norris H. Perkins

The exercise commenced at 0200 on 17 August 1941. The 66th Armor and the 3rd Battalion, 41st Infantry, made up the right fork of the division's three-pronged attack.[10] The reconnaissance elements of the 66th moved at 0400 and began their search south for the Red forces. The head of the regiment's column reached Aacoco by 1630. By nightfall on the first day the regiment reached the vicinity of Pickering. There was no unit movement during the night.[11]

The next day, 18 August, the regiment encountered the heavy antitank fire of the 32nd Infantry Division at the Red defensive line astride U.S. 171, four miles south of Pickering. The 82nd Reconnaissance Battalion covered the east flank of the 66th's west column from near Pickering all the way to the south and west of De Ridder. While the 1st and 3rd Battalions of the 66th engaged the Red forces on U.S. 171, the regiment's 2nd Battalion and the 1st Battalion, 67th Armor, worked around the west flank of the Red forces. This force got into Rosepine by 1430. The 144th Regimental Combat Team (RCT) was attached to the regiment and went into position astride US 171 north of Pickering. When darkness fell on 18 August the regiment was still deadlocked with the Red 32nd Infantry Division antitank defenses.[12]

During the evening of 18 August VIII Corps issued orders for the entire 2nd Armored Division to assemble in the vicinity of Cravens, Pitkin, Leander, and La Camp on the eastern flank of the corps. At daylight on the nineteenth the division moved to sweep around the east flank of the Red forces. Their mission was to attack in the direction of De Ridder to break through and destroy the Red forces and installations opposing the friendly 2nd and 36th Divisions. The 2nd Armored's flank attack was coordinated with the attack of the Blue 2nd, 36th, and 45th Divisions.[13]

During the maneuvers, many infantry unit commanders believed that by blocking the road along which a tank unit was attacking, the tanks could be easily stopped. Many of these infantrymen had the mistaken idea that by being in a forest they were safe from tanks. But during the maneuvers the tankers often would envelop an enemy road-blocking position by going through the pine forest to come in behind the position. The light tanks of the 66th were able to knock down trees up to eight inches in diameter. The tank would move up against the tree and then simply drive forward, knocking the tree down. Lieutenant Perkins of Company H enjoyed the tree "slapping the ground like a giant whip. and what was really fun was watching the enemy soldiers run out like a bunch of scared rabbits."[14]

Unfortunately for the 66th, it proved impossible to extricate itself from its battle with the 32nd Division. The operations order was amended for the 66th and the other elements of the west column to continue their attack on De Ridder from the north. The exercise was terminated at 1500 on 19 August while the 2nd Armored attack was in progress. During the exercise the division captured 339 vehicles, 82 artillery pieces, 79 cavalry vans, and 2,890 prisoners. Following the end of the maneuver the 2nd Armored Division units moved into bivouac locations near their final positions.[15]

On 21 August Lt. Gen. Walter Krueger, commander of the Blue Third Army, held a critique for the commanders of his forces. Among those present were the officers of the 2nd Armored Division and the 66th Armored Regiment. Following the critique, these officers returned to their units to pass on the lessons learned to their subordinate officers and men. The overall objective of this process was to find problems wherever they existed and to correct them as soon as possible. At the next exercise, commanders would check to see if the problems had been corrected. Lieutenant General Krueger had the following opening comments on the purpose of the maneuvers:

> These...maneuvers present real opportunity for making progress toward the objective of welding the Third Army into an effective fighting team. In this phase...each corps is enabled to operate as a single unit,...testing its subordinate units, its staffs, and its services against an opponent who is ever ready to seize upon and magnify the results of every misstep. The elimination of these mistakes is our immediate purpose, so that each corps will become, within itself, a formidable and dependable

fighting machine, and, more important, an effective member of the greater team–the Army.

Elimination of mistakes requires that they be sought out and held up to view, so that there may be common understanding of the nature of the error and of the specific direction in which corrective effort must be applied. It is for this reason that critiques dwell so largely upon defects in this operation, and seemingly ignore the fine work and the splendid efforts that, in fact, are noticeable to every hand.[16]

The general reminded the officers that the resources (forces and equipment) they would have to accomplish a mission would seldom be of their choosing but that "all must learn to do the job with the means available."[17] He noted that the VIII Corps' decision to spearhead their attack with the 2nd Armored Division was very aggressive and reduced the need for other reconnaissance. The drawback was that the early and continued commitment of the armored forces against organized resistance led to heavy tank losses. This reduced the tank force available for the final attack and led to a piecemeal rather than massed use of the armor. Indeed, the 66th's prolonged battle with the 32nd Division along Highway 171 was the type of battle General Krueger wished to avoid.[18]

Lieutenant General Krueger also reminded his officers that continuous reconnaissance of the terrain was critical for the success of armored forces. Tanks can best direct their attack towards a vital area or enemy element only after determining the type of terrain in the area. "To barge ahead, gain local successes in numerous places and then be stopped by a natural obstacle is a waste of power."[19]

Some problems in both the real and simulated supply systems were noted. Lieutenant General Krueger lectured, "If we cannot do this in our maneuvers, how can we expect to do it when we get real interruptions by enemy action?"[20] Commanders were told in no uncertain terms that they must have their units simulate the resupply of ammunition to the units as realistically as possible. This involved using the real amount of transport, lift equipment, and troop labor that would be required to resupply real ammunition loads. Such practice is necessary because ammunition is heavy, bulky, and used at a rapid rate. The general summarized the importance of resupply training: "It will avail nothing to penetrate deeply into the enemy lines and then find that units have no gasoline or ammunition."[21]

The flow of information between units, not only above and below but laterally, was noted as needing improvement. The units above must ensure that their orders reach their subordinates in sufficient time to allow them to plan and execute the orders. Subordinates were responsible for submitting the reports and information necessary to keep their superiors informed of their status. Lateral communication was important in sharing all types of information with the units on the flanks to improve the entire command's preparedness.[22]

The final topic addressed during the critique was discipline, not the normal type of military discipline, but instead maneuver participants' cheating. Examples included a unit crossing a bridge marked as destroyed, and vehicles operating without maneuver markings that indicated to which side they belonged. The old American spirit of competition was outweighing the sense of fair play at times during the maneuvers. The general reprimanded his audience: "Clearly, there is a need for better discipline outside of just plain obedience to orders and instructions. Without such obedience there is no Army, just a mob."[23]

An interesting letter regarding this very problem was written at Headquarters, Third Army, Office of the Commanding General, on 23 August to Major General George S. Patton, Jr., the famed commander of 2nd Armored Division. The letter chastised General Patton for numerous tanks not having the proper Red or Blue markings during the maneuvers. It requested that he take corrective action to ensure that tank markings be visible at a reasonable distance. The letter was signed "Very Sincerely, Ike, Dwight D. Eisenhower, Colonel, General Staff Corps, Chief of Staff."[24]

One of the missions the 66th Armored performed between the exercises was the test of the capability of the ground to support vehicles traveling cross country. On 22 August, Headquarters, 2nd Armored Division, issued a memorandum directing that the regiments conduct tests to determine if their vehicles could cross the local terrain without becoming mired. They eventually gauged how soft or marshy the ground was by how far a man could push a test stick into the ground with ordinary pressure. For the wheeled and half-tracked vehicles, they determined that any ground where the stick could be pushed more than six inches was very risky. The evaluators noted that a vehicle driver, stopped by soft ground, could often extricate himself by opening his door and gauging the effect of applying power to avoid the wheels or tracks slipping.[25]

After the first exercise when a large number of vehicles were mired crossing deceptively soft ground, the regiment's evaluators tested two types of light tanks, the M2A4 and the M3 (diesel engine), in several areas. They found that the tanks could cross an area where the stick (one inch in diameter, four feet long) could be thrust into the ground thirty-six inches. This type of very marshy terrain could only be crossed by a tank in the proper gear traveling at a smooth, steady pace. The tanks' return trips in their own tracks were also evaluated. In the thirty-six-inch area, it would not have been possible for more than two tanks to travel in the same tracks. The evaluators noted that this test was done under dry weather conditions and would have been impossible in wet weather. All of the areas tested were covered in grass or brush and did not appear to be anything but a field of solid ground. This information was quickly shared and helped the soldiers avoid getting stuck in the innumerable marshy areas of Louisiana.[26]

The 2nd Armored Division changed sides for the second exercise, FM No. 2, of the maneuvers. The scenario remained the same as the first exercise with the Blue attack to the south temporarily halted along the line of Hemphill, Hornbeck, and Kisatchie. Attached to the Red V Corps, the division moved their bivouac areas eight to ten miles southeast of De Ridder at 1900 on 24 August.[27]

The 2nd Armored's initial mission was to move around the west flank of the Blue forces and attack to destroy Blue installations and forces in the Mansfield–Pleasant Hill area. The division arrived at a staging area on the west flank and just south of the limiting line near Jasper–Burkeville, Texas, and moved one column, composed only of wheeled vehicles, along the western flank. This both screened the tank columns from the enemy and got the wheeled vehicles to the staging area in the shortest time. At their roadside staging area the units refueled and ate breakfast prior to the 0500 exercise start time.[28]

Throughout the maneuvers the units were under the observation not only of the maneuver controllers but also the generals who commanded the participating units. When the soldiers did not maintain the proper fifty-yard interval between vehicles during road marches, they sometimes found that someone was watching. General Patton once appeared in a light plane over a group of the 66th Armored's tanks that were bunched in a swampy area. Patton had a loudspeaker mounted on the plane so that those below could receive his comments sooner rather than later. As Perkins recalled, "you never heard such a stream of profanity come down out of the sky as General Patton telling you to get those blankety-blank tanks apart. The soldiers were cowed and the civilians edified."[29]

The V Corps, with the 1st Cavalry Division on the east flank and the 2nd Armored Division on the west, crossed the limiting line promptly at 0500 on 25 August. The 2nd Armored Division, in three columns, rushed north through Texas at maximum speed. The reconnaissance group of the regiment, supported by a battalion from the 41st Infantry and a battery from the 78th Field Artillery, crossed the Sabine River at 1130. The VIII Corps had not destroyed or guarded the bridge the 66th Armor crossed, because it was some 100 miles north of the limiting line and well in the VIII Corps rear area. Only six hours after its start, the 66th had moved 180 miles and was attacking into the enemy rear areas. At 1400 the lead elements moved south of Mansfield without encountering any Blue forces. At darkness the regiment bivouacked near Mansfield.[30]

Orders from 2nd Armored Division Headquarters directed the attack to resume at 0450 on 26 August. The 66th Armor was directed toward Robeline to the southeast some fifty miles. When darkness fell on the twenty-sixth, the regiment had secured the northern exits of Robeline.[31]

The Blue VIII Corps was being crushed between the 2nd Armored Division, with the hammer coming from the north, and the main force of V Corps serving as the anvil. At 0500 on the twenty-seventh, the 2nd Armored and the 37th Infantry Division of V Corps attacked VIII Corps, administering the coup de grace. The 66th, assisted by the medium tanks of the 67th Armor, captured Hagwood at 0727. Passing through Hagwood, the lead elements of the 66th had reached Natchitoches when the exercise was terminated at 0820. The 2nd Armored Division, with the 66th Regiment covering the most distance, had achieved a smashing victory. After playing a major role in ending the exercise a day early, the 66th Armored moved to a bivouac near Marthaville.[32]

The eight pages of critique notes on this exercise contain almost no mention of the 2nd Armored. One of the few criticisms was that a tank column was closed up during an air attack. The attack had been made by planes with friendly markings, a portent of real battles to come. The division received a positive comment for having its tanks well dispersed and under cover along Highway 6 east of Robeline at 0735 on the last day of the exercise.[33]

The Louisiana Maneuvers had been carried out not only for the normal training purposes, but also for evaluating the performance of the officers at all levels. Officers' careers were made or broken on their performance during these maneuvers. Fully understanding this, officers sometimes took risks. Lieutenant Perkins was sent out on a reconnaissance by the commander of Company H, 66th Armor, when he did "the most reckless and wild thing of his whole life."[34] While out on the reconnaissance alone in his jeep he found himself on a small lane when an enemy half-track spotted him and pulled out behind him. He thought, "Oh, oh, they must have gotten me cornered."[35] He soon came to a wooden bridge from which the enemy had removed the planks from the entire center portion, leaving a gaping space. The bridge had a fifteen-foot ramp sloped at about fifteen degrees on either end.[36]

MAP 7
Field Maneuver #3
Louisiana Maneuvers
5–7 September 1941

Lieutenant Perkins remembered seeing a Marine recruiting poster that showed four men in a jeep towing a 37mm gun soaring several feet over a hillock. He figured that if a jeep with a load like that could fly, he should have no problem jumping the gap in the bridge. He backed the jeep up a short distance to get a running start, hitting the ramp at over fifty miles per hour. He hit the near-side ramp with a tremendous bang and not only jumped the gap but soared completely over the ramp on the opposite side. The jeep landed hard on its front wheels with the lieutenant maintaining control with the four wheel drive and plenty of gas pedal.

> The wildest thing I ever did. It was really stupid. It may have saved my career because if I'd been captured, not with my company, I would have been blamed for it.[37]

The Louisiana Maneuvers now moved from corps versus corps to field army versus field army. The Third Army was composed of the V and VIII Corps with the 2nd Armored Division held in reserve. The Third Army held a Command Post Exercise (CPX) on 1–2 September 1941 in an area south of Leesville. The CPX was a war game that involved only the command posts of the units, in this case down to battalion level. The purpose of a CPX is to train the commanders and their staffs in how to maneuver and fight without actually moving troops on the ground. This allows command and staff procedures to be refined while the junior officers train their soldiers in small unit tactics and basic soldier skills at the company level and below. During the CPX, the 2nd Armored only made plans for possible operations because they remained in reserve until the end of the exercise.[38]

The large-scale field maneuvers could be destructive to private property as thousands of tanks and other vehicles invaded the countryside. During one exercise at night, a tank driver, operating with the blue blackout lights, misjudged the position of a row of mailboxes. Mistakenly thinking that the mailboxes were on the left side of the road he went to the right. The tank ripped through the fence and ran over several pieces of farm equipment. Then, without a pause, the driver went through the fence again and continued on down the road. The old farmer had a rude surprise the next morning, followed shortly thereafter by a visit to the claims office.[39]

Following the CPX the field exercises resumed on 4 September. Field Maneuvers Numbers 3 and 4 were run together from 4 through 9 September. The 2nd Armored Division was attached to the Blue Third Army. The Red IV Corps was located on the opposite (east) side of the Red River north of Alexandria (with some troops on the west side of the river). When FM Number 3 began at 0700 on 4 September, the 2nd Armored Division was in reserve.[40]

Lt. Russell Bakey of H Company behind the wheel of an early ¼-ton truck soon to be the famous Willys jeep. August 1941.

Norris H. Perkins

Tankers posing in their gas masks. August 1941.

Norris H. Perkins

Refueling a M2A4. Lt. William McCully pours the gasoline while one of his crew holds the fire extinguisher at the filler pipe to prevent a fire starting from the gas vapor encountering static electricity. September 1941.

M-3 Stuart of H Company with Lt. Russell Bakey. September 1941.

M2A4 of F Company mired in the junglelike forests of Louisiana. Lt. Chester Stitler, regimental maintenance officer, is standing at the left. September 1941.

Norris H. Perkins

Repairing a damaged bridge using logs. September 1941.

Norris H. Perkins

On the afternoon of the second day, the division received orders to move north and attack via Kisatchie–Kurthwood to relieve pressure on the north flank of VIII Corps. The 66th moved as a part of the westernmost (right) of the division's two columns. The forces of the 1st Cavalry were encountered near Hornbeck and south of Florien. Later, Red tanks and infantry were encountered near Kurthwood. The attack resumed at 0600 on the morning of 6 September towards Kisatchie. Heavy enemy resistance was encountered at Kisatchie before the exercise was terminated at 0700.[41] When the exercise ended, the 2nd Armored had accomplished its mission, and was in a good position to block the withdrawal of Red forces opposing the VIII Corps.

Field Maneuver Number 4 began at dark on the same day FM 3 had ended. The 2nd Armored Division was ordered to cross the Red River in the vicinity of Natchitoches and attack the rear of the Red forces. The 66th Armor moved with the 2nd Armored Brigade as part of the right column. At around 1000 the 82nd Reconnaissance Battalion found a site on the Red River suitable for building a pontoon bridge. A battalion of the 66th, the 41st Infantry, and a battalion of the 141st RCT established a bridgehead on the enemy side. Since the construction of a large pontoon bridge normally required twenty-four hours to complete, the commanders put every soldier in the area to work; they finished the bridge at 0900, a mere ten hours after construction started. Units began crossing immediately and continued until 0530, 9 September. After crossing, the vehicles were refueled and the men ate and rested. At dawn on 9 September the attack resumed with the division in two columns striking south, deeper into the Red forces rear area. When the exercise was terminated at 0800 the 2nd Armored Brigade and the 66th had gotten to the vicinity of Colfax. After the exercise, the units moved into bivouacs near Montgomery.[42] The tanks of the 2nd Armored Division were successful in bringing another exercise to termination almost a day ahead of schedule.[43]

Following the critique on 11 September, the 2nd Armored Division switched to the Red Second Army. The Blue Third Army was located generally between the Sabine and Red Rivers in the area of Mansfield. The 2nd Armored Division, serving under the I Armored Corps, was ordered to cross the Red River and advance to hold the line from Fort Jessup and Many west to the Sabine River. The 66th Armored Regiment was the only armored unit in the East Force under the commander of 2nd Armored Brigade.[44]

Departing from concealed bivouacs south of Friendship at 0500, 15 September, the east force moved to Coushatta where the force split. The

MAP 8

Field Maneuver #4
Louisiana Maneuvers
7–9 September 1941

1st Battalion, 66th Armor, along with reconnaissance, infantry, artillery, and engineer elements, moved south and crossed the Red River near Clarence. The main body of the regiment and the rest of the East Force crossed near Coushatta and moved rapidly south. The 1st Battalion group moved from Clarence southwest to Fort Jessup and then south to Mount Carmel. The units reached their positions in the afternoon after encountering minimal resistance. The division held its positions as the Blue VIII Corps built their forces in front of the 2nd Armored's holding positions. Patton's tanks were finally unleashed on the morning of 18 September. After reconnaissance located a weak spot in the Blue line, a force consisting of the 3rd Battalion, 66th Armor, the 1st Battalion, 41st Infantry, and Company A, 82nd Reconnaissance Battalion, rushed through that point. By nightfall the force reached Toro, well into the Blue area, before being recalled. During the night, 2nd Army ordered units back to the defensive line of Many–Fort Jessup.[45]

On the afternoon of 19 September the 1st Cavalry Division attacked the right flank of the Red force. The cavalry had crossed the Sabine River

A Company tanker removing tree branches from the suspension of his M-3 tank, "Alamo." Note the early model revolver holster. September 1941.

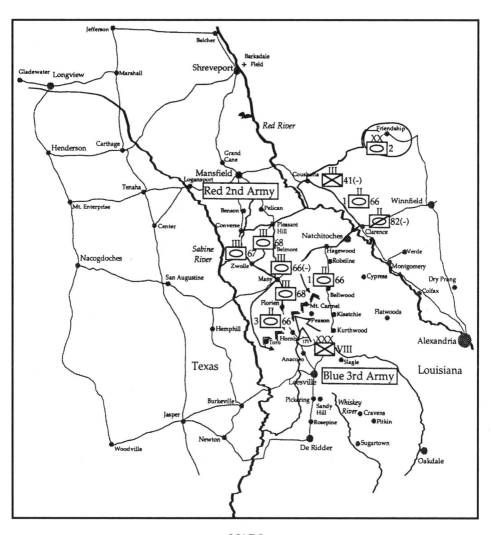

MAP 9

Field Maneuver #5
Louisiana Maneuvers
15–19 September 1941

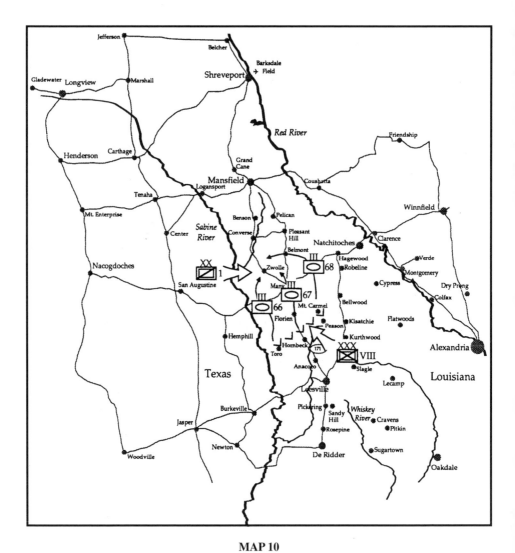

MAP 10
Field Maneuver #5
Counterattack, Louisiana Maneuvers
19 September 1941

from Texas just as the 2nd Armored Division had done earlier in the maneuvers. The 2nd Armored counterattacked with all three of its armored regiments. With the 66th attacking from the south towards Zwolle and the 67th and 68th attacking from the east, the Blue attack was halted, bringing the exercise to a close. The 2nd Armored Division demonstrated its speed and flexibility in the counterattack. The three regiments facing south and in contact with the enemy had quickly withdrawn and marched thirty miles north to execute a successful combined counterattack.[46]

In the final exercise of the Louisiana maneuvers, FM 6, the 2nd Armored Division changed to the Blue side and became a part of the I Armored Corps. The scenario had the Blue Third Army attacking north between the Sabine and Red River to defeat the Red forces in the Shreveport area. The division spent 23–24 September in the Hollongsworth–De Quincy area as the Blue Army reserve.

On 25 September at about 0530 the division received orders for a night advance west of the Sabine River to attack the west flank and rear of the Red forces.[47] The division's 87th Engineers began building a pontoon bridge at Merryville, which they completed at about midnight. The division's wheeled vehicles crossed the river at Orange and comprised the left (west) column. The tanks of the 2nd Armored Division and the 2nd Infantry Division crossed at Merryville and were the right (east) column. The 66th and 67th regiments moved north through Jasper and then north towards San Augustine while the 68th followed a parallel route to the east.[48] The columns were delayed repeatedly by destroyed bridges and enemy antitank guns. Both columns skirmished with units of the 4th Cavalry Regiment and the 2nd Cavalry Division north of the towns of Nacogdoches (west) and San Augustine (east). In the late afternoon of 26 September all the units refueled and checked their vehicles before continuing their push north after dark.[49]

The wheeled vehicle column, composed of the 41st Infantry (- one battalion), the 78th Field Artillery Regiment, and Companies C and D of the 82nd Reconnaissance Battalion, halted south of Henderson between 0100 and 0400 on the twenty-seventh. By noon, the west column crossed the Sabine River at Gladwater and advanced to Jefferson. By dark the wheeled column, led by the commander of the 41st Infantry, Col. Paul W. Newgarden, had severed the enemy communications north of Shreveport. The tank column in the east advanced to Carthage by noon on the twenty-seventh. The 2nd Armored Division ordered bridges constructed across the Sabine River at Teneha and Carthage.[50]

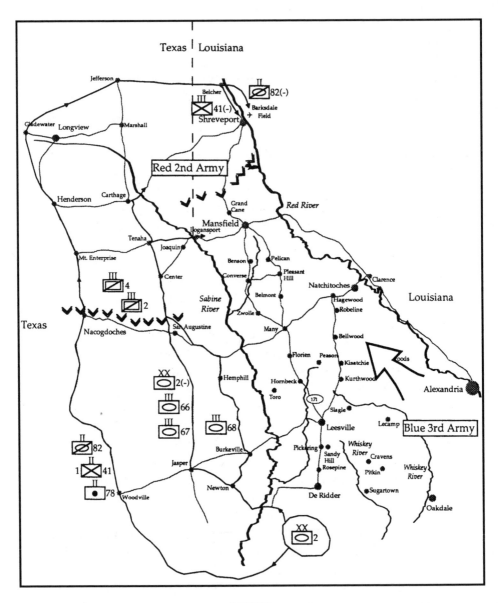

MAP 11

Field Maneuver #6
Louisiana Maneuvers
23–28 September 1941

Early on 28 September, elements of the 82nd Recon crossed the Red River and conducted a raid on the Red Army Air Corps at Barksdale Field, capturing the operations office. The 82nd succeeded in preventing any Red aircraft from departing the airfield for the rest of that day. The 41st Infantry Regiment entered Shreveport around noon and captured several key installations and much of the town. While the Red forces were preoccupied with stopping 2nd Armored Division tanks, Patton's infantry and reconnaissance units wreaked havoc in their rear area.[51]

Patton's tanks were in the process of crossing the Sabine River back into Louisiana when the exercise was halted at 1820 on 28 September.[52] The 66th Armored was still on the west side of the river at this time. That night the exhausted units bivouacked where they had stopped.

1st Lt. Curtis Clark had joined the 66th in February after graduating from the University of Massachusetts. During the Louisiana Maneuvers he served as the 2nd Battalion executive officer primarily handling the maintenance of the battalion's tanks. Interestingly all of the company commanders, a position subordinate to battalion executive officer, were captains. Clark remembers the many lessons learned during the maneuvers. The officers and men were very green, and coordination and organization had to be learned and practiced. The sergeants were the only ones who knew anything. One objective was just learning how to get around as a unit. Staying alert for the hazards of Louisiana, such as water moccasins falling out of trees onto the tanks, helped teach awareness in combat. Clark remembers most of them had no idea of war. The maneuvers hardened them and they all got to know each other and the routine of command and operations in the field.[53]

The comments and conclusions portion of the 2nd Armored Division's Report of Operations in Louisiana indicates a solid improvement in most areas over the Tennessee maneuvers. The report praises vehicle maintenance at all levels. The soldiers of line units were observed spending sufficient time performing preventive maintenance on their vehicles.[54] Preventive maintenance primarily consists of performing a series of checks as listed in a manual for each type of vehicle to ensure that everything is functioning correctly. For a large vehicle, such as a tank, these checks can take several hours.

A paragraph entitled "General Conclusions" listed the functions Major General Patton believed that an armored unit could best perform:

> Supported by motorized infantry, to make a direct attack at the beginning of an operation for the purpose of securing key points the loss of which will delay the enemy or prevent his concentration [of forces].

A marshy area which looked like a grassy field has mired a M2A4. The M3 Stuart is preparing to try to pull it out. September 1941.

Norris H. Perkins

By use of mobility, speed and surprise to attack the enemy rear.

A coordinated attack over a narrow front aided by every type of fire [support]. The purpose is to penetrate and then exploit.[55]

In summary, Patton believed armored forces should use their mobility, speed, and firepower to quickly get behind the enemy's defenses. Once there, the armor units could destroy the enemy command, communications, and support areas, bringing the conflict to a rapid conclusion.

The "Special Conclusions" paragraph noted several points that would increase an armored unit's chance of success:

Skillful leadership and a fierce determination on the part of all ranks to annihilate the enemy.

The employment of the division before the enemy can amass antitank weapons, blow bridges, sow mine fields, and shift his troops to meet the attack.[56]

Other special conclusions covered a wide range of topics from reconnaissance to logistics. The report recommended the use of multiple entrances

H Company Stuart. (*L-R*) Sergeant Dinan, Lieutenant Bakey, Private Valentine, unknown. September 1941.

Motorcycle courier of H Company followed by a tank column. September 1941.

to bivouacs to prevent traffic jams on the approach road. The difficulty involved in moving a large number of vehicles into a forest rapidly at night and without any visible lights is hard to envision. When the unit comes to a defile, the opposite end of the defile must be secured before the column can enter, in order to prevent a disastrous ambush.[57]

In his critique on 11 September, Lieutenant General Krueger, Commander of the Third Army, said that the 2nd Armored's operation had been done with great resolution and daring. The general called the division's bridging of the Red River in ten hours commendable. Vehicle congestion on the south side of the river was the only serious defect of the operation. General Krueger went on to say that the congestion was inevitable due to the poor roads and approaches to the area.[58] Another cause of the congestion was that a large number of crews had left their vehicles to help build the bridge. Without the several hundred extra men, the construction of the bridge would have taken several hours longer to complete.[59]

The general had some sharp criticism for a group led by thirty-one vehicles of the 66th Reconnaissance. This unit had driven into an ambush,

Train carrying the tanks of the 66th crossing the Mississippi River en route back to Fort Benning. September 1941.

Norris H. Perkins

and several vehicles refused to stop after running over and exploding practice mines. This was bad enough, but what really enraged him was the state of preparedness. Several vehicles had their weapons covered and were not carrying the required ammunition.[60]

Sgt. John Mayo, a tanker in Company H, summarized the soldiers' thoughts on the training that the maneuvers provided:

> So we had a lot of good training in the summer of '41 and, uh, then, that's the way everything fell together, and by the time we had to go overseas we were a good fighting force.[61]

CHAPTER 7

Dress Rehearsal:
The Carolina Maneuvers

In November 1941 the 66th Armored Regiment, with its parent unit the 2nd Armored Division, participated in the First Army Field Maneuvers. The Carolina Maneuvers, as they were more commonly known, were conducted in an area along the boundary of North and South Carolina. The maneuver area was generally bounded by Charlotte, North Carolina on the north; the Pee Dee River on the west; Columbia, South Carolina on the south; and the Broad River on the east. Numerous rivers and creeks generally flowing from north to south divided the area. Once again the bridges were going to be critical to the success of armored units.[1]

The tanks of the regiment and their crews moved by railroad from Fort Benning on 31 October. The wheeled vehicles of the regiment, including the half-tracks, departed Fort Benning on 30 October and made the 354-mile road march in three days, with thirty-four hours actually spent on the road. The first bivouac was at Monticello, Georgia, with the second night at Clinton and Laurens, South Carolina. The two movements united at the division bivouac southwest of Chester, South Carolina.[2]

The regiment's strength during the maneuvers was 87 officers and 1,131 enlisted men.[3] The Reconnaissance Company, Machine Gun Company, and the Mortar Platoon were still grouped as the regiment's provisional support battalion. This maneuver, the third in six months, would give the officers and soldiers the additional training that only large-scale exercises could provide.

The first exercises of the maneuver placed 2nd Armored Division under the Red IV Army Corps along with the 4th Motorized Division and the 31st Infantry Division. The scenario was that a hostile Blue force had landed at Savannah, Georgia and Charleston, South Carolina, had quickly captured Columbia, and was now north of Columbia covering further landings. The mission of the IV Corps was to first defeat the Blue forces north of Columbia. After forcing the withdrawal of the Blue forces, the Red forces were to retake Columbia and hold its communications facilities for Red use.[4]

The 2nd Armored Division's mission was to advance south to destroy the Blue forces wherever found between Highway 21 and the Broad River. At 1130 on 4 November, the 4th Division headquarters issued Field Order No. 3, which directed the division's advance in three columns.[5] The 1st Battalion, 66th Armor was to advance on the left axis, F3, that ran along Highway 21. The main body of the regiment was on the center axis, F2, which was between Highway 21 and Highway 215.[6] In the late afternoon of 4 November the units left their bivouac areas to form by columns behind the boundary line of Carlisle-Blackstock.[7]

At 0630 on 5 November IV Army Corps ordered the advance south to begin. Both the left column, with the 1st Battalion, and the center column, with the main body of the regiment, encountered heavy resistance from Blue forces, slowing their advance. By noon the left column, F3, had reached Woodward with its reconnaissance elements forward at White Oak. The center column, F2, was at or approaching Bethlehem Church at noon. During the afternoon the Blue resistance increased and little progress was made to the south. The main body of the 66th on F2 encountered so much resistance that the 1st Battalion, 68th Armor was diverted to assist the units on F2. After dark the units maintained contact with the enemy, established outposts for guards, and bivouacked.[8]

The Red forces resumed the attack at 0600 the next morning. Only light and scattered resistance was encountered during the morning. Again around midday, the 66th Armored units, advancing on F2, met heavy enemy resistance astride Highway 218 south of Horse Creek. Units on F3 were ordered to make a flank attack to help clear the way on F2. By dark the division had advanced to the line of Oak Grove Church and Blythewood. During the afternoon the 4th Motorized Division had joined with the 2nd Armored's right flank between the Broad River and Highway 215.[9]

Shortly after midnight 2nd Armored issued Field Order No. 5 directing the division to resume the attack at 0600 on 7 November. The order also placed the 66th Armor under the 2nd Armored Brigade on F1. This was done because F1 and F2 had crossed over each other the previous day. The order also changed the direction of attack from south to southeast. The 1st Battalion, 66th Armor made rapid progress along F3 on the right. The

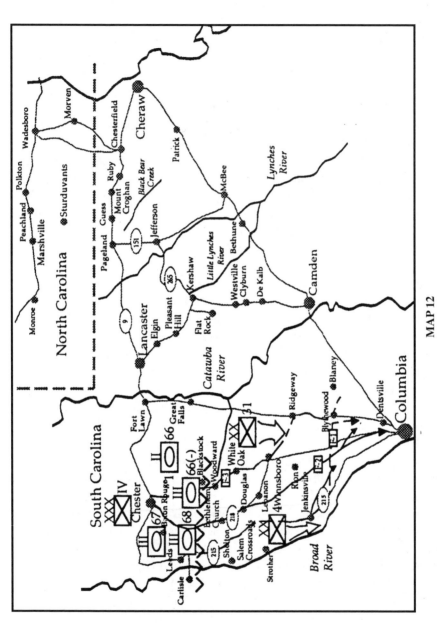

MAP 12
Exercise #1
Carolina Maneuvers
5–6 November 1941

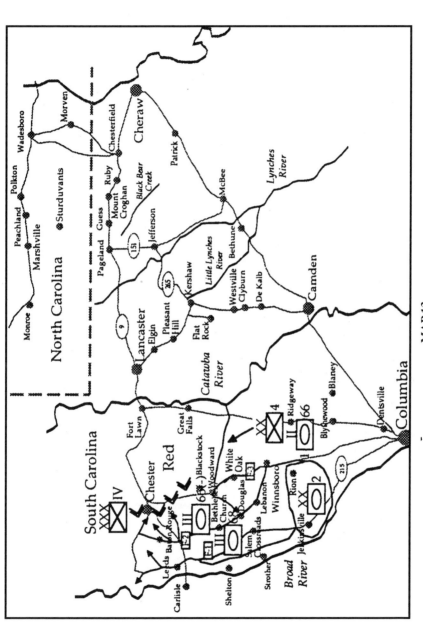

MAP 13
Exercise #2
Carolina Maneuvers
7 November 1941

regimental units now on F1 encountered heavy enemy resistance. Near
Blythewood the 1st Battalion moving south along Highway 21 linked with
the 68th Armor and the 41st Infantry. Together these Red units surrounded
the Blue force at Blythewood. When the exercise ended, the regimental
elements on F1 were six miles north of Dentsville and the 1st Battalion on
F3 was two miles west of Blaney. Reconnaissance troops of the division
had reached the outskirts of Columbia. All parts of the 66th Armor bivouacked in place that night. On 8 November the units marched to the area
of Rion and Jacksonville.[10]

Lieutenant Norris Perkins, the executive officer of Company H, advanced to company command through the misfortune of his company commander, Captain Lumpkin. Lieutenant Perkins described the accident:

> Then Captain Lumpkin did me a great good turn. We were riding down
> a steep mountainside in a pine forest on the Carolina maneuvers. He
> was simulating fire on the enemy. He turned his turret to the side to aim
> off through some trees, and a pine tree hit his 37mm cannon, spun the
> turret around, stripped the cogwheels, put his shoulder out of joint, sent
> the tank back to ordnance and put me in as company commander. My
> big break.[11]

The next exercise, designated 2nd Phase of IV Army Corps Maneuvers, had the 2nd Armored Division changing sides to the Blue forces and
joining the I Armored Corps. The Red IV Army Corps was located to the
north in the vicinity of Chester. The two forces had been fighting in the
area of Laurens, Anderson, Greenville, and Spartanburg to the west of the
maneuver area. The new mission of the Blue 1st Armored Corps was to
defeat the Red IV Army Corps and to seize the railhead and highway facilities in and around Chester.[12]

The Blue plan directed an attack with three divisions abreast: 2nd
Armored Division on the west, 4th Motorized in the center, and the 1st
Armored Division on the east. Because of a very limited road network, the
4th Motorized could not enter its zone until after the 2nd Armored had
passed through Lebanon on the left and the 1st Armored had cleared White
Oak on the right.[13] Headquarters, 2nd Armored Division, in Field Order
No. 6 issued at 2330 on 9 November, directed a division advance in three
columns, with the majority of the 66th Armor on the center route (designated F2).[14] A small detachment of the division was assigned to the right
avenue, F3, and was intended to cover a route to be used later by the 4th
Motorized on the 2nd Armored's left flank. All Blue units were restricted
to the south of the Dawkings-Monticello-Ridgeway line until the official
start of the exercise.[15]

At 0705 on 10 November the movement restriction was lifted and the Blue forces began their advance northward. By 0900 the main body of the 66th had secured the Highway 22 bridge over the Little River. The 66th and the 67th Armor on F2 fought through heavy Red opposition at Zion Chapel and Purity Church during the afternoon.[16]

The Blue attack continued northward at first light on 11 November. After crossing the Sandy River, the F2 column split. The 66th Armor continued north through Baton Rouge to attack Chester from the west, while the 67th approached Chester from the south. By late morning the 66th had captured the vital railway facilities in Chester, and when the exercise ended at noon Chester was firmly in Blue hands.[17] During this exercise, the forces of the 2nd Armored Division had very successfully employed the armor tactic of using a concentrated force of armor to first smash quickly through enemy lines and then drive hard for the enemy's vital rear areas. Any enemy strong points were bypassed and left for follow-on forces to reduce if necessary. This was seldom required because the arrival of sufficient armored forces in an enemy rear area usually destroyed the enemy's capability or will to resist any further.

The next part of the Carolina maneuvers was the 1st Phase of the General Headquarters (GHQ) directed exercises. For this training, the 2nd Armored Division remained under the command of I Armored Corps, which had changed over to the Red side. The scenario for this exercise had the Wateree River as a border between the Red country in the west and Blue country in the east. The Blue forces massed between the Wateree River on the west and the Pee Dee River on the east with the intent of invading the Red country. The mission of the Red forces of I Armored Corps was to advance rapidly to the Pee Dee River and then destroy, surround, or drive off all Blue forces in the area. The 2nd Armored Division's mission was to seize the northern part of the Corps area to the Pee Dee River from Cheraw on the division's south flank to Morven in the north. The division's Field Order No. 9, issued on 15 November, placed the 66th Armor on F1, the northernmost of the division's three routes of advance.[18]

The advance to the Pee Dee River began at 0600 on 16 November. Because the 1st Armored Division, on the northern flank of F1, had the priority in crossing the bridge at Fort Law, the 66th did not begin crossing until 0940. The regiment moved rapidly along Highway 85 and Highway 52 to approximately six miles east of Morven, very near the Pee Dee River. At this point the regiment encountered heavy Blue resistance in the late afternoon and remained engaged into the night.[19]

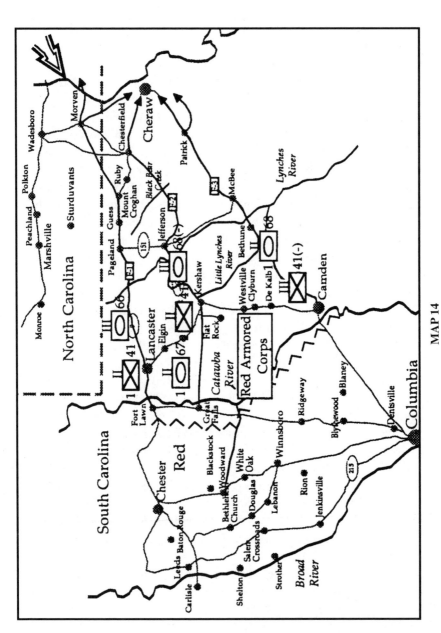

MAP 14
Exercise #3 Part 1
Carolina Maneuvers
16–17 November 1941

Company chow line operating out of a railroad car en route to Carolina. November 1941.

Vince Hooper

S.Sgt. Norman Thompson, H Company maintenance sergeant, aboard the company maintenance section's M-2 half-track. November 1941.

Norris H. Perkins

M2A4 light tank of the H Company commander about to cross a small stream. November 1941.

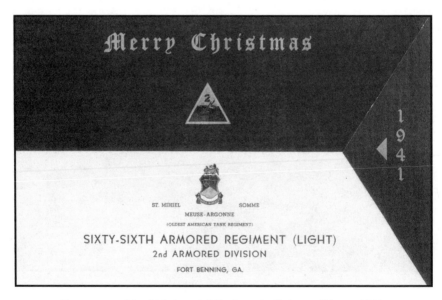

Front cover of the 66th Armored Regiment's Christmas Dinner. 1941.

During the night of 16–17 November the regiment received orders to conduct an attack south along Highway 52 to capture the town of Cheraw. The other units of the division on F2 and F3 would attack from the south and the west. While the main body of the regiment turned south to attack Cheraw, a small force led by Lt. Col. R. O. Wright successfully opposed a Blue reinforced brigade, and attacked from the northeast. By a series of brilliant maneuvers this small element was successful against a much larger opponent, an action mentioned as a highlight in the division's report of the exercise. By noon the regiment had encircled the town. By 1800 the main body of the 66th, together with the 67th and 68th Armored Regiments from F2, had captured Cheraw and destroyed the railroad facility and the bridge over the Pee Dee River. At 2000 the Red units were ordered to destroy all remaining facilities and supplies to prevent their use by Blue forces. Following the demolition, the Red forces were ordered to withdraw to areas west along the Lynches River. The 66th Armor went into bivouac around the town of Jefferson and remained there through 18 November, resting and servicing their vehicles and equipment.[20]

The 2nd Armored Division issued Field Order No. 11 at midnight on 18 November directing a renewed attack for the morning of the nineteenth. The attack began from the bivouac areas at 0630. All three columns made contact with the enemy Blue forces by 0800. The northern column advanced through Pageland and by noon had reached Lowrys. The southern column moved from Jefferson straight towards Cheraw. The 66th on F1 advanced to within three to four miles of Wadesboro while the units on F2 and F3 encountered determined resistance throughout the afternoon. A forest fire in the midst of one attack further hampered the division. In the late afternoon of 19 November the division ordered a withdrawal to the previous bivouac areas.[21]

Field Order No. 12 directed an attack to the northwest between the towns of Monroe and Pageland. The 66th moved to F2 where it was to follow the units on F1 in an attack in column. The night reorganization of the division delayed the attack until 1145, two and a half hours later than planned. By 1430 the attack had pushed east some eight miles. At that time, the 1st Armored Division to the north was in a dangerous situation, and further advance of the 2nd Armored was deemed inadvisable. At 1515 the attack was halted and the units ordered to withdraw to a division assembly area around Brady Store.[22] On 21 November the attack resumed with the intent of relieving some of the pressure on the 1st Armored Division. When the exercise ended at 0840, the attack was well under way and progressing well.[23]

The second phase of the GHQ directed maneuvers had the 2nd Armored Division continue under command of the Red I Armored Corps. The scenario had the Red forces defending a bridgehead over the Wateree River at Camden. The 2nd Armored Division's mission was to advance rapidly northward to hold an east-west line between Monroe and Wadesboro against the attacking Blue forces.[24] The division plan called for an advance in three columns. The 66th Armor comprised the tank force of F1, the western (left) column.[25]

At dawn on 25 November, the 66th left its bivouac seven miles south of Mt. Croghan and crossed the restraining line at the town of Guess.[26] The regiment first made contact with the Blue forces at 0700 one mile north of the state line. By approximately noon the 66th had advanced to the vicinity of Sturduvants.[27]

During the night of 25–26 November, the 2nd Armored Division issued fragmentary orders that directed the withdrawal of the main tank units to the south of Highway 9, the original restraining line. The order to the 66th directed it and other units of F1 to conduct an attack into the zone of the 4th Motorized Division. This attack was to reduce an enemy salient on the regiment's left flank but failed in the face of heavy Blue opposition. Throughout the day of 26 November the regiment withdrew back along their zone of F1. By nightfall, the 66th Armored Regiment was on the south bank of Big Black Creek.[28]

During the night, the regiment received orders for an attack to the north to be launched at 0600 on 27 November. But the next morning the Blue forces attacked first. The regiment had to conduct a counterattack prior to being able to reach their line of departure for their planned attack. The 66th advanced north to Pageland where they and their infantry support, the 1st Battalion, 41st Infantry, encountered heavy resistance from a Blue infantry regiment in the town. By 0900 the town had been secured and the units on route F1 established a defensive line two miles out from the north and east of Pageland. Strong enemy pressure had caused the regiment and the other units on F1 to face east by noon. The elements of F1 had their right flank on Highway 9 and their left flank one mile north of the state line. The 66th Armor's attack seriously disrupted the Blue forces' attack, causing it to become piecemeal and ineffective. The regiment maintained their stubborn defense around Pageland throughout the rest of the day. That night the regiment withdrew through the 4th Motorized area to an assembly area south of Primus. The 2nd Armored became the Red reserve force in the assembly area north of Kersaw.[29]

During the day of 28 November, the 2nd Armored occupied the center of the Red forces perimeter, which defended the Camden bridgehead.

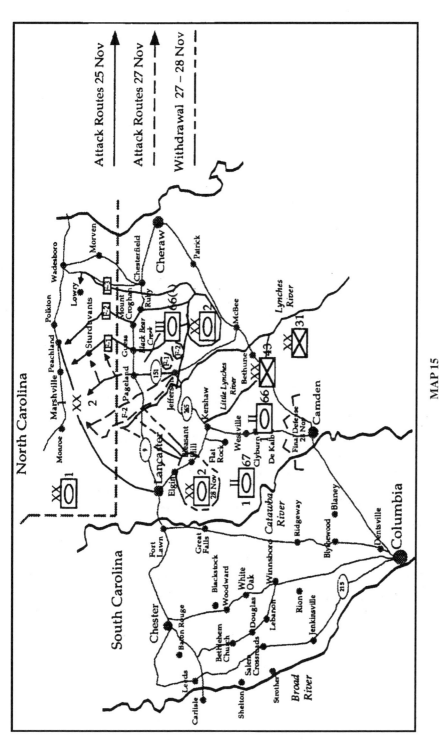

MAP 15
Exercise #4
Carolina Maneuvers
25–28 November 1941

The division gradually withdrew from their initial positions north of Primus. The division's delaying action had successfully used small-scale attacks by armor to harass and delay the attacking Blue forces. Companies and battalions of tanks used their mobility and firepower to disrupt the Blue offensive.[30]

The exercise and the Carolina maneuvers ended at 1628 on 28 November 1941.[31] The 2nd Armored Division moved from the vicinity of Leeds, South Carolina and returned to Fort Benning on 2 December 1941.[32]

The 2nd Armored Division published as part of the annexes covering the exercises their standard conclusions or lessons learned. The subject of maintenance was addressed in some detail, comprising an entire annex in the Report of Operations. The comments noted that the maintenance had been successful in keeping the division rolling. The situation had improved over previous maneuvers, but only slightly, and this owed a great deal to major maintenance done at Fort Benning following the Louisiana Maneuvers. The disadvantage was that much minor maintenance work was overlooked, leading to problems during the maneuvers. The lack of spare parts continued to be a serious problem.[33] A curious side effect of this was that the mechanics came up with ingenious ways to keep a vehicle running without the needed replacement part. The mechanics used baling wire and parts of civilian cars and tractors as temporary repairs.

The report of these maneuvers also tagged communication between organizations handling maintenance as a serious problem. The lack of radios in maintenance units made it very difficult to relay information about the location and trouble of disabled vehicles. An interim fix of assigning one individual per platoon or company to keep track of the status of all of the unit's vehicles was tried.[34] On the surface, this may sound easy, but is not necessarily so in a field-maneuver environment. The vehicles of a single small unit could easily move over a hundred miles in one day's maneuvers. A vehicle disabled early in the day might be repaired by its crew, move another fifty miles, and become disabled again in a more isolated spot. Vehicles were moving at all times, day and night, both on and off the roads, and in all types of weather. Keeping track of some twenty vehicles in the fast-paced maneuvers was often a challenge, even with radios.

The need for some type of lighted facility in which to perform maintenance under blackout conditions at night also was noted. The need for time to perform maintenance on the vehicles between operations remains true whether in maneuvers or combat. The concept was that in combat, with vehicles lost to enemy action as well as to normal mechanical problems, the maintenance time required might equal the operational time. If an operation took five days, then it would probably take five days to maintain and prepare the vehicles and equipment for another operation.[35]

Many trucks did not have assistant drivers assigned, a problem that was exacerbated when the driver was a mechanic. The mechanics were frequently needed to work on vehicle repair throughout the night and then required to drive their own trucks during the day. An exhausted mechanic-driver could become a hazard in either role.[36]

Several important lessons were learned in the maneuvers which would later be obvious in the war. Armor units require friendly air protection to successfully conduct operations.[37] This was proven when the better equipped, more experienced German armor units were decimated in France in 1944 because they could not defend themselves against the dreaded Allied fighter-bombers that ranged the skies virtually unopposed.

The extreme difficulty of changing the task organization of large units at night was fully realized. Time was required to relay the orders to all units, change communications, and move units to new assembly areas.[38] After the completion of these items and many other small and supporting tasks, the units still had to prepare for the new operation. Performing a major operation, like task organizing, in darkness with no lights is generally at least twice as difficult and takes at least twice as long as the same operation would take in daylight.

A "tanker's rule" has passed through the generations from the Carolina maneuvers to the present day: "Don't take your tanks to town." The final report contains the following comment about taking tanks into an enemy-held town:

> Attack of armored elements through a town held by enemy troops is unnecessarily costly. Infantry should be used to clear the town before moving through if it is absolutely necessary to go through the town, otherwise the town should be avoided.[39]

Each of the three combat arms has its strengths and weaknesses. The town belongs to the infantry, just like the open countryside belongs to the tank. In the town the enemy infantry enjoys the advantages of concealment and surprise. The buildings and walls of towns allow the infantrymen to close within point blank range of tanks with antitank weapons. Since tank crews usually operate with all hatches closed ("buttoned up") to protect themselves from enemy rifle and machine gun fire while in urban areas, they need their infantry to protect them from enemy infantry getting close enough to do the tanks harm. For its part, the infantry needed the massive firepower of the tank to destroy enemy positions hidden behind walls far too thick for the small arms fire to penetrate. The essential mutual support between tanks and infantry in urban areas is just one area in which combined arms are a tactical necessity.

The report also noted the violation of one of the principles of war— assault the enemy with the greatest possible concentration of forces to overwhelm the enemy at the chosen point or points:

> Piece-meal attacks by tank elements were too frequent. Insufficient support by infantry and artillery of attacks was provided with resultant heavy tank losses. The need for more effective coordination of effort and less headlong uncoordinated action is indicated.[40]

This conclusion, like the others, was not directed at any particular units, but was made to all units in both armies. It is doubtful, considering Major General Patton's constant preaching of combined arms in the 2nd Armored Division, that this comment applied to any of the division's armored regiments.

Another general conclusion concerned the concept that the tanks can seize ground, but only the infantry can hold it. This means that infantry are required to secure any objective against enemy counterattack. Infantry are much better suited to digging in and holding a stationary position. The report stated, "Failure to have infantry on hand to protect tank elements at objectives tended to nullify the effect of the success achieved by the tanks."[41]

The 1941 Maneuvers brought the United States Army out of the mere existence state of the Inter-War Years to a modern army. These maneuvers proved the value of tanks in the army. It confirmed that the German army's use of tanks in Poland and France could be duplicated by American tankers. The officers and men of the 66th Armored Regiment learned many valuable lessons in the maneuvers that would save lives and lead to victories in the war that America entered only days after the conclusion of the Carolina Maneuvers.

PART III

The Mediterranean Theater 1942–43

CHAPTER 8

Tanks at Sea:
The Final Preparations: 1942

The 66th Armored Regiment (Light) and the rest of the 2nd Armored Division had just returned to Fort Benning in 1941 when the Japanese attacked Pearl Harbor. After 7 December there was no longer any doubt about the importance of the training and maneuvers the men had gone through that year. Now the regiment's training, which had been intense all year, became more serious and determined. The atmosphere was one of "It is later than you think" as the newsreels showed one Axis victory after another.[1]

John G. Getsinger graduated in June 1940 from North Carolina State with a degree in chemical engineering. Along with his diploma he received a commission as a second lieutenant in the infantry reserve from the R.O.T.C. program. With the country still in the depression, Getsinger was fortunate to have a job waiting for him in an Asheville tannery. Because ninety percent of the tannery's production was allocated by the Defense Production Board for sale to the armed force, Getsinger received deferments whenever the army inquired about putting him on active duty. Believing that the country might stay out of the war, he bought a car and got married. Getsinger remembers how everything changed:

> Ruth and I were married July 25, 1941. The war in Europe was not much in our thoughts. When Pearl Harbor occurred I was shocked. I didn't even know where Pearl Harbor was. The day after December 7, I went in and told my boss and the company president that I felt constrained to go on active duty. They understood and I wrote a letter to Fourth Corps Area Headquarters in Atlanta saying that any previous

request for my deferment should be disregarded and that I was ready for active duty. I had a reply stating that my patriotism was appreciated and that I would receive orders soon placing me on active duty. Every day I expected orders. The whole country was galvanized. Everybody was volunteering. The newspapers and radio were filled with news of the war, all bad. I waited and waited and waited. Christmas and New Years came and went. About the end of January I decided the army didn't want me, and I began to feel sorry for myself. Finally on February 14, 1942 I received a telegram saying orders were being issued placing me on active duty February 24 at the Armored Force Replacement Training Center at Fort Knox, Kentucky.[2]

In December 1941 the 2nd Armored Division was reorganized, based on the lessons learned from the 1941 maneuvers and observations of the armored forces fighting in Europe.[3] The previous organization of the armored division had consisted of one large armored brigade comprised primarily of three armored regiments. This organization, however, did not lend itself to employing subordinate units separately. The new organizational design of the armored division allowed for the independent employment of two combat forces. These two forces were designated as Combat Command A and Combat Command B (CCA and CCB). These combat commands were routinely composed of the same units but could be changed, depending on the tactical situation. The support units of the division, such as engineers and supply, were reorganized so that they could support the two combat commands with two separate elements of their unit, each capable of independent operations.[4]

The three armored regiments (66th, 67th, and 68th) underwent a major change as a result of the reorganization. The regiments lost their heavy and light designations. After many years of being a light tank regiment, the 66th became an armored regiment with two types of tanks. The 66th, and its sister regiment, the 67th, would now have two battalions of medium tanks and one battalion of light tanks each. The third regiment, the 68th, was disbanded, and its personnel and equipment were transferred to the remaining regiments. The 66th Armored Regiment became, for the most part, the primary fighting force of CCA. The tank battalions of the regiment also underwent reorganization. Each battalion changed from three light tank companies to two medium and one light tank companies. The company organization was modified with the addition of four tanks, going from thirteen to seventeen tanks; the company now consisted of three tank platoons of five tanks each and two tanks in the company headquarters section. The division reorganization was completed on 8 January 1942.[5]

New 28-ton M-3 Lee medium tank commanded by Lt. Rutherford Fleet of H Company crossing a bridge which rated for only six tons as the loader looks nervously over the side.

Norris H. Perkins

M-3 medium tank being recovered by a M-1 Ward La-France wrecker at Fort Benning.

Norris H. Perkins

M-3 medium tank being recovered by a M-1 Ward La-France wrecker at Fort Benning.

Norris H. Perkins

M-3 medium tank being recovered by a M-1 Ward La-France wrecker at Fort Benning.

Norris H. Perkins

On 19 January Major General Patton handed the command of the 2nd Armored Division over to Brig. Gen. Willis D. Crittenberger. Like Patton, Crittenberger moved up from command of the now disbanded 2nd Armored Brigade. Patton was appointed to command the I Armored Corps on 16 February 1942.

A regimental general order from April 1942 shows the basic organization of the regiment and the number of enlisted men authorized for each unit. The companies directly under the regimental headquarters were Headquarters Company (154 men), Service Company (184), Maintenance Company (181), and the Reconnaissance Company (193). Each of the regiment's two medium tank battalions consisted of a Headquarters Company (140 men) and three tank companies (144 each). The 1st Battalion, with its light tanks, had smaller companies: Headquarters Company (131 men) and the three tank companies (105 each). The regiment had a total of 2,302 enlisted men.[6]

Through the winter and spring of 1942, the regiment was in the process of receiving and training hundreds of new recruits in addition to conducting intense training for the more experienced soldiers. The training schedule of Company H, 3rd Battalion, 66th Armor for Monday, 2 February 1942 is an example of just how intense a unit's training could become. The planning and coordination necessary to train a company of men day after day during this period of heavy training is obvious.[7]

Company "H", 66th Armored Regiment

Fort Benning, Georgia

Training Schedule for Monday, February 2, 1942.

7:00 A.M. to 4:00 P.M.   No. of Men

  1. Five men to 1st Battalion Gun Room to fire .50 calibre machine gun.   5
     Sgt. Yeo goes as instructor.   1
  2. Six tanks with 75 sub-calibre to Frey Range   16

8:00 A.M. to 11:30 A.M.

  1. 24 new men—Preliminary instruction in .30 calibre machine gun in barracks.
     All available non-coms as instructors with Sgt. Sellers in charge.
     Have 10 or 12 guns brought up before 8:00.   30
  2. All other men in company available 3½ hours instruction in
     Tommy Gun by Sgt. Young and Sgt. Owens, E.   24

1:00 P.M. to 3:00 P.M.

  1. Communications School—Advanced Students   6

2. Intelligence School   3

1:00 P.M. to 4:30 P.M.

  1. 12 men pistol instruction, these men to fire on Tuesday
     Sgt Vaicuilis and Sgt Spivey in charge
  2. 24 new men—to continue Machine Gun instruction under same instructors.   30
  3. All other available men   (a) 1½ hours tommy gun instruction
                           (b) 2 hours tactics lecture by Co. Comman.   24
  4. 1:00 P.M.—All officer candidates to Dispensary   14

7:00 P.M. to 9:00 P.M.

  1. Communication school—Beginners   15
ALL DAY
Maintenance crew at shop   10
Orderly Room   2
Mess (Mess Sergeant, 2 cooks, 3 KP's)   6
Supply   2
Radio Work   3
Guard and Fatigue   8

Shortly after its reorganization, the 66th began receiving new medium tanks. These new M3 "General Lee" tanks were a major change from the regiment's old light tanks. These new tanks, weighing twenty-eight tons and standing ten feet, three inches, were nearly twice the weight and twice the height of the tanks the regiment had been using. The M3 was a stop-gap tank that the army rushed into production in the fall of 1941, primarily to give the British a tank with a 75mm gun. In late 1941 the British army found itself in desperate need of a tank with a 75mm gun capable of fighting the German tanks in North Africa on equal terms. With the British armament industry stretched to the limit, they sought assistance from President Roosevelt's Arsenal of Democracy. At the time, the U.S. did not have a turret design capable of mounting a 75mm gun, so the best alternative was a prototype that had a 75mm gun mounted in a sponson on the right side of its large hull. A 37mm gun was mounted in a turret on top of the large hull. The hull-mounted 75mm gun of the M3 proved invaluable to British armor units fighting in North Africa.[8] The American model of the M3, known as the "General Lee" had a commander's cupola with a machine gun while the British model, known as the "General Grant" did not have the cupola. In spite of this fact the tankers of the 66th called their new American model M3s the "Grant" tank.

The tankers of the 66th had some difficulty becoming familiar with the M3's size and weight. The motor sergeant of Company H said, "...it looked like a damned cathedral coming down the road."[9] During their early

M-3s of H Company lined up in the field at Fort Benning. February 1942.

Norris H. Perkins

Dodge M-6 Gun Motor Carriage with 37mm gun and two Ford Amphibians.

Norris H. Perkins

Officers planning meeting of H Company. *(L–R)* Lieutenant Bakey, Captain Perkins, and Lieutenant Fleet during the Carolina Maneuvers. 1942.

Early M4A1 Sherman tank with three-piece final drive housing and direct vision slots.

training with the "General Lee" around Fort Benning that spring, the men had quickly discovered that a twenty-eight-ton track became stuck in swampy areas more quickly than the old light tanks did.[10] The change in tanks was quickly followed by a new respect for marshy areas after some of the tank crews experienced several unpleasant stays in the Georgia mud.

Shortly after receiving their new tanks, the tank crews named their new mounts. The name chosen for a tank had to begin with the letter of the company to which the tank and crew belonged. Some of the tank names in Lieutenant Perkins' Company H were Hannibal, Hungunner, Hurricane, Holy Joe, Hotspur, Hawkeye, Hellcat, and Halleluiah. The company's tank retriever, which looked like an M3 from a distance with its fake 75mm gun, was christened Hardup.[11]

Lt. John Roller, a native Virginian, graduated from Virginia Polytechnic Institute in spring 1942. He arrived at Fort Benning and was assigned as a platoon leader in Company D.

In late June 1942 the 2nd Armored Division departed Fort Benning for the last time, en route first to the Carolina maneuvers and then to ports in Virginia in preparation for movement to an unknown location overseas. The division's 390 tanks and other tracked vehicles were loaded onto railroad flatcars and moved to a railhead on the North and South Carolina state line. The wheeled vehicles moved by road and linked with the tracked vehicles at the division assembly area.[12]

Between 6 July and 14 August the majority of the division participated in the 1942 Carolina Maneuvers.[13] This was the 66th Armor's first large-scale maneuver with the new medium tanks, and the last in the United States before sailing off to war. These maneuvers provided units a chance to practice using their new tanks during a large-scale tactical exercise. Not all of the regiment had received new tanks, and those crews were sent to Camp Sutton, North Carolina.[14] During the exercises, one of the tanks of Company H was involved in an accident, which the company commander, Lieutenant Perkins, recalled:

> We had a fire in an M-3 Grant tank. It was sitting on the edge of the road in the maneuver area, tilted, and wouldn't start, so we got one of the maintenance crew to get in to see if he could figure out why it wouldn't start. While he was sitting there, a tilting full gas tank leaked, overflowed a little, and some of the gasoline seeped into the fighting compartment and vaporized. He stepped on the starter, a spark ignited the fumes and a seething mass of red flames came out of the hatch in the right side sponson. I was standing about four feet away, jumped up on the tank so I could see in and, in those three or four seconds, I was

Lieutenant Perkins of H Company proudly poses in front of his new M-3 tank at Fort Benning. March 1942.

M-3s of H Company crossing the Pee Dee River on a pontoon bridge during the 1942 Carolina Maneuvers. Note the sway of the bridge caused by the tanks.

Norris H. Perkins

Lt. Ben Pate with a M4A2 Sherman tank with welded hull, direct vision slots and early suspension (track return rollers mounted on top of bogie frames). Fort Bragg.

Norris H. Perkins

trying to make up my mind whether I was going to be a hero and try to go in and get the guy. But fortunately he crawled out, whimpering and groaning, with the skin falling off his face and his wrists. That was Sergeant Childers. They were second degree burns, he healed came back to the company and, from then on, he was known as Pinkey...His face was red because it burned off so much skin it never grew back tan again.[15]

At the end of July, and halfway through the maneuvers, the 2nd Armored Division changed commanders. Major General Crittenberger left to take command of the III Armored Corps. The new commander was Maj. Gen. Ernest N. Harmon, who had been the Chief of Staff of the Armored Force before this new appointment.[16]

The 1942 Carolina maneuvers were the Second Armored Division's last peace-time maneuver and gave the unit one more chance to improve the skills that would mean life or death in the near future. The maneuvers proved especially valuable for the units in becoming familiar with their new medium tanks. When the maneuvers ended, the division assembled near Aberdeen, North Carolina, and then moved to Fort Bragg, North Carolina. Fort Bragg was the new temporary base of the division as it began a new phase of training. While normal tactical training continued, units were sent in turn to Norfolk, Virginia, for amphibious training.[17]

Lt. John Getsinger of F Company describes his duties as 2nd Battalion billeting officer and a close call with military rules:

In moving the battalion (three companies, seventeen tanks each, three headquarters tanks and about 100 other vehicles), I was given the map location of a bivouac area about 25 to 50 acres in size by the regimental billeting officer and a time of departures. Usually the distance would be about 30 miles and we usually traveled at night under blackout conditions. Usually in daylight, I selected the route to be traveled, the order of march, the area assigned to each company (including Bn. headquarters company) and made sketches of the whole thing. I took one enlisted man (private) from each company who selected areas for each platoon in his company and made sketches for it. They also served as traffic regulators at key road junctions during the march, and each guided his company into its spot in the bivouac area. They took great pride in their work and I was proud of them.

We left Fort Benning in June, 1942, I believe, and I never slept in a regular building again until I arrived in England in December, 1943. We traveled from Benning to Anson County, N.C. by highway. The first bivouac we pulled into was about 5 miles from Ruth's parent's home. The Bn. commander told us at a fast first meeting that there would be no women allowed in the area. I was walking back from the meeting when I saw Ruth and her mother in our car well inside the area. I ran to the car and told her to move over and drove out of the area as fast as I could. I heard nothing about it afterward, but my Bn. commander was not one to tolerate excuses. Ruth had been driving along the road and recognized the insignia on a 66th A.R. soldier and he told her where the 2nd Bn. was. So much for security.[18]

At the Norfolk Naval Yard, the men learned to climb rope ladders, load themselves and their tanks aboard ship and then land on sandy beaches. All of this amphibious training was in preparation for the invasion of North Africa, which was a closely guarded secret known only to a small number of Allied leaders. The companies of the regiment made numerous amphibious landings on the beaches around Chesapeake Bay and Virginia Beach.

Sgt. John Mayo of Company H was in the first wave during one of these landings. His group was responsible for laying a wire mesh across the soft sand to eliminate the possibility of any of the vehicles becoming mired while coming ashore. After getting the wire mesh in place, the men established local security by emplacing machine gun positions around the area's perimeter. When the doors of one of the landing ships opened, Sergeant Mayo saw Major General Patton riding one of the light tanks ashore. After Major General Patton arrived on the beach, the group's nervous young lieutenant went to report to the general, but seemed unable to stand at attention. Sergeant Mayo remembers thinking, "Buddy, you better get to attention. You're fixin' to get reamed."[19] Just as Major General Patton began correcting the lieutenant's posture problem, the lead tank coming up the beach abruptly stopped. The tank's track had hooked the wire mesh and ripped up about twenty feet of it. Sergeant Mayo was in his machine gun position when

> all of a sudden I heard the General roar. SERGEANT! Well, I knew he was calling me. So I jumped and double-timed over to him and I saluted him,....,I says, Sir, Sergeant Mayo reporting as ordered, and...he laid his arm around my shoulder just like a father talking to his son and he said to me, he says, Now, see, the sergeant in the tank, he realizes there's something wrong. So he stopped his driver. He says, he realizes he is ripping up the wire. But, he says, he can't see what's going on but, he says, you and I, we're on the ground and we can see what's going on. He said, if the sergeant goes ahead, he rips up all of the wire, but he's trying to fight the enemy by hisself and the rest of the vehicles are stuck in the sand behind him. He says, now, we don't want to get in a

"Hawkeye" of H Company being prepared for action in this posed photograph.

Company of Sherman tanks lined up along the roadside at Fort Bragg.

hurry, and we don't want to get excited, and then he raised his voice, when he said, WE WANT TO GET THE GOD DAMNED TANK OUT OF HERE! I said, yesser.

I double-timed over to the tank and I hollered at the sergeant, I said, give me your wire cutters,...So he threw me the wire cutters I knew he had in the tank because he had the same type tank...,and I clipped about four strands of wire and rolled the wire back out and I flipped the wire cutters up to him...I waved him off, and he took on off, and I laid the wire back down and kicked some beach sand over it so it wouldn't curl up, and then I double-timed back to my machine gun nest. As I went back by Patton I heard him say, God damn it, that's what I'm talking about, he says, I'm talking about teamwork all the time.[20]

Lieutenant Getsinger of F Company describes the move from Fort Bragg to their secret destination:

We knew that some of us would be shipping out soon (rumor mill). We learned that the first Bn. (light tanks) would be going. I was transferred to B Co. to replace an officer that they considered to be incompetent for combat. In a few days (about October 15) we left by train in great secrecy. The train had all blinds closed and MP guards to let nobody off or on the train. We found ourselves in Norfolk. We boarded ship and went to the Chesapeake Bay for a few days of training. We didn't know where we were headed but most of the personnel were going on one ship and the tanks on another. The plan called for us to climb down rope nets at night into small boats, to go to the vehicle ship, and climb up a rope net to the deck. All of this was to (and did) take place off shore from where we were to land. I was faced with the prospect of leading a platoon into combat that I barely knew, in tanks that I had never rolled a foot in.[21]

The amphibious training of all elements of the 2nd Armored Division continued into the autumn of 1942. The units, fully equipped, would load onto ships that sailed into the Atlantic, out of sight of land, then return to the landing area in the pre-dawn hours. With the ships blacked out, the men climbed down the rope ladders into the landing craft and formed for the assault. Training in securing and expanding the beachhead followed the beach landing. The landings were practiced many times, until one day in late October, the ships continued sailing east instead of returning to the American coast.[22]

CHAPTER 9

Operation Torch: The Invasion of North Africa

In September, under conditions of absolute secrecy, the elements from 2nd Armored Division were chosen for the impending invasion of North Africa. The 1st Battalion of the 66th was assigned to Landing Team 3 of Sub Task Force 3 in the Western Task Force. The 1st Battalion was equipped with the M3 light tank called the General Stuart. The light tanks of the 66th and 67th were assigned to the invasion force, because they were better suited for amphibious operations than their much heavier counterpart, the M3 medium tank. The 1st Battalion left Fort Bragg in September to prepare to join the invasion force.[1]

Lt. James Burt was serving as maintenance officer Landing Team 3 and their M3 Stuart light tanks. He and the men had been working to equip their tanks with deep water fording kits that would allow the tanks to travel in water approximately two feet over the top of the tank's turret. This work was being done in absolute secrecy in the Carolina forests. As maintenance officer, Burt knew the fording system intimately, having worked with his men in finding and then solving problems with the system. After completing the work the tanks were moved by rail to the port and loaded aboard ships. Lieutenant Burt had about sixty percent of the tanks loaded when he received a visit from Maj. Gen. Lucian K. Truscott, the assistant division commander. Truscott asked, "How is Blue Freeze?" Lieutenant Burt remembers only staring blankly at the general and saying nothing, having no idea what he was talking about. The next morning several officers arrived to investigate Lieutenant Burt's competency. It was then that Lieutenant Burt found out

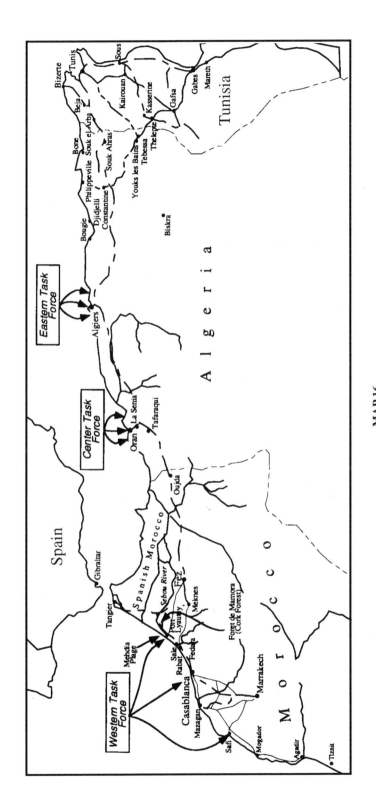

MAP 16
North Africa
November 1942–June 1943

that "Blue Freeze" was the code name given to the deep water fording kit. No one had ever told Lieutenant Burt the name of the super secret project.[2]

The Western Task Force, commanded by Major General Patton, had the mission of capturing Casablanca and French Morocco. Sub-Task Force 3, one of the three sub-task forces, was commanded by Major General Truscott and was to capture Port Lyautey, which lay eighty miles north of Casablanca on the Atlantic coast of Morocco. Attached to this force was Landing Team 3, consisting of units from the 2nd Armored Division and to which the 1st Battalion, 66th Armor belonged. The commander of the 1st Battalion, Lt. Col. Harry H. Semmes, commanded the team.[3]

At dawn on 8 November 1942, Sub-Task Force 3 made a difficult landing through the rough surf at Mehdia Plage, a beach five miles west of Port Lyautey. The 1st Battalion, 66th Armor, lost one M3 light tank, one half-track, and one scout car when the landing craft carrying them was upset in the heavy surf. The landing force also came under artillery and small arms fire from a small Vichy French force defending the beach. The first wave of Americans cleared the initial French resistance and established a beachhead. By 0800 only Company C of the 41st Infantry and a platoon of the 17th Engineer Battalion were ashore, supported by seven tanks of the 1st Battalion, 66th Armor.[4]

One of the unsung heroes, Sergeant Pruett, mess sergeant of D Company, in front of his mess tent. Spring 1943.

John B. Roller

Capt. James Burt of C Company was serving as special maintenance officer for the landing force. During the practice landings a Marine Corps Landing Vehicle, Tracked, commonly known as a Water Buffalo, had been loaded aboard the ship. The intended Marine crew never arrived, so Captain Burt and his mechanics had requested permission to learn how to use the vehicle. The mechanics soon mastered the use of the vehicle on water and land. Captain Burt remembered what happened when the ship arrived off the coast of North Africa:

> About one o'clock in the morning, the ship's lieutenant and Colonel Semmes called me and said, "We know you and your boys know how to run this thing, and we have got to throw it away unless you'll take it in."...my maintenance vehicle was in the bottom of the ship, the last to go ashore. The Marine thing was on the holds but had to be moved so they could start unloading. We agreed to take it in. The First Lieutenant then asked if I knew how to find the North Star. I said, "Sure, with the Big Dipper, hence, the North Star." He said, "Now, face the North Star and point your left arm at it. Then put your right arm at 90 degrees. Then look over your shoulder halfway. That's 45 more. That's 135. That's Africa. Goodbye." The system worked because the compass on the craft rolled greatly in the surf. We hit the beach where we were supposed to. Many Navy Coxswain were some miles off. With the Marine craft, we were able to go straight into the surf, hold our squareness and make several trips back to the ship.[5]

The seven M3 light tanks suddenly had their hands full when the French attacked the beach with a force of thirty-two tanks. Fortunately for the Americans, the French tanks were First World War vintage Renault FT-17 light tanks. These two-man Renaults, with a 37mm gun, were the same tanks that most of the U.S. tank corps had used in 1918. A fine tank in 1918, the Renaults were badly outclassed by the American Stuart tank of 1942. The 1st Battalion tanks quickly counterattacked and pushed the French back to a wadi three miles inland. A lengthy tank battle then began at the wadi, with the outnumbered Americans assisted by U.S. naval aircraft. The battalion's tanks were later reinforced by eleven M3 tanks from the 70th Tank Battalion. By 1500 hours the French tank force withdrew, leaving behind twenty-four destroyed tanks. In their first battle of the war, a small portion of the 66th Armored Regiment had fought a tank battle and won.[6]

These first amphibious landings in North Africa against the halfhearted French resistance taught the Americans a lesson which would prove valuable later. The landing craft known as lighters could only hold one tank and were easily upset in rough seas. Nearly half of the lighters were lost during the landing, showing the serious need for a better vessel. The lighters were soon replaced by the Landing Ship, Tank (LST), which could safely land a large number of tanks very close to the beach. LSTs helped to solve the problem of disorganization on the beachhead, which had been caused when the lighters that did make it to the beach were scattered along the beach for several miles. All of the units had problems trying to assemble their forces in the predawn darkness, with so many of the landing craft lost or scattered along the beach. An enemy attack early in the landing would have been disastrous.[7]

Following their defeat on 8 November, the French forces withdrew inland and did not reappear until after the armistice on 11 November. Landing Team 3 and the 1st Battalion, 66th Armor tankers spent the intervening time patrolling south of Port Lyautey in anticipation of a French counterattack. The 2nd Armored Division established their forward headquarters at Rabat, French Morocco, on 13 November 1942.[8]

Immediately after the landings, there was very little available in the way of replacement parts and supply for the relatively small proportion of the 2nd Armored Division that was ashore. John Derden was serving as a B Company maintenance sergeant with the 3rd Armored Landing Team. He describes a problem that arose and how it was solved:

> The M5 light tanks in my company began to have leaking stabilizer seals. Nobody had any spares. I took one of the seals apart to see what could be done to fix the leak and discovered it was a lead seal. I took the old seal and used the seal retainer to form a mold of the seal. I then took some .45 caliber rounds apart and melted the lead bullets down to make some new seals as good as the originals.[9]

While the 1st Battalion was en route to North Africa, the rest of the 66th Armor trained at Fort Bragg. From September through early November, they left Fort Bragg and traveled to Fort Dix, New Jersey, by train. The tanks were prepared for shipment from the Brooklyn Navy Yard. While the regiment waited for the order to board ships, they occupied their time with close order drill and calisthenics at Fort Dix. During weekend passes, the men traveled to New York City, where the New York Giant games and Jack Dempsey's bar were popular attractions.[10]

The second week of December 1942 saw the 66th Armor begin loading their tanks and other vehicles aboard ships both at the Brooklyn Navy Yard and the New York City docks. During the loading, the regiment's officers ran into one stumbling block after another. At the city docks, a longshoremen's strike was in progress and the soldiers were forbidden to assist in the loading. Next the Army Quartermaster Corps personnel re-packed the equipment from all of the vehicles. As a consequence, when the tankers arrived in North Africa they found their equipment badly mixed. Some of the tanks had cannon rammer staffs from a field artillery unit. The mechanics of Company H had spent days overhauling and tuning the vehicle engines; now the Quartermaster Corps mechanics hurriedly did the same thing, but they lacked the same experience and expertise.[11]

Many of the regiment's tanks, nearly 200 in all, were loaded aboard the massive *Sea Train Texas*, a ship that previously had carried locomotives and rail cars. Most of the men of the regiment boarded the Holland-America liners *Argentina* and *Brazil*. The men of Company H of the 3rd Battalion, commanded by Captain Perkins, boarded the *Sea Train Texas*. There, the company was fortunate enough to have plenty of room on deck for exercise and training. The soldiers also helped the ship's crew pull watch duty looking out for the deadly German U-boats. This convoy, carrying the majority of the 2nd Armored Division, formed and started across the Atlantic on 10-11 December.[12] The *Texas*, with its precious cargo of tanks, was tucked tight in the center of the convoy alongside the battleship *New York*. The catapult launching of a reconnaissance plane three times a day from the battleship provided the tankers with exciting entertainment.[13]

During the voyage, Captain Perkins' men practiced rapid adjustment of tank cannon fire by using dummy mechanisms constructed from cardboard and trash. An instructor would tell the practicing crew where their last shot had hit a target panorama painted on canvas. The crew would then use the dummy mechanisms to adjust the aim of the tank cannon as rapidly as possible. Two years later one of the platoon sergeants wrote to Captain Perkins that the innovative gunnery training at sea had paid off in combat.[14]

As the convoy neared Africa, it ran into a bad storm. Captain Perkins recalled what it was like:

> On our own ship we were required to continue our guard duty on the decks even though you couldn't see more than a few feet in front of your face. I dutifully made rounds on deck and, at one station, I was unable to find Corporal Hetherington at first but finally discovered him on the deck clutching some railings, almost washed over the scuppers by a wave that had come down the deck. Terrifying, because if he had gone overboard nobody would have found him...Eating our meals during this storm was an acrobatic experience. The dining tables had elevated edges to keep the dishes from sliding off and we were clutching at dishes to keep them from going over the side of the table while

locking our feet together with men on the other side of the table to keep
from sliding away from the table.[15]

At the height of the storm, several heavy triple decker bunks aboard one of
the troopships broke loose and killed six men. When the storm subsided,
all hands were called on deck for a funeral, the men standing in formation
as the victims of this tragic accident were buried at sea.[16]

The convoy arrived at Casablanca on 24 December 1942, and by the
end of Christmas Day, the regiment had disembarked. Most of the men in
the regiment had made the crossing aboard two Holland-America Lines
passenger liners, the *Argentina* and the *Brazil*. Lt. W. M. Page recalls the
66th's arrival in North Africa:

> Upon entering Casablanca harbor an impressive sight was the
> French cruiser *Jean Bart*, which had been damaged and sunk during
> the November 8 hostilities. The stern rested on the bottom, under wa-
> ter, with bow, bridge and gun turrets angled upward and above water.
>
> Word had spread on the *Brazil* that a festive Christmas Eve din-
> ner would precede debarkation—but threat of a German air raid led
> to our being ordered to vacate the ship immediately, without the prom-
> ised dinner. First night ashore for the *Brazil* passengers was Christ-
> mas Eve, cold and rainy. The threatened air raid did not materialize
> on Christmas Eve, and the fact that our expulsion from the ship with-
> out dinner was triggered by a false alarm added to my vividly re-
> called unhappiness.
>
> When Christmas morning came, one soldier was heard to com-
> plain that he found nothing in his stocking but a cold foot. That morn-
> ing we saw our first camels, plodding along a nearby road with riders
> who might have resembled the Magi but surely were not.[17]

The soldiers in Captain Perkins' company spent most of the two days
helping unload all the vehicles from the *Texas* and driving them to a field
outside of Casablanca.[18] After the soldiers of the regiment claimed their
vehicles in the field, the regiment moved to a bivouac in the hills overlooking Casablanca. From their vantage point on New Year's Eve, the men
witnessed a night air raid on the harbor by a number of German four-engined
bombers. Captain Perkins described the action that he witnessed while lying in his sleeping bag inside his pup tent. He took the precaution of don-
ning his helmet as he watched.

> Several 4-motor German bombers raided the harbor at Casablanca and
> we saw the fantastic anti-aircraft curtain of fire, thousands of projec-
> tiles with tracers converging in the sky over us. Scores of spotlights

Regimental chaplain Luke Bolin.

Luke Bolin

were frantically searching for planes and, when they would catch one in their light, the plane would twist and turn trying to get away, while the anti-aircraft fire concentrated on it. We saw at least one plane get hit over the harbor. Another plane dove out of the searchlights and came pretty close over our bivouac and, just as he passed us going north (we were north of the harbor), something apparently hit the plane and the tail gunner, perhaps reflexively, fired a burst of machine gun fire out of the rear of the plane. The plane went into a dive and crashed out of sight.[19]

On 8 January 1943 the newly arrived units of the 66th Armored Regiment moved to the Forêt de Mamora, located about fourteen miles northeast of Rabat. This vast wooded area, known as the Cork Forest, served as semi-permanent bivouac for the entire 2nd Armored Division.[20] There, for the first time in six months, the 66th Armored Regiment was together in one location. The division's mission was to guard the border to Spanish Morocco, which lay about thirty miles north of the forest, because of possible action against the Allies by Franco's Spain. After the Allied landings, Spain had moved a large number of troops to the border between French Morocco and Spanish Morocco. The Allied command was afraid that General Franco might repay his debt to Hitler by harassing or attacking the Allied forces.[21]

In February 1943 the 66th sent home a soldier who had served with the regiment since his enlistment in August 1940. George Campbell was a big youth from Monroe, Louisiana when he was able to take advantage of a recruiting sergeant's hangover on a Monday morning. Suffering the effects of a weekend with the bottle, the sergeant hastily enlisted Campbell so he could suffer through the Monday morning in peace. George Campbell found he was living a boy's dream as a soldier in Machine Gun Company of the 66th at the age of fourteen.

Campbell served as a motorcycle scout in Reconnaissance Platoon performing dispatch delivery and scouting missions. In January 1942 Machine Gun Company was disbanded and he was assigned to Headquarters Company of 2nd Battalion. His ruse lasted until his mother became ill and the Red Cross workers heard some interesting things from neighbors about the son who had joined the army several years ago. Campbell was soon in front of his company commander who told him he was being sent home after three and a half years in the army.

George Campbell was not finished doing his part to win the war. In December 1943 he enlisted in the U.S. Navy. He turned out for his first inspection at the San Diego Recruit Training Center wearing the three service ribbons he had earned with the U.S. Army. When the inspecting officer spotted Campbell he had some questions. "What's your name?" Campbell quickly responded with his name and service number as a small group of petty officers looked on in disapproval. "How old are you?" Campbell answered truthfully that he was eighteen. "How long have you been in the Navy?" Then tapping the row of ribbons with his finger, the officer asked, "Do you know what these are?" The young sailor responded "Yes sir, I do." The officer said, "You know people have to earn these." Campbell said, "Yes sir, I know. I did earn them." Campbell explained that he had served some time in the army and that the service had been earned. The officer told Campbell to take off the ribbons while he checked out the young sailor's story. Ten days later Campbell was told to put his ribbons back on his new uniform.[22]

Lewis Sasser, Jr. graduated from the University of North Carolina and was drafted into the army in March 1941. He was sent to Officer Candidate School at Fort Knox and was commissioned as a second lieutenant in August 1942. In November he married Celeste, and the couple spent as much time together as possible until he departed in early February 1943. Celeste and Lew last saw each other at a USO dance at Camp Kilmer, N.J. He arrived in North Africa on 19 February and was assigned to Headquarters Company of the 66th on 5 March, 1943. His letter of 20 February descibes some of local people and conditions:

> The weather here is wonderful. The nights are so cool you have to sleep under two or three blankets but they are beautiful. The days heat up to where you can go around in just your coveralls. Slept on a cot last night with one blanket doubled under me and two tucked around me and was still plenty cool.
>
> Don't really wash but once a day. About noon when the sun is well up and use my helmet for a very good wash basin. Can even shave in luxury with this and manage a pretty good bath.
>
> I'd give anything if you could you could see the people here. There are a few French who look practically civilized but the Arabs are quite a sight. Most of them are such filthy people as you've never seen. They wear a cloak-dress affair and is generally patched or more generally pure rags. Some wear sandals with no socks or quite generally no shoes at all and feet just flat as the country. Their homes look like haystacks and are packed. The stock, as it is and including camels, are hobnailed. They also have burros, chickens, goats, steers, cows, camels, sheep, etc. but in small quantity to a family. The local oranges and lemons are wonderful and cost about 5 cents.[23]

The time in the Cork Forest was spent in all types of maintenance and training, especially tactics such as fire and maneuver. One platoon would be in a position to cover the advance of another platoon. The platoon providing cover could lay down a base of fire at the enemy to suppress them as the maneuvering platoon advanced. The two platoons could leap-frog forward with the platoons taking turns providing cover. The tanks often trained with all of their hatches closed ("buttoned up"), just as they generally fought in combat. In training, the "enemy" tanks fired their machine guns at the advancing tanks for practice; with the tanks buttoned up, there was very little danger, but it provided good practice in shooting at moving targets.[24]

Commanders continually devised new firing maneuvers. Captain Perkins, ever the innovative commander of Company H, took his company out for gunnery practice one day.

> I once demonstrated to my company the accuracy of the 75 by taking them out and lining them up on a hill in French Morocco. We picked a tree that was standing on a little ridge one mile away and I told the company that the first crew to knock that tree down would get $5.00 from me. Each crew was to fire one round, then wait for the others to take their turn and then fire another round and bracket it, get an over or a short and adjust fire. I fired first in order to get the range so I could have some idea about the accuracy of range estimation by the crews, using my field glasses. I got a short and an over, reached down and moved the traversing wheel a fraction of an inch and told the gunner to fire again. Our high explosive shell hit the trunk and knocked the tree down at 1 mile, saving me $5.00 but spoiling our game.[25]

Lt. Col. Harry Semmes, the 1st Battalion commander, developed an exciting tactical innovation in Morocco. In an attack, when it was important to force enemy soldiers to seek cover instead of fight, Lieutenant Colonel Semmes had the friendly artillery fire airbursts directly over the buttoned up tanks. The artillery shells would be set to burst twenty to thirty yards in the air, raining deadly fragments over the entire area, killing exposed enemy soldiers while only scratching the paint on the tanks. This technique proved very effective in combat later and was widely adapted by U.S. tank units.[26]

During the long cold evenings in the Cork Forest, some of the men began burning gasoline in a Number 10 tin can set into the ground. These little campfires provided the men a place to gather and relax at the end of their day, although they blackened the men's faces with the carbon thrown off by the smoke. In spite of the high cost of gasoline carried to Morocco, the commanders allowed these fires in the interest of morale.[27] Lt. W. M. Page describes some of the other ways gasoline was used in the Cork Forest:

Capt. Norris Perkins of H Company in his hut in the Cork Forest. March 1943.

The champion baseball team of H Company posing in the Cork Forest in spring 1943. S.Sgt. Bill Rape stands at the far left and later 1st Sgt. Tom Domarecki stands third from left.

Norris H. Perkins

We burned it in C-ration and other cans, primarily to heat our cold rations, to heat water for instant coffee, etc. Also gasoline was freely used for cleaning greasy combat jackets and other clothing (soak, scrub and hang out to dry).[28]

During the time in the Cork Forest, the soldiers were frustrated by their inaction while the 1st Armored Division fought the Germans in Tunisia. A group of about fifty officers and NCOs from 2nd Armored Division were given temporary duty as observers with 1st Armored Division for approximately one month. The group traveled the several hundred miles from the Cork Forest to the Gafsa-Maknassy area of Tunisia in trucks. Officers from the 66th included Major Herbert Long, Lt. W. M. Page and Lt. Cameron Warren.[29]

Sergeant Gatzke's diary for the first five days of March 1943 gives an impression of the daily activities in the Cork Forest:

mo 1   Active tetanus, Typhoid vac. Reconnaissance & Demolition class. Made a hand grenade.

tu 2   Maintenance. Gave calisthenics. 10 miles of hiking to hear General Harmon, just back from fighting, give a speech, at Division Bowl.

we 3   Loaded tank with ammunition. Stabilizer class. Rained all day. Read book " The Caretaker's Cat"

th 4   Combination arms problem. Fired 7 rounds 75 mm. One didn't go off.

fr 5   Maintenance all day. Training film at night. 2nd relief guard at kitchen 11pm to 3am[30]

It was also in the Cork Forest that the officers of the 66th met French and British army officers for the first time. Their impression of the French officers was basically unfavorable, beginning with a difficulty in getting the French officers to rise in time for breakfast. The French tank officers had an "arrogant and disdainful attitude toward machinery" that, considering their branch of service, the Americans found incredible.[31] The Americans found both the French and British officers too class-conscious and separated from their soldiers. The British officers, however, impressed the Americans with their excellent training, discipline, and bravery.[32]

All mail from soldiers was screened by censors to ensure that no information that might be useful to the enemy was being revealed in the letters. Most soldiers quickly learned to keep their letter content to daily routine, amusements, family and friends. Sergeant Gatzke's diary for 14 April 1943 mentions an encounter with the censor:

Sgt. Arden Gatzke. His diary of every day from North Africa to Berlin provided a unique soldier's view of the war. Lebenstedt, Germany, June 1945.

Arden Gatzke

Got letter back. Censor wouldn't pass it because I had written "wearing our woolen uniforms in this heat we have to have our sleeves down & collars buttoned, which lowers morale."[33]

Lt. Col. Harry Semmes, commander of the First Battalion, was a veteran of the U.S. tank corps in World War I. He had told some of his officers about a French tank officer who had trained and befriended the American tankers in France in 1918. It came as quite a surprise to Lieutenant Colonel Semmes when the same French officer arrived, leading a group of Free French tankers which was assigned to be trained by the 66th. These French tankers formed the cadre of the French 2nd Armored Division which entered Paris the next year.[34]

After the disastrous defeat of the 1st Armored Division at Kasserine Pass in February 1943, the 2nd Armored Division was ordered to transfer nearly 2,000 officers and men to the 1st Armored Division as replacements. The 66th bid farewell to 8 officers and 178 men in just two days. The replacements were transported by train to Bou Chebka, Algeria, where they were assigned to fill depleted 1st Armored Division units.[35]

When Captain Perkins received the order to transfer a group of his men, he decided not to weed out his less desirable soldiers, as many commanders did at the time. He made what he felt was an ethical decision by transferring his entire 3rd platoon with no personnel changes. The men, both those who stayed and those who went to the 1st Armored, were impressed by their commander's courage and believed his decision was a good one.[36] Captain Perkins then reorganized the entire company, dividing the best men in each position equally among the three platoons. Perkins recalls that the new company was considered by all to be an excellent one.[37]

After giving a considerable number of men and vehicles as replacements to the 1st Armored Division on 6 April, Major General Harmon was appointed as the new commander of that division. When Harmon left 2nd Armored Division, he took his chief of staff, Col. Maurice Rose, and his G-3, Lt. Col. Lawrence R. Dewey, with him. Brig. Gen. Allen Kingman, previously the commander of Combat Command A, assumed command of the 2nd Armored Division.[38]

Lieutenant Sasser wrote to Celeste on 6 March describing some of the accommodations in Cork Forest:

Thought I would get you off a few lines bright and early this morning before lunch. Is quite a nice day here and have spent it getting my pup tent well placed and my stuff assorted about as well as I could.

Do not have reveille here till 7:15 which is good as there is no sense in getting up before daylight and daylight breaks about 7:30. Four of the other officers here in my company built themselves an "Arab Hut" out of pup tents, assorted wood and old canvas. Is quite large, floored with Arab rugs and has wood chairs and tables. Have hung my valapack here and is quite nice for in the evening as we can cook up a few eggs with charcoal and have a place to sit around and write or shoot the bull. Someone is using the desk now so I have this pad on my knee. Last night I had a couple of eggs and an orange which really hit the spot while I was writing you.

The chaplain and I have pup tents without because he snores and I am a newcomer and would entail some modifications for me. Are bivouaced in in a forest of cork trees and is quite pretty, interesting and nice. The fact that there is some shade during the day helps a lot. So far everyone has been perfectly swell to me and barring rain, the area is wonderful.

Has anything been cut out of any of the letters you have received thus far? Don't know whether they are checked again after we censor them or not.[39]

On 22 April 1943 all of the units of the 2nd Armored Division were moved out of their comfortable bivouacs in the Cork Forest to new ones near the coast by Port Lyautey. When the regiment arrived at the new area, they were surprised by a new threat: the Arab thief. Soldiers began missing blankets, overcoats, and other pieces of clothing and equipment. During the noon meal one day, a tank crew from Company H saw an Arab, bearing a large quantity of blankets and other items, running toward a nearby forest. While one soldier carried the word back to Captain Perkins, the others gave chase. Captain Perkins quickly gathered a large number of soldiers, loaded them onto a 2$^{1}/_{2}$-ton truck and led them in his jeep. As he rapidly approached the first Arab village, he noticed warning signals being passed from there to other villages. In the first village he demanded, in French, the immediate return of all U.S. equipment. The Arabs at first pretended not to understand the language and then feigned innocence. Captain Perkins had his men go through every hut and tent in the village, where they discovered several U.S. items. The Company H raiding party then moved on to the next village and repossessed all the U.S. equipment found there. Then, wanting to be thorough, Captain Perkins raided two more villages along the coast, returning with a truck bed filled two feet deep in recovered U.S. military items.[40]

Upon returning to his company bivouac, 1st Sgt. Philip Brooks grimly told Captain Perkins that they had been visited by the division commander and a visiting general for an unannounced inspection. When the first sergeant had to explain that Captain Perkins and most of the company were out chasing Arabs, he was told to have Captain Perkins report to the division commander immediately. Perkins recalled:

So, with great fear that my career had ground to an end, I drove up to the Battalion Headquarters and from there on up to Division Headquarters. I presented myself to the Division Commander, General Kingman, and explained what happened. At that moment, Colonel Charles G. Rau, ..., of the 66th Armored, came tearing up in a jeep, jumped out and came over and said, saluting, "Excuse the interruption, General, but there is some sort of an uprising among the Arabs down the coast. I was afraid I was not going to be able to get through some of those villages. Some of the men looked pretty threatening." The General turned to his Operations Officer and said, "Post triple guards throughout the division for one week". He then turned to me and said, "Captain Perkins, I must admit that you have shown some initiative", and dismissed me.[41]

After a short period along the coast, 66th Armor moved by train and convoy to a bivouac about fifteen miles northwest of Perregaux, Algeria, arriving there on 5 May 1943.[42] On the same day, Brig. Gen. Hugh J. Gaffey assumed command of the 2nd Armored Division. Brigadier General Gaffey, who had been Patton's chief of staff at II Corps, was promoted on 12 May. Brigadier General Kingman returned to training French armor forces.[43] Col. John H. Collier again assumed command of the 66th on 29 May.[44] Colonel, and later Lieutenant General Collier was affectionately known as Pee Wee because he stood only five feet, two inches tall and weighed 110 pounds.[45] In Algeria the regiment continued tactical and gunnery training. This training was improved by the lessons brought back to the regiment by Major General Harmon and many other officers who had observed the 1st Armored Division in Tunisia.[46]

Lt. Donald Critchfield attended a mine and demolition school during this period. The twenty students studied locating and defusing all types of German mines. Lieutenant Critchfield describes the "graduation exercise" of the school:

Culmination was sweeping, location and defusing live mines in a field placed by the Nazis. The day was hot, as North Africa usually is in summer but I was lucky—locating a "Bouncing Betty"—a canister with a three pronged detonator buried in the sand—unscrewed the detonator and tossed the A.P.M. (Anti-Personnel Mine) on a growing pile. I then sought refuge from the heat in a nearby ambulance when there was a terrific explosion lifting the ambulance in the air. I was told some unfortunate candidates stepped on a plastic detonator with a piece of priming cord leading to a buried 500 lb. German aerial bomb. Needless to say these were some who did not graduate that day.[47]

At Port Aux Poules the regiment, as part of CCA, spent two weeks training at the 5th Army Invasion Training Center (FAITC). There the regiment was trained in all aspects of amphibious operations, from firing their tank weapons off a moving landing craft, to assaulting and consolidating a beachhead. The tankers were also trained in such skills as attacking pillboxes and street fighting; these skills were expected to be important in expanding inland from a beach.[48] The tankers were trained on the impressive new Landing Ship, Tank (LST). These vessels, because of their shallow draft, could carry up to sixty tanks and armored vehicles and five hundred men right up to the beach. The LST carried an array of 40mm rapid-fire cannon and .50 caliber machine guns for anti-aircraft defense. In addition, all the vehicles that were transported on the upper deck could use their weapons.[49] These new ships were a vast improvement over the easily upset lighter ones used to land the regiment in North Africa six months earlier. Lt. John Getsinger of B Company provides some additional details of the LST:

They were 100 yards long, had two decks for carrying vehicles, and an elevator for taking vehicles to and from the upper deck. Tanks were carried on the lower deck. It had bow doors that opened outward and a ramp that lowered for the vehicles to roll out on. The ship had a flat bottom and shallow draft so it could get as far up on the beach as possible. Toward the stern was the bridge where the steering was done, and there was a ward room for eating and small cabin for officers, including us, to sleep in.[50]

Lieutenant Sasser described the regimental headquarters tank section and their uniforms in a letter to Celeste on 22 May:

Have only got 18 men to worry about and with the two Sgt. Joneses to help that's no problem at all. In fact, they're all good tankers and can take care of themselves, if the need arises.

Most of the other units have gone into khaki but we are still in our wool o.d.'s. Doesn't make much difference as we wear coveralls most of the time anyway. Do have to put on our wool o.d. pants, shirt and tie tho for supper each evening but as it gets cool after dark there is no objection to that.[51]

On 21 May, the 2nd Battalion, 66th Armor, and other small elements of CCA moved by ship to Phillipeville, Algeria, and then by road to Jemapes. The remainder of the 66th and CCA received orders on 29 May to move to bivouacs near Bizerte, Tunisia. Some elements moved by ship arriving near Bizerte between 3 and 6 June. The wheeled vehicles road marched to Bizerte with all elements arriving at their bivouacs by 6 June. The 2nd Battalion rejoined the regiment near Bizerte on 19 June.[52]

A selection of Sergeant Gatzke's diary entries for May 1943 show some of the training the companies of the 66th were engaged with in Tunisia:

sa. 8   Indirect firing in tank. Me tank commander, Moes gunner, Meeks loader. Back 8 pm.

mo. 10   School. Firing 30 Cal. machine gun, 45 pistol, tommy gun & rifle.

th. 13   Moving target range AM firing 30 cal. machine gun. Typhus shot.

tu. 18   Crew drill. Displayed tank equipment.

As part of this movement the 2nd Armored Division left its tanks in Algeria for the 1st Armored Division and picked up the 1st Armored Division's tanks in Tunisia.[53] CCA, under the command of Col. Maurice Rose, was attached to Maj. Gen. Lucian K. Truscott's 3rd Infantry Division.[54] The 66th was the only tank unit in CCA and its primary fighting force.

Lt. James Burt of C Company was in charge of the advance detachment. His little detachment of men in a jeep and a half-track quickly moved overland to Tunisia to receive the equipment left by 1st Armored Division. Burt recalls what happened on their arrival:

We found the 1st Armored Division equipment, all the tanks, all the artillery, all the trucks, all the everything, parked, tightly parked on a vast barren field. A small detachment of the First waited for us to relieve them. They were in a hurry to get away. They had no documents of inventory, so we cruised the entire park, all the equipment of an entire division, and I signed a receipt for so many "acres of armament." No one ever complained, so I guess it was all right.[55]

The soldiers were able to listen to the German propaganda program on the radio as Lieutenant Sasser describes in this letter:

Everyone gets a big kick out of the nightly German program in English. It is run by "Mae of the A.E.F." She starts her program by introducing herself as a "gentile friend" who is our friend. Then she

Chaplain Luke Bolin going to visit soldiers in the hospital. Tunisia, June 1943.

Luke Bolin

plays a worn-out recording of an excerpt from one of Roosevelt's 1932 speeches saying "no American boy will fight on foreign soil," in what is supposed to be his voice. A very good male commentator then gives the German side of the news with just enough truth in it to be interesting, usually followed by a biased thumbnail sketch of some big Allied stateman showing the weaknesses in his record or his similarity to Hitler or his antipathy toward the Jewish race. Sometimes they're down on the Jews, then the British and then the French but they stay down on the Jews for the most part.

After the commentator has finished Mae tells that all this is too deep for us to worry about, let's relax with good music and think about the sweetheart or wife back home and what's she doing. She then plays a few recordings of which "Smoke Gets in Your Eyes" and "Give me a Heart and Home to Come Back To" are her favorites. She has a very good voice, speaks without any accent, and apparently was an American or spent some years in school in the country. She definitely tries to appeal to the sentimental and uses very good U.S. slang. Along with this she attempts to prove that we're really all "gentiles" together and this war is a big misunderstanding. Finally when the time comes to sign off, she goes into great detail about how things are not so good back home but then let's think about that little white haired lady in that one-horse town—our mother.

Frankly, I think the propaganda effect is nil but it is interesting to try and figure out what they're attempting to accomplish. Instead of undoing our morale any, it seems to me that it builds it up more for after listening to the program, everyone is more thankful than ever that he's an American.

Thursday night they put on their best program "Home Sweet Home" with a band, and some humor (used to be Fritz and Fred) and Olga is the feminine insertion. The situation is still quiet and peaceful with no staff officers around. About the only useful thing I accomplished was the cleaning of 2 pairs of coveralls, my legging, and my field jacket today. Has been a wonderful relief to wander around in the uniform suiting your fancy or none at all for a couple of days. We generally have to spend most of our energy worrying about who doesn't have his leggings on, his tie tied with his wool shirt or his top overall button buttoned. The coveralls buttoned all the way up is the worst one tho and a reason for great concern.[56]

In Tunisia some of the officers visited the Tunisia battlefields and examined captured German and Italian vehicles and equipment. The primary

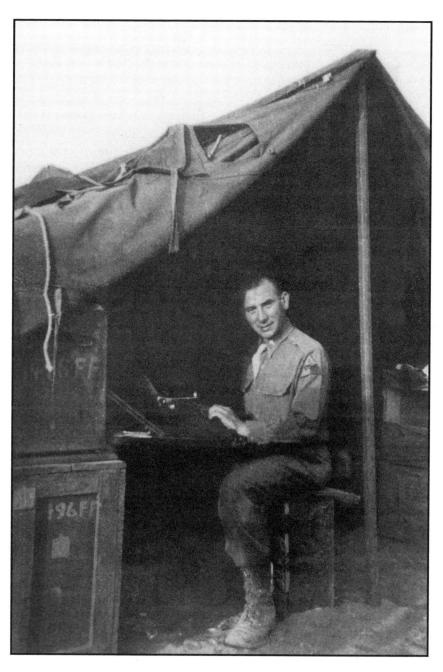

Regimental chaplain Luke Bolin at his typewriter in Tunisia. June 1943.

Luke Bolin

mission of the 66th and CCA in Tunisia was to prepare for an amphibious invasion on an enemy beach somewhere in the Mediterranean. The training focused on physical training, vehicle maintenance, tactics, and firing on tank ranges. In further preparation for the upcoming invasion, the 3rd Infantry Division (Reinforced), to which CCA was attached, was designated as Task Force J. Throughout June the regiment participated in Task Force J exercises. By 25 June the task force completed loading on board ships, put to sea, and conducted practice landings along the North African coast. Some of these landings were done on beaches with barbed wire obstacles, flares, and "enemy" soldiers.[57] After the practice landings, the vehicles remained on board while the troops returned to their camps.[58]

During the waterproofing of the vehicles a problem was encountered. Lt. John Getsinger of B Company relates the problem and the solution he found:

> Our vehicles were to be waterproofed before loading to enable them to run with the engines under water for a few minutes in getting from the ship to dry land. There was a petroleum-based material for sealing the electrical system and all the joints that might leak and cause harm. Hoses were provided to carry air from above water to the carburetors. Copper tubing about the size of a pencil in diameter would allow the fuel tank's pressure to be stable so fuel could be pumped to the engine; also a copper tube was required for the breather cap on the lubricating oil system. The hoses and tubing were to be sealed at the joints with the petroleum gook.
>
> The only trouble was that there was no copper tubing. I never knew why; somebody screwed up.
>
> It was just days before the invasion. The company commander, Capt. Hugh O'Farrell sent me, as maintenance officer, out to see if I could find tubing. I took the company maintenance sergeant (Riley) with me. We went in a jeep to Tunis. I was thinking this was typical army, sending the ignorant to do the impossible. Tunisia was a war-torn, backward country with no hardware stores, no factories, no plumbing shops. Where the hell was I supposed to find tubing? We were passing the deserted air field. There were abandoned German planes on the field. It hit me! Planes have hydraulic lines. We turned in the field, pulled up to this big transport plane and climbed inside. The walls of the fuselage were absolutely lined with aluminum tubing of the size we needed. Being a chemical engineer—trained at that great institution, N.C. State, I knew immediately that aluminum would do as well as copper for the temporary use intended.

The sergeant and I started ripping tubing off the wall. An MP came to investigate and demanded to know what we were doing. After I explained to him, he agreed that we could continue. We had enough tubing for our company in a few minutes and hightailed it back to the company area.

The company commander was delighted and immediately notified the regimental commander of the find. We went back to the field later that day, and the planes were absolutely swarming with soldiers from the 2nd Armored Division and others, all gathering tubing.

That could have been my biggest contribution to the war effort. Somebody else might have thought of it, but I was the one who did. I thought of the old poem: "For want of a nail a shoe was lost. For want of a shoe a horse was lost. For want of a horse a rider was lost. For want of a rider a battle was lost. For want of a nail a battle was lost."[59]

During the time the regiment was not training, they were working to waterproof their vehicles for the landing. The Sherman tanks of the regiment required extensive preparation all the way up to the top of the turret to keep water out of the tank. A large shroud was mounted on the back deck to handle the air intake and exhaust of the engine. The joints and cracks of the shrouds, the turret ring, and other smaller places all had to be sealed with tape and a sealant compound known as mastic. The gun barrels were all closed with tape that could be shot off when reaching the beach. The shroud could be knocked off by traversing the turret. This system allowed a tank to fight if necessary as it exited the water.[60]

The tankers were trained on the new Landing Craft, Tank (LCT), the much smaller relative of the LST. The LCT could carry three to four medium tanks that could fire over the sides of the craft, if necessary. Captain Perkins' frightening experience during one of the practice landings in Tunisia illustrates the hazards of amphibious operations with tanks.

We landed on a beach before dawn, a beach that had not yet been cleared of real German mines and barbed wire entanglements. I had our tanks all sealed up, of course, and was peering through the dark trying to see where we were. We went off the landing craft and what I didn't know was that the boat had stopped at a sandbar and we were driving down the ramp into deeper water. I had my arm over the side and water came up to my fingers. These tanks were 10' high so we were in 9' of water. It just terrified me because, gosh, if the water poured in, we were done.

I slammed down the turret hatch, told the driver to gun it and keep going and don't stop no matter what happened. I shouted on the intercom, "If we stall, I'm going to open a hatch and we're all going to crawl out and there's going to be water flowing in, so hold your breath if I tell you." Well, we came up on the beach and made it all right. That was pretty scary, not being able to see.[61]

The destination of the invasion force that had been training in North Africa for over six months was one of the Allied forces best kept secrets. At the Casablanca Conference, in January 1943, President Roosevelt and Prime Minister Churchill agreed to invade Sicily that year. The British successfully deceived the Germans into believing that Sardinia was the primary objective with an attack on Sicily as a feint. The objective of Operation Husky, the code name for the invasion of Sicily, was the city of Messina that lay only two miles across the Straits of Messina from the Italian mainland. The Allied invasion force was comprised of two armies, one British and one American. The British 8th Army, under Field Marshal Sir Bernard Montgomery, was to land on the southern tip of the island from Syracuse, move south around the tip and over twenty miles beyond the port of Pozzallo. After landing, the British were to capture first Syracuse, and then the primary objective of Messina.

The U.S. 7th Army, under Lieutenant General Patton, would land along a long stretch of southern coastline from Licata in the west to Scoglitti in the east. The American force consisted of three infantry divisions: the 1st, 3rd, and 45th. The 1st and 3rd Infantry Divisions were supported by attachments of CCB and CCA, respectively. The 66th Armor, as part of CCA was attached to the 3rd Infantry Division (Task Force J), and were assigned landing beaches around Licata.

Between 1 and 5 July the regiment completed loading vehicles, equipment, and ammunition plus checking the waterproofing of their vehicles. Beginning on the afternoon of 5 July, the troops began boarding their vessels. Troop loading was completed by noon on 7 July. The vessels immediately moved out of Bizerte Harbor to an anchorage five miles offshore. From there, they weighed anchor at 0500 on 8 July and sailed to Sicily.[62]

Brig. Gen. John H. "Pee Wee" Collier (center), commander of the 66th Armored Regiment and later CCA.

U.S. Army Military History Institute

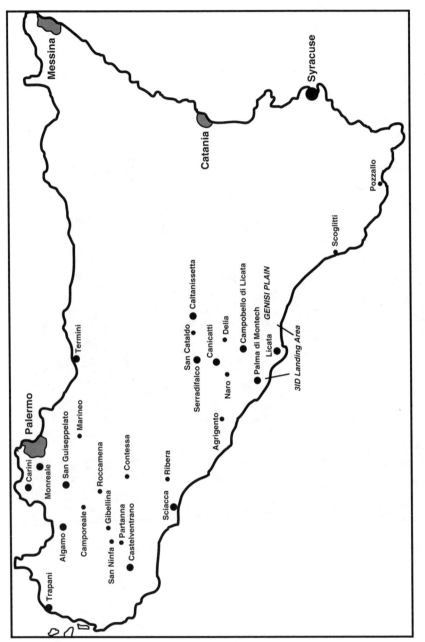

MAP 17
Sicily
July–November 1943

CHAPTER 10

Operation Husky: Sicily

The invasion plans for Operation Husky had the 66th Armor participating as two separate elements. The 3rd Battalion embarked aboard the small LCTs and was assigned to support 3rd Infantry Division units in the first wave. Company G of the 3rd Battalion, attached to the 7th Regimental Combat Team (RCT), would land at "Red" Beach. The 15th RCT, supported by Company H, would land at "Yellow" Beach. Landing at "Blue" Beach was Company I in support of the 30th RCT. The 3rd Battalion headquarters would land with Company H at "Yellow" Beach. The rest of the 66th made up the reserve of the 3rd Infantry Division.[1]

On 9 July some 3,000 ships and landing craft, bearing 160,000 men, 600 tanks, 1,800 guns (artillery pieces), and 14,000 vehicles, were moving toward the south coast of Sicily. Traveling in five LCTs were Captain Perkins and his seventeen tanks of Company H, 3rd Battalion, 66th Armor. Prior to leaving Tunisia, Captain Perkins was the only one in his company allowed to know any information concerning their destination. He had spent a considerable amount of time memorizing the features of the area where his company and the 15th RCT were to land. Captain Perkins had made several copies of his orders and helpful information, but, because his company was on five different vessels, he had no way of getting the copies to his men. This problem was solved unexpectedly when the company's LCTs were holding position in the convoy by circling. Captain Perkins described how his distribution problem was solved:

> ...one of my senior platoon leaders, Lieutenant Cameron J. Warren, with guts and initiative, stripped naked, jumped into the middle of the

173

sea and waited for my LCT to come by and pick him up. We lowered
our landing ramp down into the water and here came this naked man
walking up the ramp asking me, "What's cooking?" I gave him a full
copy of all of my orders and plans in several sets which I had had the
foresight to make, and, with them in waterproof containers, he jumped
back in the water and handed one to each of the other boats as they
came by.[2]

On the afternoon of 9 July, with the invasion fleet beyond the point of
recall, a sudden Force 7 gale struck the fleet. The storm tossed the smaller
vessels around like toys, threatening to sink them. The larger vessels
struggled to maintain their course and speed as thousands of crowded, over-
heated men became violently seasick. Then, shortly before midnight, the
storm dissipated as suddenly as it had appeared.[3]

At 0130 hours on 10 July the Allied fleet arrived off the coast of
southern Sicily. At the H-Hour of 0245 the three tank companies of the 3rd
Battalion, 66th Armor, began landing on their designated beaches. As the
LCTs moved towards the beach, Sergeant Rape of H Company went to his
tank, climbed on to the top of it, pulled out his Coleman stove and began
preparing a morning pot of coffee. Some of his men were kidding him
about getting shot off the top of the tank. Sergeant Rape calmly looked
down at them and replied, "Surely, if we made it through that storm last
night, surely we can make it to the beach."[4] The LCTs landed the tank
companies approximately ninety minutes after the first assault of infantrymen had hit the beach.[5] Because of the deception plan and the storm, the
invasion caught the Italian and German defenders completely off guard.
The 3rd Infantry Division landings met only scattered or weak resistance
from Italian forces.

After getting ashore, Company H followed in close support of 15th
RCT as they moved about three miles along the coast to Licata. The Italian
defenders surrendered the town as the 3rd Infantry Division forces closed
in on them from east and west. The team commander ordered Company H
to move two and a half miles north to secure the city airport against enemy
counterattack. The company quickly reached the abandoned airport, which
was strewn with wooden piling obstacles (to prevent Allied aircraft from
landing), and continued moving inland.[6]

Sergeant Gatzke recorded the invasion in his diary:

sa. 10 Invasion of Sicily at Licata 830am. First battle I was in. Fired
13 HE shells. 2 German shells landed close. Traveled 25 miles.[7]

When the company reached the Genisi Plain, just beyond the airport,
they deployed along a one-mile front and moved forward, a platoon of five

tanks at a time. Suddenly a hidden gun opened fire on Captain Perkins' tank as it moved by a tree. He alerted his company over the radio and moved forward to locate the enemy gun. A second shot ricocheted off the tank's turret and a third damaged the track. The 3rd Platoon leader knocked out the gun as his platoon pulled abreast of their commander. This firefight between Company H and a battery of Italian 75mm antitank guns ended with the destruction of all five enemy guns. Captain Perkins' tank, even after being hit twice, was still able to locate and destroy two of the five well-camouflaged guns.[8]

In victory, however, there was a question of what to do with the defeated Italians. Prior to the landing, Captain Perkins had been told by the team commander not to take any prisoners, because there were no personnel in the landing force to handle them. But with the destruction of all their guns, small groups of Italian soldiers began to appear, holding white flags. Captain Perkins thought:

> ...if we shot them the others would not surrender so readily and might even put up effective resistance and cause us casualties. So I disobeyed orders, rose up in my tank turret, exposing myself from the waist up, and waved the enemy soldiers back past us toward the coast. Immediately, dozens of surrendering soldiers came running down the mountainside, some of them holding stretched out bed sheets between them, etc., anything white, to signify surrender. We simply motioned them back toward the coast and expected they would be no problem to anybody. Those Italians were only too happy to get out of the war.[9]

Beginning at 1500 hours the rest of the regiment, as part of the 3rd Infantry Division reserve, began landing on "Yellow" and "Blue" beaches. At 1830 the regiment began unloading at the Licata harbor docks. The unloading continued until dawn. During this time, a German bomber scored a direct hit on the Company F ammunition truck aboard LST No. 15. The vessel burst into flames, and three tanks, the T-2 recovery vehicle, and several other vehicles were lost; one officer was killed, and two soldiers later were reported missing in action. Fortunately, the company's other fourteen tanks were already ashore. By noon on the eleventh, all of the 66th Armor was ashore in Sicily.[10]

Lt. John Getsinger was revisited by a dream from his childhood and never made it ashore in Sicily.

> When I was a boy, I used to read "pulp" adventure magazines with stories about World War I. I especially liked the ones about the fighter planes and air combat. I began to have this recurring dream which continued on into adulthood. I would dream I was in the front

yard of my home in Dardens. I would hear planes and look up and there would be a big air battle going on between American and German planes. I could hear the machine guns firing and see planes being shot down. Then one of the German planes would start diving toward me. I would run into the house into the parlor room and fall down on the floor. I could hear the machine gun firing and the bullets hitting. Then I would roll to face the outside wall and see the sun shining through the bullet holes in the wall.

On the morning of July 10, 1943, we were aboard LST No. 1 (the first one ever built) in the Mediterranean off shore from Licata, Sicily. We were part of an armada of several hundred ships. Battleships and cruisers were pounding the shore, and two of our ships, one an LST, were on fire from German air attacks. There was more air combat than I saw at any other time during the war. I was standing on deck watching the show as we were headed toward the beach for our landing. I saw American and German planes in dog fights, and the Americans were getting the best of it, as I saw German plane after German plane get shot down. When I looked at our landing spot on the beach, I saw enemy artillery bursts intermittently hitting there. I had an idea about our unloading scheme and went to the ward room to tell the company commander about it. I had just started talking to him when a German plane strafed our ship. I was hit in the foot and fell on the floor. I rolled over toward the wall and saw sunlight shining through the bullet holes and memory of my dream flooded over me.

Well, I never set foot on Sicily. I went back to Africa aboard the same LST and spent the next several months in a hospital housed in Quonset huts near Constantine.[11]

During the evening of 10 July the regiment began to assemble in an area about two miles north of Licata. Companies G and H were released by their infantry teams and rejoined the regiment at about 2000 hours.[12] The regiment received oral orders at 0100 hours on 11 July to seize the town of Naro later that morning. The advance guard consisted of the 3rd Battalion, 41st Infantry, supported by Company D, 66th Armor. The main body included the 2nd Battalion (- Co. D) and the 3rd Battalion (- Co. I). The 1st Battalion of the regiment brought up the rear as the CCA reserve. The lead vehicle of the main body crossed the initial point (IP) on Highway 123 at 0720. The command encountered only minor enemy resistance and had possession of Naro at 1030 hours. The biggest problem during the move on Naro was frequent bombing and strafing by enemy aircraft. Further, about 1300 the Army Air Corps took up where the Germans and Italians had left off and began bombing and strafing the forward elements of the American regiment. The tankers were fortunate not to suffer any casualties from the repeated attacks by American P-38 Lightnings and P-51 Mustang fighters, which had mistaken the regiment for a German Panzer Division in the area. Amazingly, there were no vehicle losses or personnel casualties during these air attacks.[13] After moving through the town, the advance guard, with Company D, continued north astride the road to Canicatti, halting on the high ground about three miles north of Naro. The main body of the regiment moved into an assembly area one mile northeast of Naro, beginning at 1830. By midnight on 11 July, the entire 66th Armored Regiment, with the exception of Company I, was located in one place for the first time since leaving Tunisia.[14]

12 July began for the regiment in the same way the previous day had ended, with the unit under attack from American aircraft. At 0830 the 1st Battalion angrily watched as an American P-38 fighter attacked and destroyed their gasoline truck. And again, whenever the American aircraft were not attacking the regiment, the Germans were. But unlike before, the aerial attacks by both sides on the morning of the twelfth did result in some personnel casualties in the regiment.[15]

Combat Command A orders called for an attack to seize Canicatti to begin at 1300 hours on 12 July. The attack would be led by Company H of the 66th Armor with the soldiers of Company G, 1st Battalion, 41st Armored Infantry, riding on the tanks. The rest of the 3rd Battalion, 41st Infantry, riding in their half-tracks, and the 3rd Battalion, 66th Armor followed the Company H spearhead. The 2nd Battalion of the 66th followed in column, while the 1st Battalion and the Reconnaissance Company were held in CCA reserve. The attack would begin from a rocky ridge (occupied by CCA) overlooking the open, rolling valley that led to Canicatti, four miles away. Canicatti, a town of 28,000, was flanked by steep hills that made any bypass impossible. Half a mile below the ridge, there was an enemy-occupied village where an enemy unit of four self-propelled guns had fought the elements of CCA the previous evening and were now knocked out or abandoned.[16] Lieutenant Warren led a small group of his men into the village and returned with twenty-five Italian prisoners.[17]

Company H then advanced towards Canicatti, deployed in a line almost a mile long. The three platoons moved forward by bounds, cautiously covering the first three miles to the town in about thirty minutes. When the company was about three-fourths of a mile from the edge of the town, German artillery began falling on each of the platoons.[18] Because the infantry had been instructed to dismount at the first resistance, almost all of the Company G infantrymen dismounted from the tanks.[19] The tanks, however, picked up speed and began zigzagging, so that all of them made it into the town safely. The three platoons went through the town in columns on three parallel routes. Because the town was reported to contain a large number of enemy snipers, the tanks raced through the streets firing their machine guns at all windows, roofs, and other possible sniper positions. The lead tank in each column fired its main gun continuously, hitting the second stories of buildings about one block ahead to suppress any possible enemy soldiers. Because of the danger of an enemy antitank gun getting a flank shot at the tanks when they crossed through intersections, the lead tank would fire a delayed fuse high explosive round into the intersection to throw a cloud of dust and smoke to cover the tanks' movements.[20]

The company exited the opposite edge of the town and began to climb the higher ground outside of the town. Captain Perkins was with the platoon that had exited the northwestern edge, when they came under antitank fire from the high ground north of the town. When the first enemy shot missed, Cpl. Kenneth Grogan, Captain Perkins' driver, sought cover behind a nearby stone wall. The tankers observed some of the enemy gun muzzle flashes coming from about 2,500 yards away and began to return fire. Captain Perkins' tank again was narrowly missed by several rounds, and then was hit squarely on the muzzle end of its gun. Perkins described the effect of the hit and his reactions:

> It tore the whole gun loose from the gun mount, breaking my arm and loader Tim McMahan's thigh. It spun the turret to the left, blocking driver Grogan's hatch and his escape route through the turret. The projectile ricocheted down, hit the hull and turned the front slope plate of the tank red hot.

> Gunner Harold Smith and I got out of the turret in seconds. The bow gunner T. D. Smith went out through his red hot hatch and Grogan followed him, after another shot tore off part of the open hatch cover. Grogan and the two Smiths used an orchard ladder for a stretcher, a tommy gun for a splint, and carried McMahan away from the tank while still under fire...[21]

Corporal Grogan later commented to a reporter during an interview about the battle:

> Explosive shells showered hot metal all over the tank but failed to hit it direct. Then one hit smack on the end of our gun. The whole tank seemed like a ball of fire. Everybody bailed out, fearing the tank would go up in flames.[22]

After bailing out of the crippled tank, Perkins and three of his crew ran back to a building about one hundred yards behind the tank. There, Captain Perkins almost passed out because of his badly shattered left arm. When they realized that the loader, Sgt. Tim McMahan, was missing, Perkins and Grogan returned to the tank where they found McMahan with a broken leg. They retrieved the radio code book from inside the tank, splinted McMahan's leg and carried him back to the building. Captain Perkins then mounted a platoon leader's tank and continued to lead his company from the back deck of his platoon leader's tank until he was forcibly taken away by the medics an hour later. For his bravery and leadership during the action at Canicatti, Captain Perkins later received the Distinguished Service Cross.[23]

Running low on ammunition and under antitank and artillery fire, Company H withdrew to the better cover of the buildings on the northwest edge of the town. Company G, with three tanks attached from Company I, was ordered to reinforce Company H by maneuvering around the west side of the enemy positions on the high ground. The ground north of Canicatti rose at an increasing angle to a pass about two miles north of town. A road ran between the bluffs leading to the pass and the town of Serradifalco on the other side. As Company G moved to the high ground it came under heavy "friendly" artillery fire. Lieutenant Colonel Quillian's artillery forward observer, a second lieutenant, was told that higher ranking observers were controlling the artillery fire and it would not be changed. Apparently, ground force's control of artillery needed improvement almost as much as that of the Army Air Force. Company G finally made it onto the high ground and was able to effectively engage the enemy gun positions at about 2000 hours.[24] The 2nd Battalion, 66th Armor, reached Canicatti at 1520 hours and began to skirt around the east side of the town, coming under antitank fire. They left Company E to guard the Canicatti-Delia road that led into the CCA right flank. The 2nd Battalion arrived on the north side of town just after dark, where they encountered more antitank fire and some mortar shelling.[25] Three Italian 90mm self-propelled antitank guns, four 75mm antitank guns, and several machine gun nests had been captured or destroyed before nightfall.[26]

Sgt. Arden Gatzke's diary for 12 July summarized the day's action:

Fired 13 HE shells indirect, like artillery. Went into Canicatti. 3rd tank into town. Germans almost trapped us but not quite. Jack Hollands & Joe Young's tanks shot up 3 armored cars, 2 motorcycles and 4 jeeps. German shell hit straight into muzzle of Capt. Perkins tank. Shoved the gun back and broke Capt. Perkins arm and Sgt. McMahans leg. They were evacuated and Lt. Warren took over Co.[27]

Although the soldiers of the 2nd Armored Division had trained hard prior to the invasion of Sicily, the action at Canicatti pointed out some weaknesses. First, the coordination between the infantrymen and tankers needed improvement when working together in small teams. Previous training had focused on tank and infantry units attacking a common objective that required little coordination at the small unit level. Thus, the infantry lacked the radios and other equipment necessary to communicate with the tanks. It also became apparent that standard procedures for small unit tank-infantry coordination in various situations were also needed. Some infantrymen had dismounted the tanks when they first came under artillery fire before reaching Canicatti because of the instruction to do so at first resistance; resistance needed to be defined in the orders. The infantrymen who dismounted were in more peril because they had to walk the remaining three-fourths of a mile into town without tank protection and were exposed in an open area for a much longer time. Fortunately for Company H, the infantry was not needed to get through Canicatti. Towns are where tanks and infantry are more dependent on each other than anywhere else. The infantrymen must protect their tanks from enemy infantry armed with short-range, antitank weapons hiding amongst the buildings. The tanks provided their infantrymen with firepower to destroy enemy machine gun positions and tanks. But infantry and tankers still had much to learn about each other's strengths and weaknesses: communication, standard operating procedures, and training were still needed to create an effective combined arms unit.[28]

Control of friendly artillery and aircraft was a significant problem during the first three days in Sicily. The regiment spent as much time under "friendly" air attack as they did under that of the enemy, which meant that not only could the Air Force not protect the ground forces from enemy aircraft, but also they actually assisted the Germans in harassing the American forces. The tankers had no problem identifying the exact type of aircraft that was attacking them. But unfortunately, the American pilots could not identify American Sherman tanks, with large white stars painted on them, moving inland from the beaches. The pilots continued their attack even after the desperate tankers threw out the friendly recognition signal of yellow smoke grenades. The problems with air support in Sicily resulted in Air Force liaison officers being assigned to ground units, which greatly improved the coordination between the two elements. The problem with "friendly" artillery during the Canicatti battle was a rare occurrence.

Artillery units had a great deal more experience supporting combat units, and artillery forward observers were invaluable to the units they supported.

During the night of 12–13 July German and Italian forces counterattacked the Company H positions north of Canicatti. Company H, now under the command of Lieutenant Warren, repulsed the attack with the help of very effective artillery fire brought down by one of the regiment's forward observers. Staff Sergeant Joe Young was assigned, along with four other tanks and a group of infantrymen, to guard one of the roads into town. Staff Sergeant Young positioned his infantry along a stone wall to watch for any approaching enemy. The infantrymen would whistle a signal back to the tanks upon sighting an enemy force. The five tanks were hidden with each of the five covering a part of the road.

> Sure enough I received the signal and after we let the point of the enemy column come into our trap we caught the last and first vehicles and then just picked off the rest of them. Quite a party.[29]

The enemy force lost three armored cars, three light trucks, two antitank guns, and two gasoline trucks, all destroyed. The regiment captured over 250 prisoners and approximately 15 vehicles as a result of the action that night.[30]

At dawn on 13 July the 41st Armored Infantry, supported by the tanks of the 2nd Battalion and the guns of the 14th and 62nd Field Artillery Battalions, attacked and seized high ground west of the pass, surprisingly with no opposition. Once the pass was secure, the road north into the Sicilian interior was open. At 1330 hours on 13 July the 15th Infantry began relieving the 66th Armor positions around Canicatti. As the units were relieved, they moved back to an assembly area northwest of Campobello.[31] The regiment, with the rest of CCA, was designated as part of the Force reserve and placed on thirty-minute alert.[32] The last units of the regiment closed at 2000 hours.

That evening Lt. Col. Amzi "Rudy" Quillian, the 3rd Battalion commander, had the daily battalion meeting at his command post, which had been set up in an orchard on the top of a knoll.[33] Lt. Cameron Warren, whom Quillian appointed to take command of Company H, wrote in his diary about the meeting:

> The Col. put it this way. "I am recommending Lt. Warren for promotion to Captain on the basis of his battlefield performance and he will take command of Company H." My heart was grateful. I was overwhelmed and fearing my voice or what would come out I remained silent. The enemy was still at hand and the Col. passed on to other

business. But in a few short words I felt a new load placed on my shoulders. The weight rested evenly. I was sure of my men but I could feel myself grow graver and sterner as the new requirements were laid down by the Col.[34]

Beginning on 14 July the regiment had a brief period of rest, their first since landing in Sicily. At noon on 14 July the regiment's Reconnaissance Company was assigned to CCA control. The Reconnaissance Company conducted continuous surveillance in the area south of Serradifalco, San Cataldo, and Caltanissetta until 18 July.[35]

The morning reports of Reconnaissance Company for 15 and 16 July show some of the unit's activities and casualties:

15 July All platoons out on regular recon missions. Pvt. Robert L. Mathis wounded in action on Hill 464 north of Celia, Sicily by enemy mortar shell fragments. Wounded in left foot and shoulder. Evacuated to hospital. Wounds not serious.

16 July 3 miles north of Canicatti, Sicily and all 3 platoons on recon patrol. CP located approximately 3 miles north of Canicatti. Pvt. Fred C. Williams, Jr. slightly injured in motorcycle spill 6 miles north of Canicatti. Pvt. Jimmie M. Henderson, shock, blinded from artillery shell striking about 20 ft. from him on highway 5 miles north of Canicatti; not serious.[36]

The rest of the regiment stayed in the assembly area near Campobello until 18 July, maintaining their vehicles and resting.[37] On the morning of 17 July Company F was attached to the 7th RCT and moved to join them in their assembly area north of Agrigento. That same morning the 1st Battalion was alerted by a false alarm of an enemy attack in the north. These false alarms were common in Sicily as the Allies tried to locate and eliminate the German forces on the island.

On 18 July Company F and Company I returned to the regiment, the latter having been out on attachment since the landing. Also on 18 July CCA was released from attachment to the 3rd Infantry Division and returned to 2nd Armored Division control.[38] At 0130 hours on 19 July the regiment, as part of CCA, road marched via Campobello–Licata–Palma, arriving in an assembly area two miles south of Agrigento at 1000 hours the same day. The 66th Armor was then ordered to Palermo on the Ribera–Sciacca–Castelvetrano route and then to move northwest to Palermo. The main body of CCA, with most of the 66th, departed at 1650 hours and closed into a bivouac one mile south of Sciacca at 0300 hours on 21 July. After a halt of about four hours, CCA moved out again. After hours of movement, the exhausted men arrived in an assembly area north of Castelvetrano at 0330 hours on 22 July. The Reconnaissance Company and Company E, supporting the CCA advance guard, halted at the line of departure (LD) located from San Ninfa to Partanna.[39]

During rapid movement of the tank units in Sicily, Lt. Donald Critchfield of A Company experienced something that every tank commander dreads when exhaustion, idleness, and darkness combine:

> Mostly all the fighting was done by the lead elements as the roads were one track and mountainous. I had very little sleep for 48 hours and we sat at idle in the moonlight. Blackout lights in front and back as far as the eye could see. I asked my gunner to take watch so I could catch a little sleep and he said he would. Woke to find no tanks in front and blackout lights as far as you could see to the rear. We took off on the run and it was some time till we caught the column.[40]

The regimental headquarters issued the next set of orders at 0330 on 22 July to the commanders of the 2nd and 3rd Battalions; these orders specified the order of march for the next operation. The Reconnaissance Company and an engineer detachment would lead the attack to Palermo. Company E would support the advance guard that was comprised mainly of the 3rd Battalion,

Lt. James Burt of C Company *(right)* and his cousin Zeke from B Company in an olive grove in Sicily. Burt later received the Medal of Honor for actions in the fighting around Aachen. Zeke was killed in action in Normandy. October 1943.

James M. Burt

41st Armored Infantry. The 2nd and 3rd Battalions of the 66th comprised the main body of CCA and the 1st Battalion was the CCA reserve. The 2nd Battalion was to be prepared to reinforce the advance guard. The order also included the important and correct directive, "When tanks are leading and AT (antitank) guns are encountered, infantry will pass through the tanks."[41]

C Company Lt. James Burt's platoon was a forward element on the drive to Palermo. The platoon had halted briefly to rest and eat when General Patton pulled up and asked, "Are you gassed?" Lieutenant Burt answered that they were. Patton responded, "Eat on the run if at all. Sleep on the run if at all. Mount up and continue. Don't stop except for gas. We have them on the run. Keep it that way."[42]

The Reconnaissance Company crossed the LD at 0545 on 22 July and moved quickly toward Gibellina and Camporeale, advancing without opposition until 1014 hours, when they encountered minefields covered by antitank guns and machine guns one mile south of San Guiseppe Lato. Together with the advance guard, they overcame the enemy defenses and continued northward. At 1230 hours, when north of San Guiseppe Lato, the command came to a pass blocked by mines and tank obstacles and covered by enemy antitank and machine gun positions located high above and on both sides of the pass. The Reconnaissance Company, supported by Company E and an infantry company from the 41st, were able to clear the enemy positions by 1315 hours with the assistance of CCA's artillery.[43] Once through the pass, CCA encountered only minor resistance from German troops en route to Palermo. At 1558 hours the Reconnaissance Company entered the outskirts of Palermo.[44] At 1600 Palermo abruptly surrendered, and by 1800 the advance guard, now supplemented by Company F, rolled into the city and occupied a portion of it. The rest of CCA assembled on the southern outskirts of Palermo with the last elements not closing until early the next morning. Sergeant Rape remembered:

> As we rode into Palermo one morning about daylight, it was a pleasure to see so many happy people. It was still dark, and we were told to keep our heads down and our eyes open because the enemy might be in that great crowd of people.[45]

Shortly after his company's arrival in Palermo, Capt. Curtis Clark, the commander of Company F, was flagged down on the street by a nun. The nun then invited the entire tank company into the courtyard of the convent. Once inside, the tired and dirty tankers were allowed the luxury of a well-deserved bath.[46]

The Reconnaissance Company outposted and patrolled Palermo throughout the night and until relieved by elements of the 3rd Infantry

Division. During the advance on Palermo, the regiment lost five soldiers killed and thirteen wounded. They captured over 2,700 prisoners during the operation. The morning of 23 July saw the commander of Company F take eighty soldiers by truck to quell a riot in the town of Monreale. The detail quickly stopped the looting and dispersed the crowd.[47] In less than twenty-four hours, the tankers had gone from fighting Germans to putting down Sicilian civil disturbances.

With the surrender of Palermo, the regiment ended their combat in the Sicilian Campaign. On the afternoon of 24 July the regiment moved one battalion at a time to a bivouac south of Carini, with the last battalion closing in at 1055 hours on the twenty-fifth. After arriving in the bivouac, the CCA commander assigned the regiment an area of responsibility that covered the ground west and south of Palermo. The regiment was directed to occupy the area, preserve order, round up prisoners of war, and administer the local governments. By noon on the twenty-fifth, American troops occupied all towns, and patrolling began. Personnel not involved in patrol or occupation duties were busy with physical conditioning and vehicle and weapon maintenance. At 1600 hours on 27 July the regiment moved from attachment to CCA to CCB.[48]

During the war there was a close relationship between the regimental commander, Colonel Collier, and the regiment's Protestant chaplain, Capt. Luke Bolin. Bolin recalls:

> One day in an olive grove near Palermo, with Col. Collier, on the way to church service , I said, "Colonel, you may not agree with my sermon today." He replied, "Luke, I don't ask you how to run my regiment, do I?" Then he said, " I don't tell you what to preach."[49]

Lt. Lewis Sasser described dinner one evening in a letter to his wife Celeste:

> I wrote you a V-mail for today but it blew away and couldn't find it so this is a replacement. Was in the middle of writing you during this morning when I caught a detail from the adjutant for the general of the division and had to leave immediately. Took off with a driver and after trying 3 roads took the 4th one successfully on our way. However, when

Field organ used by Chaplain Bolin in church services in Sicily. Summer 1943.

Luke Bolin

night fell we stopped at an Italian Captured Depot guarded by some soldiers for supper and a place to sleep. Before we could get our stove started up, an Italian who had lived in Philadelphia from 1921–39 came up and said a friend of his would like us to come to his place for dinner.

He vouched for the dinner and set about to show us the way. Turned our the friend was the son of the local baroness and led the way to the castle. Was practically dark when we hit the castle and immediately went in to meet the old gal and her colleagues. She had two sons and two daughters all young kids but was well along herself. Then her brother and two cousins and their families lived there and several more families whom I couldn't figure out lived there. Anyway, there were a slew of people when they finally got into the living room.

We got up to the castle about 8:30 p.m. and the baroness met us all. (My driver and I had picked up 5 men hitchhiking to find their outfit which was near our ultimate destination.) Our interpretor, Joe, was the only outsider and much in demand as none of the seven of us spoke Italian. The castle had an orthodox tower, square in design, sat on the top of a hill, and had the conventional court.

The kitchen crew started the meal for us as soon as we came. The rest of us went in the living room and sat down where we handed out cigarettes and tried to talk as best we could. The baroness was an old lady with a distinguished set of chins and a fancy, beat-up house coat draped around her. She was quite amicable, enjoyed our cigarettes and showed us the pictures of her distinguished and deceased husband who had served in many of the world's capitals.

When the dinner was finally ready, we were ushered into the state dining room, which was quite impressive. The baroness sat at the end of the table and I (being the only officer) was escorted to the other end. Twelve of us ate the late supper and twice as many more sat on each side of us to be sociable.

But the meal was really something. A bowl of real spaghetti, with grated cheese, meat and tomatoes. Couldn't eat it all and for dessert we had a fancy cheese, two types of melon, or grapes—I took some of each. To drink we had some wine from the lower cellar which everybody raved about but didn't care too much for.

Took us well over an hour to eat with the quantity and jabbering going on. After we finished, it was well after 11 and started taking our leave, which took half an hour by the time all seven of us shook hands with each of the 35 of them. Joe, our interpretor, showed us the way

G.I. humor about a young Sicilian in front of a M-4 Sherman west of Palermo. July 1943.

Luke Bolin

back and really we enjoyed it a lot and they were lovely to us oppressed for so long and practically starved.[50]

The 66th continued normal bivouac activities and occupation and patrolling duties in their area until 31 July. Beginning at noon on the thirty-first they assumed responsibility for a new area. The new and larger area was between Termini Imerse on the east, and Marineo and Roccamena on the south, and Algamo on the west, except for Palermo itself. In addition to occupying all towns and patrolling, the soldiers were to prevent any vessels from departing and to investigate any trying to land. The occupation duties for this area were often so heavy that units were able to leave only a skeleton force in the bivouac areas.[51] This left little time for the men to rest, perform maintenance on their vehicles and equipment, and train. Pfc. George Lincoln of Company H was assigned to a small patrol given the mission of occupying a small Italian town in the hills about thirty miles north of Palermo. Led by a lieutenant, the patrol established its command post in the town police station. An hour after they arrived, an Italian came in and told them that the Germans were coming out of the mountains. The lieutenant had Lincoln take the other two men to investigate. As Lincoln's tiny patrol walked along a ridge three miles from town, Lincoln spotted a single German near a stone wall beneath them. Crouching down, Lincoln signalled the other two soldiers, one to come down on the German from Lincoln's left and the third soldier to cover them from the ridge.

> ...thinking it was only one German I went sailing down the hill like an Indian, it took only a few seconds to get there. When we took count instead of one German soldier there were ten soldiers and an officer. I made them take off their shoes and march back to town. When we got back the Lt. said,"What the hell have you got there the whole German Army, now I have to get a truck to take them to Palermo."[52]

On 3 August the regiment received the word that the Allied Military Government for Occupied Territories (AMGOT) would begin taking over all civil administration matters. The 66th was ordered to continue all civil functions until relieved by the AMGOT officers, a task completed on 7 August. Because of the suspected danger of sabotage, the regiment began guarding all bridges and tunnels on 5 August.[53]

During the occupation of Sicily many officers and men from the combat units were temporaily assigned military government duties. Lt. James Burt with six or eight men, a jeep and a truck had responsibility for a small city on the northern coast. Lieutenant Burt explains some of his duties:

Every day I conferred with the civilian powers who were: Number 1—the priest, number 2—the mayor, number 3—the police chief. In my jeep was a driver. I had to change drivers about twice a day. At each stop they would take the driver in the rear room and give him a drink. He must have had a water glass full at every stop. In the office there would be a ceremonial drink for me, about a thimble full. So I could last all day, but my drivers could last only about a half a day each.

One day there was a riot by the women because their bread was too soggy. Fortunately, in my unit I had a man who was a miller who suspected trouble. So much wheat would be brought in—let us say a hundred units. It would be washed to take away the dirt and dust, and it would grow in weight when dried because it was not thoroughly dried, to perhaps 110 units. The farmer could get back 100 units of flour and the 10 extra would be his payment. It was a standardized washing and drying. But the bread came out wet. That meant that the miller had not dried enough, cheating someone. The ovens that baked the bread had no flexibility whatsoever. So many bundles of grapevines went into the oven and burned so long. The ashes were then dragged out and the loaves were set in and baked to historic perfection. If something upset the procedure it meant lower grade bread.[54]

On 6 August Lt. Col. Amzi Rudolph "Rudy" Quillian, 3rd Battalion commander, wrote to his wife, Evie:

My Darling,

This is the first time I've had the time or paper to write you anything but a sketchy letter since July 10th and earlier. Even now I may be interrupted any minute but I'm going to try to write a long letter.

Before I forget to mention it I want to tell you that I now have for my private car a Fiat touring car, captured from the enemy of course. We have painted it with American markings complete with name and that is what I wanted to tell you about. I have been so busy I didn't even have a chance to look at the car for about three days but when it was delivered to me yesterday Sheets had the name Little Sally on it which of course pleased me no end. [The Quillians' daughter Sally had been born after he left for North Africa.]

Our G-2 says its all right for us to say now that we landed on the south central coast of the island. My battalion had the honor of being the first armor to lay a track on the hostile shore. And we did O.K. by ourselves.

We have seen action several times and have gotten around quite a bit. The sharpest scrap I have been in was on July 12 when the German anti-tankers laid a trap for us but we weren't caught by it. However it was necessary to slug it out with them for a while until we could make arrangements to take care of them. During that little scrap my tank got some scars on it from a shell that hit about five yards in front of it and my radio mast was shot away. My crew and I got some of their guns and crews, I can't say how many because the confusion of a fight makes it impossible to tell exactly what happens and exactly who hit what.

As for my reactions to a fight. Going up to it before I see exactly what the ground looks like and before the shooting starts I'm scared stiff. It's the fear of the unknown—like being afraid of the dark. After the fight starts and we see something to shoot at its different. It's just plain exciting then and the most thrilling thing I've ever done. And when the scrap is over we are sorry it's stopped because its so much fun. There were some machine guns in buildings and its quite an experience to aim your tank gun at a window and see the side of the house fly away.

We get A rations now and they are wonderful. I'm gaining weight— maybe an ounce or so.

I love you and Sally

Rudy[55]

During the month of August the regiment's area of responsibility changed numerous times, normally reducing the area of responsibility. The soldiers spent a considerable amount of time finding and securing prisoners and abandoned weapons. Everything from hand grenades to large howitzers were lying around the countryside. Much time and energy was expended following up on wildly exaggerated rumors of German soldiers in the hills of the island. Reports of several hundred Germans usually yielded at most one or two of them. The real threats were the numerous minefields and abandoned ammunition dumps, which, at 0930 hours on 8 August, caused the regiment to suffer its most severe loss of life since the battles in 1918.[56] Two miles east of Comporeale, in railroad tunnels guarded by the regiment, two massive ammunition dumps exploded under unknown circumstances. Thirteen soldiers died in the massive explosion, which also destroyed two half-tracks and a jeep.[57]

Mostly though, life in Sicily during the months of occupation was pleasant with many interesting diversions. Lt. W. M. Page remembers the food of Sicily:

Outdoor life in Sicily had its compensations. We frequently found ourselves in fields where garlic, tomatoes, melons and grapes were abun-
dant. The garlic did wonders with C-rations. Melons were the same as
American watermelons except for being smaller, about the size of can-
taloupes. Ripe olives were a novelty, being inedible balls of grease that
made quite a splash on tanks bivouacked in olive groves.[58]

The regiment went on alert at 0410 hours on 8 August, because two
Italian cruisers had been reported in the area. The beach patrols were doubled,
but, like all the other threats of Axis counterattacks, this one proved false.[59]
During their patrols, the soldiers had to be on guard against a wide variety of
dangers, from land mines and unexploded bombs to the dreaded booby traps.
Booby traps were created by placing a hand grenade or other explosive device in a position where an enemy soldier would be likely to trigger it by
moving an object holding the explosive device. Soldiers often set off booby
traps when they picked up a seemingly discarded enemy weapon or opened a
door. Some booby traps could even be very small, like the booby trap foun-
tain pen found by one patrol, that was intended to blow a victim's hand off.
Local civilians reported that large numbers of these unique booby traps had
been dropped by aircraft.[60] Another danger was an enemy ammunition dump,
which was discovered to be leaking a persistent chemical agent.[61]

As of 20 August the regimental area ranged from the western edge of
Termini Imerese on the east, Marineo, Roccamena, and Algamo on the
south, Trapani on the west, and to the coast on the north, except for Palermo.
Bivouacked at Carni, the regiment remained under CCB of 2nd Armored
Division. Beginning on 24 August elements of the 3rd and 45th Infantry
Divisions began relieving the regiment of portions of their area. The new
area under regimental control was San Guiseppe Lato on the east, Contessa
Entellina and Gibellina on the south, Algamo on the west, and the coast on
the north.[62] This area was divided into five sub-areas, each assigned to a
battalion, the Reconnaissance Company, or the attached Reconnaissance
Company of the 67th Armor. The 66th continued to man outposts, patrol,
and guard ammunition dumps, bridges, and other key locations.

The regiment's Protestant chaplain, Capt. Luke Bolin, traveled widely
as he ministered to the units of the 66th. He made the most of his travels by
finding out what men needed most and then trying to provide for them
materially as well as spiritually. In a letter to his wife on 3 September he
tells about some of his work:

Darling I have gained a bad reputation over here—maybe it is good.
Once during combat I met some infantry that needed sox—they always

The mountainous terrain of Sicily as seen looking across a bay on the northern coast of the island. September 1943.

John B. Roller

Lieutenant Hartson and Lieutenant Roller in the olive grove bivouac of D Company. September 1943.

John B. Roller

Lt. William A. Nicholson, platoon leader in D Company, in an olive grove bivouac. September 1943. Nicholson was killed in action in Normandy on 13 June 1944.

John B. Roller

Sicilian women with a wide variety of containers waiting to draw water. September 1943.

John B. Roller

Streetside in Capaci, Sicily. October 1943.

John B. Roller

The town of Partinico southwest of Palermo showing a typical Sicilian street. October 1943.

John B. Roller

Lt. John Roller of D Company astride a burro beside its proud owner. November 1943.

John B. Roller

want sox and water. In a nearby town we had captured an Italian Quartermaster warehouse. There Pete and I secured about 300 pairs of socks and gave them to the Infantry. In another badly bombed city Pete and I visited a civilian hospital that had about 15 patients but no medical supplies. We knew where some could be found—in a railroad station. We took them to the hospital and one old lady kissed me on both cheeks. Recently I secured enough donuts from the Red Cross to give a small amount to all the men. In another endeavor—strictly legal—I secured enough razors to give one to each company barber. I now shave with one myself. Some of the officers have been kidding me about "Looting." I was talking to the Col. the other day and he asked me what I had been looting. No, all of it has been legal and the men have enjoyed all of it.[63]

Gradually, in September, the tankers were able to devote an increasing amount of time to individual and crew training as they prepared for their next mission. On 8 September the regiment went on alert against possible enemy airborne assault. No attack ever materialized and the regiment returned to its occupation and training routine on 11 September.

Sergeant Gatzke's diary entries for some of the days in September tell about training and recreation:

mo 13 To the Catacombs in Palermo. Had steak & spagetti in an Off Limits restaurant. Two military police also eating there.

tu 21   To 75 mm range at noon. Tank Co. for tomorrow's exercise.

we 22 Platoon exercise. Back at 5 pm. Slightly drunk on cognac.

tu 28   CQ at noon. Relieved Frank Bisogno. Cloud burst at 6 pm. Tent blew over. Got soaking wet. Floor all mud, so Capt. Warren slept on the table and I slept on some .30 cal. boxes. Read Time and Newsweek magazines.[64]

On 13 September Chaplain Bolin wrote to his wife about life in occupied Sicily:

I am writing this letter not because I have any news but to tell you something about where I am at present. I wish I had words to describe what I can see as beautiful as it really is. I am sitting on the 2nd floor of a beach house on the Mediterranean. The officers have the 2nd floor and the men the 1st. To my right I can see mountains and a beautiful village. The sky is clear except for some clouds over the mountains. I can look down on the first floor and see GIs reading and relaxing in big chairs. A group of men are diving off of a float about 50 yards out in the water. There are also several officers and four or five nurses enjoying the hospitality of this place. Small boats with large white sails are cutting the water in front of me. In the distance the blue (it is blue) water and sky seem to converge. From inside I can hear the sound of paddles hitting ping pong balls and somebody playing a piano and several men singing.

Darling, this war seems a million miles away. Truly, war is 1% fighting and 99% waiting. If one thing were added, this place—this sunny afternoon—would be perfect—and it will take no stretch of your imagination to know who I am thinking of.[65]

During October 1943 the 66th Armor continued guard and patrolling responsibilities as well as training. Beginning in October the regiment's occupation duties were reduced to two daily coastal patrols, one semi-weekly patrol inland, and railroad bridge and tunnel guards. Four days later, on 4 October 1943, the guard was eliminated.

Sergeant Gatzke's diary for early October showing the regiment as it moved closer to departing Sicily:

we 6 Problem. 56 rounds fired. I shot 30. Brought our tanks back 730 pm. Dark, raining.

th 7 Cleaned guns and tanks. Theobald & I to Palermo. Pretty well lit up.

fr 8 Got tanks ready to turn in.[66]

On 13 October Lieutenant Sasser wrote to Celeste about the uncertainty loved ones in the States experienced, not knowing where their soldiers were or what they were doing:

Feel terrible when I read your letters and realize how you must worry and wonder where I am and what we're having to put up with. The trouble is that you have been worrying all thru this Italian mainland business and here I've been sitting in Sicily the whole time. About the time you'll decide you don't need to worry will be when you should. Just seems to work out that way. You did pretty well on the Sicilian campaign, the only trouble was that we didn't know how much news you all were getting and couldn't know if you had any idea who was where. The truth is that you seem to be pretty well informed. Guess that's one of the things we're fighting for—at least where it's feasible to tell things. For us, the worst part is the time preceding when you know something's going to break, maybe what and maybe not exactly but all the time can't dare mention any part of it. Should be getting used to it by now. Was suprised to hear that you all knew all about the fleet waiting off Italy on Sept. 8th from the papers because we saw it and were wondering ourselves what the full story was. Getting the news for 15 minutes over the radio like we do is a great help in getting a rounded picture of what goes on.[67]

By the end of October, all combat and most general purpose vehicles were turned in to supply units, and the regiment assembled in a staging area near Carini for their impending departure. Only a couple of officers in the regiment knew the destination.[68] On 7 November the 66th Armor left Sicily with the rest of the 2nd Armored Division.

In early November, Lt. Donald Critchfield found himself in the hospital and in danger of being left behind when the regiment shipped out.

> I had caught a good case of yellow jaundice and was hospitalized in Palermo. The cure was easy, but tiresome, a bag of hard candy a day which after awhile found its way under the mattress. Had a good friend in Lt. Philip Cudd who came most every day and played cribbage and keep me posted. Cudd was as handsome an officer as ever came out of central casting—tall blonde wavy haired Norwegian from Minnesota (later killed in France). One day he told me the division was soon to sail from Palermo (going home was rumored) and he felt that if I stayed I would surely find myself in 1st Armored in Italy. He arranged a jeep to be under my window the night of embarkation and I made the leap. Sailed west through the Straits of Gibraltar and then north in a truly luxurious cruise ship.[69]

Lt. W. M. Page provides some information of the convoy and its voyage to England:

> The convoy that left Palermo area with most of the 66th and other 2AD units was joined by ships leaving North Africa with the rest of our division and also 9th Infantry Division. It was a sizeable convoy. We spent some 21 days on a route that went far west from Gibraltar (to avoid submarines based in France) and around the north end of Ireland into the Glasgow area where we landed and went by railway to Tidworth.
>
> As we boarded ship for departure from Sicily, our destination was secret and undisclosed. It was joyously rumored that with our service in North Africa and Sicily behind us, we would be returning to the U.S.A. Thus it was quite a jolt, when well out to sea, we received a message of <u>congratulations</u> upon being "selected" to train in England for the upcoming invasion.[70]

Sgt. Arden Gatzke's diary entries for the day he departed Sicily and some of the days he spent at sea:

> th 11   Left mudhole in woods 830am. Boarded HMS Monterey 1030am. C deck room 255.

sa 13   Calisthenics. 1st Coca-Cola since leaving the states Dec. 12 1942.

su 14   No cal. Submarine alert. Abandon Ship Drill (ASD) to see how long it took to get everyone to their particular life boat.

we 17   ASD 7 min. Sex lecture.[71]

Another soldier who did not like the idea of never returning to the 66th was Lt. John Getsinger of Reconnaissance Company, who had come to be very separated from his unit. After being wounded in the foot on the LST the day of the Sicily invasion, he had been sent to a hospital in North Africa.

> When the hospital was ordered to move, I talked the doctor into discharging me even though my foot was not quite healed. I was ordered to a casual camp, which was commanded by a 1st Lt., to wait for my foot to heal. There were only about four officers in the camp including a doctor. The camp commander took a liking to me and wanted me to stay there. I was really lost in the back waters of the war. My conscience wouldn't let me stay, so when my foot healed, I made him cut orders sending me to a replacement camp outside Tunis. On the way there I encountered a major I knew formerly with the 2nd Armored, and he told me that the 2nd had gone to England after the Sicilian campaign ended.
>
> When I arrived at the replacement center I told the adjutant, a major, that I wanted to rejoin my outfit. He looked doubtful but said he would see what he could do. From time to time when I checked with him he would say he was going to send me to the 1st Armored Division in Italy. I would say 'No Sir.' One day it made him mad and he said, 'What do you mean, No Sir' I said, 'No Sir, I want to go back to my outfit.' A few days later he ordered me to Algiers to board the British ship, *Franconia*, to Liverpool. When I got on board ship I found that there were 125 American casuals and 8000 British from the 8th Army on board. The ship had been pressed into service when the war started, and except for its gray color on the outside, it retained all of its luxury liner status. We ate on white linen cloths with real silverware. They had even retained the ship's staff. Except for bunks and crowded staterooms, we officers were in luxury. Enlisted men below decks were in misery with bad food. I visited with some of the American soldiers. They were cheerful, because being resourceful Americans, they had brought fruit and American canned rations in their packs.
>
> When we arrived in Liverpool, so many men crowded to the shoreward side of the ship that it took a severe list. The captain of the ship

said over the speaker system he would not dock the ship until it it was aright. They all rushed to the other side and it listed the other way. It was funny until your remembered that many had been away from home for four years and most for two or three years.

When I got back to my company, everyone seemed glad to see me. It was like a homecoming to me.[72]

The regiment arrived in England on 24 November and moved to Tidworth Post or Barracks in Wiltshire in preparation for the upcoming invasion of France.[73] Needless to say, after a year in the field the men appreciated the brick barracks. Lt. W. M. Page provides a few details of the regiment's new home:

Tidworth Barracks was quite a large army post, brick construction of perhaps 1900 vintage. Different sections of the post bore names associated with British army involvements in India, the 66th being quartered in in the Candahar barracks. Officer quarters were in separate brick buildings outside of their sleeping quarters.[74]

Lieutenant Sasser was billeted in an English home in the winter of 1943.

Am bunking with Zitnik in a typical English house with no central heating and our room is the only one with no fireplace. So we visit till bedtime. Have a double-decker bed with mattress and makeshift pillow (straw in pillow case), sheets, electric light, desk, large window (for cold air to enter) closet, wash basin, two nice straight-backed chairs, shelf space and all the comforts of home.[75]

From Tidworth the regiment began an intensive training program on the ranges and training areas of the bleak and windswept Salisbury Plain. The training include a significant amount of range firing from small arms through tank cannon. The units conducted a variety of maneuver exercises across the Salisbury Plain.[76] Lieutenant Page remembers some of the training that took place at remote locations and some of the problems of getting there:

...during the earlier months of 1944, units of the regiment engaged in tank gunnery at remote British ranges where errant projectiles would reach the open sea rather than dropping into populated areas. We first went to Minehead, on the north coast of Devon about 90 miles west of Tidworth and next to Pembroke, at the southwestern extremity of Wales and much farther from Tidworth.

During our time in England, tank and truck convoy passage through villages with narrow and crooked streets was quite a challenge, compounded by having to conform with the British practice of driving in the left lane rather than our customary right lane.[77]

Maj. Lindsay C. Herkness, Jr. joined the regiment in late 1943 after serving as assistant G-3 for the division since 1941. He had graduated from West Point in 1939 and served with the 2nd Cavalry. After graduating from the Cavalry School at Fort Riley in 1941 he had joined 2nd Armored Division at Fort Benning. His first assignment with the 66th was as executive officer of 3rd Battalion. In spring 1944 he was promoted to lieutenant colonel and given command of the 2nd Battalion.[78]

One of the regiment's first tasks in England was receipt of their new tanks, vehicles, and other equipment from the massive army depots in southern England. Everything was issued, checked, and then tested on the training areas and ranges. The regiment's training covered all levels, from individual and crew through platoon and company to battalion and above. Maj. Gen. Edward H. Brooks, who previously activated the 11th Armored Division, assumed command of the 2nd Armored Division on 17 March 1944. The outgoing commander, Major General Gaffey, was appointed chief of staff of the 3rd Army.[79]

During the intensive training that spring, Lieutenant Colonel Herkness was conducting a maneuver exercise on the Salisbury Plain with his battalion when he received a distinguished visitor. The new 2nd Armored Division commander, Major General Brooks, arrived with British Prime Minister Winston Churchill. After reporting to his visitors, Herkness explained the armored attack maneuver they were witnessing. Churchill then remarked, "It is rather like cavalry tactics, is it not?" Herkness, commissioned as a cavalry officer, answered that the tactics were the same. The prime minister told Herkness that he had served as a cavalry subaltern in India. Herkness responded that he had been a subaltern at Fort Riley. General Brooks, noting Herkness' bold use of the British rank subaltern in his response, glared at Lieutenant Colonel Herkness. Churchill sat down with Herkness, and the two cavalrymen had a talk that lasted nearly an hour. Herkness remembered that Churchill had that special charisma that made one feel as if you shared a special bond with him and he would always know you.[80]

In the spring short furloughs were allowed, and the men enjoyed the cities and countryside of England. The regiment then moved to one of the invasion marshaling areas for training in May 1944. This training was basically the same as that the regiment had practiced around Norfolk, Virginia, in 1942. The soldiers learned how to assemble their vehicles, and to board and disembark the LSTs. Upon completion of the amphibious training the units returned to Tidworth. At the end of May the authorized regimental strength was 122 officers, 12 warrant officers, and 2,364 enlisted men. The regiment went on six-hour alert notice on 1 June for movement to the marshaling areas, and the troops began making final preparations for amphibious landing, including initial waterproofing of the vehicles. The first phase of waterproofing included treatment of those areas that would not interfere with the driving of the vehicle. The regiment then moved to the marshaling area, loaded their vehicles on the LSTs, and completed the waterproofing process.[81]

At 1145 hours on 5 June the Headquarters of the 2nd Armored Division ordered the 66th to move to their marshaling areas beginning at 0224 hours on 6 June. As the soldiers prepared to leave Tidworth barracks that night, hundreds of aircraft could be heard passing overhead as D-Day began. The regimental headquarters, reconnaissance company, and the 2nd Battalion with the light tanks of Company A attached moved to their marshaling area near Dorchester. The 3rd Battalion with Company B (light tanks) and the rest of the 1st Battalion marshaled near Winchester. Near Frawley the regimental maintenance and service companies were organized for the invasion.[82]

Portrait of 2nd Lt. John Roller, platoon leader in D Company, taken in Sicily, 5 September 1943. Note the tanker boots.

John B. Roller

Maj. Herb Long, executive officer of 3rd Battalion. Spring 1944.

Only one came home. The five officers of A Company from left to right: Lt. John Roller, Lt. William Nicholson, Capt. Sten Bergstedt, Lieutenant Corbin, and Lt. John Hartson. All but Roller were killed in action in 1944. England, Spring 1944.

English children giving the famous symbol of the Allies, "V" for Victory. Spring 1944.

1st Lt. John Roller astride a Military Police WLA motorcycle, a slightly modified for military use Harley-Davidson. Spring 1944.

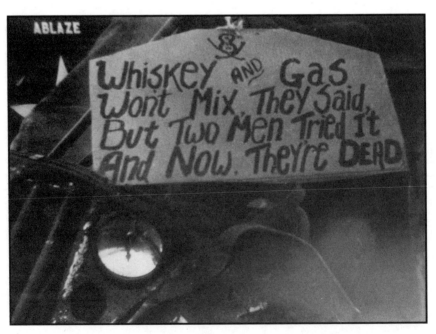

Safety message, the wreckage of a jeep with a warning sign. Spring 1944.

Machine-gun training with the M1919A1 .30 caliber. Spring 1944.

John B. Roller

The great Joe Louis boxing for the soldiers. Spring 1944.

John B. Roller

Lt. John Roller displaying a 75mm Sherman tank round. England, February 1944.

John B. Roller

The famed "Brown Bomber," Joe Louis, in the doorway before his boxing match. Spring 1944.

John B. Roller

Capt. Sten A. Bergstedt, nicknamed "Bergy" or "the Swede," commander of A Company. February 1944. He was killed in action in September.

John B. Roller

English orphans trying out a Sherman tank during one of the visits to the regiment organized by Chaplain Bolin. Winter 1944.

PART IV

Omaha Beach to Berlin
1944–45

CHAPTER 11

Close Combat in the Hedgerows: Normandy

In the heavily guarded marshaling areas of southern England the 66th made final preparations. Vehicle waterproofing was completed, and final assignments of vehicles and personnel to the vessels were made. Maps were issued to the officers and all personnel were briefed on where they would be landing on the coast of Normandy.[1]

As many of the soldiers awaited crossing the channel in a state of nervous boredom, many of the unit leaders had no time for anything except the last-minute preparations and checks of their soldiers and equipment. The executive officer of the regiment's Reconnaissance Company, Lt. John Getsinger, provided an example of how many leaders felt on the last days before landing in France:

> I had many duties to see to all day and into the night. Finally, I knew I had to attend to my personal effects. I donned my "icky" feeling uniform which was treated to protect our skin from gas or chemical attack. I applied the special paste to my shoes for the same purpose, hastily grabbed my gas mask and personal effects, picked up my pack, and rushed out of the building to see the tail lights of the last vehicle from the barracks disappearing into the distance. With my heavy load, I ran the mile to the motorpool where our vehicles were. I climbed into my half-track in the vehicle commander's spot just as the order was given to move out. I raised my right arm and swept it forward to signal the vehicles behind me, my legs buckled, and I collapsed in a heap from exhaustion. I did not lose consciousness. My first thought was

that I was glad the Germans couldn't see me. I could imagine them saying "and you're coming over here to kick our butts?" It was then that I realized I hadn't taken time to eat all day, and it was now 4 A.M. the 6th of June. I opened some K-rations for quick energy. I felt like Popeye when he eats a can of spinach with the strength flowing to my muscles.[2]

That night and into the next morning thousands of Allied soldiers witnessed a sight that those who survived the coming ten months of combat would remember the rest of their lives. Lieutenant Getsinger remembered:

> On my run to the motorpool I had seen many cargo planes pulling gliders with airborne troops at low level. Also, I could hear many other planes at higher levels. I knew it had to be D-Day. As dawn broke, I knew I was looking at a sight that probably would never be seen again. The sky was literally filled with planes from horizon to horizon. It was difficult to understand why some of them didn't collide, but none did that I saw. British bombers were returning from night raids in their typical scattered non-formation, and American bombers of all kinds were heading for France. Even today I get goose-bumps thinking about that display of power.[3]

The regiment loaded aboard its vessels and left England on 8 June. These steps, however, were not without their setbacks. During the loading, Cpl. Harry D. Martin won the Soldiers Medal for risking his life trying to extinguish a fire on a half-track, and during the crossing, German E-Boats attacked and hit two of the convoy's Landing Ship, Tank (LSTs) that bore elements of the regiment. Although it did rain heavily, the regiment was fortunate that the channel was calm during the crossing.[4]

When the 66th Armor began landing in Normandy on 9 June, it was part of Combat Command A (CCA) of the 2nd Armored Division, a part of the 1st Army under Lt. Gen. Omar Bradley.[5] The regiment's Reconnaissance, Maintenance, and Service companies, along with Companies D (less one platoon) and E, landed first on Omaha Beach on 9 June. Lieutenant Getsinger of the Reconnaissance Company recorded these memories of arriving at Omaha Beach:

> When we arrived near Omaha Beach at dawn on the morning of the 9th, I realized I was seeing another sight that probably would never be seen again. The channel seemed to be filled with ships. This was my third invasion. In the first, I counted about 90 ships. In the second, I counted about 350. Today, you could not see the horizon for ships, you couldn't count the ships for the ships. As we made our way toward

shore I could see our artillery firing with their gun's trails literally at the edge of the water....We disembarked and went into our assembly area without opposition, thanks to those who had gone before us on the 6th, 7th and 8th, many of whom were killed and badly wounded. Ambulances on the beach bringing wounded to be taken back to England sobered us.[6]

The 3rd Battalion with Company B attached and Company C landed the next day.[7] The regimental headquarters and 2nd Battalion (less Company E and two platoons of Company D) with Company A attached moved ashore on 11 June. The last units of the regiment to land were the headquarters elements of the 1st Battalion on 12 June. As the units landed, they moved from the beach to a transit area where the vehicles shed their waterproofing before moving to an assembly area near Mosles. The units of the 66th, already ashore, departed at 1450 hours on 11 June for a new assembly area near Cremy, completing the movement at 1950 hours.[8] Held in reserve through 12 June, the units concentrated on preparing the tanks, vehicles, and weapons for action and conducting reconnaissance of routes to the south and southwest for upcoming movements. By the end of the day, the entire regiment was assembled and ready for action.[9]

Involvement in action came almost immediately. Shortly after midnight on 13 June a task force consisting of the Headquarters, 66th Armor, the 2nd Battalion (with Company A attached), and the 3rd Battalion, 41st Armored Infantry, all commanded by Colonel Collier, the commander of the 66th Armor, received orders to assist the 101st Airborne Division. The 101st, which parachuted into Normandy in the predawn hours of 6 June, had been in almost continuous combat since that day. Lt. Donald Critchfield, a platoon leader in I Company remembered the paratroopers he encountered:

> They were an angry bunch and boarded our tanks and quickly exhausted our supply of 50 caliber ammo and I've never saw so many dead—before or since. The 101st had apparently landed in a Panzer Grenadier Division on maneuvers.[10]

Elements of the 17th SS Panzergrenadier Division were counterattacking the paratroopers.[11] The 17th was one of the mechanized infantry divisions of the Waffen-SS. The Waffen, or Armed branch of the SS, was a private army under the command of Reichsfuehrer-SS Heinrich Himmler, although it was under the operational command of the Army in the field. Renowned as fanatical fighters, the soldiers of the Waffen-SS were usually better equipped, trained and more experienced than their regular army counterparts.

MAP 18

Normandy (A)
June–August 1944

In a letter home Captain Warren related his impressions of the fighting:

Some elements of my outfit, not the company, launched an attack soon after we landed against Hitler's best troops the SS and Herman Goering's paratroopers. The attack jumped off in a blinding rainstorm supported by our airborne troops. Our paratroopers are positively magnificent fighting men—in my opinion, the best in the business. The Krauts were launching an attack of their own when we hit them. The situation was very critical. For our boys in tanks, it was their first trip to the plate— a few saw some action in Sicily. The fight was to death for both sides— and extremely bitter fighting—the Boche had played some underhanded tricks and nobody was in much mood to take prisoners. Very few were taken by either side. After six hours of steady but slow progress we reached our objectives and the attack was extremely successful. Our long hard training was thoroughly tried and tested and found to be not wanting.[12]

The mission of the regimental task force was to hold the Vire River bridge just west of Isigny and to contact and assist the 101st Airborne and the 175th Infantry Regiment which was also in the vicinity. At 0322 hours on 13 June, the task force, led by the infantry battalion, marched to an assembly area at Les Veys near Isigny, arriving at 0800 hours. While the infantry patrols moved south to make contact with both friendly and en- emy forces, the S-2 of the regiment made contact with the 327th Glider Infantry Regiment of the 101st and received the dispositions of friendly units and the suspected enemy locations and strengths.[13]

During the morning, Company D was ordered to an assembly area on the eastern edge of Carentan in preparation for a mission to assist the 101st in clearing the Germans out of the western edge of Carentan. Before they could launch the operation, the company was ordered to return to the 2nd Battalion due to the imminent threat of an enemy counterattack attempt forming west of Carentan with the objective of retaking the city. By late morning, new orders were received for the task force to launch an after- noon attack. The operations order directed Company A to secure the Vire River bridge near Les Veys against a possible German attack from the south- west.[14] The task force, led by the 3rd Battalion, 41st Armored Infantry, and Company D of the 66th, was directed to attack the enemy west of Carentan by advancing astride the Carentan–La Campagne road. The first objective of the attack was the high ground and road intersection at La Campagne. After taking La Campagne, the task force was to advance southeast astride the La Campagne–Meautis road and seize the village of Meautis. Additional fire support was made available through a naval gunfire spotting party attached to the task force. The spotting party had available the massive sixteen-inch guns of the battleships *Nevada* and *Texas*, firing from some twenty miles away.[15]

At a small bridge along the road to Carentan, Maj. Curtis Clark, the S-3 of the regiment, was able to make good use of the naval guns to remove a dangerous threat. A well-hidden German 88mm gun was sighted in on the bridge and was intent on destroying the bridge and anything attempting to cross it. The Americans quickly determined that it took the German gun crew sixteen seconds to reload, thus providing a gap in which to dash across the bridge. Major Clark was near the bridge in his half-track when a U.S. Navy jeep arrived with two very clean and smartly dressed naval spotters. Major Clark, surprised by the immaculate appearance of the Navy men and his good fortune, quickly apprised them of the situation. Shortly afterwards the deadly accurate naval gunfire eliminated the 88 and the regiment moved on towards the 101st.[16]

At 1430 hours on 13 June, elements of the 66th went into battle for the first time in France. The task force crossed the line of departure held by the 101st Airborne just west of Carentan.[17] The weather that afternoon was dismal and raining, greatly limiting visibility. Also, the terrain in Normandy was the most difficult on which the regiment had ever fought or trained. The countryside was divided into innumerable small fields by hedgerows and sunken roads. The hedgerows, living fences grown over the centuries until most of them were over ten feet wide and higher than a tank, were impenetrable in all but a very few places. The narrow sunken roads, worn as deep as fifteen feet into the ground, hemmed in the tanks that were on them and acted as antitank ditches to the tanks trying to cross them. In all, the terrain was best suited for infantry fighting on the defensive, as the 17th SS Panzergrenadier Division was doing around Carentan. Using the hedgerows as concealment, an ambush at point-blank range with an antitank gun was an effective way for the Germans to eliminate American tanks. An example of this was an incident in which a lone German tank hidden in a sunken road between two hedgerows destroyed twenty-five American tanks and armored vehicles and then was able to escape.

Several days later S.Sgt. Hubert Gwinn, a tank commander in H Company, wrote a letter to his old company commander, Capt. Norris Perkins with some of his observations about Normandy:

> This country is much different from any we went through. The fields are anywhere from one acre to two and are surrounded by a very high hedgerow and a bank impossible to cross except in some places.

There has to be close coordination between the infantry and tanks, or else snipers will pick you out of the turret. The infantry swear by the tommy gun and say the carbine is no good because you have to hit a vital spot to stop a man. Dead Jerries are thick as flies and they line the hedgerows. Very few prisoners in some sections. Jerry's a low down——so it works both ways.[18]

At 1430 hours Company D of the 66th Armor crossed the LD under heavy German mortar and artillery fire.[19] The company, commanded by Capt. Sten Bergstedt, advanced with one platoon on either side of the road and the third platoon in reserve just behind the lead platoons.[20] Initially, the German resistance consisted of rifle and submachine gun fire. After a steady advance of about 500 yards, however, the enemy resistance stiffened, with the addition of heavy machine guns and antitank and tank fire. Company D returned fire, spraying the hedgerows with the tanks' .30 caliber machine guns. The poor visibility among the hedgerows and sunken roads turned the attack into a series of small-unit actions as the tankers and their accompanying infantrymen fought the Germans for every hedgerow.[21] At around 1600 hours, Company D reached the village of Douville and was relieved by Company F. During its advance, Company D had killed a large number of Germans and destroyed a German Mark IV tank and three 75mm antitank guns. For its part, Company D had lost one tank, and two crewmen were wounded while expending 225 main gun rounds, 75,000 machine gun rounds, 750 rounds of .45 caliber sub-machine gun rounds, and 25 grenades.[22] Company F, commanded by Capt. William Nicholson, passed through Company D and continued the attack. Shortly after taking over the lead, Captain Nicholson spotted and then destroyed a German self-propelled gun sitting ahead in the road. Coming under heavy machine gun fire, the commander backed his tank off the road, where he was killed by a sniper. Command of the company then passed to Lieutenant Tonkin, the 1st Platoon leader, who was severely wounded minutes later when his tank was hit by several rounds from German Panzerfausts, a deadly short-range antitank grenade launcher, similar in principle to the American bazooka.

The company's attack on the right flank had also been moving slowly forward in the difficult conditions. Led by Lieutenant Swartz, Company F's 2nd Platoon had been in action along the right flank shortly before the company took over the lead. Lieutenant Swartz destroyed a German 75mm self-propelled gun at a range of only seventy-five yards, again showing the poor visibility caused by weather and terrain. Determined to keep the attack going, Lieutenant Swartz dismounted several times to make contact with the other elements in order to coordinate their efforts when unable to

Lt. John Roller posing with paratrooper at their link-up.

John B. Roller

reach them by radio. Company F led the difficult attack forward against mounting German resistance until a shortage of ammunition and the approaching darkness made it necessary to halt about one mile west of Cantepie at about 1800 hours.[23] The company had lost one tank to a mine and had destroyed one German Mark IV tank and two 75mm self-propelled guns. Company E, which was in the supporting role behind Companies D and F during the attack, was also heavily engaged on both flanks of the task force attack. One platoon was successful in repulsing a minor German counterattack with the assistance of paratroopers from the 502nd Parachute Battalion.[24] Although the tankers found working with the airborne infantry very rewarding, most attempts at coordination with the task force's own infantrymen from the 41st Armored Infantry were frustrating. The 41st's infantry were reluctant to accompany the tanks through the difficult hedgerow terrain even though infantry support was badly needed. The reluctance may have been due to inexperience and the difficult weather and terrain situation. The paratroopers, however, had been fighting alone for a week and were glad to have the firepower of the American tanks. With the approach of darkness, the paratroopers and infantrymen formed a defensive line, and the tanks of the 3rd Battalion withdrew to an assembly area directly behind the defensive line.[25]

The 1st Battalion, 66th Armor, commanded by Lieutenant Colonel Parker and consisting of Companies I (Sherman medium tanks) and C (Stuart light tanks), launched an attack at 1630 hours. Together with the 501st Parachute Infantry Regiment and the 14th Armored Field Artillery Battalion, the tankers attacked southwest along the Carentan-Auverville road. A rolling artillery barrage preceded just ahead of the tanks in their attack to the high ground near the road intersection northeast of Auverville. Advancing at the pace of the foot soldiers, the team seized the objective at about 2100 hours. Company I led the attack and destroyed three German 75mm assault guns with the loss of one Sherman. After taking the objective, the 1st Battalion withdrew to an assembly area behind the infantry.[26]

During this battle, Lt. Lamar Russell, C Company light tank platoon leader, had just witnessed the destruction of two reconnaissance vehicles and their crews led by Lieutenant Shackelford 100 yards to his front. An infantryman from the unit that was advancing up the other side of the road from C Company ran up to Russell's Stuart tank. The soldier said, "My buddy is hurt across the road and I need help; I'm going back over there whether you go or not." Lieutenant Russell quickly took a poll of his crew to see what they thought about the situation. Sergeant Apgar, the gunner, responded, "That is why we are over here." Russell rapidly maneuvered his tank into the area where the infantryman had gone. With their bow and coaxial machine guns blazing they were able to wipe out the German patrol which was causing the infantry problems. With the Germans eliminated from the area, the medics were able to get in to treat the wounded infantrymen.[27]

Lt. Jim Burt, a platoon leader in C Company, used an effective technique to fight through the hedgerows with the paratroopers of the 101st. When a passage through the hedgerow was found or created, the Americans were faced with the problem of dealing with the German troops waiting in ambush on the other side of the hedgerow. Working closely with the men of the 101st, the tankers found an effective way of countering the ambush. With the paratroopers mounted on its back deck, the Stuart tank would crash through the hedgerow opening with all guns blazing. The 37mm gun of the Stuart would fire canister rounds to the left, the bow machine gun fire to the front and the paratroopers fire to the right. The massive firepower directed in three directions simultaneously proved to be very effective. Amongst the hedgerows the Stuart light tanks made up for their light armor and gun by having the only tank canister rounds. Lieutenant Burt remembered that the tired and angry paratroopers had fought with a savage determination resulting in high German casualties and few prisoners. He recalls the German radio propaganda calling them "Roosevelt's Butchers."[28]

Sgt. Arden Gatzke, a Sherman tank gunner, also remembered the link with the paratroopers:

> They had been fighting since D-Day and were out of ammunition and food and had been fighting hand to hand. We gave each one ammunition for his rifle. A couple broke down and cried when they got this ammunition so they could go kill some more Germans who had killed so many of their buddies. There were dead German and American soldiers laying all over. Anywhere from one to fifty in a football size field.[29]

The 66th Armored Regiment's first day of combat in France had been a difficult preview of the battles to come in 1944. The regiment was now fighting a tough enemy who had superior tanks and defended on difficult terrain. Although Colonel Collier's task force had fallen short of its objective, it was successful in halting the German counterattack to take Carentan. The regiment's two attacks had killed an estimated 500 to 600 Germans and destroyed seven 75mm assault guns. The small number of German prisoners (four wounded) taken from the SS was evidence of their determination. The regiment lost two soldiers killed and eight wounded. William Rape, a platoon sergeant in Company H, poignantly remembered their first day in Normandy:

We went down to Carentan about D plus 8 to rescue the 101st Airborne Division who were cut off by the Germans. Those paratroopers were very grateful when we got there. We gave them food, ammunition, and anything we had that they wanted. I hope I never see anything like this again. When it was over we drove up the road aways. The road had a high bank on each side. The German soldiers were marching in columns on both sides of the road. We caught them with artillery and machine-gun fire. I had never seen as many dead in all my life. Some were leaning on the bank and looked like they were still alive. I saw the 29th Infantry boys go over and take their guns and shake them to see if they were alive. Trees were blown down, and many cows and horses were killed. I remember pulling out into a field, stopping, and getting out of my tank and sitting on a log. I said aloud, "I believe everything and everybody but us is dead."[30]

At 0530 hours on 14 June, both task forces of the 66th Armor resumed their attacks. These attacks were preceded by heavy, ten-minute artillery barrages and neither encountered German resistance. Colonel Collier's task force with the 2nd Battalion reached the La Campagne road junction at 0800 hours. They remained there until relieved at 1500 hours by the 502nd Parachute Infantry, whereupon they moved to an assembly area near Douville. The 1st Battalion task force cleared the area south of the Auverville-La Campagne road to the Cantepie-La Godillerie trail. Also relieved by the 502nd they rejoined the rest of the regiment. In the late afternoon, Company I supported an attack on Méautis with the 501st Parachute Infantry. The attack was successful in driving the Germans out of the town, and that night the company returned to the assembly area.

The most significant event of 14 June was the reorganization of the regiment. This was the result of a 15 September 1943 reorganization of the armored divisions. In this revision, the three tank battalions, consisting of one light company and three medium tank companies, replaced the division's two armored regiments. Probably because of their seniority in the armored force and the views of generals such as Patton, the 2nd and 3rd Armored Divisions did not become new "light" armored divisions. The two regiments of the 2nd Armored Division, the 66th and 67th, were not separated into the battalions but instead retained their regimental organization. The reorganization of 1944 organized the battalions into two companies of medium tanks (M4 Shermans) and one of light tanks (M5 Stuarts). The new organization was somewhat confusing because all of the companies kept their original letter designations. For example, 1st Battalion no longer had Companies A, B, and C. Beginning on 14 June the regiment was changed

as follows: 1st Battalion retained Company C (M5) and gained Companies
F and I (M4) ; the 2nd Battalion received Company A (M5) and kept Companies D and E (M4); and the 3rd Battalion took Company B (M5) and
maintained Companies G and H (M4).[31]

Throughout the war, the man who kept the tank company supplied with
everything they needed was the company's senior noncommissioned officer,
the first sergeant. First Sergeant Domarecki of H Company considered his
most important task to be managing the replacement of killed, wounded,
and sick men with the best possible men. He kept a roster of the company
and those who were available as replacements. On a good day the first sergeant would have eight or nine replacement men riding in his half-track.
The critical report for keeping the personnel and supply system informed
of the company's needs was the morning report which went to the battalion
sergeant major every morning. The morning report provided the numbers to
insure the company received enough rations, gasoline, and ammunition.

Tank cannon or main gun ammunition available included Armor piercing, canister, and white phosphorus. Canister rounds worked like shotgun
shells and were used against infantry. White phosphorus, which burns
fiercely, was used to set targets afire, produce covering smoke and against
enemy infantry under cover.

The normal method of resupply was for the first sergeant to lead the
supply trucks forward after dark to where the tanks had stopped. Gasoline
was carried from the trucks up to the tanks in five-gallon cans. Cannon
ammunition was contained in three round sills. The resupply normally took
about two hours to complete.[32]

During one of his days serving as the Maintenance Officer, Lt. Jim
Burt was out with a tank retriever recovering knocked-out tanks.

> We had orders that we should prepare to withdraw, that our position
> was being taken by the 4th Infantry Division....There was another
> knocked out tank along a farm road, a narrow trail with hedgerows on
> each side. The tank hit a mine and had not burned, so it was worthy of
> retrieving. I left my crew alone because they were plenty busy and
> went to the tank which had struck a mine. I reasoned that it might not
> have hit the first one. I had a L.L. Bean hunting knife and probed for
> mines and found five or six. The tank, sensing there might be mines,
> had been as far to one side of the trail as possible and therefore had
> missed several which were right in the obvious vehicle rut. As I found
> a mine with my hunting knife I would uncover it, remove the fuse, put
> the fuse on one side of the road and the mines on the other side. No one
> was around. Then I was aware of a presence, and I did not know if it

were friend or enemy. So I slowly looked over my shoulder and there was Eugenio Bonafon, my high school classmate who I had played baseball and football with back in Massachusetts. Eugenio was known as "Beppo" in high school. His outfit was coming into the sector the next day and he was making a reconnaisance. We had a wonderful visit. I wrote home that night. I learned later that he wrote home that night. That night we pulled out. His unit pulled in, and the next day he was killed in that same locale.[33]

On the morning of 15 June, the regiment's Reconnaissance Company (less one platoon), with two platoons of light tanks from Company C attached, moved out on a reconnaissance in force mission.[34] This task was to determine the enemy's strength and positions from Auverville south to St. Andre de Boron and then southwest to Saint Eney. The force moved in two columns and ran into heavy enemy resistance about 1,000 yards outside of Auverville, the 37mm guns of the Stuarts being no match for the 75mm German assault guns. At 1000 hours both columns withdrew back to Auverville where they were reinforced by the Headquarters Company of the 1st Battalion, a troop of the 4th Cavalry Squadron and one company of the 41st Infantry. The larger force, now commanded by the 1st Battalion commander, Lt. Col. Carl Parker, crossed the LD at 1200 hours and was abruptly halted at the same point as the previous effort. Lieutenant Colonel Parker called for additional reinforcements when one of the columns became surrounded by enemy infantry and Panzerfaust teams. Before the reinforcements of Company I (less one platoon) and a company of the 41st Infantry could arrive, the force was ordered to withdraw at about 1930 hours. After regrouping near Auverville, the elements of the 66th moved to a nearby assembly area.[35] Meanwhile, the 2nd and 3rd Battalions of the regiment spent most of the day on short notice alert in the CCA area at La Campagne and Douville. The soldiers worked on the maintenance of vehicles and weapons and the evacuation of German vehicles and dead soldiers from the previous day's battles.[36]

The regiment (less the 1st Battalion) spent the remainder of the month of June in a bivouac near Cremy. The 1st Battalion was attached to the 101st Airborne Division and bivouacked near Auverville. These units of the 66th received personnel and vehicle replacements and performed vehicle and weapons maintenance and repair. The men also conducted physical and tactical training and reconnoitered routes for possible use. Most of this time was spent on one-hour notice alert. It was during this period that seven men were awarded the Silver Star and ten received the Bronze Star for gallantry in action near Carentan.[37]

Daily life in the field, however, also consisted of routine concerns such as food preparation and writing letters to the folks back home. In a letter to his fiancee, Carol, Capt. Cameron Warren described the American soldier's unique approach to food in the field:

> Cooking in the field is quite educational. Everyone cooks by his own vehicle—an excellent ration—ham & eggs dehydrated, biscuits & jam— dry cereal and coffee constitute breakfast. Little hard biscuits, lemon- ade, cheese, "shoo-gum" as the French say and cigarettes are in the noon ration. For supper, maybe, string beans, corn beef, fruit bar, but- ter (canned), biscuits are all very good and plenty of it. The meat var- ies—but the educational part comes in traveling from vehicle to vehicle seeing the different ways men prepare the food. Paddies, melted cheese sandwiches, hashes, stews. It's great sport trying to outdo the other fellow in the culinary art.[38]

During this lull, the motor sergeant of Company H manufactured hedge cutters, which were mounted on two tanks from each platoon. The hedge cutters were cut from scrap iron and mounted on the lower part of the tank's belly. Shaped like massive triangular teeth, these cutters allowed tanks to ram their way through most hedge rows. Staff Sergeant Rape's platoon became the first in the company to receive the new M4A1(W) Sherman tank.[39] This was the first Sherman to feature the new 76mm gun with a high muzzle velocity. Although a major improvement over the short barrel 75mm gun, it soon proved inadequate against the very formidable German Pan- ther and Tiger tanks. The (W) stood for Wet because the ammunition racks were surrounded by liquid containers to reduce the considerable risk of fire in the gasoline-powered Sherman.

Lt. Lewis Sasser wrote to his wife, Celeste, on 21 June about the cold grey Norman weather and their long separation:

> Has been a right nice day but for the first day of summer I have been about to freeze. Still have on wool underwear and a combat jacket but that doesn't seem to help much. Just a cool breeze blowing and seems to be trying unsuccessfully to rain. The sun hasn't been out all day.
>
> This is the 500th day we've been apart according to my figures. Can't help but wonder how many more hundreds of days it'll be before we see each other. Remember the first 100 I thought was about all I could stand and here I still am. At least I seem to average around 6 months to a country which is about right—get a pretty good idea of the place and by that time you're ready for another.

I'm still so cold I just have to get in bed or rather my sleeping bag, and have been freezing writing this much.

Today was just another day—just laid around and same old stuff—hurry up and wait—today I waited.[40]

Sergeant Gatzke's diary for a few of the last days of June gives an idea of some of the activities the soldiers were engaged in:

sun 18   Standto 15 min. 0500 Slept most of day. First letters arrived in France

tues 20   Guard 0300-0420, standto 0600—15 min. Oriented new guy, Mike Elliott from Madison, Wi.

fri 23   Off guard 0015, standto 0500—15 min. Saw American plane hit by ack ack. Pilot bailed out. Couple hours later he came walking in from the German lines.

sat 24   Guard 0400-0500, standto 0500—15 min. Short run. Led calisthenics. Still dodging artillery every day.[41]

On 1 July 1944 CCA ordered the 66th Armor (less the 1st Battalion) to move to an assembly area near Le Mesnil to support the 2nd and 3rd Battalions of the 41st Armored Infantry in the front line. The orders directed the regiment to be prepared to meet any enemy attack, reconnoiter possible routes and positions, and, if requested, assist the artillery by using the tank guns for indirect fire. The regiment departed Cremy at 1600 hours and arrived in their assembly area near Le Mesnil at 1945 hours.[42] There the commanders of the regiment met and planned for possible operations while the soldiers prepared their vehicles and weapons. That night the Reconnaissance Company moved into the front to maintain contact between the 41st Infantry and the British 2nd Battalion, the Gloucester Regiment. On 3 July the 1st Battalion was relieved from attachment to the 101st Airborne and attached to the 83rd Infantry Division.[43]

During the war it was common for American units to post signs warning following units of nearby dangers. One of the most frequently seen signs was "Mines cleared to the ditches," indicating that while the road was cleared of enemy mines nothing beyond the edge of the roadside ditch was safe. While traveling along a road in Normandy, Sergeant Getsinger saw an interesting and humorous variation left by the soldiers of the 1st Infantry Division. The roadside sign read, "Germans cleared to the ditches."[44]

In Normandy, the light tanks of the 66th soon found a method to deal with the larger and more powerful German tanks that they encountered often with little or no warning. Lieutenant Burt, the Executive Officer of C Company, said that the Stuarts began carrying a round of smoke in the 37mm chamber. The Stuart would fire the smoke round at the German tank, blinding it, and then quickly maneuver to get a flank shot. If flanking the German tank was not possible, the light tankers would bypass their heavier opponent and call in the close air support in good weather or artillery fire in bad weather.[45]

On 3 July Regimental chaplain Luke Bolin wrote to his wife about life in Normandy:

> Had a good sleep last night but today the rain makes everything miserable. It had rained some about 2/3 of the days I have been in France. Sometimes it rains hard but usually it drizzles. You've heard of slit trenches, I suppose. Well, I am getting experience digging them. My latest is a masterpiece. I decided to sleep in it so I put my pup tent over it, pulled in the bed, blew up my airmattress and find it very comfortable. In case of a raid it takes a lot of courage to get out of the sack and into a trench so I solved the problem by sleeping in it. Fortunately, I have seen few Jerry planes but plenty of ours. They are music to one's ears.
>
> It's a treat to see hundreds of allied bombers go over with fighters covering them. The fighters go buzzing all around them and Jerry doesn't seem anxious to try to interfere. You've no doubt read of Allied air supremacy. It's a comforting fact.[46]

On 4 July the 1st Battalion, commanded by the S-3, Major Long, supported an attack by the 330th Infantry Regiment of the 83rd Infantry Division. The 1st Battalion of the 330th was on the left and was supported by one platoon each from Companies C and F. On the right, Company F (less one platoon) of the 66th supported the 330th's 2nd Battalion. The 330th launched the left flank attack at 0445 hours on a narrow 1,000-yard front following a ten-minute artillery barrage. The attack first encountered German defenses about 0630 hours, and this resistance steadily increased until the attack was halted around 0830 hours. On the right, one of the infantry companies suffered serious losses including its three ranking officers. The 1st Platoon leader of Company F was killed when a Panzerfaust team destroyed his tank. Surrounded by German infantry, the tank platoon organized a 360-degree defense and requested reinforcements. The unit was finally extracted about 1530 hours, having lost two tanks.[47]

The left flank attack with the 1st Battalion, 330th Infantry, and one platoon each from Companies C and F, 66th Armor, did not begin until 1800 hours. The 3rd Battalion, 330th Infantry, with the surviving five tanks of the 1st and 3rd Platoons, Company F, also attacked. The tanks proved invaluable in driving the Germans out of several groups of buildings and a church tower they were using as fighting positions and for artillery spotting. One of the platoons lost two tanks to mines while the other lost two tanks to Panzerfausts. After the loss of the two tanks, the latter platoon withdrew because of engine, main gun, and communications problems with each of the remaining tanks. In spite of the tank losses, the attack reached its objective at 2230 hours. After covering the infantrymen while they consolidated on the objective, the last tanks returned to their assembly area about 0130 hours on 5 July. The 1st Battalion had one man killed and seven wounded in the day's fighting.[48]

On several occasions units of the 66th fought alongside the regiments of the British Army. The impressions the British made upon the Americans are nicely summed up in this letter from 3rd Battalion commander, Lt. Col. "Rudy" Quillian to his wife, Evie:

> ...I have had occasion to get to know some of the British pretty well. They are remarkable people. Their outstanding quality is their unhurried and methodical approach to everything they do—which is good. The pay off is to see them stop to brew up their tea during a battle, but they fight well both before and after tea. One British tank commander we talked to was quite resentful that "Jerry", as he called them, had knocked out his tank while he was "brewing up".[49]

The 1st Battalion, 66th Armor, again supported two attacks by elements of the 83rd Infantry Division on 5 July. The 3rd Battalion, 329th Infantry, made an attack southwest along the left on the Carentan-Periers road supported by 2nd and 3rd Platoons, Company I, and the 2nd Platoon, Company C. Attacking along the opposite side of the road was the 1st Battalion, 331st Infantry, supported by the 1st Platoon, Company I, and the 3rd Platoon, Company C. The units launched the attack at 0900 hours following fifteen minutes of artillery preparation. To the left of the road, mines disabled two tanks in the first fifteen minutes. The attack proceeded slowly against moderate enemy resistance and extensive minefields. The troops reached the objective at 1900 hours, and the two platoons of Company I and one platoon of Company F were relieved by the 746th Tank Battalion at 1930 hours. En route back, the Germans ambushed the American tanks with an unidentified antitank weapon. The result was the destruction of two tanks and the loss of five men; three were dead, and two left missing in action. The tankers believed that unseen German Panzerfaust teams were responsible for the destruction. Later, a Maintenance Company T-2 recovery vehicle was damaged by a mine while recovering the disabled tanks.[50]

To the right of the road, the 1st Platoon, Company I, and the 3rd Platoon, Company C, had just crossed the Line of Departure (LD) when a Panzerfaust destroyed a platoon leader's tank. The terrain was difficult, making it hard for the remaining tanks to move forward. When the tank platoons caught up with the infantry elements, they were ordered to assault a piece of high ground just beyond a group of buildings. During the ensuing assault a German tank or assault gun destroyed two Shermans. Another Sherman hit a German tank or assault gun causing it to burst into flames. The 746th Tank Battalion relieved the regiment's tank platoons at about 1800 hours. The 1st Battalion had lost four men killed and thirteen wounded, with two more missing in action.[51]

The 1st Battalion was relieved from attachment to the 83rd Infantry Division and rejoined the regiment near Le Mesnil late on 6 July. There, from 7 to 16 July, the regiment remained on alert status while receiving personnel and vehicle replacements. They serviced the vehicles and trained the replacement soldiers during the days in reserve. During this period German planes bombed elements of the regiment, a rare event with the almost complete Allied air superiority over Normandy.

On 8 July Chaplain (Capt.) Luke Bolin wrote to his wife about the war. He told her of the unique challenges faced by regimental chaplains as they tried to visit and minister to several thousand soldiers often spread over large areas fighting a war:

> Yes, darling, I believe the cause for which we fight is just but don't let anybody fool you. War is not glorious. It's inhumane, ghastly, deadly. The more we see of it the more we despise it, but the more determined we are to end it. Americans are not blood thirsty, but in a pinch they can be ruthless as any of our enemies.
>
> As you realize, it is very difficult to have church services, but I try to get to all my men sometime during the week if I can't make it on Sunday. Some time ago I was conducting a service and a barrage of friendly artillery opened up and almost drowned us out. It literally shook the earth. But our own artillery or the drone of allied planes is music to my ears! And we certainly have plenty of both.[52]

On 9 July Lieutenant Sasser, a tank platoon leader, wrote to his wife about some experiences during the fighting in early July and sleeping in a slit trench:

> Can tell you now that I have seen action—not that I don't think you'd already figured that—but some of these outfits stay so far back all they ever see are the air raids and artillery. For a while there we spent a good

part of the time tracking down snipers and in a tank that's quite enjoyable. You know you have the advantage on them unless they happen to have a bazooka. The old boys would fire small arms into the area and we'd take a tank and chase them down but usually unsuccessfully. The artillery all nite long was quite a nuisance for a while and had to take up sleeping regularly in my slit trench in order that I be safe. Never would wake up when they would start coming over and consequently figured I'd better play safe and stay there....Lots more trouble to have a slit trench to sleep in as you have to dig out more to make room for your bedding roll. But, there is no more miserable feeling than to have to pull yourself out of a warm sleeping bag and move to a cold, wet ditch in the middle of a good night's rest. The worst calamity is to dig a nice trench and then have to move—takes all of the initiative out of you.[53]

On 17 July the 66th received their first M4A3E8, Sherman tanks, nicknamed the "Easy Eight." These new tanks featured an improved suspension system which improved cross country performance and the more effective 76mm gun. That same day the regiment moved to an assembly area near Sur Le Chemin Du Gril, and from the seventeenth to the twenty-fourth they concentrated on maintenance, training, and rest. During this time, the troops painted some of the tanks in a camouflage pattern for the first time. Although rarely done during the war, the camouflaged tanks blended in with the countryside better than the solid dark green colored tanks.[54]

Chaplain Bolin wrote to his wife on 19 July about an interesting officer in the regiment:

I wrote you once about Lt. Shires—Abe. He's the most calm, cold-blooded man I ever saw. Nothing excites him. I asked him to come to church yesterday and said this to him, "We're big buddies and last time I had church here you sat 15 yds. away playing poker and didn't come. I'm disappointed!" He replied, "Well, I heard the sermon and the Lord blessed me. Here's the money I owe you!" Then he gave me 500 francs. Can you beat it![55]

Lt. Lewis Sasser wrote to his wife during the lull about his desire to escape from the HQ Company and the artillery:

Told you I was thinking about getting out of HQ Company if I could as my 3 light and 2 medium tanks here have little chance of ever getting to act as a platoon in combat and thus my chances of promotion are not so good. Besides have all the extra stuff of Supply and Mess Officer to fool with here and would rather have a platoon of tanks in a line company. Might get a chance to put a few rounds over near old Jerry instead of ducking his half the time and being knocked down by our artillery letting him have a few the other half. It's wonderful tho how easy it gets to be able to tell the outgoing from the incoming mail. Ours makes more noise but theirs has a more moving noise to it and we do move too. It's funny how the men will put down a trench a foot deep to begin with and then when a few come over those trenches seem to automatically sink deeper. No one says anything but all the shovels are busy and if we are in the same place for more than a day or so a good percentage of the trenches have a roof over them. End up with some pretty livable places. I've been in this company for over a year now and know everybody so well kind of hate to leave. Do know all the officers in the Regiment well and that will be a help wherever I go and having been here as long as I have known a lot of the men come for schools and details. Glad of the change anyway and will let you know how I like it. Wish me luck.[56]

It was also during this time that Capt. Cameron J. Warren, the commander of Company H, had a chance to write a letter. On 22 July 1944 he wrote home to his parents about many things, from the weather and his health to sniper and artillery fire:

...One thing you soon learn if you are ever where the news is being made is that the reporter's written account of it is often a little fiercer sounding than it really was and of course the same events seen by the soldier and reporter make two separate and distinct impressions on the two men's minds. For example, to the soldier it may have just been another day's work while to the reporter it might have looked heroic. Since he cannot see how he, himself, could have done the same job and quite naturally so because he is not trained to do it....

Lost my pup tent the other day to Art'y fire. The shell hit about 10 feet from it and riddled it like a sieve—But I had my bedding roll in a slight depression and it came thru unscathed. My French-English dictionary, lying on level ground inside the tent, was caught by shell fragments as were 4 air-mail envelopes laying beside it. I'll enclose one as a souvenir to you. You've probably heard of the London cabby who was asked if he was afraid of the rocket bombs. He replied he wasn't in the least because "O'le Hitler e's got to find London, which is easy enough, but then e's got to find Ammersmith Street and then 84 Ammersmith St. to hit me and then likely as not I'll be down to the corner Pub."

Well, like the cabby I was down eating chow when the shell hit.[57]

Knocked-out German Mark V Panther tank. July 1944.

Sherman tank crew takes down their improvised shelter near LaCommunne, France. 24 July 1944.

Shermans hidden under their camouflage nets in the hedgerow country. July 1944.
Cameron J. Warren

Crewmen relaxing and writing letters beneath their lean-to and camouflage net. July 1944.
John B. Roller

Group of French resistance fighters armed with German Mauser 98K rifles. August 1944.

Luke Bolin

CHAPTER 12

Breakout and Pursuit: August 1944

On 20 July the regiment received orders from Combat Command A (CCA) of the 2nd Armored Division for Operation Cobra.[1] Cobra was the Allied plan for a massive and very concentrated attack intended to break the Allies out of the bloody stalemate among the hedgerows in Normandy. The Germans were using the difficult terrain to their best advantage and had reduced the Allies to a costly crawl. Delayed from the originally planned date of 20 July due to severe storms, the Cobra attack plan called for two U. S. corps to create a gap in the German lines and hold the shoulders of the penetration open, thus allowing the 1st Infantry and 3rd Armored Divisions to break out into the open country. The storms that swept across Normandy were the worst in decades. The violent seas in the English Channel destroyed or damaged the massive pre-fabricated Mulberry Harbors set in June to unload ships across the invasion beaches.

The 66th Armor, as a part of CCA, had the mission of seizing the area bounded by Le Mesnil Herman-St. Samson De Ban Fosse on the left (east) side of the penetration. As the only tank unit in CCA the regiment was to be prepared to defeat any German counterattack expected from Conde Sur Vire in the east or Hambye in the south.[2] Combat Command A moved to the attack in two columns with the 2nd Battalion in the west and the regimental headquarters and the 3rd Battalion in the eastern column. Two platoons of the Reconnaissance Company spearheaded the advance with these orders: "Move rapidly to objective, post guides at critical points along routes, clear routes of march employing attached engineers, overrun light enemy resistance, and outpost objective until relieved by advance guard."[3] The

1st Battalion followed in support of the two lead battalions. An unparalleled aerial bombardment of the attack corridor by 1,500 heavy bombers, 380 medium bombers, and finally 550 fighter-bombers preceded the attack and devastated the area.[4] Massive German Tiger tanks weighing over 50 tons were flung into the air and overturned onto their turrets. In fact, some areas were so badly cratered by the bombs, they became an obstacle to the American tanks.

Finally on 26 July Operation Cobra was launched at 0945 hours. CCA crossed the LD and moved toward their objective of the high ground near Le Mesnil Herman. The 2nd and 3rd Battalions advanced astride the Canisy-Le Mesnil Herman road with considerable difficulty because of the hedgerows, sunken roads, and new bomb craters. The regiment penetrated seven miles into the German lines, capturing numerous prisoners and destroying German vehicles and weapons that survived the bombing. The troops seized Canisy at approximately 1900 hours, with the loss of three Shermans to that point. At Canisy the two columns split; Colonel Collier led the 3rd Battalion east toward St. Samson de Bon Fosse, and Brig. Gen. Maurice Rose, the CCA commander, moved the 2nd Battalion south toward Le Mesnil Herman.

Lt. Lamar Russell commanded a platoon of Stuart light tanks of C Company during Operation Cobra. His platoon's mission was to guard the right flank of the main column. Whenever there was a break in the hedgerows, Lieutenant Russell led his platoon into the field where it would circle the open area in search of enemy tanks and troops. In one field, four German tank crews emerged from the corners of the field with their hands up. The Germans probably had their tanks destroyed or disabled during the massive bombardment earlier. Lieutenant Russell shuddered to think that any one of the German tanks "could have sent all 5 of my tanks (37mm Lt) to glory."[5]

Capt. Cameron Warren described the fighting in a letter home from his hospital bed in England:

> The Air Corps gave us marvelous support the first day and we bucked the hedgerows all day. We jumped off about 0900 and about 0930 we hit a thin line of Germans. After killing a considerable number they gave up and we got a nice bag of prisoners. But we didn't stop. By 1830 we had made about 3¹/₂ miles (about 100 hedgerows). That was really a days work and not fooling. Our boys did some excellent shooting and our losses were light. We passed many wrecks of German tanks and various other sundry vehicles that our P47s had knocked out. Sure was good to see. We lost a tank to bazooka fire. Everyone got out.

Some were burned pretty bad but all are going to be back for duty soon. He got hit early in the game and it made us pretty mad and also probably scared too—but we all expect to lose one now and then.

Well before the nite was over they finally relieved us and we followed along behind awhile and before the day was out we had our objective a total distance of around six miles. We were deep in enemy territory and so most everybody slept in the tanks. Snipers got one or two—not from my bunch but we again got some more prisoners and killed a few more. The next afternoon we were off again and it was the same old stuff—arty, tanks and infantry—and hedgerow after heartbreaking hedgerow. We had penetrated about 4 more miles and that nite we really sweated it out. Finally we got our own arty down all around us for a little protection. The next morning we were off again and I got hit around noon about 1$\frac{1}{2}$ miles and right on our objective (Villebaudon).[6]

Mario de Felice was an Italian-born and -trained physician. He had moved to the United States and established his medical practice just in time to be drafted in 1941. He was commissioned as a first lieutenant in the Medical Corps and assigned as the surgeon for 2nd Battalion. On 27 July in the fighting near Le Mesnil Herman Lieutenant de Felice attempted to move forward to evacuate three seriously wounded men from their knocked-out tank. The rough terrain and dense forest prevented getting the surgeon's half-track to the wounded. The surgeon dismounted and went forward with three of his medics. The group reached the wounded and began to treat them in spite of an intense mortar barrage. A mortar round landed just feet away, killing two of the medics and two of the wounded. In spite of being painfully wounded Lieutenant de Felice did not pause to check his own wounds but continued to work on the wounded tanker. For his heroism Lieutenant de Felice was awarded the Distinguished Service Cross. Later as a captain, he declined promotion to major and the position of regimental surgeon to remain with the 2nd Battalion.[7]

During the 2nd Battalion attack, Lieutenant Colonel Herkness' tank was knocked out. Herkness mounted the back of another tank and continued to lead his battalion in the attack while being exposed to artillery and mortar fire, as well as enemy small arms fire. When the attack bogged down in the difficult hedge row and sunken road country, Lieutenant Colonel Herkness dismounted the tank and went forward on foot to direct the clearing of two burning German tanks. While in the sunken road Herkness suddenly encountered two German officers from the headquarters 2nd Battalion had overrun. One of the Germans fired his pistol at the same

Lt. Col. Lindsay C. Herkness, Jr. 2nd Battalion commander.

Lindsay C. Herkness, Jr.

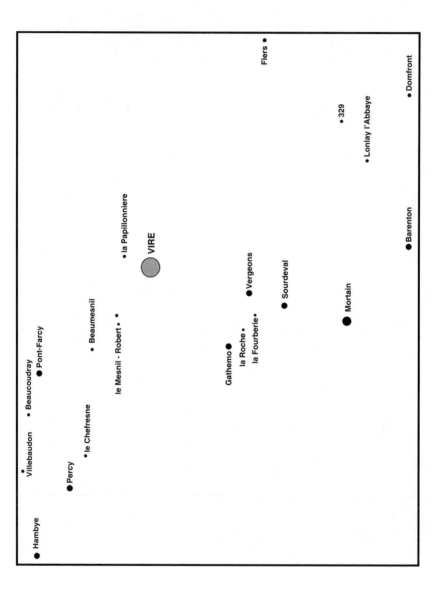

MAP 19
Normandy (B)
June–August 1944

moment Herkness fired his .45 automatic. Herkness had learned to fire as he turned sideways towards his target, and the move saved him as the German's bullet grazed his side. The first German was felled by Herkness' shot and the second one fled. Herkness refused evacuation and continued to lead his battalion after accepting some first aid. His arrival later at regimental headquarters in a blood-soaked uniform attracted some interest from his fellow officers. Lieutenant Colonel Herkness later received the Distinguished Service Cross for his courage and leadership during the successful attack.[8]

By 2100 hours the two columns had reached St. Ebremond de Bonfosse (east) and St. Martin de Bonfosse (south). At 2300 hours the east column began moving into their objective of St. Samson where they resupplied and prepared to meet any German counterattacks. The south column reached Le Mesnil Herman about 0200 hours on the twenty-seventh and secured it by 0800 hours.[9]

In the late afternoon, the regiment sent two task forces to conduct reconnaissance in force missions. The 1st Battalion followed the road southeast toward Tessy Sur Vire, while the 3rd Battalion explored the road southwest to Villebaudon. Both task forces ran into heavy German resistance from enemy infantry and Panzerfaust and antitank gunfire.[10]

These once-peaceful roads in Normandy were irrevocably disturbed by fierce fighting. Staff Sergeant Rape recounted some of the civilian costs of the war in hedgerow country:

> ...we regrouped and took cover behind a farm house. The Germans put a heavy barrage of artillery on us trying to flush us out. They could not flush us out and decided to shell the farmhouse. Several people were killed, and one woman ran out with a baby in her arms. She ran toward my tank motioning me to take the baby inside. I noticed the baby's stomach was ripped open and his intestines were hanging out. One of the soldiers from the 29th Infantry handed me the baby up on the tank, and I handed it down inside to my gunner, Frank Bisogno. I remember saying, "Oh my God, how can I fight a war with a baby in my arms?" After a while, I spotted a medic in the area and turned the baby over to him.[11]

The southern element moved within two miles of Villebaudon before dark. That night Lt. Col. "Rudy" Quillian, the 3rd Battalion commander, was mortally wounded when hit in the back and legs by 37mm and machine gun fire from another American unit.[12] Lieutenant Colonel Quillian died in a hospital in England on 4 August and is buried in the American cemetery on Omaha Beach. Lieutenant Colonel Quillian left behind his

Lt. Col. Amzi "Rudy" Quillian, 3rd Battalion commander. Died of wounds received in Normandy.

wife, Evie, and baby daughter, Sally, whom he had never seen. He had written a letter for his daughter, Sally, in the event that he did not return and mailed it to his wife. The letter to Sally from the father she never knew is contained in the epilogue. Maj. Hugh R. O'Farrell then took command of the 3rd Battalion. The day had been a particularly bloody one for the regiment with nine killed and twenty-one wounded.[13]

Sergeant Gatzke's diary for 26 June records some of the events that took place in his platoon:

> wed 26   Moved out 0030. Got to attack position 0900. Fought 10$\frac{1}{2}$ miles to objective. Had a very sore nose and a pair of bent glasses when tank came to an abrupt stop when it hit a ditch while I was looking through the periscope. Lt. Montgomery's tank had a camera attached to the 75mm and took pictures where the gun was aimed. His tank got hit and burned with no pictures being taken. PFC Byrnes died from burns and became Co. H first fatality.[14]

During Operation Cobra, numerous soldiers of the regiment performed acts of bravery and were awarded decorations. Cpl. William Giblin won the Silver Star for gallantry on 27 July. Although badly burned when his tank was hit, he rescued his company commander from three German soldiers who had captured him. Giblin then captured the three German soldiers. The Distinguished Service Cross was later awarded to Capt. Mario DeFelice who moved his medical half-track forward through an artillery barrage to help the wounded. With his half-track surrounded by Germans he cared for the wounded without regard for his own safety, even when the medic next to him was killed.[15]

On the afternoon of 28 July, the 66th received orders to participate in an attack southward to take the high ground of Percy-le Chefresne-St. Marie. The 1st Battalion led the left column, the 2nd Battalion the middle one, and the 3rd Battalion the right flank march. The middle column moved at 1400 hours and advanced to Moyen before being halted by the determined resistance of a considerable force of Panzergrenadiers (mechanized infantry) supported by tanks. The middle column remained on the high ground north of Moyen until elements of the 29th Infantry Division relieved them at 2030 hours. The left flank units fought a German force of tanks and the legendary German 88mm antiaircraft guns deployed in the antitank role near Le Mesnil Opac. During this battle, the 1st Battalion task force destroyed five German Mark IV tanks and four antitank guns without suffering any losses. The advance continued under mortar and artillery fire until halted by heavy resistance at 2100 hours. The right elements had a much easier day, securing Villebaudon with little resistance and continuing to

move south toward Percy. This force, led by Major O'Farrell, resumed the
attack to the south at 0730 the next morning and took Percy at 1530 against
heavy enemy resistance.[16] Later, Lt. Finis Smith, a platoon leader in Company
H, wrote to his old company commander, Captain Perkins, at Fort
Knox about the action and the casualties:

> Tried to take Percy from another direction. Lost 8 tanks in 15 minutes—5 G, 3 H, (including Gwinn's second tank) Kays MIA—head
> torn off and one that I can't remember. McCully and about 10 or 12
> enlisted wounded.[17]

The next morning, the left units under Major Cox, the 2nd Battalion
executive officer, moved from the vicinity of Le Mesnil Opac at 0800 and
headed toward Pont Farcy but had difficulty finding a ford to cross a stream
near La Chapelle. During this time the force fought a tank battle and destroyed
three German tanks. The task force was finally ordered to disengage
at 1800 and move to an assembly area.[18] During this two-day attack
the regiment lost twenty-one killed, eighty-five wounded, and seven missing.
Five sergeants of the 66th were awarded Silver Stars as a result of the
battles on 28 July. One of them, S.Sgt. Calvin McBride, pulled two men
out of a burning tank while seriously wounded himself.[19]

Another soldier, Sgt. Arden Gatzke recorded the combat of 28 July in
his diary and paid tribute to a friend who had been killed in the fighting:

> Under artillery fire all day. Attacked Percy just as it was getting dark.
> Got clobbered with anti tank fire. Five tanks burning all around us.
> Finally got orders to move back. I then found out that just before the
> attack Henry Wellnitz got caught in an artillery barrage and got a piece
> of shrapnel in the neck and died. He and Chet Polanski were the men of
> each side of my cot when I joined the Company back in January of
> 1942. We had gone together many times on passes in the States, Africa,
> Sicily and England. His death hit the company pretty hard. He was the
> best liked man in the company. Always ready for a good time or to
> create some laughter. No more.[20]

The 2nd Battalion and its attached elements attacked east toward Tessy
Sur Vire on 30 July. The battalion fought against heavy resistance and then
repelled a strong German counterattack. Under heavy artillery fire, they
reached and secured the objective of the crossroads at Villebaudon. Then,
at 2100 hours, the tanks withdrew to an assembly area north of Villebaudon
while the supporting infantry held the town.

The 1st Battalion moved to an assembly area southwest of
Villebaudon at 0545 hours on 31 July. Later that morning the battalion

launched an attack on the high ground near Dumont east of Villebaudon. At 1400 hours they encountered German tanks in a forest on the far side of a deep ravine. The tanks fought while the reconnaissance elements vainly sought a way across the ravine. American troops eventually destroyed four German tanks in the battle, but the battalion was under heavy German artillery fire during much of the time. About 2100 the battalion was ordered to secure the area for the night.[21] The last day of July was a rough one for I Company platoon leader, Lt. Donald Critchfield. He had one tank hit and burned and then mounted a second tank to continue leading his platoon. His second tank was also hit by German fire and burned. The second tank's destruction sent him to the field hospital.[22] During the last two days of July the regiment captured 1,200 prisoners and two Mark V Panther tanks; they also destroyed six Panthers and two Mark IVs as well as eight 88mm guns.[23]

The chaplain was perhaps the only person to whom a unit commander could confide his most personal feelings. During the war Regimental chaplain Luke Bolin and the Commander of the 66th shared many of their private thoughts. During the fierce combat in Normandy, Colonel Collier told Bolin,"Luke, they tell me if this war lasts a little longer, I will get my general's star, but I tell you I don't care if I ever get that star."[24]

As the month of August 1944 dawned, the 66th Armored Regiment, as a part of CCA, 2nd Armored Division, was in contact with the German forces to the east of Beaucoudray. Shrouded by mist, the combat team, led by the 3rd Battalion, launched an attack toward Tessy Sur Vire at dawn on 1 August. The American column rolled quickly through a force of German reconnaissance and personnel vehicles it had surprised in the poor visibility. Company G, 66th Armor, in the lead ran into the first heavy resistance on the outskirts of Tessy Sur Vire, where German Panzerfaust teams destroyed two of their tanks, and mine and antitank fire in the town cost another one, capturing the tank crews.[25]

Farther back in the American column, two German Panther tanks attacked the left flank at 0830. They were outnumbered by the American tanks who destroyed one and forced the other to retreat. Later, the Panthers returned to hunt the Americans from hidden positions and destroyed two more Company G Shermans. The 3rd Battalion regrouped and resumed the attack at 1430 hours with Company H on the left (north) and Company G on the right of the Villebaudon-Tessy Sur Vire road. The battalion again encountered heavy resistance from German tanks, and four more Shermans were lost. In spite of the heavy losses the battalion secured their objective of the high ground northwest of Tessy Sur Vire at 1800.

Lieutenant Smith's letter to Captain Perkins related the intensity of the fighting that day:

> ...about 4AM started out, came back behind Villebaudon and started mission of taking Tessy Sur Vire. Had about 30 M4s in Bn & 15 lights when we got here; about dark had 9 of each: Co. H—6, Bn.—2, Co. G—1. Had more casualties in H that day than any other time. 2 men killed; Sgt. Young and several other seriously wounded. Gwinn lost his 3rd tank that day & Spivey his second. G Co. lost all officers except Roberts and B Co. lost two.[26]

In what became his last day in combat in Normandy, Staff Sergeant Rape remembered the day's events:

> ...we tried to take Percy, France. In the process we lost several tanks...We withdrew to regroup. Several of us got out to plan our next move...While we were trying to regroup, we were heavily attacked by mortar fire...Cpl. Calasina was hit in the eye and face. Cpl. Bisogno and I pulled Calasina to a bomb crater. I held him in my arms and comforted him until the medics came. I never saw him again after that. I didn't realize the severity of my wound until the medics came to take Calasina. I was taken to an airfield close to Omaha Beach. After spending one night there, I was flown to Manchester, England where I stayed in the hospital 30 days. After this, I was sent back to the front...I landed again at Omaha Beach, walked up the bluff, and got in a truck convoy. Four or five days later I caught up with my outfit at the Seine River.[27]
> Author's Note: A search of the records indicates that Corporal Calasina survived his severe wounds.

The 3rd Battalion had lost fifteen Shermans and one Stuart light tank in the attack.[28]

At 1130 hours the 1st Battalion launched an attack to seize Hill 112, one mile southwest of Tessy Sur Vire. The battalion advanced, its left flank guiding along the same road where the 3rd Battalion had attacked only a short time earlier. By 1400 when the advance had covered a half mile, aerial reconnaissance located three German tanks hiding in ambush just ahead of the battalion. The Americans requested air support, and fighter-bombers quickly disposed of the enemy tanks. The attack continued through heavy German artillery and flank attacks by marauding German tanks.[29]

At 1300 hours the 2nd Battalion was ordered to join the regiment's attack. The 2nd Battalion, moving along the left (north) side of the road, caught up with the 1st Battalion at 2130, and the two battalions resumed the attack together. The 2nd Battalion reached its objective at 2300; it had destroyed five German Panther tanks, with the loss of only one light tank. Not as fortunate, the 1st Battalion secured its objective at midnight with only twelve Shermans and fifteen Stuarts remaining, leaving the battalion at less than forty percent strength in its primary striking force, the medium tank. It was a grim day for the battalion, which had suffered the largest loss of tanks and highest number of casualties thus far in the war. The heavy combat of 1 August resulted in eleven men receiving the Silver Star. The most notable award went to T/4 Henry E. Volz of Company G. Volz organized and led the remaining tanks of his battered company into the attack after all the officers of the company were put out of action. Two other enlisted men stayed on their disabled tank and dueled with the antitank gun that had crippled them until they drove the German gunners from the field.[30]

Capt. Cameron Warren wrote his fiancee, Carol, on 3 August from his hospital bed in England:

> England
>
> 3 Aug 44

Dearest,

Had a little tough luck and caught some anti-tank shell fragment in my left leg and nose. It's temporarily knocked me out of the big show but as the papers show she's still going strong. I lasted a good ways into it three days and got hit outside of one of my tanks when it was knocked out by an anti-tank gun, all the crew got out. The splatter of the shell hit me. I should be well in 2–3 weeks. I can't give you my final Gen Hosp address yet as I'm to move there tomorrow or next day. As soon as I know it I'll V-mail it to you. My nose is healed already not even a scar. The fragment that entered my leg is still in there. They couldn't get it out but might be able to later on. Its in about $1\frac{1}{2}$" in the muscles right under the knee.

Darling our outfit really turned in a great performance. I was extremely proud of them. They're still going strong I'm sure and I'm itching to rejoin them.

I was out today, a lovely evening on crutches. I really can navigate up a storm on them oophs I'm breaking my arm. This place has lovely green lawn all round, pretty nurses too—jealous? I did manage to bring thru with me all the pictures of my swell gal and family—also my mussete bag so am faring well. I returned to England on an LSP

Hosp. Ship, landed at same port I left from—felt awfully foolish retracing my steps that way.

Up till the time I left however not a single man had died in my outfit for which I was extremely grateful. Believe those who faced us suffered a much worse fate.

Fred Waring is on the hospital radio now—beautiful, "Shining Hour" is playing, "I had to call you up" just Lord how I wish I could. Your raise sounds swell. I always knew you were underpaid and overworked. I'll sure come to your party especially would the ice cream taste good. Have had none in over a year. England you know has outlawed it for the duration. The hospital did fetch up a nice chocolate milk this eve though Yum Yum. Your letter of the 13th is last from you. I imagine I'll have a dickens of a time getting mail until I rejoin the company. Continue writing there unless I write you otherwise.

I believe the war in Europe will be over in 44, hows that—you know I'm an old conservative so that should make you feel good. Of course when I get back is another matter—we've still the Japs and its hard to forsee that now but I might go that way first before getting hme. Well they're turning out the lights now so will finish this in morning, Goodnight sweetheart.

Just a good morning note to you before posting this. Believe I'm to another hospital a general from here sometime today. Its a lovely clear blue sky day out unusual for England. Good for the Air Corps too on France's roads which is good.

Darling be awful good and take good care of yourself, next time you go champagne drinking count me in. Bet your eyes really sparkled overtime. I miss you every minute. I'm awful proud of the job you're doing. Each passing day brings the time shorter when I can tell you personally how beautiful and lovely and kind you are.

All my love

Cam[31]

During 2–3 August the regiment consolidated their objectives around Tessy Sur Vire before turning them over to the 30th Infantry Division. The regiment repaired and serviced their vehicles and received personnel and vehicle replacements. By the end of the day, the regiment was restored to eighty Shermans, fifty-six Stuarts, and fourteen armored cars. In addition, ninety-three soldiers and thirteen officers came in as replacements.

The 2nd Battalion, reinforced, then led a CCA advance southeast from the area of Tessy Sur Vire towards Vire at 0600 hours on 4 August. The advance met only weak and scattered resistance all the way to Beaumesnil, where a minefield caused a brief delay. The advance resumed and reached le Mesnil Robert; there, a lone Panther tank challenged the Americans. After knocking out the tank with artillery fire, the Reconnaissance Company withdrew, and the tanks of Company D took over the lead. The attack continued against stiffening enemy resistance until it ground to a halt near La Papillonniere. The Germans, positioned on the high ground there, quickly destroyed five of the battalion's tanks. Consequently, the battalion was ordered to withdraw a short distance and consolidate for the night.[32]

The 1st and 2nd Battalions of the 66th Armor, reinforced by the 2nd Battalion, 119th Infantry and two platoons from the 17th Engineers, attacked at 0800 hours on 5 August to secure Hill 219 west of Vire. The battalions pushed through moderate enemy resistance to secure the area at 1015 hours. The tanks formed a perimeter defense, which overlooked the five roads leading out of Vire to the south and west, and, during the afternoon, repulsed several small German counterattacks. At 1800 the 1st Battalion was ordered to seize the high ground directly south of Vire. When the battalion commander tried to return to his unit after receiving the attack order, he found that the Germans had completely surrounded Hill 219. The orders were modified, and one tank and one infantry company made the attack. The small force was quickly repulsed by overwhelming enemy fire and was ordered back to Hill 219 for the night. During the attack one soldier won the Silver Star for a double feat of bravery. With his tank disabled by fire, T/4 Floyd Allen rescued three wounded crewmen. He then crawled back to the tank under fire, extinguished the flames and drove the tank to safety.[33]

At 0830 hours on 6 August, a 1st Battalion force again tried to take the high ground south of Vire. The attack made a little progress but was eventually halted by heavy German fire. An infantry division was later required to seize this area.[34] The regiment's ability to battle the Germans was increasingly hampered by dwindling ammunition and supplies. After two days with no resupply, small groups of tanks had to fight through the encircling German forces to the regiment's supply trains and then return to Hill 219. The 3rd Battalion, which had been in reserve, joined the attack and, after fighting through German antitank and mortar fire, drew abreast of the 1st Battalion at 1500 hours. All three battalions of the regiment were now grouped on and around Hill 219 southwest of Vire. A German tank and infantry attack hit the rear area of the 3rd Battalion at 1630 hours. The assault destroyed three T-2 tank recovery vehicles and three Shermans undergoing repairs. Company G repulsed the German counterattack after a fierce battle, but the regiment lost eleven men killed, twenty-four wounded and five missing.[35]

After Lt. G. Lamar Russell, a platoon leader in C Company, was wounded by a piece of shrapnel during an artillery barrage, he and several other wounded made their way to the aid station. When Lieutenant Russell arrived there, the aid station was surrounded by a large group of wounded, comprised of American and German soldiers and four wounded French civilians. The GIs were begging the medics to treat the wounded French first. When he was evacuated to the field hospital, he traveled there in a ambulance containing four GIs and four Germans.[36]

In Normandy, as in all wars, the meeting of old friends was a bittersweet occasion. Glad to see one another still alive, the buddies' conversation soon turned to the fate of those who were now absent from their ranks. Over forty years later, one veteran remembered one such reunion in the hedgerows of Normandy:

> From the time I arrived in the Cork Forest in 1943 to the invasion of Normandy I became a good friend of Sgt. Ken Kays. We played ball together and he was a great inspiration to me. Sgt. Domarecki told me sometime later that Kays was killed and he had to identify the body. Kays had a girlfriend back in Fairfield, Ill. and was counting the days when he could be with her again.[37]

Colonel Collier, the regimental commander, moved up to take command of CCA on 7 August. Lt. Col. William M. Stokes, Jr. was appointed the new commander of the 66th Armor. From 7 to 9 August the regiment remained on Hill 219, where it performed much needed maintenance and reorganization.

Many injuries and deaths in war are caused by accidents rather than enemy action. Sergeant Gatzke's diary for 8 August records one such incident:

> Stopped in open field at night. No moon. Pitch black. Lay down on the ground on my stomach with my feet next to the tank. Slight hollow by my chest making it uncomfortable so turned around and put my head next to the tank. A few minutes later a peep (jeep) came past and ran over both my legs with the front and rear wheel, right where my chest had been before I changed position. Had slight bruise on one.[38]

Late on 9 August Task Force A, under the command of Lieutenant Colonel Stokes, was formed and attached to the 23rd Infantry Division. The task force consisted of the 2nd Battalion, the regimental headquarters and other combined arms attachments.[39]

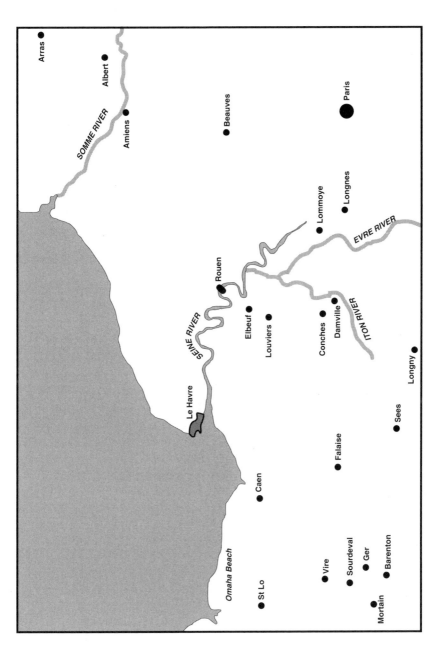

MAP 20

Northwestern France
August–September 1944

Task Force A moved in the predawn darkness of 10 August to an attack position near Champ Du Boult. At 0700 hours the task force, led by Company D, passed through the American front lines and attacked to the southeast. Moments after crossing the line of departure, Company D lost three tanks to a small group of German tanks that they in turn soon destroyed. The force had great difficulty moving through the terrain, with its swamps, hedgerows, and sunken roads but finally made it to an area southeast of Gathemo before noon, where they destroyed two German mortar positions and six large antitank guns. A platoon of light tanks from Company A cleared the town of Gathemo by 1215. Company E now assumed the lead and continued the advance against heavy German resistance to La Fourberie. The force destroyed four more large antitank guns and other German vehicles during this move. The task force consolidated near La Fourberie, where German artillery shelled it intermittently throughout the night.[40]

The next day the attack continued, again led by Company D, which advanced about one mile under constant German artillery fire and resistance ranging from rifle to large caliber antitank fire. The assault units held their ground when darkness came; meanwhile, the rest of the task force resupplied near La Roche. At dawn on 12 August, the task force again resumed the attack and by 1330 hours had secured their objective of the crossroads two miles east of La Roche. At 1500 they were relieved by elements of the 28th Infantry Division, and the 2nd Battalion rejoined CCA in the corps reserve area near La Roche. Late in the afternoon, a task force under the command of Major Cox, the 1st Battalion executive officer, was formed. Task Force Cox, led by Company I and followed by the 2nd Battalion, 41st Armored Infantry, and the 1st Battalion, 66th Armor, advanced to Vengeons. After working through a minefield, Task Force Cox halted at 2130 hours just east of the town.[41]

In his letter to his wife, Celeste, Lt. Lewis Sasser described some of the close calls he had experienced recently:

Have had artillery hit all over that tank of mine without ever getting a direct hit with anything big enough to do the job. Am convinced that I've been shot at with everything the Germans have for putting out tanks. Think I hate those anti-tank guns worse when they're firing direct. Can never be quite sure where they're coming from and they have a horrible zoom when that high muzzle velocity passes by your ears. Was under an apple tree one day trying to pick out some targets on the opposite hill when bang, bang— they started coming in. Radioed down to my driver to slap it in reverse and get in farm house defilade. Before he could get it backed up one came directly overhead and filled the turret with apples and leaves from the tree. Then after we got behind the building they hit that from the other side and the building fell over us.

So far I'm still without a scratch. Was the lead platoon coming down exposed hill when they let loose some big artillery on us and in the course of the serenade some stuff flew in the turret where I was "peeking" out and laid open a hole in my steel helmet. Had just enough protection on my head because it not only went thru my helmet but thru my crash helmet which I had under it. Felt it hit my head and thought, "Well, this is like I've always heard and hoped—it stuns you and feels numb but doesn't hurt". Took off my helmet and felt my head only to find there wasn't anything but a scratch.

That same afternoon we had to advance past an ammunition truck which we had set fire to and was burning and exploding all the time. Went as far around it as possible but just as I was on a line with it one of the explosions put a short piece of burning 2 x 4 right down my back in the turret. Didn't know what had hit me on the back and when we finally figured out what that chunk of burning matter was on the turret floor, tossed it out in a hurry. Thoroughly expected it to explode until after we'd thrown it out the turret and cooled off we realized what it was.

Will try to write you more regularly but usually when we're battling it up till dark and then the artillery zooms around too much to do anything with a pen....[42]

On 13 August Task Force Cox advanced through Sourdeval and halted at its objective one mile south of town. There, at 0830, the 3rd Battalion passed through and assumed the lead. The 3rd Battalion, with infantrymen riding on their tanks, moved south to the Ger-Mortain road and then turned east toward Ger. They were screened by the regimental Reconnaissance Company as they advanced slowly over the difficult terrain. The battalion halted for the night approximately three and one half miles west of Ger, after encountering only light and scattered resistance during the day.[43] On 14 August the 3rd Battalion advanced to three miles southeast of Ger. The 1st Battalion moved to an assembly area southwest of Ger and the 2nd Battalion remained in XIX Corps reserve.

At 0800 hours 15 August, the 3rd Battalion, 66th Armor, with the 1st Battalion, 112th Infantry, and followed by the 1st Battalion of the 66th, moved out with the mission of seizing Hill 329. The column crossed the Egrenne River at Lonlay l'Abbaye and turned northeast toward Hill 329. The column fought through occasional antitank fire as it advanced to Hill 329 and several secondary objectives of the road junctions in the vicinity of the hill. By 1330 hours they secured Hill 329 and the road network in the area of the hill, establishing road blocks.[44] Sergeant Gatzke recorded in his journal the successful turkey shoot of one of their tanks:

> Lt. Gwinn had a field day with his tank. He got in position on a German convoy and knocked out the whole works, artillery pieces, tanks, trucks, the works.[45]

Lieutenant Herbert Gwinn received a battlefield commission in Normandy. As a sergeant in Company H he had been heavyweight boxing champion of the division. He had also survived the destruction of seven tanks. After his promotion in Normandy he was transferred to Company F and soon lost an arm in the fighting.[46]

The 2nd Battalion was released from corps reserve and joined the rest of the regiment. As the 66th rolled across France, one tank crew witnessed something very unlike the characteristic French response to liberation:

> I remember our tank approaching the edge of this town when we saw an old man standing outside, hollering and raising his arm up and shouting Heil Hitler! When he realized we were Americans he knelt down on his hands and knees and started crying.[47]

On 16 August the regiment was ordered to the 2nd Armored Division assembly area near Barenton for forty-eight hours of maintenance and re-habilitation. At the assembly area, an army inspection team examined the vehicles, giving the regiment a high rating on vehicle maintenance. The inspectors also checked clothing and equipment. The next day, 18 August 1944, the regiment road marched eighty-four miles east to Sees and then moved another thirty-eight miles to Longy Due Perche. This long march was part of the Allied effort to destroy the German 7th and 15th Armies that had been squeezed into a narrow corridor centered on the town of Falaise. In another diary entry, Sgt. Arden Gatzke, a tank commander in Company H, remembered the roadmarch:

> Fri. 17 Aug. Changed oil in tank 1am. Then went on an 83 mile road march on blacktop roads. It was HOT and the tank treads tore up the blacktop and the fumes got into our eyes. We got to Sees, but we couldn't see. If the Germans would have attacked very few of us would have been able to fight.[48]

As the Germans sought to escape the trap, American units rushed east to close the narrow escape route. The 66th Armor, which had contributed its share of tanks and lives, had finally broken the Allies out of the hedgerow country.

After fighting for yards in the hedgerows of Normandy the tanks were finally out in the open countryside with the Germans on the run. Lieutenant Sasser wrote:

> Have seen some perfectly beautiful country and quite a bit of it too. One day we came 75 miles in $7^1/_2$ hours—not bad time for a tank column. Several days we've done 50 or more.[49]

This breakout led to the final disintegration of German forces in Normandy. The Battle of the Falaise Pocket resulted in the destruction of hundreds of irreplaceable German tanks and vehicles and the death or capture of over 80,000 German soldiers.[50]

On the morning of 20 August, the regiment, as part of CCA, attacked north with CCB on their left and the 30th Infantry Division on their right. Led by the Reconnaissance Company, the force moved northeast toward the Aure River, where it halted about twelve miles northwest of Longny for the night. The next day, with the 3rd Battalion in the left column, the 2nd Battalion on the right, and the 1st Battalion as the reserve, CCA crossed the Aure River and secured for the night at Roman and Damville, respectively. During the two-day advance, the regiment lost only one man killed and one wounded against the diminishing and weak German resistance.[51]

On 22 August the 66th, with the 2nd Battalion in the lead, crossed the Iton River and continued the attack north, securing the high ground near Bonneville at 2030 hours. During the advance, the regiment captured approximately 400 prisoners and killed some 80 Germans who resisted the onslaught. Company H, attached to the 2nd Battalion, 41st Armored Infantry, reached a point three miles northeast of Conches before stopping for the night.[52]

The entire regiment was ordered north to the Seine River on the morning of 23 August. The 2nd Battalion moved out at 0630 hours, crossed the Iton River and raced north toward Elbeuf on the Seine. The battalion destroyed some 100 German vehicles as they dashed to escape across the Seine at Elbeuf. The 2nd Battalion stopped for the night near Fouqueville, where their roadblocks took a heavy toll on German personnel and vehicles as they sought to escape. The 3rd Battalion likewise reached the Fouqueville-Elbeuf road, established roadblocks and waited for the escaping Germans to come to them. During this time, troopers of the 66th destroyed or captured one Mark IV and three Mark V Panther tanks, six rocket launchers *(Nebelwerfers)*, seven scout cars and fifty horse-drawn carts. Two soldiers of the regiment won the Silver Star for attacking a German Tiger tank and setting it afire with a thermite grenade.[53]

Again Sergeant Gatzke recorded in his diary some of the destruction as the German army sought to escape to the east:

> Thu. 23 Aug. Still going. Shot up so much equipment we lost count on what we destroyed.

> Fri. 24 Aug.   Still going. My tank alone shot up 17 German vehicles.[54]

The regiment continued its advance on 24 August with all three battalions blocking the roads leading to bridges at Elbeuf. Numerous German tanks and other vehicles were destroyed as they tried to get through the increasingly tight seal the regiment was putting around the west side of Elbeuf.[55] The ever intensifying destruction of the German army at the Falaise Gap was described by Lieutenant Smith of Company H. He wrote:

> ...caught a Bn (battalion) of infantry on the road, captured about 250 and no telling how many we killed. Destroyed a few vehicles and weapons.

> Aug 23 We advanced 31 miles through enemy territory and destroyed 64 German vehicles and have no idea of prisoners. Two of those vehicles were Mark 5 Panther tanks and 6 were Nebelwerfers.[56]

The 1st Battalion and its attachments attacked at 0700 hours to cut a road running west out of Elbeuf. A massive concentration of German direct and indirect fire halted the attack, and not even the Air Force could silence it. The battalion was ordered back to La Saussay and closed there at 2130. The 2nd Battalion also encountered tough German resistance but finally overcame it at 2000 hours and secured the right flank sector of Elbeuf. Company D lost two tanks, and the Germans lost three Mark IV and two Mark V tanks in the battle. The casualty list of the regiment was again an entire page in length, just as it had been in the bloody hedgerow fighting a month earlier.[57]

One wounded company commander wrote home to his mother from his hospital bed in England. This letter expressed his experiences and feelings since landing in Normandy:

> Death and destruction in all its horrible shapes and forms have become so common to me in the last two years and especially the last two months that the full import of it no longer registers and my emotions remain unruffled just like the G.I. who can eat "C" rations beside dead men and with great relish too. I have seen civilians, starved and naked, clutching unweaned babies walking or running barefooted, machine gunned, bombed and thrown into ditches to rot. I've seen our own tanks run over German bodies in the road because no one could expose himself to remove them.

Because of all that and much more too, Mother I am very stable now, I have learned the values. I have learned to know when I know not and also when I know. Yet don't suppose for a minute it has not made me more pitying and more kindly toward all mankind because it has. I can still appreciate a baby's whimper or the hurt feelings of a friend. I am still most human. Even more so than when I left. Any change that war has wrought in me has definitely been for the better.

One thing I have learned to love 150 men in my outfit more than anything else on earth. They are simply magnificent, fighting demons. Loyal and true—every one—ready to give their full measure—so trusting. I'm not doing them much good here where I am now except I sleep well knowing they're well-trained anyway and I'll rejoin them soon. They've already accounted for many times over their number and by now Lord knows what the future is. Well, these bustling wardboys have brought fruit cocktail now so will stop.[58]

The action died down on 26 August, and that night the 1st and 2nd Battalions withdrew to an assembly area after being relieved. The difficulties and dangers of roadmarching tanks at night are considerable. Sergeant Gatzke's diary gives one example he and his crew experienced:

...took a night march from Venon. Blackout driving. Could only see very small red lights on rear of tank ahead. Tank in front of us stopped and my driver couldn't stop in time without hitting him so he swerved to the right of the tank and came up along the side of it. Our tank tread was right on the edge of a cliff that went straight down about 20 feet.[59]

On 28 August the entire regiment moved to the division area near Lommoye, forty miles southeast of Elbeuf. On 30 August the regiment crossed the Seine River and advanced northeast in two columns against light resistance. On the thirty-first the Reconnaissance Company captured two German medium bombers during the day's fifty-six-mile advance.[60]

In a letter home to his wife, Lieutenant Sasser related his experience with liberating a French town:

Don't think I told you about getting kissed by a strange woman. Was the lead tank the other day into a fairly large town and being the first Americans to arrive and the Germans retreating the people were quite jubilant. Finally when we had outposted the town with tanks and I came back to my tank in the square quite a crowd had gathered and started the routine of hand shaking which goes along with the "Vivas this" and "Vivas that." Everybody started taking our pictures as usual and we passed out that town's ration of cigarettes. One old boy stepped up for his cigarettes and another one pounced him right off. Said he had been taking from the Germans and now that we were there the other people weren't going to have him taking from us too. What threw me though was this nicely-dressed middle-aged woman who came up to me, planted her hands—one on each shoulder—and let me have a big one on each cheek. Had to retreat to the confines of my steel-walled tank.[61]

During the month of August 1944, the 66th Armor captured 2,510 prisoners, destroyed or captured 62 tanks, 28 antitank guns, and 264 other vehicles. The regiment's losses in personnel for the same period totaled 64 killed, 196 wounded, and 37 missing.[62]

While moving rapidly across the fields of northeastern France, Lieutenant Colonel Herkness noticed two men he took to be French peasants trying to flag down the approaching American tanks. Herkness ordered his tank to a halt at the side of the road to see what information the two might have to offer. Herkness was stunned when one of the men enthusiastically greeted him with a thick southern accent. The two men were downed U.S. Army Air Force flyers who had been in hiding with the French underground.

On 1 September the regiment began advancing rapidly in two columns northeast into the Somme region of northeastern France. Passing through the Somme, the American tankers saw the many tiny British and Canadian cemeteries that dotted the landscape from the last war with Germany. During a brief halt, Captain Burt found a helmet from the First War partially rusted away lying in the brush.[63] The left column, commanded by the regimental commander, Colonel Stokes, was headed by 3rd Battalion. The 2nd Battalion, 66th Armor, and the 2nd Battalion, 41st Armored Infantry, headed the right column. The two elements advanced fifty-seven miles to the vicinity of the Somme River and the Canal de la Seusee.[64] Ironically, the 1st Battalion in the division reserve, which was following behind the rest of the division, saw the only serious action that day when it fought several enemy units that tried to pass through the battalion's assembly area near Albert.

One night in the 1st Battalion's bivouac area near Albert was an exciting one for many soldiers. CWO John Derden was late getting in after having stopped to repair the clutch on a motorcycle. Derden was in his jeep stopped in a sunken road talking to his sergeant who was standing by his half-track on the bank above the road. Suddenly a large amount of small arms and tank fire was heard close by. Chief Derden describes what followed during what had become a very long night:

> I heard what I identified as a German half-track coming our way. My driver and I got out of our jeep and got on the bank opposite from my sergeant and the rest of the crew. Almost that instant this German

half-track came down the hill too fast to stop and ran into my jeep and wrecked it. The half-track was loaded with Germans and was towing a 75mm anti-tank gun and had mounted on the half-track a dual 20mm flak gun. I got off the jeep too fast to get my tommy gun...and all I had was my .45 cal. automatic. The Germans were so close I could have almost reached out and shook their hands.

While they were trying to get untangled from my jeep and backing up I figured my sergeant would start firing with .50 cal. machine gun on his half-track and knew he would hit me because I was laying in the weeds directly opposite the Germans. He didn't fire because he couldn't get the gun untangled from a camouflage net luckily for me. As soon as the Germans untangled they unhooked the anti-tank gun and left it in the middle of the road. As they started to move I emptied my .45 at them from about 20 feet and hit some because they started to holler. The half-track sped up and failed to make a 90° turn and went into what turned out to be an old World War I trench about 100 yards from where I was. I got up and got my tommy gun from the jeep and climbed up the bank to where my maintenance crew was and we tried to get the .50 cal. MG untangled but in the dark we couldn't see how.

By this time the German half-track crew was beginning to get organized and managed to fire the 20mm gun but the half-track had turned on its side and they couldn't aim their gun in our direction. We were bivouaced on an open hill side and had several fuel and ammo trucks just above us. I knew if they hit a fuel truck and it started burning and lit the area the Germans would wipe us out with that 20mm gun. So I did the only thing I could do, I took the tommy gun and crawled under cover of some bushes to within 25 yards of the German half-track. They were all in a bunch trying to lift the half-track. I took good aim, lying flat on the ground and emptied a full 30 round clip. They really hollered and screamed and everything got quiet.

I crawled back to our position and then all hell broke loose. One of our tanks at a nearby cross roads knocked out 16 enemy vehicles that had tried to run his roadblock. As soon as this quieted down, I reloaded my tommy gun. I heard some hob-nailed boots hitting the ground in the sunken road by my wrecked jeep. I waited until they had gotten slightly past my position. The moon was shining enough so I could make out the shape of their helmets and see their black high top boots. There were three Germans walking abreast and the one nearest to me had what looked like a pistol in his hand pointed down the road. I squatted down behind the left front wheel of my half-track. I hollered "Halt" and the German nearest to me emptied his pistol at the front of the half-track and one threw a grenade over the half-track. Almost the same instant I opened up with tommy gun and got the guy that had fired at me. The two others dropped to the ground and started crawling down the road. I hit one in the rear end and he laid in a ditch and hollered for a long time. The third one got away.

After things quieted down and I got my men organized for the worst, I decided I better go to the Bn. CP and let them know that we had Germans in the Maintenance and Supply trains area. Upon arriving at the CP I found things pretty well stirred up. The half-track that ran into my jeep had also run through the Bn. CP and wounded the Bn. XO and four other men.

The next morning a search of the area produced about 30 prisoners, all of them SS troops. The German half-track with the 20mm flak gun had been abandoned but seven dead Germans lay around it. The reason for all this activity was caused by my unit bivouacking on the edge of a forest with a German SS battalion bivouaced deeper in the forest unbeknownst to us. When it got dark and we were settled down they decided to make a run for it.[65]

Several months later Sgt. Kenneth Grogan wrote in a letter about the headlong pursuit across northern France:

I never knew one company could get so many objectives in a days time. One time we were in the attack for a solid week....We didn't even have maps of where we were going during those days—It was just like a duck hunt.[66]

The reception by the French people as the 66th raced across France moved many of the soldiers that witnessed it first hand when their tanks were the first Allied forces to enter a French town. Lieutenant Sasser wrote:

Have seen some happy people and wish I had time to help them celebrate. One day we collected 35 eggs, bunches of flowers, plums, apples, pears, peaches, innumerable bottles of wine, cider and beer. The beer varies all the way from a poor home-brew to a very fine brand of bootleg. When you see people standing in front of homes that were bombed the day before and who can still stand there and wave and cheer at you in spite of their personal hardships you realize that you have really freed a lot of people. Our tank has the names of 20 or more towns written in chalk on it by people who would come up to it when we slowed down in a town and write "such and such a town liberated." Quite impressive and I have been extremely touched to see these people so happy—grown men standing there on the side of the road, in so much dust I could hardly stand it, waving both arms; old ladies waving with tears in their eyes and young gals kissing everybody on both cheeks. An experience I know I'll never forget and if I never see a Broadway reception I'll know I've had mine and that it's the real McCoy.[67]

Near the 1st Battalion command post was a refugee home run by the Sisters of Charity. When the Americans arrived, the residents greeted the soldiers and one French woman who spoke English carried a warning. She told them that several hundred SS troops were in the area. The SS had come to the refugee home earlier looking for food and had said that they would return. 1st Battalion deployed in defensive positions and waited for the SS unit to return that night. This report describes what happened in one platoon's area during the fierce night battle:

1st Lt. E. R. Morris, platoon leader of Company "I" in the southwest sector...placed three tanks in position to form a road block and about 2200 a number of vehicles came down the road at quite high speed. The engineer squad, unable to quickly recognize the vehicles as enemy, failed to pull the mines across the road in time to stop the approaching vehicles. By the time they were definitely recognized as German, three half-tracks had passed the roadblock....Sergeants Polley and Duby opened fire on the German vehicles and continued firing until the heat from one burning enemy vehicle forced Sergeant Polley to abandon his tank, which wouldn't start. Sergeant Duby continued firing on vehicles and Germans that had managed to get out of the vehicles. The following morning Lt. Morris checked the knocked out vehicles, some of which were still burning, and found 6 half-tracks, 10 trucks and 2 scout cars which towed a short barreled howitzer each.

The trucks and half-tracks were loaded with munitions, gas, and oil, and the explosions and fire were very large. Burning parts were blown out and some fell inside Sergeant Polley's tank and caused three rounds of 75mm HE to explode, but the tank did not burn and was sent to Maintenance Battalion under its own power for repairs.[68]

The regiment continued its rapid advance northeast on 2 September with the objective of seizing the high ground east of Orchies on the Belgian border. At 1100 hours the leading elements crossed into Belgium, and the left column occupied an assembly area near Bacay, Belgium for the night. On 3 September the regiment (less the 1st Battalion in division reserve) secured an area around Rumes and Croisette, five miles southwest of Tournai. The 66th performed maintenance and swept the surrounding area

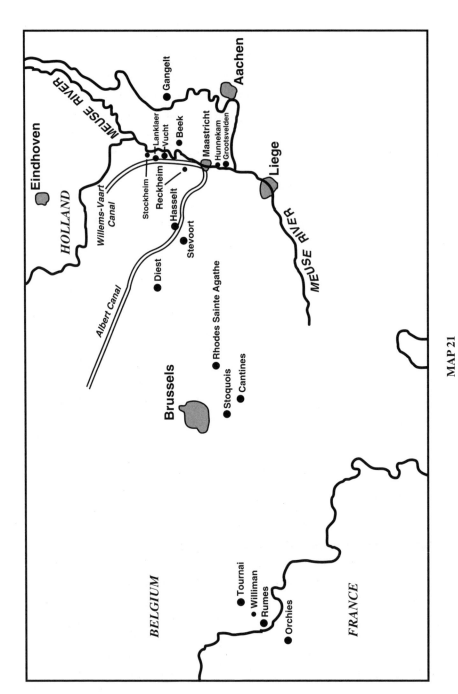

MAP 21
Belgium
September–October 1944

for German troops. The next day the regiment moved two miles northeast to Williman and set up roadblocks and patrolled the area.

The regiment moved out in two columns at dawn on 6 September 1944 to continue the advance through Belgium. The left column, with the 3rd Battalion, was commanded by Lieutenant Colonel Stokes, and the right, with the 2nd Battalion, was commanded by Lieutenant Colonel Herkness, the 2nd Battalion commander. Both columns included attachments of infantry, artillery, tank destroyers, engineers, medical units, supply trains, and maintenance detachments. The right units advanced to near Cantines, and the left reached Stoquois, south of Brussels, having covered an impressive distance of fifty miles. The next day the regiment moved another fifty miles, halting near Reutenbeeke and Rhodes Sainte Agathe seven miles southwest of Louvain. The right column continued to advance to Stevoort and the left flank units to Diest/Kermpt, near Hasselt, for approximately fifty miles with no resistance. The Reconnaissance Company secured a bridge across the Albert Canal on the twelfth. On 14 September the regiment's two columns cleared the west bank of the Willems-Vaart Canal, encountering only light resistance such as mines and harassing artillery fire.[69]

At 0500 hours on 16 September, Lieutenant Colonel Stokes was given the mission of crossing the Willems-Vaart Canal and clearing all enemy forces from the area between the canal and the Meuse River. Task Force Stokes first secured the near bank of the canal as the engineers began constructing a bridge near Reckheim. They finished the bridge quickly while the soldiers on the enemy side of the canal suffered under occasional German artillery fire. At 1000 hours on that same day the lead elements of the task force rolled into Holland. The 1st Battalion, as Task Force C, was released from division reserve and moved to Grootsvelden, Holland and attacked toward Hunnekam at 0700 hours the next day. All forces were slowed by both rainy, foggy weather and inaccurate maps that omitted dikes and streams.[70]

On 17 and 18 September Sergeant Gatzke experienced two of many close calls common to the tankers of the 66th, and especially the tank commanders, who often had their heads up out of the hatch and were more frequently dismounted from the relative protection of the tank.

Sun 17   My tank and a squad of infantry continued between the river and the canal. Infantry squad leader came to my tank to tell me there was a German machine gun firing at them from a corner of the field. While leaning over the edge of the turret those few seconds to talk to him a stream of bullets hit the padding on the turret hatch doors right where my chest would have been if I hadn't been leaning over. We fired one round of high explosive into the corner. There was no more firing from there.

Mon 18. Still going. Tank hit twice by Panzerfaust fire but no damage either time except a piece of shrapnel got embedded in my carbine which was laying on the rim of the turret right in front of my face. A short time later I saw four Germans crouched in the ditch. I pointed the useless carbine at them and they surrendered. I took the officer's P38 pistol.[71]

Task Force Stokes secured Vucht at 0745 hours on 18 September and continued the attack south. Two miles south of town the tankers ran into determined German resistance; four 88mm guns opened fire on the Americans but were knocked out by tank and artillery fire. The entrenched enemy infantry fought fiercely and were, in many areas, killed by grenades, submachine gun and pistol fire from the tankers as they passed. At 1735 the task force had taken their final objective of Lanklaer-Stockheim. The 49th Infantry Division relieved them during the night, and they went into the division reserve near Beek, seven miles northeast of the city of Maastricht, with the 1st and 2nd Battalions securing various road junctions throughout the day.[72]

Task Force C (1st Battalion) with Task Force A (2nd Battalion) on their right advanced eastward, unopposed, to cross the border into Germany north of Aachen at 1400 hours. At 1730 the Germans launched a strong counterattack with eight assault guns and a reinforced infantry regiment. Task Force C held their position while Task Force A, supported by artillery fire, attacked the German forces in the flank and rear. By 2000 hours they had destroyed all eight assault guns and repulsed the counterattack. Between 20 and 21 September the 1st and 2nd Battalions remained in their assembly area just across the German border near Gangelt. They outposted and patrolled the area and hunted for German forces. They defeated one other German counterattack and directed artillery fire onto a German unit during one patrol.[73]

On 24 September the 2nd Battalion attacked German forces in the forests west of Neideheide and Bauchem. The Germans were well-dug-in and supported by antitank guns that destroyed two Sherman tanks and damaged three others. The tanks withdrew to their assembly area behind a smoke screen.[74]

Between the twenty-fourth and the twenty-ninth the regiment engaged in patrolling and maintenance in their assembly areas. The 2nd Battalion became the CCA reserve, and the 3rd Battalion was relieved from corps reserve. On 30 September elements of the 29th Infantry Division relieved the 66th. September had been an easier and less costly month than either of the two preceding ones in France. The regiment lost only eight killed and twenty-four wounded during the entire month.[75]

On 20 September Chaplain Luke Bolin wrote to his wife about some of the Dutch people that the soldiers of the regiment found so friendly and helpful:

> I learned that there is a Protestant Church near here so I called on the minister today. He and his wife and two cute boys, 6 and 8 years old— were tickled pink. They are so happy to get rid of the Huns and now to have an American chaplain call on them caused their cup of joy to run over! I stayed for dinner, took pictures. He showed me his library— several books in English. He and his wife speak English. Saw the church, a home for kids when their parents are sick, club and industrial school for girls. He has a lovely home and a fine set up. They wanted me to stay all night but I couldn't. Probably couldn't sleep in a bed! As we walked along the street I had the hand of a boy on each side and the little one would sing the German song, "Sailing Against England," and his Dad would rebuke him ! We came to the home of an old lady who was sick—she was so pleased when I went in and spoke to her. She is unable to get out and yell at the Americans and sing like the rest. It was good to see a little civilization again but I hardly knew how to act.[76]

Tank company church service in France. Late summer 1944.

Luke Bolin

A rare treat for combat soldiers, Red Cross doughnuts.

Luke Bolin

Three Dutch women with their hair cut for fraternizing with the Germans. September 1944.

Luke Bolin

The welcome in Belgium. Jeep surrounded by jubilant Belgians. September 1944.

Sherman tank of Company F approaches the Dutch-German border in October 1944.

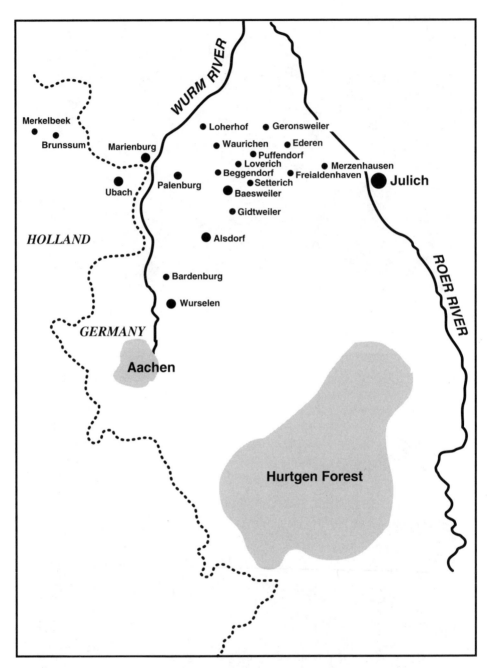

MAP 22
Aachen
September–December 1944

CHAPTER 13

The Siege of Aachen

The 66th Armor was able to take a break from the action in their assembly area near Brunssum, Holland from 1 to 5 October. The men were able to take advantage of the long-awaited showers located at nearby coal mines. For the first time since leaving England four months earlier, the men saw movies and heard live band music. They were given refresher courses in the use of flame throwers against pillboxes in anticipation of breaching the German Siegfried defensive line. On 1 October the regiment had received orders to be prepared to follow CCB of the 2nd Armored Division through a breach in the Siegfried Line made by the 30th Infantry Division. For this offensive, the regiment was organized into two columnar formations, with the left consisting of the 2nd Battalion with normal combined arms attachments of tank destroyers, infantry, artillery, and engineers, and the right with the regimental headquarters and the 1st Battalion organized similarly.[1]

In the late morning of 5 October, the 1st and 2nd Battalions left the assembly area and moved to the bridge over the Wurm River at Marienburg. The left column, with the 2nd Battalion, encountered strong enemy resistance from antitank guns, infantry, and pillboxes as it moved through Marienburg. The resistance and German artillery fire made the advance difficult as the column crossed the river and moved through Palenburg. The right column (1st Battalion) crossed the Wurm River and advanced to one mile west of Baesweiler against heavy resistance.[2]

The attack was a part of the American effort to encircle the city of Aachen, which sat astride the German-Dutch-Belgian border. This ancient capital of the Holy Roman Empire was the first German city to be attacked by Allied ground forces, and Hitler was determined that it should not fall. To the Germans, Aachen was an imperial city where German kings and emperors had been crowned for a thousand years. Its importance to German nationalism was enormous. Therefore, after the pursuit across France, Belgium, and Holland in August, the American forces suddenly ran into a stone wall at Aachen.[3]

After several unsuccessful weeks of trying to take Aachen, the Americans were now working to cut off the city from the rest of Germany. On 6 October the regiment continued its attack to seize the high ground near the village of Oidtweiler. German resistance throughout the attack was heavy. The 66th succeeded in crossing an antitank ditch after the supporting infantry drove some twenty German Panzerfaust teams from its cover. S.Sgt. Richard Hickman earned the Silver Star for commanding the tank bulldozer that filled in the antitank ditch. He bravely dismounted the tank several times under fire to guide the driver. Company I led the attack which secured the high ground near Oidtweiler late in the day. The columns were then ordered to establish 360 degree security with the Aachen-Settrich highway as their front line.[4]

The morning of 7 October saw the 66th resume the attack, with the 2nd Battalion assaulting Baesweiler and the 1st Battalion moving on Oidtweiler. The 2nd Battalion lost two Shermans, one Stuart, and an attached M10 tank destroyer to antitank mines in Baesweiler. After sweeping through the town, the battalion turned south to strike Oidtweiler from the north; at the same time, the 1st Battalion hit the same village from the south. Both battalions lost several Shermans to antitank and assault gun fires during the successful attack. At 1800 hours the battalions established defensive positions in Oidtweiler and southwest of Baesweiler.[5] Col. Ira P. Swift assumed command of the regiment from Lieutenant Colonel Stokes during this period.[6]

Second Battalion commander Lt. Col. Lindsay Herkness established his battalion headquarters in a house in Baesweiler. One of his orders as an occupying commander was that none of the numerous hogs or other livestock in the town were to be harmed. Later that day a half-track accidentally hit and badly injured a stray hog. Called to the accident scene, Herkness shot the injured animal and then told his men that there was no sense in wasting the meat so they could butcher the hog. Within thirty minutes the enterprising men of the battalion had released the town's livestock and were hunting them down with speeding half-tracks. The battalion enjoyed their first taste of German Schnitzel that evening.[7]

During this period, the soldiers of C Company received loaves of bread to supplement their rations. Some of the men sharpened sticks and attempted to toast the bread over a fire. The bread always seemed to twist and fall off the sticks into the fire. One tank commander, Sgt. Patrick Burke, observed the falling toast problem and then went to get some of the plentiful barbed wire from the obstacles of the famed German defensive belt known as the West Wall or the Siegfried Line. Burke cut and shaped a piece of the barbed wire into a long fork complete with coiled wire handle to prevent the toaster's hand from getting burned. The invention was dubbed the West Wall Toaster.[8]

Chaplain Luke Bolin wrote home on 10 October sharing a little of the frustration he was feeling:

> Somewhere in Germany
> 10 October 1944

Dearest Roberta,

> It is cold, wet and miserable. I am sitting on my bed with my feet under a blanket to keep them warm. My morale is low. I hold all the services I can for my men. I make them as dignified as possible and preach the best sermons I can. But the Div. Chaplain brought a letter. He apologetically said it wasn't for me; that he was simply passing it on to Protestant Chaplains! It burnt me up anyway. A chaplain, who probably lives in a nice heated trailer, who is never close enough to the front to be in danger, tells us to hold more dignified services, to hold at least 3 on Sunday and one each week day!! He sarcastically says that why we don't have a service every day is a dark mystery to him. It's no mystery to us and wouldn't be to him if he had a little more idea of what it means to be a combat chaplain. I told the Div. chaplain to tell him that I didn't in the least appreciate such B.S. and that if he had some conception of our problems he wouldn't put out such hash!

> Roberta, life isn't easy and I am happy to be able to impart a little hope and love into the lives of the men and they appreciate it too. Sharing some of their dangers and trying to give them hope in life and in death is indeed a rewarding experience but you know that I am too independent to take the jaw from anybody who doesn't know what he is talking about.[9]

The 1st and 2nd Battalions of the regiment were dug in on the front line generally along a line from Beggendorf-Baesweiler-Oidtweiler. The

1st Battalion, plus Company E and attached infantry, attacked through the woods north of Oidtweiler and cleared it of German troops. From 9 through 11 October, the 66th (less the 3rd Battalion in Division reserve) continued to hold the line north of Aachen, despite frequent rain turning the ground to mud. The tankers came under attack from German aircraft at night, mortar and artillery fire all the time, and even a massive 240mm railroad gun that threw shells the size of a jeep at the Americans. The German civilians, however, were well-behaved, and all claimed to hate the Nazis.[10]

Many of the GIs found Germany to be very interesting and quite "contemporary." Captain Warren wrote home on 10 October with some observations on the German homes:

> Their homes are the most modern I have seen since arriving overseas. They are quite cozy and comfortable with a lot of modern fixtures we regard as the modernistic pattern in our newer American homes— for example, nicely styled radio-phonographs—lovely oak twin beds with mirrored dresser and clothes closet to match. I am writing on a kitchen table whose top is a linoleum composition just like the newest products put out at Armstrongs.
>
> Curiously enough all the rooms, almost without exception, and I have seen many, are adorned with crucifixes of Christ, pictures depicting religious life by the score, the last supper, the pastor with his flock, and plenty of prayerbooks.[11]

On 12 October 1944 the 3rd Battalion was attached to the 116th Infantry Regiment of the 30th Infantry Division at Bardenburg. The regiment's mission was to attack toward Wurselen with the goal of cutting the routes leading north and northwest out of Aachen. The attack south began on 13 October, with each of the three tank companies (G, H, and B) attached to a battalion of the 116th Infantry. The attack advanced slowly over the next several days as the Germans fought with everything they had. Their resistance was so intense on 16 October that the American battalion was unable to advance even three hundred yards as they had done the day before. German attacks were frequent and employed heavy concentrations of mortar and artillery fire, a desperate bid to keep Aachen from being encircled.[12]

Staff Sergeant Rape was a platoon leader in H Company when he and his tank commanders radioed the German farmhouse that served as the H Company headquarters. There Captain Warren explained the situation:

> There's a light tank company cut off in a little village about a mile from here. He told me, "I'm going to send you and your platoon up there because of the fire power of your 76mm guns. There's a soldier

in a jeep who will lead you down this farm road and will show you an open field that the Germans have zeroed in on that you will have to cross." As we crossed that open field, it was getting dark. The Germans threw everything at us but the kitchen sink. When we got into the little village, I made radio contact with the company commander of the light tank company. He said, "We're going to jump off around daylight tomorrow. If we get in trouble, you come on and give us some more firepower." They jumped off the next morning as planned. After about 400 yards, the Germans started shooting those light tanks out from under them. The company commander called me and said, "Come on, we're in trouble!" We took off and came through their position and took the top of the hill. Fritz and Holland were laying down artillery fire and machine gunfire on the right flank, and my other two tanks and I were laying down artillery and machine gun fire on the left flank and straight ahead. The Germans had the infantry pinned down with machine guns in the hedgerow in front of me. I tried to find the machine gun in the hedgerow that had them pinned down through the periscopic sight on my tank. I couldn't find him so I opened the hatch and stood up to look. He hit me in the left shoulder, left hand and broke my arm. I was still conscious. I called down to my driver, "I'm hit, back up behind this hill." They got me out of the tank. As the medics were working on me, a sergeant from the light tank company said they were still cut off. I was bleeding badly when the sergeant said,"If you want to take a chance, we'll try to get you out of here." Before I was evacuated, I asked for my gunner, Frank Bisogno, and my section commander, Jack Holland. I told Jack that he would have to be platoon leader, and I told Frank that he would have to be the tank commander in my tank.

The light tank sergeant took a door from the village and made an improvised stretcher on the back of one of the light tanks. With Staff Sergeant Rape lying on the exposed back deck of the Stuart, they raced back across the same field Rape had crossed the previous evening, again under heavy German fire. The Stuart sergeant got Rape to an ambulance that carried him to a field hospital. After an immediate blood transfusion, he was taken to a hospital near Leige, where he was put in a cast from the waist up and put on a hospital train. Staff Sergeant Rape then began a journey through a series of hospitals in a body cast all the way back to the U.S. The body cast was not removed until June 1945. Staff Sergeant Rape was finally medically discharged in July 1945, ten long months after being wounded.[13]

Captain Burt's B Company was one of the three 66th Armor tank companies attached to the 2nd Battalion, 116th Infantry. Within the first several days of intense fighting in the streets, the 2nd Battalion, 116th Infantry had lost its commander, executive officer, S-3, and all the officers of the infantry companies. With only the S-2 and S-4 officers remaining in the infantry battalion, Captain Burt became the acting battalion commander. This situation was made all the more curious because the 116th Infantry was part of another division.[14]

The 3rd Battalion and its infantry reached the road on the northern edge of Wurselen on 15 October. The units held there against repeated German counterattacks and shelling until relieved on 22 October. This week-long battle was the hardest the regiment had experienced since Normandy. The 3rd Battalion suffered in both men and tanks but held the line against the German assaults.

Capt. Cam Warren was talking to his 2nd platoon leader, Lieutenant William C. McCully, on the radio during the vicious street fighting to coordinate the movement forward with the infantry. Lieutenant McCully was in mid-sentence speaking to his commander when his transmission was cut off. McCully's tank had been hit by a German tank round erupting in a fireball killing the entire crew of the Sherman.[15]

Sergeant Gatzke recorded some of the action that took place in Wurselen on 15 and 16 October:

Sun. 15 Oct.   Attacked Wurslen. Got through town after dark. Went about a hundred yards past the last group of houses and pulled up behind a brick house and brick fence. The road in front of the house was the dividing line between us and the Germans. One tank of ours got hit and the tank commander got a broken arm. As he jumped off the tank he broke both ankles. He then ran back about a hundred yards to the nearest house. Rest of the crew unhurt. We were under heavy artillery fire all night. Raining.

Mon. 16 Oct.   In the morning when it started getting light I told Lt. Coneally we better back up a little to get more protection from the house. (Lt. Coneally had just graduated from Officers Candidate School, what we called 90 day wonders. Even though he was the platoon leader of five tanks, he told me to tell him what to do until he learned a little bit of how things were run which I understood was something most of the others didn't do. He learned fast too). As we started backing up we heard the sharp crack of an 88mm shell going by. Lt. Coneally asked how close I thought it was to hitting us. I pointed to where our radio antenna had been clipped off just about four inches above the tank. Six inches lower and this would probably not be written.[16]

Captain Burt put his company executive officer and the two remaining infantry officers in a cellar where they could keep in communication with their headquarters and keep the flow of supplies, artillery and air support coming. The infantry battalion had also lost all of its artillery forward observers in the earlier fighting. Artillery support, up to and including Corps Artillery, was often requested by Captain Burt and one of his enlisted soldiers.[17]

Ever since landing in Normandy, B Company had worked with the same squadron of P-47s whenever the tankers needed close air support. During lulls in combat, the tankers of the 66th visited the squadron at their airfield and the pilots would visit the tankers. Captain Burt wrote:

> ...this cemented the linkage between our support air and ourselves and it paid off immensely all the way across Europe. We could trust them to know where we were, to know who we were.

During the bitter house to house fighting, the P-47s delivered a successful air strike on the house just across the street from the schoolhouse in which the Americans were. The Americans in the courtyard of the school were showered with the .50 caliber links and spent casing as the fighters strafed the house. On the planes' next pass they were able to see the markings on the bombs as they fell.[18]

In the urban fighting, the men of B Company and the 2-116 Infantry captured some of the best and most unusual weapons in the German arsenal. The infantry used a bazooka to blow the track off a massive German *Jagdpanther* (Hunting Panther). This awesome version of the Panther tank mounted the famed 88mm gun and was the most lethal of a long line of German tank destroyers. Upon inspection it was found that the gun muzzle was covered and the chamber was empty. Apparently the *Jagdpanther* was en route back to its unit when it became lost and fell into the Americans' hands. Another day the Americans captured a German assault rifle with an attachment designed to shoot around corners in urban combat. It resembled a ten gauge shotgun with a ninety degree barrel.[19]

In the Aachen Gap fighting, the Americans were amused by the German propaganda leaflets that were dropped one night. Using American slang, the leaflets said in part, "Oh my Aachen back." The leaflet went on to tell the Americans of the formation of the new Ninth Army under General William H. Simpson,"If you weren't aching and hurting so bad they wouldn't have organized a new army to bail you out."[20]

On two occasions the German traits of discipline and routine helped save Americans lives. Every morning for several days a German mortar crew would begin their daily routine. With remarkable precision the mortar would fall on a certain point in the street; the rounds were then walked down the street at precise intervals, turned a corner, and walked down the next street. The best part for the Americans was when they confirmed that the mortar barrage would begin precisely every seventeen minutes. The well-disciplined German mortar unit allowed the Americans fifteen-minute periods during which they could move with some degree of freedom and safety.

The second occasion was after the infantry battalion had received some replacement officers. The plan was to capture several houses, starting with sneaking some infantry through an apple orchard. The new infantry officer led his men into the orchard where he was hit and wounded. His men made it to the other side and Captain Burt related what happened next:

> I figured that he had been hit by a burp gun from a cellar window. Before too long we could get some artillery on that house, but I immediately wanted to reassure the four or five men who were beyond that point that they were OK and needed to stay put. So I trotted through the orchard and leaped as though going over a hurdle at what I figured was the burp gun alley. And sure enough, a burst went right under me. I talked to the boys and then had to return. I figured that the burp gun was on a bipod fixed position to control that alley. Would it stay that way or would it change? By then we had a pretty good idea of the German discipline, so I gambled that he would have made no change. So I returned, hurdled at the same point, and again a burst went under me.[21]

The fierce fighting in the streets of Wurselen and Aachen was not without its rare moments of humor. Captain Burt and his tank crew witnessed the following incident:

> One day in the house fighting, I observed a line of German troops in single file at dogtrot come from behind a building. I don't know how large the unit was, but six or seven of them had exposed themselves. I told my gunner to swing his turret and I drew my pistol and took aim. At that point—and things were happening pretty fast—the German soldiers in single file dogtrotting saw me, and without a command because there wasn't time, but with perfect precision, they then dogtrotted backwards out of sight behind the house. I burst out laughing and never shot my pistol and never told my gunner to shoot either.[22]

The actions of Capt. James M. Burt, the commander of Company B, resulted in his receipt of the Medal of Honor. Unique for the period of time

Pvt. Morris Radkoff, Pvt. Albert Shaffer, and Pfc. Irvin Schweig of HQ Company, 2nd Battalion enjoy a *Life* Magazine during a lull in combat. October 1944.

U.S. Army Military History Institute

Capt. James M. Burt receiving the Medal of Honor from President Harry Truman in August 1945. The medal was awarded for his actions as tank company commander during the encirclement of Aachen in October 1944.

James M. Burt

it covers, this citation for his country's highest decoration reveals the intensity of the battle:

> Capt. James M. Burt was in command of Company B, 66th Armored Regiment on the western outskirts of Wurselen, Germany, on 13 October 1944, when his organization participated in a coordinated infantry-tank attack destined to isolate the large German garrison which was tenaciously defending the city of Aachen. In the first day's action, when infantrymen ran into murderous small-arms and mortar fire, Capt. Burt dismounted from his tank about 200 yards to the rear and moved forward on foot beyond the infantry positions, where, as the enemy concentrated a tremendous volume of fire upon him, he calmly motioned his tanks into good firing positions. As our attack gained momentum, he climbed aboard his tank and directed the action from the rear deck, exposed to hostile volleys which finally wounded him painfully on the face and neck. He maintained his dangerous post despite pointblank self-propelled gunfire until friendly artillery knocked out these enemy weapons, and then proceeded to the advanced infantry scouts' positions to deploy his tanks for the defense of the gains which had been made. The next day, when the enemy counterattacked, he left cover and went 75 yards through heavy fire to assist the infantry battalion commander who was seriously wounded. For the next 8 days, through rainy, miserable weather and under constant, heavy shelling, Capt. Burt held the combined forces together, dominating and controlling the critical situation through the sheer force of his heroic example. To direct artillery fire, on 15 October, he took his tank 300 yards into the enemy lines, where he dismounted and remained for 1 hour giving accurate data to friendly gunners. Twice more that day he went into enemy territory under deadly fire in reconnaissance. In succeeding days he never faltered in his determination to defeat the strong German forces opposing him. Twice the tank in which he was riding was knocked out by enemy action, and each time he climbed aboard another vehicle and continued to fight. He took great risks to rescue wounded comrades and inflicted prodigious destruction on enemy personnel and materiel even though suffering from the wounds he received in the battle's opening phase. Capt. Burt's intrepidity and disregard of personal safety were so complete that his own men were inspired to overcome the wretched and extremely hazardous conditions which accompanied one of the most bitter local actions of the war. The victory achieved closed the Aachen gap.[23]

After being relieved and detached from the 30th Infantry Division on 22 October, the 3rd Battalion moved to the vicinity of Ubach and was placed in the division reserve.

While in division reserve Captain Warren wrote to Carol a little bit about the previous days in combat:

> ...My 1st Sgt.—a peach of a fellow—just brought me some hot co- coa—Nestle's, as a matter of fact—his folks sent it to him—got my laundry caught up on today too. The last ten days have been awfully rugged—no shoes or clothes off for about 7 days and nites—you can imagine how foul a person becomes. But if one dwelled on the grisly aspects of this thing—all the friends he's lost or things he's seen, he'd never hold himself together so, you see, we teach ourselves to forget quickly—I try to avoid looking at all dead men and it goes easier that way.... Don't worry Darling—I'll write soon again—To be a plagiarist from some smart G.I. "Oceans of love and a kiss on every wave"—C.J.

P.S. Why don't you come over for Sadie Hawkins Day?[24]

During the week that the 3rd Battalion was in action, the rest of the 66th remained on line, repelling occasional German attacks and being shelled almost daily. The period of 23–28 October was also spent holding the defensive line north of Aachen. On the twenty-eighth the regiment turned over their sector to the 1st Battalion, 405th Infantry. The 2nd Battalion moved to an assembly area near Indenboden on 29 October. The 1st Battalion moved first to Merklebeek and then to Neerbeek on the thirtieth. The 3rd Battalion remained at Ubach in CCA reserve. The regiment ended the month resupplying and performing maintenance in preparation for the winter. Troops cleaned equipment and restowed it on all the vehicles. The regiment's tanks received a new item of equipment that was badly needed in northern Europe during the soggy autumn months. The tank tracks were fitted with steel extensions or grousers, nicknamed duckbills, effectively widening the track and enabling the tank to better cross marshy terrain.[25] It was hoped that this might help alleviate tank losses for the regiment, which during October had been fourteen Shermans and four Stuarts.[26]

From 1 to 16 November the elements of the regiment remained in their assembly areas near the Dutch-German border. The units engaged in winterization of all vehicles, maintenance, and training. Sergeant Gatzke's diary entries for some of the days in the assembly areas:

> 7 tue.   Signed payroll. Roosevelt beat Dewey in election. Skipped Calisthenics.

8 wed.   Lt. Victor Schultz killed by sniper in Jallaucourt, France. He was a High School classmate of mine.

9 thur.   Snowed. Got tank "Houdini" with 76mm gun. 66 Armd. Reg. xmas card to Betty.

11 sat.   Walked a mile for a shower. Lt. Gunderson took over platoon again. Lt. Coneally still in Company. I took over as tank commander again in "Homesick" with a 75mm gun.

12 sun.   Got 6 Div. xmas cards to mail out. Been raining for past two weeks. Muddy as hell.[27]

On 5 November Lt. Lewis Sasser wrote to his wife on their second wedding anniversary. This letter provides a typical example of how a soldier traveled great distances behind the Allied front lines:

Happy Anniversary! Do mean it even if this is too much of a remote method of saying it. I had hoped I might be with you to celebrate this day but maybe next year this time we can make up for some of the time we've lost being together. Always thought of people who had been married this long as old married people but now that I've been I certainly don't feel that way. Now to tell you about the rest of my journey back Tuesday from Paris. It was some job getting back.

My first ride took me about 50 or so miles where I had to take another road and wait while the M.P. (Military Police) there found me a ride. Got several small rides that afternoon and ended up in a fair sized town. The M.P. Lt. asked me up to his quarters here which were in a house they had taken over. Got a good meal, shave, wash and listened to the radio for a while. Finally decided to see if I could find anything traveling at night and finally got a ride about 50 miles in a peep or jeep.

This ride brought me a little more than halfway back to camp and found myself in a good sized town with no traffic and every place closed. Did find a bar in a hotel that was closed but still lighted up inside. Tried to get something to warm me up and the proprietor fixed me some coffee....was finally offered a room in the hotel, which I took rather than risk waiting on a ride in the cold night.

I had the hotel proprietor wake me up at 6 and headed on again without breakfast. However, the first ride I got was with a truck going to a hospital so had breakfast there and caught a ride on in my direction...I knew once I got far enough forward I would run across some division vehicles which I did early in the afternoon. Found a quarter ton truck which took me by the Medical Battalion where I checked back in and recovered my pistol which I had left before the pass.

Lt. John Roller, platoon leader in D Company, beside his Sherman tank "Dodo." Spring 1944.

John B. Roller

I did have one unusual thing happen to me this day. When I left the hospital I got a ride to a small Belgian town where there was one M.P. directing traffic. Had arranged with him for a ride when a man came up to me and asked if I'd like to come have breakfast with him. Told the M.P. to call me if a ride came and went with the man to his home where he and his wife fixed me a wonderful breakfast: two eggs, toast, jam, coffee, and an apple. Enjoyed this second breakfast quite thoroughly and sat and talked with the couple till the M.P. found a ride. Turned out the man was a professor of government and always had an American in once a day to eat.

But, the important thing was that I finally did get back to my outfit about 4 Wednesday afternoon....

Have been thinking about 2 years ago all day. We are having Kentucky weather here now. Could use that good dinner we had that night now. This time last year I was in Sicily and hope I do as much traveling in the next year but in a different direction.[28]

On 11 November the 1st Battalion was designated as part of Task Force B of CCA, and the 3rd Battalion was assigned to CCB. During this time, 1st Sgt. Pelah Gilley was fatally injured when he rescued a small Dutch boy from beneath a falling wall on 9 November. For this act, he was posthumously awarded the Soldier's Medal, a decoration given to those who save the life of another in a noncombat situation.[29]

On 17 November the 2nd Battalion moved to Beggendorf as part of Task Force A. At 0700 hours the task force attacked northeast toward Loverich and Puffendorf. Although Puffendorf had just recently been occupied by CCB, the task force ran into heavy German resistance there. Eventually, the town was taken from the German tank and infantry units but not without the loss of four Shermans and one Sherman bulldozer tank. The rest of the regiment remained in their assembly areas on thirty-minute alert.[30]

In the fighting near Puffendorf, Lt. John Roller's tank was hit by a German tank and set afire. Roller and the men in the turret exited the tank, but the driver and assistant driver were trapped by the 75mm gun which blocked the hatch. Roller directed a crewman to get in the turret and traverse the gun away from the blocked hatch. Lieutenant Roller then tried to lift out the trapped men from the front slope of the burning tank. As he tried to pull the driver out, a second enemy round penetrated the driver's compartment and killed the driver. Lieutenant Roller received his second Silver Star for his gallant attempt to rescue the men.[31]

During the fighting around Puffendorf, WO John Derden was talking to his battalion commander when a call came over the radio from the reconnaissance platoon leader. The platoon leader needed some artillery fire on an enemy location to his front and did not want to take the time to encode the map coordinate location of the enemy. The commander was not going to authorize the artillery fire until he was certain of the intended location. Both the battalion commander and the platoon leader were from the deep South, so the platoon leader said, "Do you see the place on your map called Chittlin?" The colonel said, "What the hell is he talking about?" as he started to look at his map. The colonel began laughing when he found the word "Gutt" on the German map. The artillery fire was soon on the way.[32]

Sergeant Gatzke's diary entries mention one of the things the army did to keep tanks from sinking into the deep mud and his army "anniversary":

18 sat. Put wider tracks (duck paddles) on "Hypo." Moved to Baseweiler at 4 pm. Staying in a nice house.

19 sun. Went to an open field near Immendorf 8am. 3 years in this Army. The last one too. Time to get Purple Heart or the $10,000 one. (meaning killed) Had two drinks of vodka. Slept in a barn.[33]

Task Force A (2nd Battalion) launched an attack east towards Ederen beginning at 1500 hours on 19 November. Enemy resistance was so strong that the force stopped for the night halfway to the objective. Task Force B (1st Battalion) moved through Setterich and attacked toward Freialdenhaven. The tanks crossed the antitank ditch easily and reached a point just short of Freialdenhaven where a vast minefield stopped them at 1330 hours. With the tanks providing covering fire, the infantry passed through the minefield and secured the objective. After dark the engineers cleared two lanes through the minefield. The 3rd Battalion (less Company G) moved to Waurichen during the morning, and Company H moved to Immendorf to help outpost the village.[34]

Task Force A resumed its assault at 0800 the next morning using two columns: one attacked toward Geronsweiler, clearing the antitank ditch of German troops en route, and the other, consisting mainly of tanks, seized Ederen after a tank battle in which they destroyed two Panthers and an assault gun. Unfortunately, this victory cost the column five Shermans and a tank destroyer.[35]

Task Force B attacked at 1000 hours and reached Freialdenhaven at 1330 after mines and an irrigation ditch delayed them. At 1630 the task force moved to the high ground southeast of town. One soldier, Sgt. Wilkie Bruten, won the Silver Star on the twentieth for his gallantry and sheer determination to keep fighting. When his tank was knocked out, he ran three hundred yards under fire to a tank destroyer that he guided to knock out the German tank that had hit his own. Then, armed with only his pistol, he entered the enemy-held village and captured five snipers. Next he found a tank that was short a crewman and took command of it to continue the fight.[36]

On 21 November Task Force A seized the high ground east of Ederen after clearing the town. Task Force B attacked at 1000 hours to clear the ridges south of Merzenhausen, a mission accomplished by 1115 hours without encountering any enemy resistance. As the task force began to move into the village of Merzenhausen, six powerful Mark VI Tiger tanks were spotted moving into the village from the opposite side. With the assistance of artillery fire, Company F was able to destroy two of the Tigers. The task force consolidated for the night about three hundred yards west of the village. The 3rd Battalion, still in division reserve, moved to Loherhof.

Task Force B resumed its attack on Merzenhausen at 0900 hours with the assistance of three Crocodile flame thrower tanks and two Churchill tanks from the British Fife and Forefar Yeomanry. Although watchful Tigers destroyed all of the British tanks when the British moved over an exposed ridge line, the task force did manage to seize part of the village before dark. Reinforced by the 2nd Battalion, 41st Armored Infantry, they consolidated their gains.[37]

As winter approached, some soldiers sought to supplement their U.S. Army issue winter clothing items with some finer items from the home front. Captain Burt wrote to an outfitter he had become familiar with while working a number of outdoor jobs in Vermont before the war. In his letter to L. L. Bean he gave his shoe size and asked if they still had the L. L. Bean boot. Mr. Bean airmailed a pair of the boots to him along with a note to pay for them whenever he could. Captain Burt treasured the boots to keep away the frostbite through what would be the coldest winter in fifty years.[38]

Between 23 and 25 November elements of the 66th Armor began assembling near Baesweiler as they were relieved or released from attachment to other units. During this time the regiment maintained their vehicles and trained near Baesweiler. Individual companies were attached to various infantry units to support local attacks that usually lasted less than one day. On the twenty-fifth, the 3rd Battalion was attached to the 41st Armored Infantry. The 3rd, and later the 2nd, Battalion moved to Freialdenhaven to occupy defensive positions east and northeast of the town. On 29 November all of the regiment except the 2nd Battalion and the Reconnaissance Company were at Baesweiler.[39]

Lt. Lewis Sasser wrote to his wife, Celeste, on 1 December about the loss of the Sherman tank that he had named after her:

Am writing this from tank defilade and am only able to write you like this instead of V-mail because of the envelope you enclosed. Am not in El Celeste as she is kaput as of last Tuesday. Was a good tank and hated to lose it after it had been as lucky as it was, but her luck ran out and mine damned near did with it.

Had had good luck from the last day I wrote you up till then. We'd made our attack and were in the process of holding when some of the brass decided to send a reconnaissance over the hill to see what was there. So—my platoon won out and I took off with my platoon on line and El Celeste in the middle. Went over the hill with all guns blazing away eyes open to see what was in store for us. We found out in a hurry. We were coming down the forward slope of the hill toward an orchard outside of a town to our front. Couldn't see what was in the orchard but we were to hold a position facing it or draw back if we ran into anything. Well, we put a lot of fire into the orchard and advanced almost all the way down the valley between us and the orchard before we started receiving fire in bigger amounts than small arms. Wanted to find a little ridge or cut that we could get defilade in to protect us while we fired but there was none suitable.

About this point they opened up on us coming at them with their armor piercing shells interspersed with high explosive. Could see the gun flashes and put my gunner on them but our stuff is a little light on their tanks and they had the advantage. Looked right down the line of fire of one AP that barely missed the tank and then the next one hit a glancing blow that failed to penetrate. It felt just like a big sledge hammer had hit the tank and sparks flew which give the impression a welder had struck the metal with his blow torch, only on a grander scale. We were giving shells back to Jerry as fast as he was throwing them at us but he lucked out the next shot and that AP came right on inside.

Had already told the other tanks over the radio when I first got hit and we were starting to back off but when that shell came inside things came to a standstill. The drivers and assistant drivers hatches flew open and I threw my turret hatch open at the same time. The loader and gunner were pushing me out the turret and the rate I was going I didn't need pushing. Lifted myself up by my arms on the doors and swung to the ground in one motion. For a fraction of a minute the whole crew was standing there on the ground outside the tank and then we took off as the flames from the exploding ammunition inside the tank started pouring out the turret.

I crouched for a minute or rather a second, behind the tank and then hit a shell hole a few feet away to keep down the shrapnel and machine gun bullets they were letting loose. Caught my breath in the shell hole and took a look over the rim at the orchard from which they were firing. We were between six and eight hundred yards away and the place was alive with small arms and cannon fire from my tanks backing off and the Krauts shooting at us as we pulled back over the hill. I ran about 300 yards to go to clear the crest of the hill and be in defilade from their direct fire. I'd run about 10 yards and hit a shell hole, rest a couple of seconds and take off for another. The field was planted in sugar beets and hard traveling but there had been plenty of artillery which left holes to fall in when it seemed a shell was going to land too close. Wondered the whole way up that hill if I would make it because the air was ringing and zinging with shrapnel and bullets. Finally did and got behind one of the tanks as it backed down the reverse slope a short distance.

Found the captain's tank and went over and got in with him for a while which is a grand feeling to a tanker after having played "doggie" for a while. Sent the rest of my crew back to the rear with one of my other tanks on which the tank commander had caught a small piece of shrapnel thru the turret and we had no other way to get back to the medics. The best part was that John Bova had a pint of Seagram's Seven Crown stuck down with his maps in his tank and he gave me a few shots. It really hit the spot and said he carried it for just such occasions. An aunt of his had sent it to him in a Christmas package and I will ever be grateful to her.

I could see El Celeste burning on the other side of the hill and every few minutes she would explode. Seemed that at first only flames came up, then white smoke would belch forth and then black smoke after which there would be another explosion and more fire would pour out. It burned and exploded for over two hours and altho I haven't gotten up there again to see it I know what it will look like—the paint will be completely gone and the metal will be rusted; the bottom will be blown out and you won't be able to make out exactly what any of the charred remains therein were in their previous form. Maybe it'll just sit there indefinitely or maybe one of these days ordnance will load it up for the metal that's left or the tracks or some part of the outside that might still be usable.

Anyway, it was a good tank. It killed a lot of Germans and it went a good many miles thru France, Belgium, Holland and Germany during which time it always got in the first shot and the last—up till this. But, I'll get another El Celeste and I'll have the same crew and I expect we'll kill a few more Germans before this is over with. Been expecting it to happen a long time and now that it has I'm happy everybody made it out—usually one man or another doesn't.

Waited in Capt. Bova's tank for the tank of my platoon which I had sent to the rear to return at which time I moved over to it in the tank commander's place that had been wounded. So—I am "living out" until my crew gets another tank from the rear and returns. Sure do hope I get a new one and not one from some other company with a patch over an old hole and and all somebody else's troubles.

Fortunately, for the first time, I left that good sleeping bag you sent me on the supply truck. We pulled out in a hurry and can never use it when fighting so decided not to throw it on the back of the tank. So, I still have it but as for a lot of other stuff—it's gone forever. My camera with a couple rolls of film taken, some of your letters, a couple of your new pictures, stationery, maps, toilet articles, my good .45 Colt I'd had since new and 85 dollar, G.I. compass, gas mask, clothes, the new books you'd sent me, the new game kit, some souvenirs I never had gotten off, all my unanswered letters with addresses, a new cashmere scarf I'd just gotten from the PX, my pair of paratroop boots (about worn out tho), and a lot of stuff I won't remember for a while....

Will answer your letters good soon and hope this letter is not too dismal. Also hope the censor doesn't nip it but don't see why he should as I've been over 50 hills just like the one I last went over and the only difference is that the Jerries caught up with me this one time. Have seen him catch up with a lot of other tanks but outside of numerous scars and nicks El Celeste had previously managed to hold her own.[40]

The 2nd Battalion rejoined the 66th Armor near Baesweiler on 2 December. The next day, the regiment was assigned to CCA but remained near Baesweiler for training. Here, the 66th was reorganized by order of the regimental commander as follows: 1st Battalion—Reconnaissance Company and Company C (Stuarts); 2nd Battalion—Companies A (Stuarts), D, E, and F (Shermans); 3rd Battalion—Companies B (Stuarts), G, H, and I (Shermans). On 7 December, the regiment again was organized into task forces in preparation for the division's attack across the Roer River. Task Force A had the 2nd Battalion, Task Force B the 3rd, and Task Force C the 1st Battalion (including the Reconnaissance Company). Each task force had one platoon of engineers and one platoon of tank destroyers attached.[41] The 66th continued training near Baesweiler during the first half of December 1944 in preparation of continuing the advance into Germany.[42]

Capt. James M. Burt, Medal of Honor recipient, 66th Armored Regiment, ca. 1968.

James M. Burt

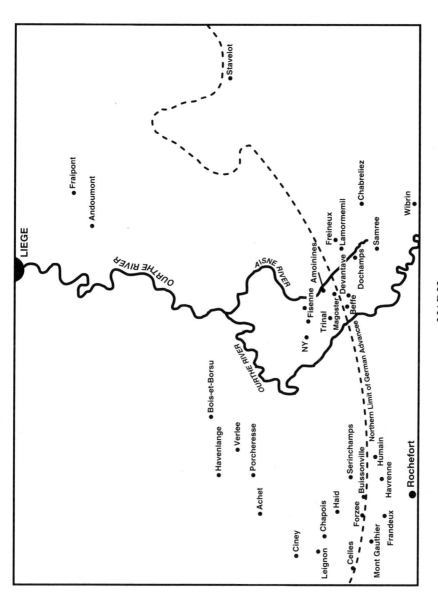

MAP 23
Battle of the Bulge
December 1944–January 1945

CHAPTER 14

Collapsing the Bulge:
The Ardennes

On 12 December Lieutenant Colonel Stokes again assumed command of the regiment. Four days later, on the morning of 16 December, Hitler shocked the Allies by launching his Ardennes offensive, better known as the Battle of the Bulge. Because the Germans attacked in bad weather that grounded Allied aircraft and across rugged terrain thought to be unsuitable for armored forces, the Americans were caught completely by surprise. The Ardennes sector, with its hilly, wooded terrain and sparse road network, was used as an area to keep untrained or tired units that needed a safe place. The 66th Armor found itself on three-hour alert status, and leaders reconnoitered possible routes. While the regiment anxiously awaited news of the German winter offensive, Col. William S. Triplett was appointed to command the 66th on 19 December.[1]

Lieutenant Sasser wrote to his wife about the possibility of a furlough:

...Will tell you something on these 21 or 30 day furloughs for combat troops back to the states. I know you'll see some of them or hear about them and wonder about me. You also know that I would love nothing better in the world than to see you. Well, my time may come sometime but am not expecting to be the first by a few. Our division sent home some of the bunch that you may have read about but no officers from my regiment went although eligible because of the regimental commander. That may change next time, however, if there is one, the priority goes to men and officers wounded twice and sent to the hospital both times—which takes me out of the first group. Then it goes on by a process of medals, length of time, combat, etc. which puts me in fair shape but there are others with more service and more medals so you see it may come to me sometime. What I don't want you to do is get your hopes up too high. I like to think that it's possible sometime but am not figuring on it till it comes. Do like to build castles in the air but I know the wheels of the Army are slow.[2]

Finally, on the night of 21 December, the regiment was ordered to Belgium. Task Force C, comprised of 1st Battalion (C Company) and the Reconnaissance Company, were the first to move on the long, cold night road march. They departed at 2230 hours and traveled seventy-five miles to Bois et Borsu, arriving at 1330 hours the next day. Task Force A, made up of 2nd Battalion (A, D, E, and F Companies), arrived at the village of Borsu, four miles east of Havelange, at 1520 hours. Task Force B, consisting of 3rd Battalion (B, G, H, and I Companies), made it to Havelange, about seventy miles southeast of Namur, Belgium by 1745 hours.[3] This march placed the 66th Armor a short distance north of the German penetration.

On the afternoon of 23 December the 66th joined the Battle of the Bulge. Task Force A was ordered to occupy the town of Ciney, a short distance north of the northwestern part of the German penetration. Moving rapidly southwest, it secured the town. Ordered by CCA to continue farther south, the task force moved to Leignon where it encountered and destroyed a small German force. The next objective was Buissonville, which lay nearly fifteen miles to the southeast. The task force resumed its advance at 2300 hours. Shortly after midnight, they met a German column coming from the opposite direction. The confrontation ended near Chapois, where the Germans were destroyed. After this firefight, the force stopped for the night.[4] Meanwhile, Task Force B moved first to Ciney and then to Leignon without incident. Task Force C occupied Ciney.

Task Force A continued its advance southeast through Haid. At a crossroads one mile south of the town, a platoon of Company A, 702 Tank Destroyer Battalion, encountered and destroyed a Mark V Panther and an armored car. The task force mission was changed to secure Forzee, which was done without resistance. Road blocks were established around the town.[5] Task Force B advanced toward Buissonville in two columns, destroying three wheeled vehicles and a 88mm gun en route. At 1500 hours, they assaulted Buissonville from opposite directions and quickly overcame the German force. They captured 20 wheeled vehicles, 9 guns, and 104 prisoners. Among the captured items were two U.S. two-and-one-half-ton trucks being used by the Germans. After the fight, American P-38 fighters strafed the soldiers despite the recognition markers they displayed and the signal

Maj. Herb Long and Lt. Col. Hugh O'Farrell of 3rd Battalion enjoying their pipes during a quiet time.

The crew of F-15 "Fancy Pants" commanded by 1st platoon leader, Lt. Donald Critchfield. Winter 1944. Tanker on the left wears the M1941 field jacket, center three wear the beloved "Tanker's jacket," and the man on the right wears the new M1944 field jacket.

of yellow smoke. Task Force C cleared Leignon of Germans and then moved to occupy Haid at 1915 hours.[6]

1st Sgt. Thomas Domarecki of H Company made a supply run to the rear every night to resupply the company during the hours of darkness. That night the first sergeant had taken his supply train of three trucks fifteen miles back to a supply depot. The supply train was en route back to the company when it approached a lone military policeman (MP) posted at a road intersection. The MP directed the H Company supply train down a road that traveled through a small hamlet. As the trucks entered the hamlet, a hidden German tank hit the gasoline truck at the head of the convoy. As the gas truck exploded in a gigantic fireball, First Sergeant Domarecki quickly maneuvered his jeep in between two buildings. While the first sergeant pulled the gas truck driver to safety, the tank very quickly destroyed the remaining two trucks. The enraged first sergeant then returned to the intersection with his submachine gun to deal with the German "MP" that had sent his convoy into the ambush. The German was nowhere to be found. Domarecki made his way back to the battalion command post to warn Lieutenant Colonel Fowler of the danger. When the first sergeant returned to the ambush site the next morning, only the burned-out shells of the three trucks remained, his jeep having been taken by the victorious Germans.[7]

Christmas Day 1944 saw the soldiers of the 66th Armor moving and fighting. At 1230 hours, Companies D and E, plus other attachments, were removed from Task Force A and placed under the operational control of the 2nd Battalion, commanded by Maj. Herbert S. Long. Their mission was to move south and relieve an encircled battalion of the 84th Infantry Division at Rochfort. Ten miles south of Forzee, Rochfort was in the center of the German penetration. Initially moving at 1345 hours, Task Force Long had to move north and clear Frandeux before proceeding farther south. The task force reversed itself and secured Frandeux by 2030 hours.[8] Task Force A (-) advanced toward Rochfort at 1515 hours. They encountered a minefield south of Forzee and were ordered to secure for the night in Forzee.

Also actively engaged in combat on Christmas Day was Task Force B. Sergeant Gatzke recorded in his diary the fight at Buissonville at 0800 hours:

> Dec. 25 Mon. CHRISTMAS DAY After staying in our tank all night parked on the side of the road next to a halftrack, a German gun further down the road, shot at and hit the half-track. The driver had been cleaning the engine of dirt with a stick. After the shot he had no more stick in his hand. He was not injured. We fired one shot at the gun and our 75mm jammed. As we started backing up to get over the crest of the hill the Germans fired at us but the shell hit and knocked down a

tree that was between them and us. Then our engine stalled and the
Germans fired again, hitting another tree. Before they could fire again,
we had gotten back over the crest of the hill. We had to take the tank
back to Maintenance in town to get it fixed. While there we ate our K
ration Christmas Dinner.[9]

Later a patrol was sent south to reconnoiter the village of Havrenne which
they found unoccupied. Company I engaged several Tiger tanks nearby. At
1600 hours Company I and an infantry platoon occupied the village. Company G was attached to the 24th Reconnaissance Group to support their
attack on Humain. Task Force C (-) moved to Forzee while elements of the
Reconnaissance Company outposted outlying areas.[10]

The 2nd Platoon of the Reconnaissance Company was establishing
outposts in the tiny hamlet of Verre, west of Celles, when they sighted a
German column moving along the road from Celles. The platoon leader
quickly maneuvered his platoon into an ambush position where it readily
destroyed five German half-tracks, six command cars, and one captured
American vehicle. One American tank and three jeeps were recaptured.
The platoon then moved to a tiny village called Mont Gauthier and established outposts.[11]

The most difficult part of the Battle of the Bulge was the snow and
bitter cold, as Europe endured the coldest winter in fifty years. When not
moving, fighting, working, or guarding their vehicles and comrades, the
men would dig a shallow ditch in the snow. Then, wrapped in their shelter
half and blanket, the men would huddle in their ditch and try to sleep. The
guards around the unit were changed every two hours in the severe cold. K
rations were sometimes heated on the exhaust flame of their tanks. A few
clever maintenance men rigged some longer handles onto skillets, to allow
the soldiers to warm their food more easily on the exhaust. Frostbite was a
very common concern in the sub-zero temperatures. Uniforms were often
supplemented with wool blanket ponchos. Blankets or other material were
cut into strips and wrapped around their feet.[12]

Just before dawn on 26 December, and right after the departure of
their supporting infantry, Company I was hit by a powerful German counterattack at Havrenne. The German force consisted of ten Panthers from
the 9th Panzer Division and ten half-tracks from Panzergrenadier Regiment 10.[13] Company I halted the attack, destroying five of the Panthers and
seven half-tracks. Later, a company of infantrymen and a platoon of tank
destroyers arrived to reinforce Company I. The company commander, Captain Henry Chatfield, received the Silver Star for his aggressive and determined leadership in defeating the German counterattack. After dark

Chatfield's force moved south through entrenched German infantry and blockaded the two roads leading north from Rochfort. Task Force A secured the road junction west of Humain while elements of Task Force B secured Serinchamps, Havrenne, and Jambodine.[14]

During one of many American attacks to reduce the Bulge, the light tanks of C Company were moving through an open field accompanied by a company of infantry. The field was covered in some twelve to eighteen inches of snow which caused the unfortunate infantrymen to resemble waddling ducks as they struggled forward. Halfway across the field the tank commanded by Sgt. Patrick Burke found one of the marshy spots hidden by the snow. As the tank became mired, the nearby infantrymen gave it a wide berth, knowing the sitting duck was likely to draw enemy fire. The rest of tanks and infantry moved on, leaving Sergeant Burke and his crew alone in the field.

After about thirty minutes, a recovery vehicle arrived to pull the tank out of its mudhole. The maintenance men had just stopped their recovery vehicle behind the tank when a German high explosive round slammed into them. The recovery vehicle was covered with the normal assortment of spare boogie wheels, track, sand bags, bedrolls which were launched into the air by the blast. Just like many tankers believed, having all the extra gear on the outside of your armor could save your life. With their ears ringing, the recovery vehicle crew were able to make a hasty retreat.

The German antitank crew then turned their attention to Sergeant Burke's tank. Switching to armor-piercing rounds, the Germans fired their first round at the mired tank. The round hit a small knoll about 50 yards in front of the tank and went about five feet over the top of the tank. This knoll between the hunter and the hunted was just high enough to keep the Germans from getting a clear shot at the tank. The first round was soon followed by another, and some ten more rounds, each glancing off the top of the knoll before sailing just over the top of the tank. Sergeant Burke and his crew were next amazed when the German antitank crew began to fire round after round at a deserted spot in the field some 200 yards to the left of the tank. The armor-piercing projectiles ricocheted off the frozen ground and flew end over end in the air. The only thing Sergeant Burke could guess was that the antitank crew had been ordered to hold their position until all their ammunition was expended. Burke and his crew spent a nervous night stuck in the field before being pulled out the next afternoon by another recovery vehicle.[15]

Task Forces A and Long attacked to the south to secure the key road junctions southeast of Rochfort in the mid-afternoon of the twenty-seventh. Advancing in several columns, the two forces were partially successful in securing the vital area in spite of heavy German opposition, difficult terrain, and the early winter darkness. Task Forces B and C outposted Havrenne and Forzee, respectively.[16]

In the Ardennes, the soldiers often faced very determined resistance from German soldiers who feared the American backlash to the Malmedy Massacre. Captain Burt, the commander of B Company, believed that the "emotional back-home outpouring, of we shouldn't take prisoners either" made their fighting very difficult:

> The troops we faced for a day or so, fearing they would not be taken prisoners, fought with greater intensity; in fact, it is very, very difficult to fight suicidals, those who are genuinely fighting to the death.[17]

On 28 December Task Force Long moved to Frandeux while Task Force A remained in place. Task Force B moved from Havrenne to Mont Gauthier, closing at 1055 hours. Task Force C moved from Forzee to Abbey St. Martin. The next day, since only German stragglers remained in the area, the three task forces of the regiment began maintenance and rehabilitation.

On 30 December the task forces moved north to assembly areas in the vicinity of Achet and Porcheresse. During the fighting of December 1944, the 66th Armor destroyed seven Panther tanks, twenty-three guns, and one hundred thirteen other vehicles. Regimental casualties included five killed, one hundred thirty-two wounded, and one missing.[18]

On New Year's Eve 1944, Capt. Cameron J. Warren, now advanced to Executive Officer of 3rd Battalion, wrote a letter home to his girlfriend Carol:

> Darling,
>
> I am saying to hell with the work and to hell with the Krauts. I am in receipt of your sweet, sweet letter of 2nd December and I haven't written you in some time. The last time I can't remember, but the Krauts are reeling backwards now, and I'm sure you know I wasn't just playing tiddlywinks the last ten days.
>
> Old Santa kinda let us down, didn't he sweetheart. 52nd Street will be kinda deserted and I feel a mite put out tonight. It was champagne I was supposed to bring wasn't it? I am with you yet cause I know at 2400 you'll be thinking of me and I of you.
>
> You have no idea what a lift your warm, glowing letter gave me. I turned to my comrades in arms and gave glowing descriptions of the merits of your sugar reports. All without exception were duly impressed and we had a drink of hoarded Scotch on it. Another small jigger sits

Changing tracks on Sherman tanks in the Ardennes. January 1945.

Luke Bolin

75mm and 76mm gun Sherman tanks of the 66th in the Ardennes. January 1945.

Luke Bolin

before me now and I drink it in dedication to you and our reunion before another new year.

I am anxiously awaiting your pictures. Yes, I keep my hair at $1/2$" to 1" length at all times. Hope you don't mind sweet, you see it's so much cleaner and more feasible in this type life. It also makes you one of the old guard around here. We're getting quite aged and clannish now. Each time we lose one it draws the bonds closer.

The esprit de corps here now is something terrific. It is a great source of pride for us to know we stopped and turned back the Krauts and that they had to call on us to do it. The battles are very exhilarating, my first as battalion executive officer. It is getting so now my only ambition is to kill Germans. Don't be alarmed that I might be becoming uncivilized, to the contrary, I feel very keenly the need for a feminine atmosphere where perfume is the most powerful pervascent and a drink of rye and soda the most lethal weapon present. Nonetheless, I realize the amount of time I'll have to enjoy these niceties of life varies in direct ratio to the amount of Krauts we kill now.

Surely you realize how I'd love to hold you in my arms tonight and you how much I love you. Don't give up patience; it'll be over within the next year I feel, although not until late in the year. Please give mummy and Grant, Becky Dodd and the Doubs, all your family and Jack my very best for the coming year and to you a silent prayer that you will think of me and miss me.

Love

CJ[19]

On 2 January 1945 the regiment moved east and southeast to new assembly areas. Task Force A marched to the vicinity of Ny after eleven hours on the road. Meanwhile, Task Force B occupied an assembly area near Fisenne and Task Force C arrived near Soy. The road march was maneuvered through extremely difficult winter conditions over the narrow and often steep, curvy roads covered with ice and snow. The last unit of the regiment did not close into their assembly area until after midnight. There were rare times when the treacherous roads proved to be an advantage. During one of H Company's moves in the Bulge, the lead tank went out of control just as it was starting down a steep hill. As the 35-ton Sherman bobsled raced down the hill sideways, it convinced a German antitank crew at the bottom it was time to abandon their position.[20]

Less than six hours later, in the frozen predawn hours of 3 January, Task Force A went into the attack, carrying infantrymen on the tanks. This

Celeste Sasser at a USO Halloween party in 1944.

Lt. Lewis Sasser killed in action January 1945.

Celeste Sasser Singleton

attack was part of the renewed Allied effort to reduce the Bulge. The task force advanced southeast in the area between the Ourthe and Aisne Rivers. The right column secured Trinal and the high ground southeast of town by 1330 hours under enemy artillery and mortar fire. The left column advanced against determined enemy resistance, losing two tanks to antitank and Panzerfaust fire. By 1430 hours the left units of the 3rd Battalion (-) had secured their objective near Magoster. The right column of Task Force A was just outside of Beffe at 1600 hours when they were ordered to consolidate for the night.[21]

On 3 January Lt. Lewis Sasser was killed by shrapnel from German artillery. Celeste Sasser remembers the day she was notified:

I was at work when the telegram arrived. My mother said a nice old black man delivered it, with tears in his eyes (2 stars indicated a "Killed in Action"). My mother phoned the office manager who gave me the news on Jan. 19, 1945, Lew's sister's 10th birthday, and I had to tell the Sassers.[22]

Celeste received these ironic words from him in one of his last letters written on 29 December. She did not receive this letter until 14 February:

...I've gotten to the place that I've quit worrying about ever being sick and if I can just keep missing those armor piercing shells I think I'll make out OK. Medical Science has developed to the place where they can pretty well patch up any hole if it's just not too big so put my faith in God and the Medics and trust to luck.

Guess you are probably up better than I on the current situation. It has been a pleasant change from the fighting in Germany, principally because the Jerries don't seem to have the concentration of artillery everywhere that they had up there. Do run into spells of it but then when we do it doesn't usually keep up all day and all night....[23]

Probably the worst task for a chaplain is to write the letter to a dead soldier's wife. The following is the letter Celeste Sasser received:

My Dear Mrs. Sasser:

I have never met you but I knew your husband so well and have seen so many pictures of you that it seems as if I am personally acquainted with you. This letter is one I certainly do not want to write but being both the Chaplain and friend of your husband I want to give you some additional information to what you have already received concerning his death.

You certainly have read about the recent German counter attack in Eastern Belgium. First Lieutenant Lewis S. Sasser, Jr. 0-013060, "E"

Co., this regiment, helped stop them and throw them back. Lieutenant Sasser was advancing with his unit on 3 January 1945 into the German Salient from the north when he was hit by shrapnel from an enemy artillery shell and was killed in action. Friends who were nearby inform me that he did not suffer but was killed instantly. His body was evacuated to an American Military Cemetary in Southeastern Belgium and a Protestant Chaplain conducted an appropriate service.

Mrs. Sasser, I knew "Sass" for a long time in Regimental Headquarters. We often lived near each other. After he transferred to "E" Company and became the leader of a platoon of medium tanks, I saw him often. His friendly disposition and fighting ability endeared him to the officers and men who knew him. He deeply appreciated all the letters and pictures you sent him. He seemed to get more mail than any of the officers of his company and they would often kid him, saying, "Well, we got another letter from our Celes today!"

Lieutenant Sasser was a man who lived a clean moral life and I am thankful that he often attended church services. The last time I talked with him was 31 December 1944. I ate dinner with him at the company and then we walked over to church. Just as the service was ready to start, he got a call to report to the company for some duties. As he left he said, "Well, Chaplain, I tried," and I replied, "I'm sorry you can't stay, but I'm glad your heart is in the right place." While he gave his life as a soldier for his country, we can believe that through faith in Christ he still lives in the other world. May that faith bless and comfort you.

Celeste, I know how badly you must feel. I know how my wife would feel under similar circumstances. My prayer is that you can take it as a good soldier—as your husband most certainly would desire— and finally become reconciled to your great loss. May memories of him bless you and may our Heavenly Father grant you His peace.

All who knew Lieutenant Sasser extend to you and all the family their deepest sympathy.

Most Sincerely,

/s/ Luke Bolin,

Protestant Chaplain, 66th Armored Regiment

That day, Sergeant Gatzke's journal recorded the tragic loss of another promising young platoon leader and his tank crew:

Lt. Coneally and his crew were killed when their tank slid off the icy roadway onto a pile of our mines that had been stacked in a pile on the side of the road. The turret was blown completely off the tank and landed across the road. All five of the crew were killed, including Clarence Terrebonne who was a friend to all.

Lt. Coneally always chose me to go along with him to check out where we could cross a stream with our tanks or see if there could be mines in the road or the best way to get someplace. One time we stood in the middle of the town square just after a squad of infantry had practically run through the town to get to the other side and continue on to the next town. As we stood there Lt. Coneally turned and looked at me and said,"You know Sgt. one of these days you and I are going to get our ass shot off doing this". He was wrong. We didn't.[24]

Amazingly, none of the nine infantrymen of Company B, 335 Infantry Regiment, 84th Infantry Division, who were riding on the tank at the time, were killed in the incident.[25]

Task Force B moved through gaps in a friendly minefield and advanced on the left flank (east) of Task Force A. Task Force B moved forward in coordination with Task Force A toward Devantave. Task Force B consolidated for the night north of Devantave. Task Force C outposted Amoinines and blocked all roads leading to the south.[26]

At 0500 hours on 4 January 1945 a force of German tanks and infantry attacked Task Force B. The tanks of Company D engaged the German tanks at ranges of seventy-five to one hundred yards in the darkness, destroying one Panther and two Mark IV tanks. The Germans withdrew at 0630 hours. Task Force A, led by Company I, attacked and secured Beffe. Task Force B assaulted toward Devantave, but rough, frozen terrain, bad weather, and enemy tanks slowed the Task Force B attack. The force consolidated for the night just short of their objective. The next day the task forces of the 66th Armor remained in their positions while sending out small infantry and tank patrols to reconnoiter the surrounding area. Several small skirmishes with German forces occurred throughout the day.[27]

At 0840 hours on the sixth, Task Force B launched an attack toward Devantave in visibility of less than one hundred yards. The tanks, carrying their attached infantrymen, moved slowly over the slippery and rough terrain. By noon, they had at last taken the town after overcoming some German infantry.

In the dark cold night Capt. Cam Warren, Company H commander, went on a solo reconnaissance of the terrain his company would be attacking through the next day. His firm belief was there is no substitute for having seen the ground. After years of growing up in Montana and working for the Forest Service, he was an expert at moving silently through the dark forests to learn the terrain. He stopped frequently and listened for any indication of danger. His reconnaissance that night resulted in a successful attack the next day in spite of snow and fog which limited visibility to between 25 and 50 yards. He later turned down a Distinguished Service Cross for his leadership and heroism in the Ardennes saying that he had done nothing unusual.[28]

Task Force A attacked south at 1500 hours and reached their objective of a blocking position on the Devantave-Dochamps road. Task Force C fought their way from Fisenne south toward Amonines. After fighting through German roadblocks, Sgt. Arden Gatzke and the others secured for the night around a farm north of Amonines.[29]

Gatzke described in his diary some of the day's action:

> Started on drive to Huffalize. Only 7 tanks left in the company. Went over the crest of the hill and the artillery and direct fire was so intense we all backed up behind the hill. A German gun or tank on our right flank opened fire and knocked out four tanks with four shots. Mine was the next to be fired at but woods hid my tank and the two others. We three tank commanders got out of our tanks and had a conference on what to do next. As we prepared to go back to our tanks a mortar shell landed amongst us. It knocked us down into the snow. The other two were okay but I had a piece of shrapnel in my neck. About five minutes later my crew asked if I could see any movement around the tanks that had been hit and were burning. As I turned my head to look, my whole body turned. I just couldn't turn my head, so I told the crew I was going back to the medics. Walked back across the field covered with about a foot of snow to the Medics. There they found I had shrapnel in my neck, chest, arms and legs. So they sent me back to the Co. A 48th Medics.

> We had gotten hit about noon. I learned that Lt. Marz, Pop Cuevas, TD Smith had been killed and McNulty had a broken leg. Never did find out what happened to the other men.[30]

Task Force A set out to take the high ground southwest of Dochamps on the morning of 7 January. The lead tanks of Company I encountered a minefield that could not be bypassed because of terrain on one side and an enemy tank covering the other side. The German tank was well-hidden in a dense forest that commanded the area. All attempts to outflank the tank or drive it away with artillery fire were unsuccessful. American bazooka teams tried to destroy it but were stopped by German infantrymen protecting the tank. The standoff continued into the night. Finally, when a bazooka team went after the tank, it had disappeared. This incident is an excellent example of the advantage or disadvantage that rough terrain like the Ardennes could give to a combatant. One tank had stopped two battalions for an entire day with the selection of a good defensive position. One element of Task Force C encountered a German roadblock of a captured American tank and M8 armored car on the road to Douchamps, which they cleared by evening.[31]

T/5 Edward Cuthbert, a Sherman tank driver in A Company, remembered the cold, the danger of frostbite and his special task during the Battle of the Bulge:

> It was cold and snowed all the time. No one took their shoes off because you would never get them back on. We lost more men to frostbite than to the Germans. I was the only one in our tank with overshoes. Every day when the supply truck with the rations came my tank commander would yell,"Cuthbert go get the rations" I would get out of the tank and be up to my hips in snow and have to walk a long way and back with C-rations. They were not worth the walk. Thank goodness no one in our crew got frostbite.[32]

Task Force A resumed the attack toward Samree on 8 January. The assault again ran into German tanks located in excellent defensive positions. Two of them knocked out one of the task force's tank destroyers. The dense forests, deep snow, and slippery ground thwarted any task force efforts to flank or kill the Germans. Task Force C moved to Douchamps where it engaged in a firefight with German forces that continued far into the night. They moved on icy roads so slippery that the column was led by men on foot. By dark they were west of Douchamps.[33]

The regiment's attack on 9 January advanced in a heavy snowstorm that limited visibility to less than seventy-five yards. The attached infantry traveled on the tanks except when the terrain dictated that they go first. Task Force B sighted German tanks withdrawing several times, but each time they were unable to engage them. The regimental commander, Colonel Mansfield, was killed at 1630 hours by a direct hit from a German shell while on a dismounted reconnaissance. Lieutenant Colonel Stokes then assumed command of Task Force B and the regiment.[34]

During the actions around Samree Capt. James Burt, B Company commander, was able to apply some knowledge from his youth to solve a tactical problem:

> My tank company was second in line. The point and lead company was stopped in a mountain defile by well placed German AT guns. The battalion commander, Lt. Col. O'Farrell asked if I could go over the wooded mountain to at or near a village beyond the defile. I said, "Yes." He asked, "How come you are sure?" I said, "No boulders, tree farmers here in Belgium have service trails every few contours. We'll

"Loretta II," a 105mm Howitzer M-4E5 of 3rd Battalion, shelling German positions near Amonines, Belgium on 4 January 1945.

A tank destroyer of 702nd Tank Destroyer Battalion and M-4 Shermans of H Company in position to attack Houffalize. 16 January 1945.

go southerly, pick a poor tree spot, crash up to the next trail, follow it a while, crash up to next one etc. We will be on top, beyond the forest and move to overlook the village." That's what we did. I reported by radio and Lt. Col. O'Farrell said to take the village. We did—it had just been abandoned. Knowing by the sound they were being out-flanked the German forces in the defile and in the village pulled out. I had grown up spending much time in New England forests, hills, mountains, defiles and also had observed European forestry habits.[35]

Both Task Forces A and B launched a coordinated assault on Samree and the hills to the southwest of the town. Strong enemy forces were expected, but they encountered only weak resistance. By 0900 hours, Samree, with its key road junction and high ground, was secure. The task forces spent the rest of the day consolidating their positions.[36]

Most elements of the regiment moved on 11 January to assembly areas near Lamormemil and Freineux where they rested and prepared their vehicles and weapons for the next operation. Task Force B conducted an attack on 13 January that was slowed by enemy minefields and difficult terrain. Task Force C attacked and secured Chabreliez and the surrounding ridges.[37]

On the fourteenth, Task Force B attacked south toward Wibrin at 1045 hours. Company G, in the lead, quickly ran into heavy enemy resistance, losing four tanks. The enemy force was estimated to include twelve tanks, numerous antitank guns, and a battalion of infantry. Despite the resistance, Company G continued forward and succeeded in reaching Wibrin. Once there, supported by Company F, 41st Armored Infantry, they cleared the town while Company H assisted in defeating the German forces defending other parts of Wibrin.[38]

On 15 January Task Force B advanced without opposition to secure the high ground northwest of Houffalize. The task force provided covering fire for the engineers while they built a bridge over the nearby river. They then moved to join Task Force C near Wibrin the next day. A regimental team was sent to an area southwest of Liege to establish an assembly area. On the seventeenth the task forces were dissolved as the three battalions of the 66th performed maintenance and rehabilitation.[39]

On 20 January the regiment was withdrawn and moved approximately forty miles to new assembly areas southeast of Liege. The 1st Battalion occupied a bivouac near Fraipont, with the 2nd Battalion at Pbry and the 3rd Battalion in the vicinity of Andoumont. Assembled in one place, the 66th entered the rear area routine of maintenance and training. This training included radio security procedures, indirect fire by tanks, and the proper use of camouflage. The men also fired their personal weapons on the range, acts that seemed curious considering what they had been through during the previous months.

There was also extensive training in chemical warfare, a serious concern of the Allies as they entered Germany. It was feared that Hitler would use his chemical weapons against the Allies in a desperate attempt to protect the Fatherland from invasion. Germany's leading role in chemical warfare during World War I and the intelligence reports on Nazi chemical capabilities was the cause of this American chemical defense training and preparation. Gas schools were conducted, soldiers appointed as unit chemical specialists, and chemical protective and decontamination equipment issued and tested.[40]

In addition to the serious training activities, movies, Red Cross clubmobiles, and passes to Belgian and French towns were available to the men. Soldier-produced plays such as "My G.I. Back" were popular with the men. Best of all, in the middle of the month, the regiment was billeted indoors.[41] However in the month prior to this time, the 66th Armor lost 37 men killed and 352 wounded. They had also captured 659 prisoners and destroyed 66 vehicles and 14 guns. In addition, they recaptured an amazing amount of American equipment: wool blankets and overshoes to a half-track and three Sherman tanks. At the end of the month, the regiment had 128 officers, 9 warrant officers, and 2,173 enlisted men. Overall, the 66th Armored Regiment on 31 January 1945 was rested, fit, and ready to return to Germany.

On 3 February the regiment left their assembly areas and conducted a night road march to another assembly area near Teuven, Belgium. This move to an area less than twenty miles west of Aachen was conducted under strict security. They covered all shoulder patches and vehicle markings and made the march under radio silence. From 4 to 23 February the 66th remained at Teuven, training and putting all vehicles, weapons and equipment in top condition for the upcoming operations, wherever they might occur. The tanks were camouflaged. Logs, sandbags, or other materials were added to boost the tanks' armor protection. The tanks fired on a range and the men trained with new ammunition. The regiment, earlier a victim of so many friendly air attacks, conducted experiments with the Air Force on the use of vehicle recognition panels.[42]

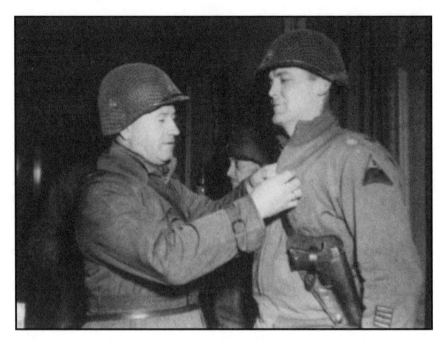

Lt. Col. Hugh O'Farrell, 3rd Battalion commander, being awarded the Silver Star by General White, 2nd Armored Division commander, for his leadership and heroism during the Battle of the Bulge. January 1945.

Soldiers of Company F enjoy a break for chow and newspapers brought by Regimental Chaplain Luke Bolin. January 1945.

"Astoria," a M-5 "Stuart" light tank of A Company. January 1945.

The officers of A Company: Lieutenant McQuillen, Lieutenant Martyn, Lieutenant Shields, and Captain Roller in front of Roller's jeep, "Action." Note the wire cutter on the front of the jeep. March 1945.

76mm gun Sherman tank of the 66th, commanded by Sgt. Edgar Cameron near Tuevan, Holland. 22 February 1945.

The Belgian Secretary of War and Brig. Gen. John Collier, commander of CCA and previously 66th commander, at a ceremony at Hasselt. March 1945.

John B. Roller

Brig. Gen. I. D. White, commander of 2nd Armored Division, being presented flowers by a young Belgian dressed up as an MP. March 1945.

John B. Roller

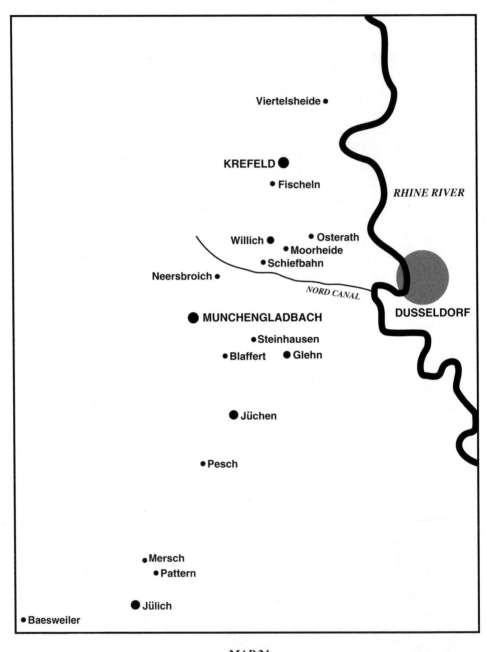

MAP 24
Ruhr Valley Campaign
February 1945

CHAPTER 15

The Race for Berlin

The regiment moved to a new assembly area near Aachen on 24 February. CCA Field Order Number 65 again organized the regiment into task forces. Task Force A consisted of the 2nd Battalion of the 66th with Companies A, D, and E, along with various combined arms attachments. The 3rd Battalion (Companies B, G, and H) was the primary fighting element of Task Force B. The 1st Battalion (Companies C, F, and I) became the CCA reserve.

Everyone in the regiment knew they would soon be engaged in action. Once again the 66th would be fighting Germans on German soil. Fierce resistance was expected by all and vividly remembered by those who had fought in the closing of the Aachen Gap five months earlier. Sergeant Gatzke sent home his new 2nd Armored Division History Book, some maps and a letter:

Dear Folks,

If I don't make this coming battle don't feel too bad about it. After all, what's life if it will help others to enjoy theirs? I've done nothing that I'll ever be sorry for and if it's God's will to take me, it's alright with me. I'm in his power. Good luck and goodbye. All my love. Arden.[1]

At 0700 hours on the twenty-seventh, Task Force A departed Aachen and marched to an assembly area near Mersch, Germany, arriving there at 1000 hours. Task Force B moved to Pattern, approximately sixteen miles northeast of Aachen, and the 1st Battalion moved to the forest southeast of Julich.[2]

Chaplain Luke Bolin reflected on a conversation with General Collier and their feelings about Germans after two years of war:

317

Gen. Collier said,"Luke, the German race seems to be born for war. We may have to destroy every one of them!" I remember I was feeling very low, too. I am not a vicious person, but to see a dead German, I almost rejoiced and it is hard for me to realize that I felt that way toward the Germans.

Sometime later when the war was about over, we were going thru a small German town. A woman asked me where we were going. I said, " Berlin" and she started to cry. " My husband is in Berlin." This made me realize that they are human and have feelings, too.[3]

On the last day of February 1945 the regiment went into action. Task Force A passed through the 29th Infantry Division and attacked northeast at 0700 hours. Enemy resistance was weak with little tank or antitank opposition. In fact, Panzer troops were captured while fighting as dismounted infantry. Good weather, open terrain, and rolling countryside made conditions perfect for tanks, a welcome change after the regiment's previous battles. The task force moved rapidly, reaching the area of Pesch and Glehn by nightfall. Task Force B followed Task Force A in the attack, and the 1st Battalion moved forward to Jüchen.[4]

In the fighting near Jüchen, Capt. Jim Burt, Company H commander, saw an indication of the desperation of the German army:

Near Juchen there was what we might call a high school ROTC. And these cadets had been put in the line to cover a retreat. One thing in which they had not been trained and had not learned was how to surrender. Our tanks passed through a potato field. I saw a foxhole with a boy. But just a few yards behind we had infantry on foot. So the boy in the foxhole was an obvious major danger to the infantry following who thought things were safe because we passed over the ground. So I shot him with my pistol as a necessity. Of course that alerted the following infantry so they proceeded then with great care.[5]

The 66th Armored Regiment was part of Combat Command A of the 2nd Armored Division on 1 March 1945. The battalions of the regiment were organized into three task forces. Task Force A consisted of the regimental headquarters, the 2nd Battalion, a platoon each of engineers and tank destroyers, and the 2nd Battalion (-), 41st Armored Infantry. Task Force B included the 3rd Battalion, the regimental Reconnaissance Company, and platoons of engineers and tank destroyers. The 1st Battalion became the major combat element of Combat Command Reserve (CCR).

CCA ordered Task Force A to attack at 0700 hours on 1 March. The objective was to seize the crossing over the Nord Canal by 1200 hours. Led by the light tanks of Company A, the task force assaulted toward the hamlet of Weilerhofe, which it secured at 0810 after eliminating an antitank gun and its supporting infantry. At 0950 hours the lead tanks of the company were only two hundred yards from the canal bridge when they came under heavy enemy fire from a battery of German 20mm anti-aircraft guns. These rapid-fire weapons, designed to shoot down high speed aircraft, were devastating when used as a ground weapon. With the firepower of an enormous machine gun, the 20mm AA gun could easily destroy a Sherman tank. The tanks quickly withdrew when faced with this weapon and called for artillery fire on the German position. The tanks found a covered position where they could fire on the Germans, and a coordinated attack of infantry, tanks, and artillery succeeded in crossing the bridge at 1200 hours. After clearing the remaining German opposition, the assault continued through Moorheide to Osterath, which Company A secured at 1845 against minor resistance.[6]

To the left of Task Force A, the 3rd Battalion and the other elements of Task Force B also attacked north at 0700 hours on 1 March, with the same mission as Task Force A. The 3rd Battalion crossed the Nord Canal without resistance and at 1130 secured Schiefbahn. After being relieved at about 1400 hours, the task force continued north and seized Willich at 1730. The battalion commander, concerned about the small force left to outpost, received permission to detach a tank platoon of Company H to help guard Schiefbahn. The wisdom of his action became obvious at 1730 when five Panthers and a company of infantry attempted to escape east through the town. The German force was stopped with heavy losses, and at a cost of all five of the Company H tanks, sent to the town. The 1st Battalion, sent to reinforce the guard units, ended the battle of Schiefbahn when it arrived in time to halt the German advance.[7]

Sergeant Gatzke wrote a recollection of the day's confrontation along with a few thoughts on the human losses he witnessed on that, another day of war:

> ...fought on to Schiefbahn, Germany. Placed my tank next to a building on Main St....
>
> I then talked to two old women sitting on the steps of their apartment. They were happy the war was nearly over and their town had not been shot up. After I got back into my tank some Germans fired at my tank and missed, but the shell killed one of the women and the other one's leg went rolling down the steps. Some people carried her into the apartment. I don't know if she lived or died.
>
> I then moved my tank on to the side street and had another tank backed up to mine facing out into an open field while my gun was

ready if anything came down the main street....Somehow some German infantry got into the building across the street in front of us with a bazooka. The shell hit and both crews bailed out of the tanks. As I came down the front of my tank two burp gunners were firing at us from the corner of the building. As I pulled my pistol from its holster it hit the edge of the turret and went rolling down to the street. When I reached down to pick it up a stream of tracer bullets went between my hand and the pistol so fast it looked like a solid stream of fire. I left the pistol lay and joined the other nine men running through the back yards jumping about eight fences five feet high with the burp gunners firing at us all the time. When we stopped we discovered no one had been hit except for one bullet hole through the coat tail. No one even got a scratch from going over the fences. Guess we never touched them.[8]

Shortly before midnight, the CCA commander ordered Task Force A to seize as soon as possible Objective Prune, a vital network of crossroads just north of the village of Fischeln, on the south side of the city of Krefeld. The Task Force A attack began with a dismounted infantry force crossing the LD at 0130 hours on 2 March. Made without the normal artillery barrage, the attack went forward quietly until the first platoon of tanks joined the advance at 0320 hours. At 0530 the task force halted until daylight because of a false sighting of enemy tanks on high ground to the flank. The advance resumed at first light on 2 March, and the tanks moved out on a broad front heading north. Objective Prune was under control by fire at 0825 hours; however, there were some setbacks. A German assault gun ambushed Company E and dispatched three Shermans before the American tanks could locate and destroy it. The German tank units were masters of camouflage, as shown by a Panther tank that was hidden in a courtyard. This tank, assisted by supporting infantrymen, fired on the U.S. troops by momentarily opening the courtyard door. Despite such tactics, though, the task force secured all of Objective Prune by noon.[9]

The 3rd Battalion, as the major part of Task Force B, advanced from Willich via Osterath to Steinrath and accomplished the goal of blocking off the road located there by 1700 hours. During the evening the task force repelled several German counterattacks. The 1st Battalion was counterattacked at 0200 hours in Schiefbahn. The battle saw house-to-house fighting until 0415 hours when the Germans withdrew. Later in the morning the battalion moved to Willich.[10]

In the street fighting near Krefeld, Captain Burt received his third and most severe wound of the war. Badly wounded in the hip, chest, stomach, and back, he was evacuated on the back of a tank and then transferred to a half-track ambulance to be taken back to the aid station. En route to the rear, the half-track approached a small group of woods that the company had passed earlier that day. Hidden in the woods was a German pillbox that earlier had remained silent and gone unnoticed. As the half-track passed by the woods, a group of German soldiers suddenly appeared with a white flag. Captain Burt remembers:

> My driver stopped and spoke to me and said there's a dozen soldiers who want to know if there's an officer in the vehicle. They'd like to surrender to a front line officer. They are afraid if they wait there too long they will be surrounded by rear echelon troops and they are fearful of such troops. Would I take their surrender? I was on a litter in the back of the vehicle but I said sure, just follow us and it will work out. After a while we came to a crossroads which had an aid station and the medics checked me over, told the prisoners to sit around and after a while there'd be some "C" rations, "K" rations and checked their medical condition with no concern for security. I think this was an example of the fraternity of the warrior. Those front line troops trusted that other front line troops, even we the enemy, would not be unnecessarily trigger happy. And we weren't.[11]

When Captain Burt got back to the hospital a nurse cut off his tattered and bloody clothing. Later, personal items that were found in his clothing were returned. The items included a New Testament, a money belt with shrapnel holes, and his wife's photograph, also with a shrapnel hole and spattered with ink from the destroyed pen that was in his pocket. Captain Burt was delighted to find that his beloved Bean boots were also returned to him.[12]

The 2nd Battalion, at Fischeln, was made the division reserve and remained on thirty minute alert status throughout the day of 3 March. Task Force B "leapfrogged" with the 379th Infantry Regiment around the western side of Krefeld. The task force first captured the airfield north of the city and then secured for the night at Viertelsheide.

During this operation Lt. Donald Critchfield's platoon was in the lead. German fire eliminated one tank after another during the advance. Critchfield lost his 5th and final tank to enemy fire since landing in Normandy. The action resulted in a Bronze Star and a cluster to his Purple Heart. After recovering in a hospital in Leige he returned to his unit.[13] The 1st Battalion, still part of CCR, moved to Steinrath and then advanced to just short of their objective north of Krefeld.

The evening of 4 March saw the 3rd Battalion move to a division assembly area near Rehydt. During the day the 1st Battalion advanced north to the canal where they began patrolling. On the fifth the entire regiment

Engineers working to finish a bridge over the Rhine near the destroyed German bridge. March 1945.

T-26/M-26 "Pershing" heavy tank F-15 named "Fancy Pants." The turret is traversed to the rear and the 90mm gun is in travel lock.

moved to an assembly area in the vicinity of Neersbroich–Blaffert–Steinhausen, all in the immediate proximity of Munchengladbach. They remained there until 27 March, conducting range firing of all weapons, platoon tactics, artillery call for fire and adjustment and maintenance. The men were able to enjoy movies, showers, and recreation during this three-week break.[14]

Late on the night of 27 March the 2nd Battalion, 66th Armor, and its normal attachments now designated as Task Force B left the assembly area near Munchengladbach. The 3rd Battalion and its attachments, redesignated as Task Force A, followed. The task force crossed pontoon bridges over the Rhine River to an assembly area north of Hunxe. After traveling on the road all night, the regiment (-) closed in the assembly area between 0500 and 0700 hours on the twenty-eighth.[15]

Sgt. Edward Cuthbert, a gunner in A Company, remembers very well when his Stuart light tank crossed the Rhine River:

> That night we had to cross the Rhine on a hastily made pontoon bridge. We were in the middle of the bridge and I could look down and see the mighty Rhine about 10 feet below me. Our tank commander was sitting on the front slope of the tank guiding our driver, Hank over the bridge. Inadvertantly Hank got the right track of the tank up on the bridge rail. Very slowly Sgt. Poulin was able to guide him off the rail and back on the tracks part of the bridge. When we reached the other side the rest of the column had taken off and were long gone. It was very, very dark. Somehow we managed to catch up and all was OK.[16]

In late March Lt. Donald Critchfield of F Company, Maintenance WO John Derden, and a skeleton tank platoon of men were sent back to the Rhine River to pick up a platoon of the new T-26 "Pershing" heavy tanks. "Its 90 mm gun made all the difference. Instead of bouncing projectiles off their armor we could penetrate—alas, it came too late." Finally, the American tankers had a tank capable of fighting a German Panther or Tiger tank head to head.

The two officers and their men received the new tanks and got on the German autobahn to head east and rejoin the regiment. Critchfield and Derden led the column of five tanks in their jeep. Along the way they heard radio traffic from the regiment and knew they were getting close. The officers got off the autobahn at the next exit to look for the unit, leaving the tanks idling back on the autobahn. Derden and Critchfield soon passed two German soldiers riding bicycles with their rifles slung over their backs. Critchfield remarked to Derden, "that we did a poor job of disarming those chaps." Shortly, they came to a huge roadblock blocking their path.

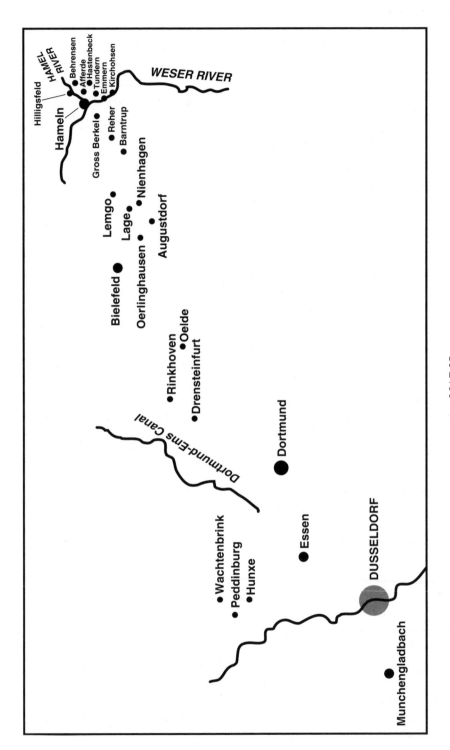

MAP 25
North German Plain
March 1945

Stopping the jeep, the pair climbed onto the roadblock and peered over. They found themselves looking at what appeared to be "the whole German Army at chow." The two officers quickly left the area, speeding past a group of armed Hitler Youth in the process. Rejoining the tanks on the autobahn they quickly moved on to find the regiment. The speed of the American advance had left large pockets of armed Germans, which had to be cleaned up by following American units.[17]

The 2nd and 3rd Battalions received orders on 29 March to attack at 0600 hours the next day. They were to pass through the front line held by the 17th Airborne Division to seize the crossings over the Dortmund-Elms Canal. Task Force B moved out of its assembly area near Wachtenbrink at 0600 hours and advanced rapidly to the canal. Encountering no resistance, the task force covered the twenty-eight miles to the canal by 1030. The bridge had been blown, but the infantry quickly crossed by turning a canal barge sideways across the canal to make a giant footbridge. By 1700 hours the engineers finished a pontoon bridge, and the tanks moved across the canal. Once across, the task force coiled,[18] refueled, and waited for the moon to rise.[19]

Task Force A left its assembly area at Peddinburg at 0600 hours and advanced toward the canal on Force B's left flank. Using the same bridge, they crossed the canal and continued eastward to Rinkhoven, where they stopped to refuel in the early morning hours of 31 March. The task force continued east after refueling and encountered occasional enemy opposition. The German forces were infantry, armed with machine guns, Panzerfausts, and the deadly 20mm anti-aircraft guns. By midnight on the thirty-first, the task force had advanced some thirty miles to Oelde and was still moving east. The 1st Battalion followed between the two task forces as the reserve.[20]

Task Force B moved out at 2030 hours and traveled throughout the night. Just outside of the town of Drensteinfurt, the lead tanks engaged a German training garrison unit, which had been defending the town and fighting hard with Panzerfausts, mortars, and a single assault gun. The task force moved around the town's defenders on both flanks, while U.S. artillery rained down on them. They finally took the town and some two hundred prisoners at about 1100 hours.[21]

The task force continued its drive east at 1230 hours on the thirty-first. When they encountered pockets of resistance, they either quickly destroyed them or bypassed Germans and left them for reserve forces to eliminate. When darkness came Task Force B coiled near Oelde, two days and many miles from when it had started.

Pfc. Donald Evans was serving as the gunner on a Stuart light tank in 1st Platoon of Reconnaissance Company. His platoon had been performing recon missions ahead of one of the task forces of the 66th for several days. His crew was short one crewmember following the injury of the bow gunner the day before. The platoon had just completed a night road march at 0530 on 31 March.

> As dawn was beginning to break, our column was ordered to halt for a much needed break for both man and machine. I don't think many of us knew our geographical location nor did we really care. It was just another day of war. It was a quiet morning as though there was no war anywhere. We knew the war was winding down but having been at it so long we didn't think it would ever come to an end. Everyone just piled out of their various vehicles, sought out buddies and lit up the little gasoline stoves to make coffee, open some particular ration for breakfast and shoot some bull with one another. Because the area was so quiet everyone just seemed to throw all caution to the wind.

The tranquility of the platoon's early morning was shattered when a German truck suddenly appeared. One of the tank gunners quickly riddled the truck with bullets from the tank's .50 caliber machine gun. The driver was fatally wounded and the other German occupant of the truck taken prisoner. Evans remembers:

> After traveling all night we were now some distance into the German line and with the presence of this enemy vehicle in our midst it should have alerted us to the fact that the enemy was now very close.

The platoon resumed their breakfast break for another fifteen minutes until receiving orders to mount up and be prepared to move. Sergeant Selby, Evans' tank commander, moved in the bow gunner's seat to get some rest, leaving Evans in the turret. A scout section jeep came alongside and the soldier, Buren Mercer, in the rear of the jeep asked if he could serve as Evans' loader. It was a cold, windy March morning and the inside of a tank turret was out of the wind. Evans continues the account of that fateful day:

> Mercer, known as "Shorty" was a very likeable guy...everyone liked him and always ready to give him a hand. Climbing into the tank that morning was to be the greatest mistake he would ever make. It cost him his life. Our vehicle was about the fifth one in the column and while standing in the turret and awaiting the order to proceed the platoon leader came by and informed me that we would now be the point vehicle and ordered us to the head of the column. No one but no one wants to ride point and I tell you this order shook me up. When you

realize that the only people in front of you is the enemy lying in wait it puts a different perspective on your mission....

We had scarely gone 30–45 seconds when I noticed a huge red flash on the right side of the road. I immediately dropped into position to reach for the gun and turret switches and at that instant a ball of fire lit up the interior of the turret. What had probably been a Panzerfaust penetrated the steel on the right front at about the position of the .30 cal. machine gun directly into the face of "Shorty" Mercer. I was to learn later this had taken off his head and the ensuing fire burned most of his body. What a quirk of fate. I'm sure his body took a lot of punishment that I would have received had he not volunteered to be my loader.

I immediately bailed out as did the driver. At the moment I did not realize I had suffered so badly. Instantly, there was an enormous amount of gunfire as both sides fired on one another. As Asher and I lay huddled in the ditch I then realized I was not able to see. With parts of my face and hands burned and neck swelled so I could hardly swallow I thought surely I would die.

And of course our platoon following the orders we had been given...broke off the engagement and went on with the mission. Things pretty much quieted down then except for the ammo exploding and the tank afire. Tank drivers are armed with .45 caliber pistols in shoulder holsters, therefore when Asher bailed out he had his pistol and was able to capture a German soldier immediately. When the firing ceased he instructed the German to tell his comrades to surrender. Of course with the odds as they were they were not about to do that....With all my problems I still had no pain. Not being able to see Asher kept me informed of the situation.

Soon a small German Army car approached our position. A German officer got out and Asher challenged him to put up his hands. He refused and Asher immediately shot him several times. I knew then there would be no mercy for us when we were taken. There still was no move by the Germans to come to us. As we laid in the ditch I thought I would surely die there. Strangely enough at that time dying did not scare me. I just did not want to die there as I thought my body would not be found and my family would not know that I was dead.

I had often worn a German P 38 pistol on my belt and the night before I had taken it off and put it aside in the tank, knowing that if I was ever taken prisoner I would probably be shot with it. Now laying along that road and possibly facing capture, with my burned hands I was pulling from my jacket medals taken from captured Germans the day before.

Now with a very bright day upon us the skies were filled with our fighter planes looking for targets and roads to strafe. This became another worry. Asher and I then decided to get up off the ground and walk to the rear with our hands up to see what would happen. Instantly a small group of German soldiers were upon us. We were taken directly to an officer who spoke English. This officer addressed Asher and said, "You shot and killed a German officer!" He was quite mad. Of course Asher denied the charge and the German shouted, "We saw you, We saw you!" As I stood there with arms raised and not being able to see and knowing the situation with Asher killing the officer and me as a helpless POW and a German officer really mad I knew this was the end of the line. I just knew any minute the German would blow me away. Now I was really scared. The silence was terrifying. Finally the officer said,"Well I guess its part of war, you may put your hands down." With a sigh of relief I said to myself "Thank you Lord."

We were loaded into a small 4 door German Army car....Several times we made stops and each time a crowd would gather around the vehicle. Many, many American fighter planes were now roaming above looking for targets. I had expected any moment to become a victim of some strafing aircraft. All the while we were being treated very well by our captors and the civilians that always gathered at each stop. My wounds were beginning to come to life and I was experiencing much discomfort.

Finally we make a stop and we are told to leave the car. It is an army installation. The fear of being shot is continually with us. Asher as usual fills me in on all things. A medical officer looks me over and says no one there is able to give me any aid. Prior to becoming captive, Asher had applied my first aid bandage and sprinkled some of the wounds from my sulfa powder package—not being able to swallow the sulfa pills.

After a few more moments another medic came by and Asher asks that he give me some morphine to ease the pain. The officer is quite arrogant and shouts,"Where is your morphine, you Americans are supposed to have everything!" He did however produce a syrette and gave me a shot. We were then left alone and I stretched out...and went off to sleep. When I awoke, I don't know how much later, I was on a litter being carried up a flight of stairs inside a building. There two German girls which I believe were nurses stripped off my clothes and put me into a bath tub. They then dressed me with a night gown and put me into a bed. Asher was not around, just the enemy, no one speaking

English. I was now a very lonesome man. Not sure of my surroundings or my future....

There were five wounded German soldiers in this room also. I was amazed that I was receiving such good attention being the enemy. Not being able to fend for myself I was hand fed by the nurses. Cigarettes came from the wounded Germans. That evening a German Army medic speaking fluent English visited with me for a couple of hours. He was very friendly and very interesting. He would convey my needs to the nurses. He returned each morning and each evening during my stay there.

Other than dressing my wounds I received no other aid as they claimed there was no doctor available to treat my eyes. As infection set in the pain worsened. Occasionally I was administered a sedative which brought relief.

Every day I prayed that American troops would enter the town so I could...get some much needed treatment. Finally early on the seventh day the German medic...excitedly proclaimed that my comrades were coming as a scout car was seen near the village. To say the least I became quite excited myself as I quickly set up in bed. For the first time in a week life took on a new meaning. I was so anxious to see some GIs and I expected any moment for them to come through the door. However nothing happened...as the hours passed my day turned into dismay and disappointment....Night came and I finally fell asleep.

Awakened early the next morning there seemed to be an air of expectancy among the nurses and the wounded Germans. Shortly after finishing breakfast there was a roar of vehicle engines in the street below and a few bursts of .50 caliber machine gun which seemed to be just outside the window. In a few seconds a group of GIs came charging into the room. I don't have the words to express the feeling that overcame me. I know I shed a few tears of joy. They inquired of my condition, how I was being treated and what did I need. I assured them that I was very well treated and all I wanted was to leave there. They took my name, rank, serial number and unit. I was informed my unit would be notified and some medics would shortly pick me up.

The nurses then readied me to depart their company. Everything that I arrived there with was returned to me. Everything. When the ambulance arrived I said good-byes and was gone. Under the circumstances it had not been too bad a stay. My only regret has been that I had not gotten any names and addresses of those people that I may have visited with them on one of my return trips to Europe after the war.

Capt. Cam Warren beside the sign pointing
to the 3rd Battalion Headquarters, Germany.
Spring 1945.

Cameron J. Warren

Sherman tanks of Company H on the North
German Plain. April 1945.

Cameron J. Warren

Visit by Cardinal Spellman. Spring 1945.

John B. Roller

Three days after my recapture I was back in England, a patient in
U.S. Army Hospital #4129, adjacent to Tidworth Garrison from where
I left the previous June for the landing in Normandy. I was then returned to the U.S. and discharged from the Thomas M. England Hospital in Atlantic City, N.J., August 30, 1945.[22]

At 1710 orders from CCA called for the immediate formation of a
special task force. Commanded by the 2nd Battalion executive officer, Maj.
Cameron Warren, the task force consisted of Company D, 66th Armor,
Company E, 377th Infantry, Battery A, 65th Field Artillery Battalion, and a
section of tank destroyers from the 702nd Tank Destroyer Battalion. The
mission of Task Force Warren was to move as fast as possible to seize a
mountain pass through the Teutoburger Wald. This pass was on the autobahn
a short distance southeast of Bielefeld. The Teutoburger Wald, a dense forest covering a line of mountains, was the next natural obstacle.

Maj. Cameron Warren recalls the orders he received from Brig. Gen.
"Pee Wee" Collier, the CCA commander:

> General Collier said, "Major Warren, I'm creating a task force and
> putting you in command. Your mission is to move out as soon as pos-
> sible and take one of the three passes through the Teutoberger Wald.
> You'll have a company of tanks, a company of infantry, a battery of
> field artillery and a medical section. It's 25 miles to the pass and it's
> imperative we secure this as we expect the Germans to make a stand
> there and we want to beat them to the punch. Colonel O'Farrell and the
> 3rd Battalion will be following along behind to give you back up sup-
> port. Keep in contact by radio and keep us informed as to your move-
> ment. Your tanks are being gassed now. Move out as soon as possible.
> Any questions?" Warren asked, "Do I have complete freedom as to my
> tactics and the line of march?" Collier answered, "Do whatever you
> need to get that pass. I don't care how—just get it." "Yes, Sir" was my
> response.

Major Warren describes his thoughts and the hasty planning of the
mission:

> My heart was in my mouth. No rest tonight. I felt as if it was up to me
> to win the rest of the war single-handed—I was so charged up. Of course,
> it did no good to dwell on that very long—there was work to be done.
> I hurried back to my headquarters, assembled my major commanders
> and plotted my strategy—What was the best way to take this pass?
> What defenses could I expect? Surely any Mark V Panzers in the vicin-
> ity would be deployed. You could bet on that. We hadn't had much

resistance during the day. In fact the day's march was quite routine. My own feeling was that the Germans were reeling and ready for the knock-out blow—at least in our area between the Americans and the British. I felt maybe the time was right for the bold stroke—a chance to put Robert E. Lee's, Sherman's and George S. Patton's surprise tactics to work.

> Q. How fast will the tanks go?
>
> A. 27 miles per hour.
>
> Q. What's the shortest distance between two points?
>
> A. A straight line.
>
> Q. What's a straight line look like on the map?
>
> A. The autobahn.
>
> Q. How much daylight did we have?
>
> A. Maybe 2 hours or so—depending on how quickly we finished gassing and got under way.

Realization: Gee!! If we really got the element of surprise we could be at the pass before dusk. Wouldn't that be something.

> Q. What strategy gave the best chance of low casualties?
>
> A. Well, obviously surprise—surprise.

So the answer became obvious. Resistance had been light that day. The Krauts wouldn't expect us to keep driving into the night.

Task Force Warren was soon fueled and ready to begin their move. Major Warren describes the operation to seize the pass:

> I ordered the infantry to mount up on the backs of the tanks. I ordered the tanks to get on the freeway and "put 'er to the floor." I rode in the 4th tank from the front. Each tank stayed 50–100 yards apart. 1st tank—75mm gun straight ahead. 2nd tank gun 90 degrees to the right. 3rd tank gun 90 degrees to the left and so on—alternating left and right....Sure enough we achieved complete surprise. We had only been under way a few minutes when we lost radio contact with headquarters. We were beyond the 4 to 6 mile range of our standard tank radio set. I had no way to tell "Pee Wee" how we were doing. I could hear them frantically calling for reports but my responses obviously weren't getting through.
>
> About 5 miles out we met a farmer coming down the road towards us riding on a tremendous load of hay. He was astounded when we gently nudged him off the road. Three or four miles farther, a German staff car drove into our column. It was 6 or 8 tanks deep into our ranks

before realizing these were not German but American tanks. It quickly crashed into the ditch as we sprayed the occupants with machine gun fire and continued to roll. I did not want to stop and take prisoners—no need to be diverted from our main mission.

Then we looked off to the right in a field about 300–400 yards away and I knew surprise was complete. A large bus—looking much like a school bus was disgorging soldiers. They were being formed up in close order drill three abreast in long columns and being marched off for what purpose I'm not sure. It looked just like a parade ground. We opened fire and scattered them as we rolled on. Our intrepid little band was making a foray deep into enemy country and we wanted to make the pass by dark if possible. Let Hugh O'Farrell handle the prisoners or engage them in the fight if they still had the stomach for it. It had to be one of the most surprised bunch of Hitler's army there ever was. They couldn't have thought we were within miles of them. Within less than an hour I figured we had come 22 miles and we were only three miles from the pass.

Up ahead several trees had been cut and blocked the road. They must have been cut before our march ever started. This meant the Germans were planning some kind of stand to defend the pass. I quickly coiled the tanks off this vulnerable autobahn where you could sight a panzer tank gun up to its maximum range. We moved into the comforting shadows of the trees and bushes off the freeway. I dismounted the infantry and ordered an advance by them on the road block. After a brief fire fight we flushed out eight soldiers commanded by an officer with a wooden leg. It was another sign that the Reich was reaching to the bottom of the manpower barrel. We disarmed them, pointed them to the rear, and resumed our march.

We moved around the road block pushing the trees out of the way. I decided we were getting close to "Tiger" country so became much more wary of exposing the column. We stayed off the freeway where possible, moving up both sides of the road keeping a sharp eye out for good enemy tank positions that could cover the highway.

By now darkness was fast descending and I decided to "circle the wagons and wait til dawn." The roar of our tanks was sure to draw attention and I soon learned some of the enemy were around. I made the rounds of my commanders, checking on their defenses and sentries. To my horror too many times, I found a group of soldiers all asleep from their long day—and the lighting dash for one of the few mountain passes left between ourselves and Berlin. They apparently thought that rest was more important than safety. It is not a good feeling in a spot like this—telling friend from foe can be tricky.

We were near a small village so I entered it alone on foot to scout the area. I moved up a dark side street to the central intersection, my .45 in hand. I was in shadows and there was ample moonlight to see. During the war we marched with blackout lights so much I believe our night vision was quite good. I made my way along a two storey building built right up to the sidewalk on the corner. As I poked my head around the corner I saw a German sentry marching up and down in front of the entrance to the building. Ah Ha!! This was a German Command Post and obviously the "Kommandant" was asleep upstairs. No time to be a hero. I retreated down the dark side of the building, knowing the enemy slept among us. I had found out what I wanted to know— no big enemy encampment here—probably just a small outpost but then again who knows.

I formulated plans in the wee morning hours. We resumed our march towards the pass at daybreak. I moved the infantry on foot up the flanks of the pass with the tanks in close support. By noon we had the pass, were taking prisoners, and securing the high ground. Casualties were light. Another step towards Berlin had been taken.[23]

The Americans finally secured the pass at 1600 hours. One hour later they were withdrawn to refuel and reassemble to return to Task Force B.[24] That evening Major Warren learned about what happened in the wake of his dash for the pass when he reported to General Collier's headquarters.

"O'Toole", as we affectionately called the big sandy haired, gruff spoken colonel from the Third Battalion of the 66th, had run into a hornet's nest from the "Krauts" we took by surprise. He was busy all night trying to get up to us. I was told there were plenty of fire fights all along the route. I don't think Lt. Col. O'Farrell, with whom I was personally quite close, particularly looked kindly on the dirty "mop up" job I had so cavalierly left to him. We buried the hatchet a little later with a couple of good belts of scotch and he acknowledged that the 2nd Bn. probably had recently attained the lofty stature and fighting ability of his 3rd Bn. O'Farrell had been my commander in the bloody battle at Wurselen, Germany a few months earlier. I looked up to him as a real fine officer—one of that great fighting breed that the South provided to the Armed Forces and notably to the Armored Forces in great numbers.[25]

Task Force B continued on 1 April to advance east against scattered opposition. Late that evening, the task force moved into and began clearing

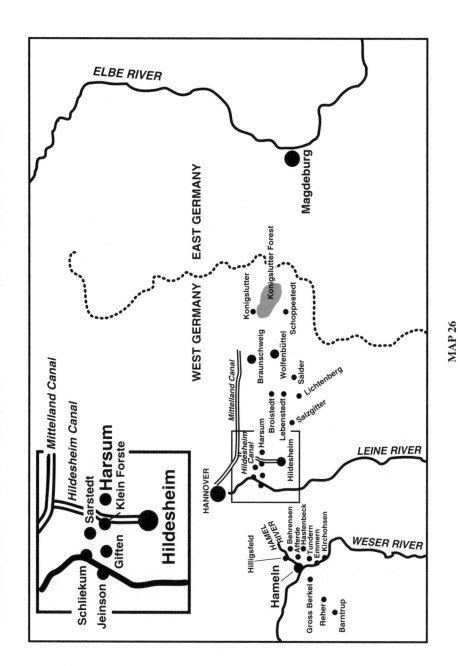

MAP 26
Drive to the Elbe
March–April 1945

A grain sack of the German Waffen-SS. Spring 1945.

John B. Roller

German Ju-87 "Stuka" dive bomber captured intact on a German airfield. Spring 1945.

John B. Roller

the town of Augustdorf at the base of the Teutoburger Wald range. Task Force A traveled on the autobahn and, after refueling, moved forward to the Wald where the artillery, mortar, and assault units were set to support an attack. This assault began at about 1100 hours and quickly overcame the enemy infantry and the one Mark IV tank. The day's fighting netted 244 prisoners and the destruction of two 88mm guns.[26]

After a relatively quiet day in assembly areas on 2 April, the regiment began moving again on the third. The 1st Battalion, attached to the 1st Battalion, 119th Infantry, attacked at 0530 hours to seize Oerlinghausen. The battalions ran into heavy resistance, and it was 2200 hours before they secured the town. Task Force A began its advance at 1300 moving northwest to get on the autobahn. The task force crossed the Teutoburger Wald through the pass taken by Task Force Warren and advanced astride the road to Lage. After passing through elements of CCA, the task force advanced thirteen miles to seize the town. The units shot down one German Me 109 fighter and destroyed two 88mm guns, capturing 236 prisoners and liberating twenty British prisoners of war.[27]

On 4 April at 0800 hours, Task Force B left the vicinity of Augustdorf. They advanced rapidly through Nienhagen, Barntrup, and Reher against scattered resistance that consisted primarily of road blocks, only some of which were defended. At nightfall the task force consolidated at Gross Berkel and began preparing for crossing the Weser River. Task Force A seized Lemgo in the morning and by dark had advanced thirty-five miles to the town of Hameln. Meeting moderate opposition at some points along the way, the tankers destroyed two German King Tiger tanks. These powerful tanks, armed with an 88mm gun and possessing very heavy armor, were extremely difficult for a Sherman tank to destroy. German planes again attacked the column, and the battalion shot down another aircraft. The 1st Battalion followed behind the two task forces and was southwest of Lemgo on the night of 4 April.[28]

On the morning of the fifth, the tanks of the 2nd Battalion covered the infantry crossings of the Weser River. At 1530 hours the engineers completed a pontoon bridge and the tanks crossed, rejoining the infantry in Tundern at about 1700 hours. At 1900 the task force secured the town of Afferde that lay east of Hameln. The 3rd Battalion entered Hameln and cleared the town on the Weser River by reducing road blocks and taking 112 prisoners. Some of the tanks destroyed a train on the opposite side of the river. The 1st Battalion, in support of the 119th Infantry, advanced from Arzen, crossed the Weser, and went on to take Voremberg. A task force was detached briefly, and it seized the bridges over the Weser at Emmern and Kirchohsen.[29]

Sergeant Gatzke wrote of the day's travels, which included an encounter with some zealous Hitler Youth:

> Crossed Weser River at Hameln famous for the 'Pied Piper of Hameln'. Ran into a group of Hitler Youth. Infantry had a hard time getting by them. They were Die Hard fighters. Traveled another twenty-five miles.[30]

Task Force B advanced to Hilligsfeld on the morning of 6 April, to secure both the town and the bridges over the Hamel River north of the town. After defeating the German infantry and its supporting anti-aircraft guns, they secured the area at approximately 1100 hours. An attack on Behrensen was canceled because of heavy enemy infantry resistance, and the Americans bypassed the town. By 1630 hours, Task Force B had fought through road blocks and scattered opposition to seize the two bridges over the Leine River in the town of Schulenburg. They captured one of the bridges intact, only because some of the infantrymen riding on the lead tanks jumped off them and pulled the burning demolition charge fuse out of the explosives.[31]

While fighting through a town Company D encountered a road block covered by two of the deadly "88mm" guns. The tank dozer had just opened a hole in the road block when it was knocked along with one of the company's M24 "Chaffee" light tank. Two men were killed and two badly wounded in the tanks. Capt. John Roller, the company commander, left his tank and ran forward through the enemy fire. He dragged the wounded men to safety behind a building. The heroic action earned Roller his third Silver Star.[32]

The 3rd Battalion, as part of Task Force A, moved south out of Hameln and crossed the bridge that the Task Force B engineers had built the previous day. At noon on the sixth, the task force traveled from Hastenbeck through Afferde. They advanced through moderate enemy resistance that consisted primarily of road blocks and 88mm guns, now aimed at the advancing Shermans and not at the bombers flying high overhead. The task force passed Coppenbrugge and advanced along the steep, wooded road toward Eldagsen, the task force objective. After advancing twenty-four miles, they halted for the night.[33]

Task Force B secured several other bridges over the Leine River on 7 April. The task force remained in the area of Schulenburg until the tenth, in order to defend the bridges against counterattacks and to clear the area of German troops. During the night of 7 April, small Panzerfaust teams made several unsuccessful attempts to penetrate the task force perimeter and destroy the American tanks. Task Force A attacked at dawn to secure the

The meeting of East and West. Artillery officer attached to 3rd Battalion, Capt. Cam Warren, and two Soviet noncommissioned officers.

The famous German 88mm gun in an antitank role on the outskirts of a German village. Spring 1945.

towns of Gestorf, Jeinson, and Schliekum. The Germans fought back with a number of heavy anti-aircraft guns mounted on rail cars. The American tanks moved seventeen miles during this action and destroyed a number of German guns, including one 170mm and four 150mm railroad guns. Ahead of the main body, a reconnaissance platoon seized a bridge over the Leine River and held it against German counterattacks. The rest of the force crossed the bridge and moved to seize Sarstedt, where the unit secured for the night. Elements of the 1st Battalion captured Barnten and then Giften by 1430 hours while under enemy artillery and aircraft attacks.[34]

At 1730 hours on the eighth, the 1st Battalion attacked through the Klein Forste to the Hildesheim Canal. While tanks provided cover, the infantry crossed the canal, and the engineers built a new bridge. After crossing, the task force captured Harsum and formed outpost area.

On 10 April, Task Force B went back on the offensive and quickly advanced from the area of Schulenburg to Lichtenberg and the Salder River. The 1st Battalion, operating as three sub task forces, advanced against enemy resistance to seize Lebenstedt. The 3rd Battalion destroyed one Mark IV tank and six 88mm guns on the tenth during their move forward to Broistedt.[35]

The regiment's daily advances increased every day as the Third Reich crumbled. Task Force B advanced south of the city of Braunschweig to take Schoppestedt on 11 April. The 3rd Battalion seized Wolfenbüttel and cleared it. The men were taking larger numbers of German prisoners, with each battalion averaging 200 to 300 daily. As Nazi Germany crumbled, the Germans increasingly used the close-combat Panzerfaust and the long range and deadly flak (anti-aircraft) guns as their main weapons, primarily because they were the only ones capable of stopping the thousands of American tanks.[36]

Sergeant Gatzke's journal on 11 April read simply, "We went 57 miles in one day and reached the Elbe River." A few days later, he was with the medics for complete physical exhaustion; he slept for forty-eight hours, rising only a few times to eat something. The company had been moving and fighting day and night since crossing the LD on 30 March.[37]

On 12 April, the soldiers of the 66th received the news of the death of their commander in chief, Franklin Delano Roosevelt. Captain Warren remembered being in his tank, moving across the North German Plain, when the news came over the tank's radio. He remembered crying and thinking how sad it was that FDR had not lived to see the end of the war.[38] The regiment, still assigned to CCA, arrived just northwest of the city of Magdeburg. While the regiment helped surround the city, CCB was struggling to get a bridge over the Elbe River. The regiment took positions and established road blocks to the north and northwest of the city remaining in defensive positions around Magdeburg from 13 through 17 April. They were anticipating strong German counterattacks to break the encirclement. The Germans made numerous small assaults without success. After cutting off Magdeburg, the 66th and CCA joined the 30th Infantry Division in capturing the city on 19 April after massive artillery and air strikes.[39]

On 20 April 1945 the regiment began moving with the rest of the 2nd Armored Division back to the vicinity of Braunschweig and Wolfenbüttel. The next day, elements of the regiment were involved in the destruction of one of the Germans' last-ditch counterattacks in the Konigslutter Forest just east of Wolfenbüttel. On the twenty-first the 66th Armor began area security and occupation duties, for which the veteran soldiers of the regiment were able to use experience from the earlier occupation of Sicily.[40] The 66th Armor was heavily involved in establishing centers for the thousands of displaced persons in the area. These people included everyone from Germans who had fled across the Elbe River escaping the Russians, to Russian and eastern European slave laborers from the Nazi war industries. By the twenty-fourth the regiment had moved as many as 5,000 people through the displaced person's center.[41]

On 22 April the Russian armies completed their encirclement of Berlin. Because of the Allied agreements at Yalta the American forces did not advance more than a short distance east of the Elbe River. The disappointment of the soldiers at not being able to go all the way to the capital of the Reich is clear in this sentence from the last paragraph of the regimental report for April 1945:

> It was felt by all members of the command that the regiment could
> have, without great difficulty, gone on to Berlin or taken any objective
> to the east if so ordered when it was ordered to return west.[42]

During the month of April 1945, the 66th Armor took 7,420 prisoners and destroyed or captured 352 guns, 723 vehicles, 24 tanks, 44 aircraft, 11 entire trains, and 14 locomotives.[43] The small number of tanks and large numbers of aircraft and mostly anti-aircraft guns show how desperate the German forces had become in the last month of the war.

Adolf Hitler committed suicide on 30 April, and two days later the city of Berlin surrendered. During the first week of May, German armies in different parts of the Thousand Year Reich surrendered to the Allies. The unconditional surrender of the Third Reich was signed in Berlin on 8 May 1945.

Sgt. John Fabian, who had just joined Company A of the 66th in March remembered how they made use of some of the German facilities:

> In Wolfenbüttel we came across a German 88 factory which we used to set up an assembly line to recondition and spray paint our tanks, preparing them for entrance into Berlin.[44]

The regiment remained in the vicinity of Wolfenbüttel and south of Braunschweig, performing occupation duties until 7 May. Orders were received on that date to consolidate the 66th in the vicinity of Lebenstedt, a suburb of Salzgitter southwest of Braunschweig. By 10 May all of the regiment had closed in at the assigned area. There the men moved into recently vacated German army barracks. After spending a few days organizing and cleaning their new accommodations, the 66th began the process of regaining the once very neat and orderly appearance of the unit before their last year in combat. Uniform regulations were enforced and the troops thoroughly cleaned, painted, and re-marked the insignia on the vehicles. On 24 May the men's mail was no longer censored. The veterans and the new replacements resumed unit and individual training.[45]

In June 1945 elements of the regiment received two significant unit decorations. The Belgian unit decoration was awarded to the units of the 2nd Armored Division for the liberation of Belgium and the Battle of the Bulge. The 2nd Battalion, 66th Armor, was awarded the Presidential Unit Citation for its role in the St. Lo breakout in Normandy from 26 July to 12 August 1944. The joy and pride of these events and honors were sobered by remembering the cost. 1st Sergeant Domarecki of Company H remembered that of the 160 original members of the company, only nine of them remained. Some men had fortunately been transferred or promoted out of the company, but many had been wounded too badly to return or had been killed.[46]

On 17 June the regiment, along with the rest of the 2nd Armored Division, received orders to prepare to move to Halle in the Soviet occupation zone. The move was an intermediate stop en route to Berlin, to serve as part of the occupation force for the city. The regiment road marched eighty-three miles to the area of Trebnitz, Germany on the twentieth. Additional orders, received on 26 June, outlined the regiment's move to Berlin and once there, its occupation responsibilities. Advance billeting parties left for Berlin on 1 July. On the third the 66th Armor moved 184 miles in approximately seventeen hours and proudly rolled its tanks into Berlin.[47]

The men celebrated American Independence Day in the captured capital of the enemy they had fought for three years in North Africa, Sicily, France, Holland, Belgium, and Germany. The regiment was billeted in buildings mainly in the Zehlendorf area of southwest Berlin. As the units of the

66th were moving into their comfortable accommodations in Berlin, something happened that gave Capt. Jim Burt, the H Company commander, a great sense of pride:

> The First Sergeant gave me a room that was large enough for six, and I protested because some of the men were crowded. And he said that the men in the 2nd Armored knew their figures, they knew that their officers bled when they shouldn't. They knew that officer casualties were a much higher percentage than enlisted men and that their officers deserved the most and nothing was too good for them. That was a very, very good feeling.[48]

Sgt. John Fabian of A Company recalls some of the American efforts to make life in Berlin more comfortable:

> The weather was extremely hot, so some GIs decided to convert the air raid water pool across the street into a swimming pool. They even installed a makeshift diving board. Sadly enough, shortly upon completion it was declared off limits due to the possibility of increasing bacteria.[49]

Chaplain Luke Bolin described Berlin in a letter to his wife on 12 July:

> Roberta, I have now seen Berlin. We had orders not to leave the American area, but the Russ, Br. and several Americans were going all over the place, so I did too. Now we can take tours. I went out this afternoon to lay out a route covering the sights. I told the Col. at supper, so he asked me to go with him after supper to see the plan. Of course, I did. Think I got some good pictures this afternoon. I went thru the Reichs Chancellery, where Hitler had his office. It is kaput. Drove down and up Unter den Linden, saw the Library, Tomb of the Unknown Soldier, Kaiser's Palace, Cathedral, Museum, and Gallery etc., all of which were likewise kaput. Simply the shells remain. The Brandenburg Gate remains, but is damaged. The Reichstag has been bombed heavily. The Tiergarten is, to my surprise, a park but badly messed up with wrecked vehicles, blown trees, graves of the dead who fought there, and general debris. The Olympic Stadium is on the west side. It is a tremendous place, able to seat 90,000, and damaged very little. The center of Berlin makes me remember reading about the sacking of Jerusalem, Babylon, etc., and leaving them desolate, except for the howling of wild animals. Surprisingly enough, more and more people are getting on the streets, but where they live in the center of town, is a mystery to me. Very few do and they live in basements. The Air Corps did a good job but in old style war it is impossible to justify the destruction of churches,

hospitals and even private homes. But in modern, total war it is not only understandable, but necessary. Seeing this makes me realize what is in store for Japan. If they have an ounce of sense, they'll quit soon, but that is doubtful.[50]

Life in the German capital was always interesting, as the men worked with the British and Russians in their joint occupation of the city. One first sergeant was surprised when a number of German men of military age approached him and wanted to volunteer to help the Americans fight the Russians. Relations with the Russians on the soldier level were generally cordial. There was considerable buying, selling, and trading of items between the Allies. One American soldier sold his watch to a Russian for an amazing three hundred dollars. Watches with large faces were especially popular. A carton of American cigarettes could bring over one hundred dollars. Other highly prized items the Soviet soldiers sought were shoe polish and toilet paper. Life there was pleasant, with the comfortable billets, movies, and a service club. The men even had a club on Berlin's great lake, the Wannsee, where they could swim and use a small fleet of boats.[51]

While he was in Berlin, Maj. Cameron Warren, Regimental S-1, had received word from his stepfather to visit his father's old friend Gen. Harry Vaughn. Vaughn was President Truman's close friend and served as military aide. Warren took his jeep to where the presidential party was staying at the "Little White House" in Potsdam. After leaving his pistol with the guards he was shown into General Vaughn's office. After chatting for a while Vaughn asked if Warren would like to meet the president. Warren said sure and Vaughn brought him into the president's adjoining office to met President Truman. The president spent about fifteen minutes talking to the young major. Warren remembers that the president talked primarily about how hard he was working "to get the boys home."[52]

During one of their days in Berlin, Captain Burt and his driver wandered around Berlin in their jeep. They arrived at the Reichs Chancellery where they met a Russian officer and his driver. Together they explored the building and found an office which had bins and drawers full of Nazi medals. The group assembled full sets of the decorations before departing.[53]

Sgt. John Fabian recalls his three different visits to the Reich's Chancellery:

> The first time I was in the Reichs Chancellery I was with a buddy from N.J. We came upon a room that was partially destroyed. We found ourselves knee deep in medals. We stuffed many different types into the bags we had, took them back to the billets and gave them away to fellow GIs.

The light tanks of A Company along a road in Grunewald, the great forest of Berlin. July 1945.

John B. Roller

M4 Shermans of the 66th lined up along the autobahn in the Grunewald for the grand review of 2nd Armored Division. July 1945.

John B. Roller

On our next visit to the Chancellery the room was completely empty of medals. On the third visit Russian soldiers were standing on the front steps selling them to anyone who was interested.[54]

After years of conducting his church services outdoors, Chaplain Bolin was finally able to use a church in which to hold his services.

Had three services yesterday and did alright but some men had to clean their tanks. They clean them almost every day but they are about as dirty as ever after a few miles drive. Had one service in a beautiful, rather modern church. It's windows had been blown out but other than that it was in good condition. It was built in 1933 and in the front of the sanctuary are hundreds of symbols, many Christian but some German eagles and Swastikas! I understand that some of the members were Nazis and wanted the Nazi symbols in addition to the Christian ones! As one enters the church he sees on the right a relief of Hindenburg with Iron Crosses on each side and on the left Hitler with Swastikas on each side! That made it convenient to give the men a good object lesson on what happens to religion when it gets tied to the state. The Swastikas and Hitler won't be there next Sunday![55]

On 16 July the tanks of the 66th Armor lined the autobahn running through the great Grunewald forest in Berlin and were reviewed by President Harry S. Truman, Prime Minister Winston S. Churchill, and other Allied leaders. The 66th again turned out for a review on 18 July for Gen. George C. Marshall, Gen. Henry "Hap" Arnold, Adm. Ernest King, and Field Marshal Sir Allen Brooke, Chief of Staff of the British Army. Their previous commander, Gen. George S. Patton, and Secretary of War Henry Stimson reviewed them on the twentieth. Patton wore a highly polished helmet adorned with his four stars and the patch of the 2nd Armored Division.

At the end of July 1945, the 82nd Airborne Division relieved the regiment and the rest of the 2nd Armored Division from their duties as the first American occupation unit in the former Nazi capital. From August to mid-December the 2nd Armored Division performed occupation duties in the area of Hanau, Gelnhausen, and Bad Orb, a short distance east of Frankfurt am Main. During this time most of the veteran soldiers returned to the United States while the newly arrived replacements stayed with their units. Finally, on 18 January 1946 the 66th Armored Regiment left Marseilles, France. On 29 January, after three years, three months absence, the regiment returned to the United States. In February 1946, the 66th Armored Regiment moved to its new home of Camp Hood, Texas.[56]

Lt. Donald Critchfield of F
Company relaxing in front of
his pup tent after V-E Day.
Donald A. Critchfield

Motorpool of A Company with a row of M-24 "Chaffee" light tanks on the right and their
predecessors, the M-5 "Stuart" light tanks, on the left. The photograph was taken on V-E
Day at a former German army barracks in Lebenstedt.

John B. Roller

The old and the new. A M-26 "Pershing" heavy tank named "Hell on Wheels" beside a M-4 Sherman.

John B. Roller

Capt. John Roller, A Company commander, receiving his third Silver Star from Brig. Gen. John "Pee Wee" Collier. April 1945.

John B. Roller

The "All American" M-24 "Chaffee" light tank of A Company commander, Capt. John Roller. May 1945.

Capt. John Roller posed atop one of the German anti-aircraft guns near Berlin. July 1945. Note the seven kill rings around the barrel.

M-5 "Stuart" and M-24 "Chaffee" light tanks of A Company. Spring 1945. Note the names on the tank: Ann, Army, and A-For-Lee.

American-made $2^{1}/_{2}$-ton trucks of the Red Army on the Leipzig-Berlin autobahn. The convoy of the 66th en route to Berlin is at the right. July 1945.

Capt. Cam Warren receiving the Bronze Star at Bernburgh, Germany on 25 June 1945.

Cameron J. Warren

Capt. Cam Warren next to his jeep in Berlin. July 1945.

Cameron J. Warren

Crews lined up before their M-5 Stuart light tanks just before the grand review. This photograph gives some idea of the awesome line of armored might that lined the autobahn for several miles. July 1945.

John B. Roller

Lt. Donald Critchfield of F Company in front of a neat stack of bricks which Berliners have salvaged from the bombed building for use in rebuilding the city. July 1945.

Donald A. Critchfield

Sign of 2nd Battalion. On the left is Lieutenant Colonel Herkness, commander from England to Germany. On the right is Lieutenant Colonel Cox, commander from the Bulge to Berlin. July 1945.

John B. Roller

The ruined Reichstag. July 1945.

John B. Roller

Tankers of A Company in Potsdam: Cpl. Joe Kollar, Pfc. Russell
Alsip, Pfc. Ed Cuthbert, Pfc. Jack Fabian, and Pfc. Dewey Wells.
July 1945.

Destroyed Soviet Josef Stalin-II heavy tank along a Berlin street. July 1945.

Knocked-out German Mark V Panther tank with Berlin children. July 1945.

John B. Roller

Massive portrait of the "Big Three" allies erected in Berlin. July 1945.

John B. Roller

American soldiers and vehicles in front of the bombed-out Ministry of Propaganda. July 1945.

John B. Roller

Soviet soldier filming in Berlin with a crowd of German civilians. July 1945.

Luke Bolin

Bombed-out buildings in Berlin. Back of photo reads: Typical, there are miles of this. July 1945.

John B. Roller

Ruins of one of the large villas near the Grunewald. July 1945.

John B. Roller

Capt. John Roller, commander of A Company, in front of German He-111 bomber and Me-110 fighter bomber. Roller wears the popular "Ike" jacket uniform.

Back of photo reads: "Three GIs sell a Russian a watch. Girls at right show lots of leg—all night—one chocolate bar." July 1945.

Soviet soldiers pose for a photo outside the battle-scarred ruin of the Reichschancellery. July 1945.

A young German poses next to the dug-in turret of a Mark IV tank located in a former garden plot. July 1945.

The men of H Company pose in front of variety of their tanks. Berlin, July 1945.

Cameron J. Warren

Epilogue

Following the birth of his daughter, Sally, Lt. Col. Amzi "Rudy" Quillian wrote a difficult letter home. Quillian mailed the letter from North Africa to his wife to be given to his daughter in the event of his death. Lieutenant Colonel Quillian, the 3rd Battalion commander, died of wounds received in Normandy in August 1944. The following is his daughter Sally's story of the letter from her father:

The letter was something I avoided reading for 41 years, until the 40th anniversary of D-Day in Normandy. It was addressed to me from someone I never knew. In retrospect, I wish it had been read aloud by my crib every night.

Instead, I remember my mother saying I should read the letter from my father when I was old enough to understand. But you don't have to be able to read to understand how to begin to avoid painful emotional subjects, especially ones that make adults cry. I never knew much about World War II because the school semester always seemed to be over by the time we got to it.

In 1984 a series of events led me back to the letter. A retired Army general moved next door, and as soon as he learned my father had been a West Point graduate killed in WWII, he wrote the academy for his records. Among the items sent to me was a copy of his eulogy which had appeared in *The Assembly*, West Point's quarterly alumni magazine.

The memorial article started, "In a little country church yard in Hall County, among the hills of northeast Georgia, stands a block of granite with the simple inscription, Lt. Col. Amzi Rudolph Quillian, Gentleman and Soldier. Born September 12, 1911—Died August 4, 1944."

Rudolph's broken body, with those of thousands of his comrades, lies in the Normandy American Cemetery overlooking Omaha Beach, but his spirit is here—in the rolling red hills among which he grew up, in the blue mountains he loved, and in the little Methodist Church which he joined at an early age..."

The article continued with information I was aware of, but was put together in chronological order for the first time. He graduated from North Georgia Military College in Dahlonega prior to receiving an appointment to the United States Military Academy. At West Point he was on the honor committee and his sport was boxing.

After he graduated in 1937 he was commissioned to the 66th Infantry (Light Tanks) at Fort Benning. This became the 66th Armored Regiment of the 2nd Armored Division, under then Brig. Gen. George S. Patton, training at Benning and in Louisiana and the Carolinas until deployment to North Africa in November 1942.

He earned the Silver Star at Canicatti, Sicily. The 2nd Armored Division, nicknamed "Hell On Wheels," was deployed to France, and his battalion landed at Omaha Beach on D-Day plus six.

Receiving this information coincided with the intense media coverage of President Reagan's visit to Normandy to commemorate the 40th anniversary of D-Day, 6 June 1944. In May of 1984, it was possible to read the eulogy and follow all of the final events of his life on the maps in the issues of *Time* and *Newsweek*. For the first time I picked out St. Lo where he was mortally wounded when returning to part of his battalion after the St. Lo breakthrough. He was wounded 28 July and died seven days later.

The letter began:

Africa, 29 April 1943. My Dear Sally, The reason for this letter is that because of the business I'm engaged in it is possible that I may never get to see you. If that should be the case I want to at least leave you one or two of my ideas.

If you had been a boy I would be full of fatherly advice and I would encourage you to grow up to be a good soldier like I hope your father will prove to be. Since you are a girl—of which I am glad—I will leave all the advice for your mother to give you because she is better qualified to advise you than I am.

...If I do get to see you this letter is pointless and should be destroyed but if I shouldn't, I want you to know how I feel about the reason for it. We are living in a time now when soldiers must be willing to die for their country—I won't go into detail because I know you will read it all in your history books.

Of course I am willing to die if necessary but before I do I expect to make many of the enemy die for their country. Don't think we are martyrs either because this is an interesting and fascinating game and we are rather keen about it. I have under my command some of the best and bravest soldiers in the world and regardless of whether or not some of us fail to come back, the Germans will say we gave them the toughest fight they ever had.

Always remember that you have a fine and honourable name—all three of them. All my love—except your mother's share, Pop (P.S.) This is the first time I've thought of what I want you to call me. I like Pop after your grandfather Pop Ansley.

Well, well, I thought. Having a daughter must have been as strange for him as not having a father had always been for me. I guess I had felt kind of sorry for him, but suddenly the letter let me know that he was a thoroughly professional soldier doing a job he had chosen because he understood what was at stake, even though he knew the risks. At any rate, my conclusion was that if we had known each other, we would have been great buddies.

Sally Quillian Gates

Notes

CHAPTER 1

1. Mary Lee Stubbs and Stanley R. Connor, *Army Lineage Series Armor—Cavalry Part 1: Regular Army and Army Reserve* (Washington, D.C.: Office of the Chief of Military History, United States Army, 1969), 363.

2. Kenneth Macksey, ed., *Tank Facts and Feats: A Record of Armoured Fighting Vehicle Achievement* (New York: Stanley Publishing, 1980), 51.

3. Christopher F. Foss, *The Illustrated Encyclopedia of the World's Tanks and Fighting Vehicles* (London: Salamander Books, 1977), 15.

4. *A Co. Tank, 301st Battalion Tank Corps* (Philadelphia: Wright Co., 1919), 33–34.

5. Ibid.

6. This phrase first appeared on the top of the U.S. Army recruiting poster for the Tank Corps in 1918. It remains a motto of the U.S. Armored Force to this day.

7. This poster is shown in many of the books on WWI. It can be found in A.J.P. Taylor, ed., *History of World War I* (London: Octopus Books, 1974), 173.

8. Stubbs and Connor, *Army Lineage*, 363.

9. *A Co. Tank*, 34.

10. Ibid., 35.

11. Ibid., 38.

12. Ibid., 40.

13. Ibid., 40–42.

14. Ibid., 42.

15. Ibid., 42.

16. Stubbs and Connor, *Army Lineage*, 363.

17. *A Co. Tank*, 46.

18. Pyle, David A., "World War I Survey," Carlisle Barracks, Pa.: U.S. Army Military History Institute, n.d., 2.

19. Foss, *Tanks and Fighting Vehicles*, 16.

20. Macksey, *Tank Facts and Feats*, 54.

21. *A Co. Tank*, 46.

22. Ibid.

23. Ibid.

24. Dale E. Wilson, *Treat 'Em Rough!: The Birth of American Armor, 1917–20* (Novato, Calif.: Presidio Press, 1990), 54. This excellent and enjoyable book provides an outstanding history of American tanks and all tank units of WWI.

25. Ibid., 46–47.

26. Headquarters 301st Center, Tank Corps AEF, "Memorandum to Chief of Tank Corps, American E. F. France, Subject: Movement of Troops" (Camp Worgret, England: 301st Center, August 23 1918), 1.

27. Note: The squad roll contained all the nonessential items that each squad of ten men had to haul as baggage.

28. Headquarters, 301st Center, Tank Corps AEF, "General Orders No. 47" (Camp Worgret, England: 301st Center, 2 August 1918), 1–2.

29. *A Co. Tank*, 50–51.

30. Maj. R. I. Sasse, "Operations of the 301st Tank Battalion—T. C. Sept. 29th to Oct. 23rd 1918" (France: 305th Brigade—Tank Corps, 1918), 6.

31. *A Co. Tank*, 50–51.

32. Ibid., 51.

33. Ibid.

34. Ibid., 54.

35. Sasse, "Operations of the 301st," 3.

36. Historical Section, U.S. Army War College, "Memorandum for the Historical Section, U.S. Army War College" (Washington Barracks, Washington D.C.: Army War College, 9 March 1923), 1.

37. Sasse, "Operations of the 301st," 2.

38. Rose E. B. Coombs, *Before Endeavors Fade: A Guide to the Battlefields of the First World War* (London: Battle of Britain Prints, 1979), 102–3.

39. Sasse, "Operations of the 301st," 3.

40. *A Co. Tank*, 54.

41. Sasse, "Operations of the 301st," 6–7.

42. Ibid., 7.

43. Ibid., Appendix F.

CHAPTER 2

1. Ibid., 7–8.

2. Ibid., 8–9.

3. Ibid., 9–10.

4. Ibid., 10.

5. Ibid., Appendix F.

6. Sgt. Carl E. Rosenhagen, "Co. 'C' 301st Heavy Tank Corps" (n.d., Unpublished Memoirs, Patton Museum, Fort Knox, Ky., [post 1926, probably after 1945]), 3–4.

7. Ibid., 3–4.

8. Ibid.

9. Sasse, "Operations of the 301st," Appendix F.

10. Rosenhagen, "Co. 'C' 301st," 6–7.

11. Ibid., 11–15.

12. Sasse, "Operations of the 301st," Appendix F.

13. Ibid., 11.

14. Ibid., 13–14.

15. Ibid., 13–14.

16. *A Co. Tank*, 56.

17. Ibid., 96–97.

18. Sasse, "Operations of the 301st," 21.

19. Ibid., 22–24.

20. Ibid., 25.

21. *A Co. Tank,* 112–14.

22. Ibid., 112–18.

23. Ibid.

24. Sasse, "Operations of the 301st," 34.

25. Ibid., 36–40.

26. Ibid., 38–41.

27. Rosenhagen, "Co. 'C' 301st," 17.

28. Sasse, "Operations of the 301st," 38–41.

29. *A Co. Tank*, 59.

30. Ibid.

31. Ibid., 59 and 142.

32. Ibid., 142

33. Ibid.

34. Ibid.

35. Ibid., 143.

36. Ibid., 154–58.

37. Ibid., 158–59.

CHAPTER 3

1. First Tank Regiment, "History of the First Tank Regiment (Light)" (n.p.: First Tank Regiment, [1930]), 1.

2. Ibid., 1.

3. Headquarters, 16th Tank Battalion, letter to Adjutant General of the Army entitled "Silk Streamers for Colors." (Camp Meade, Md.: HQ, 16th Tank Battalion, 9 February 1923), 1.

4. The Army Adjutant General to Commanding General, III Corps Area, letter entitled "Redesignation of Infantry (Tank) Units" (Washington, D.C.: War Department, 13 August 1929), 1.

5. First Tank Regiment, "History," 1.

6. "History of the First and Second Tank Regiments" (n.p.: First Tank Regiment, [1931]), 4.

7. The Army Adjutant General to the Commandant of the Tank School, Letter entitled "Redesignation of Infantry (Tank) Units" (Washington, D.C.: War Department, 13 August 1929), 2.

8. Headquarters First Tank Regiment, "Roster of Officers of the First Tank Regiment and Attached Units" (Fort George G. Meade, Md.: Office of the Regimental Commander, 1 September 1929), 1.

9. Headquarters, 66th Infantry (Light Tanks) Regiment. "History 66th Infantry (Light Tanks) 1932" Fort Meade, Md.: HQ 66th Infantry Regiment (Light Tanks) 1933, 9.

10. 1st Lt. Bob Childs, "Report on Operations of First Platoon, Company 'B', First Tank Regiment from June 21, 1932 to August 4, 1932" (Fort George G. Meade, Md.: 5 August 1932), 1.

11. Ibid.

12. Ibid.

13. Geoffrey Perret, *America in the Twenties: A History* (New York: Simon and Schuster, 1982), 478–80.

14. Ibid., 480–81.

15. Childs, "Report," 1.

16. Ibid.

17. Colonel H. N. Cootes, "Report on Operations, 3rd Cavalry Regiment" (n.p.: 3rd Cavalry Regiment, n.d.), 1.

18. Childs, "Report," 1.

19. The report refers to alleged communists because Lieutenant Childs apparently had some doubts about the Communist involvement with the Bonus Army.

20. Childs, "Report," 2.

21. Susan Winslow, *Brother, Can You Spare a Dime?: America from the Wall Street Crash to Pearl Harbor* (New York: Facts on File Publications, 1976), 42.

22. Childs, "Report," 1.

23. Cootes, "Report," 3.

24. Perrett, *America in the Twenties*, 421.

25. HQ, 66 Inf. "History 66th Inf., 1932," 10.

26. Ibid., 7.

27. Ibid.

28. Ibid., 7–8.

29. Ibid., 8.

30. The date was officially designated by the 4th Endorsement, AG 314.73—(2-20-30) Misc. (Returns) War Department Army General Order (AGO) dated 5 April 1932. The Organization Day passed officially to the 66th by the 13th Endorsement, 320.2 Inf. (11-1-32) (Returns) War Department Army General Order (AGO) dated 12 December 1932.

31. Ibid.

32. Headquarters, 66th Infantry (Light Tanks) Regiment, "History, 66th Infantry (Light Tanks) 1932" (Fort Meade, Md.: HQ, 66th Infantry Regiment [Light Tanks], 1933), 1.

33. Ibid., 2–3.

34. Ibid., 4–5.

35. Ibid., 11.

36. Ibid.

37. Headquarters, 66th Infantry (Light Tanks) Regiment, "History, 66th Infantry (Light Tanks) 1933" (Fort Meade, Md.: HQ, 66th Infantry Regiment [Light Tanks], 1934), 1.

38. Headquarters, 66th Infantry (Light Tanks) Regiment, "66th Infantry (Light Tanks) Swimming Pool" (Fort Meade, Md.: HQ, 66th Infantry Regiment [Light Tanks], 1933), 1–3.

39. HQ, 66 Inf., "History 66th Inf., 1933," 2.

40. Ibid., 2–3.

41. Ibid., 2–4.

42. 66th Armor Regiment, "Anti-Machine Gun League, Order of the Little Red Tank, Tank Chapter No. 1 History" (n.p.: 66th Armored Regiment, n.d.), 1.

43. Ibid., 1.

44. Ibid.

45. This letter was designated AG 537.3I.R.

46. Headquarters, 66th Infantry (Light Tanks) Regiment, "History, 66th Infantry (Light Tanks) 1934" (Fort Meade, Md.: HQ, 66th Infantry Regiment [Light Tanks], 1935), 3.

47. Ibid., 3.

48. Ibid.

49. Ibid., 4.

50. Ibid., 2–3.

51. Ibid., 5–6.

52. Ibid., 6.

53. Ibid.

54. The (-) sign following a unit designation indicates that some part of the unit is detached. The number and/or size of the detached unit is not specified.

55. HQ, 66 Inf., "History 66th Inf., 1934," 6–7.

56. Ibid., 6–7.

57. Ibid., 7.

58. Ibid., 7–8.

59. Ibid., 8.

60. The letter was designated AG451, Misc.M–D.

61. Headquarters, 66th Infantry (Light Tanks) Regiment "Letter to the Adjutant General, U.S. Army, Subject: Requisition for Machine Guns" (Fort Meade, Md.: Office of the Regimental Commander, 11 March 1935), 1.

62. In the case of 3rd Battalion the (-) sign referred to Company I, which was attached to 1st Battalion.

63. Headquarters, 66th Infantry (Light Tanks) Regiment, "History, 66th Infantry (Light Tanks) 1935" (Fort Meade, Md.: HQ, 66th Infantry Regiment [Light Tanks], 1936), 3.

64. Ibid., 3.

65. Ibid.

66. Headquarters, 2nd Battalion, 66th Infantry (Light Tanks) Regiment, "History of Second Battalion Sixty Sixth Infantry (Light Tanks), 1936, (Ft. Benning, Ga.) HQ 3rd Bn. 66th Inf. (Light Tanks), 5–7.

67. HQ 2nd Bn., "History 1936," 4.

68. A tasking is a requirement given by a superior unit headquarters to one of its subordinate units. A tasking can require a unit to provide anything they have from soldiers to equipment for any period of time to perform any sort of job or training.

69. Headquarters, 66th Infantry (Light Tanks) Regiment, "History, 66th Infantry (Light Tanks) 1936" (Fort Meade, Md.: HQ, 66th Infantry Regiment [Light Tanks], 13 January 1937), 5.

70. Ibid., 3–4.

71. HQ 2nd Bn., "History 1936," 7.

72. Ibid., 4–5.

73. Headquarters, 3rd Battalion, 66th Infantry (Light Tanks) Regiment, "History of the Third Battalion 66th Infantry (Light Tanks), less Company I, for the Year 1936" (Fort Devens, Mass.: Office of the Battalion Commander, 5 January 1937), 9.

74. HQ, 66th Inf., "History 66th Inf., 1936," 2.

75. Headquarters, 2nd Battalion, 66th Infantry (Light Tanks) Regiment, "History of the Second Battalion 66th Infantry (Light Tanks) 1936" (Fort Benning, Ga.: Office of the Battalion Commander, 7 January 1937), 9.

76. HQ, 3rd Bn., "History of 3rd Bn.," 11.

77. This document was designated TO558-T.

78. This document was designated TO560-T.

79. HQ, 66th Inf., "History 66th Inf., 1936," 1.

80. Headquarters, 66th Infantry (Light Tanks) Regiment, "History, 66th Infantry (Light Tanks) 1937" (Fort Meade, Md.: HQ, 66th Infantry Regiment [Light Tanks], 1938), 5.

81. Ibid., 2.

82. Warren, Cameron J., interview with author, 25 June 1995.

83. HQ, 66th Inf., 1937, 2.

84. Ibid., 2–3.

85. Ibid..

86. Headquarters, 66th Infantry (Light Tanks) Regiment "Letter to the Adjutant General, U.S. Army, Subject: Journal of March" (Fort Meade, Md.: Office of the Regimental Commander, 26 October 1937), 3.

87. Ibid., 3.

88. Ibid.

89. Ibid., 3–5.

90. HQ, 66th Inf., "History 66th Inf., 1937," 3.

91. This order was designated TO No.7–81.

92. Office of the Chief of Infantry, "Letter to The Adjutant General; Subject: Activation of Headquarters and Headquarters Company and Maintenance Company, 66th Infantry" (Washington, D.C.: War Department, 29 September 1939), 1–2.

93. Operations and Training Division, G-3, "Memorandum for the Chief of Staff; Subject: Tank Units" (Washington, D.C.: War Department General Staff, 12 October 1939).

94. Ibid., 1–3.

CHAPTER 4

1. Col. A. C. Gillem, "Conference for Officers, 2nd Armored Division Lessons Drawn from a Concentration of the Provisional Tank Brigade" (Fort Benning, Ga.: 66th Armored Regiment, 7 October 1940), 1.

2. Ibid., 2.

3. Ibid., 3.

4. Ibid., 4.

5. Ibid.

6. Ibid., 5.

7. Ibid., 6.

8. Ibid.

9. Ibid.

10. Ibid.

11. Ibid.

12. Ibid., 7.

13. Ibid., 8.

14. Ibid., 9.

15. Ibid., 9–10.

16. Ibid., 11.

17. John Cranston, "1940 Louisiana Maneuvers Lead to Birth of the Armored Force" (*Armor*, May–June 1990, Volume XCIX, No. 3), 30–32.

18. Bradford G. Chynoweth, "Recollections of My Army Career, 1890–1941, Box 3," Date unknown, location unknown (Archives, U.S. Army Military History Institute, Carlisle Barracks, Pa.), 25.

19. Gillem, "Conference for Officers," 14.

20. Ibid., 13.

21. Ibid., 13–14.

22. Lt. Col. B. G. Chynoweth, "Letter to Colonel E. L. Gruber, Chief Control Officer" (Tank Camp, Harmony Church, Ga.: 1st Battalion, 66th Infantry, 20 April 1940).

23. Ibid., 14.

24. Cranston, "1940 Louisiana Maneuvers," 32.

25. Gillem, "Conference for Officers," 14–15.

26. Ibid.

27. Cranston, "1940 Louisiana Maneuvers," 32.

28. Public Relations Office, "A Brief History of the Second Armored Division" (England: HQ 2nd Armored Division, 1 March 1944), 1.

29. Ibid., 4.

30. Ibid.

31. Unknown, Profiles in Courage Concerning Our Honorary Regimental Commander—Colonel Herbert S. Long, Jr. 1913–86.

32. Public Relations Office, "A Brief History," 4.

33. Headquarters, 2nd Armored Brigade, "Training Memorandum No. 21" (Fort Benning, Ga.: HQ, Office of the Brigade Commander, 24 October 1940), 11.

34. Ibid.

35. Headquarters, Fort Benning, "Letter to Colonel A. C. Gillem, Jr., 66th Armored Regiment (Light Tanks), Subject: Commendation" (Fort Benning, Ga.: Office of the Commanding General, 26 November 1940).

36. Public Relations Office, "A Brief History," 5.

37. Hylinski, Bernard. Telephone interviews with author, 27 February and 20 March 1995.

38. Alvin C. Gillem, Jr., "Division School—January 6, 1941 The March to Panama City" (Fort Benning, Ga.: HQ, 66th Armored Regiment, January 1941), 1.

39. Ibid., 2–3.

40. Ibid., 3.

41. Ibid., 3–4.

42. Ibid., 4.

43. Domarecki, Thomas, telephone interview with author, 23 December 1994.

44. Dr. Norris H. Perkins, "Adventures in Armor" (Dr. Norris H. Perkins Papers, Portland, Ore.), 11.

45. Public Relations Office, "A Brief History," 5.

46. Domarecki, telephone interview, 23 December 1994.

47. Long, Herbert S., Profiles of Courage: Col. Hugh R. O'Farrell.

48. Warren, Cameron J., interview with author, 25 June 1995.

49. John H. Mayo, "War Memories" (Dr. Norris H. Perkins Papers, Portland, Ore.), 3.

50. Ibid.

51. Public Relations Office, "A Brief History," 5.

52. Ibid., 5.

53. Mayo, "Memories," 3.

54. Perkins, "Adventures," 4.

CHAPTER 5

1. Headquarters, Second Armored Division, "Annex Number 1 to Report of Operations Second Army Maneuvers" (Fort Benning, Ga.: HQ, Second Armored Division, 10 July 1941), 1.

2. Headquarters, Second Armored Division, "Report of Operations—Second Army Maneuvers" (Fort Benning, Ga.: HQ, Second Armored Division, 15 July 1941), 1.

3. Headquarters, Second Armored Division, "March Table Second Army Maneuvers" (Fort Benning, Ga.: HQ, Second Armored Division, June 1941), 1.

4. Headquarters, Second Armored Division, "Field Order Number 3, Second Army Maneuvers" (Chickamauga Park, Ga.: 15 June 1941), 1.

5. Headquarters Second Armored Division, "Annex Number 3, to Report of Operations—Second Army Maneuvers"(Fort Benning, Ga.: 15 July 1941), 1.

6. HQ, 2AD, "Report of Operations—Second Army Maneuvers," 1.

7. HQ, 2AD, "Annex Number 3," 1.

8. Ibid.

9. William Lloyd Rape, "Memories of World War II," September 1985, (Dr. Norris H. Perkins Papers, Portland, Ore.), 3.

10. Ibid.

11. Dr. Norris H. Perkins, "Adventures in Armor Talk," 5 April 1986, (Dr. Norris H. Perkins Papers, Portland, Ore.), 3–4.

12. Ibid.

13. HQ, 2AD, Annex No. 3, 1.
14. Perkins, "Adventures," 5.
15. HQ, 2AD, "Report of Operations," 2.
16. Headquarters, Second Armored Division, "Annex Number 4, to Report of Operations—Second Army Maneuvers" (Fort Benning, Ga.: HQ, Second Armored Division, 15 July 1941), 1.
17. Headquarters, Second Armored Division, "Annex Number 5 to Report of Operations—Second Army Maneuvers" (Fort Benning, Ga.: HQ, Second Armored Division, 15 July 1941), 1.
18. HQ, 2AD, "Report of Operations," 2.
19. Ibid., 3.
20. Headquarters, Second Armored Division, "Annex Number 6, to Report of Operations—Second Army Maneuvers" (Fort Benning, Ga.: HQ, Second Armored Division, 15 July 1941), 1.
21. Headquarters, Second Armored Division, "Train Schedule" (Camp Forrest, Tenn.: HQ, Second Armored Division, 28–30 June 1941).
22. HQ, 2AD, "Field Order No. 8" (Decherd, Tenn.: HQ, 2AD, 27 June 1941).
23. HQ, 2AD, "Report of Operations," 4.
24. Ibid., 4.
25. Ibid., 3–4.
26. Ibid., 3–4.

CHAPTER 6

1. Burt, James M., letter to author, 5 February 1995.
2. Headquarters, Second Armored Division, "Report of Operations, Corps Field Exercises and Army Maneuvers" (Fort Benning, Ga.: HQ, Second Armored Division, 23 October 1941), 1.
3. Warren, Cameron J., notes.
4. Mayo, "Memories," 7.
5. Headquarters, Second Armored Division, "Annex Number 4, to Report of Operations—Corps Field Exercises and Army Maneuvers, August and September 1941" (Fort Benning, Ga.: HQ, Second Armored Division, 16 October 1941), 1.
6. Ibid.
7. HQ, 2AD, "Report of Operations," 2.
8. HQ, 2AD, " Report of Operations," 2.
9. HQ, 2AD, "Annex Number 4, " 1.
10. HQ, 2AD, "Report of Operations," 2.
11. HQ, 2AD, "Annex Number 4," 1.
12. Ibid., 1–2.
13. Ibid., 2.
14. Perkins, "Adventures," 7.
15. HQ, 2AD, "Annex Number 4," 2.
16. Public Relations Bureau, "Comments by General Krueger" (Camp Polk, La.: Public Relations Bureau, 21 August 1941), 1–2.
17. Ibid.
18. Ibid.
19. Ibid., 3.
20. Ibid., 6.
21. Ibid., 6–7.
22. Ibid., 8.
23. Ibid., 9.

24. Headquarters, Third Army, Office of the Commanding General, "Letter to Major General George S. Patton, Jr. (Camp Polk, La.: HQ, 3rd Army, 23 August 1941).

25. Headquarters, 66th Armored Regiment (L) "Memorandum to Commanding General 2d Armored Division. Subject: Testing Ground for Cross-Country Operation" (DeRidder, La.: HQ, 66th Armored Regiment [L], 24 August 1941), 1.

26. Ibid.

27. Headquarters, Second Armored Division, "Annex Number 5, to Report of Operations—Corps Field Exercises and Army Maneuvers, August and September 1941" (Fort Benning, Ga.: HQ, Second Armored Division, 16 October 1941), 1.

28. Ibid.

29. Perkins, "Adventures," 7.

30. Ibid., 7.

31. HQ, 2AD "Annex Number 5," 2.

32. Ibid.

33. Ibid., 7.

34. Perkins, "Adventures," 7.

35. Ibid., 7.

36. Ibid.

37. Ibid.

38. HQ, 2AD, "Report of Operations," 3.

39. Perkins, "Adventures'" 8.

40. Headquarters, Second Armored Division, "Annex Number 7, to Report of Operations Corps Field Exercises and Army Maneuvers, August and September 1941" (Fort Benning, Ga.: HQ, Second Armored Division, 16 October 1941), 1.

41. HQ, 2AD "Annex Number 7," 1.

42. Ibid., 2.

43. HQ, 2AD "Report of Operations," 4.

44. HQ, 2AD, Field Order No. 17" (Zwolle, La.: HQ, 2AD, 15 September 1941), 1.

45. HQ, 2AD "Report of Operations," 5–6.

46. Ibid., 6.

47. Headquarters, Second Armored Division, "Annex Number 9, to Report of Operations—Corps Field Exercises and Army Maneuvers, August and September 1941" (Fort Benning, Ga.: HQ, Second Armored Division, 16 October 1941), 1.

48. HQ, 2AD "Report of Operations," 7.

49. HQ, 2AD "Annex Number 9," 1.

50. Ibid., 1–2.

51. Ibid., 2.

52. Ibid.

53. Clark, Curtis, telephone interview with author, 25 January 1995.

54. HQ, 2AD "Report of Operations," 8.

55. Ibid.

56. Ibid., 9.

57. Ibid.

58. "Notes for Critique by General Krueger—September 11, 1941" (National Archives, Suitland, Md. Branch). 3–4.

59. Ibid.

60. Ibid.

61. Mayo, "Memories," 7.

CHAPTER 7

1. Headquarters, Second Armored Division, "Report of Operations—IV Army Corps and GHQ Directed Carolina Maneuvers" (Fort Benning, Ga.: HQ, Second Armored Division, 10 December 1941), 1–2.

2. Ibid.

3. Headquarters, Second Armored Division, "Annex No. 1 to Report of Operations—IV Army Corps and GHQ Directed Carolina Maneuvers" (Fort Benning, Ga.: HQ, Second Armored Division, 10 December 1941), X.

4. Headquarters, Second Armored Division, "Annex No. 2 to Report of Operations—IV Army Corps and GHQ Directed Carolina Maneuvers" (Fort Benning, Ga.: HQ, Second Armored Division, 10 December 1941), 1.

5. Ibid., 1.

6. HQ, 2AD, "Report of Operations" (10 December 1941), 3.

7. Annex No. 4, 1.

8. Ibid., 1–2.

9. Ibid., 2.

10. Ibid.

11. Perkins, "Adventures," 5.

12. Headquarters, Second Armored Division, "Annex No. 5 to Report of Operations—IV Army Corps and GHQ Directed Carolina Maneuvers" (Fort Benning, Ga.: HQ, Second Armored Division, 10 December 1941), 1.

13. Ibid., 1.

14. HQ, 2AD, "Report of Operations" (10 December 1941), 4.

15. Annex No. 5, 1.

16. Ibid., 1–2.

17. Ibid., 2.

18. Headquarters, Second Armored Division, "Annex No. 6 to Report of Operations—IV Army Corps and GHQ Directed Carolina Maneuvers" (Fort Benning, Ga.: HQ, Second Armored Division, 10 December 1941), 1.

19. Annex No. 6, 1.

20. Ibid., 2–3.

21. Ibid., 2.

22. Ibid.

23. Ibid., 3.

24. Headquarters, Second Armored Division, "Annex No. 7 to Report of Operations—IV Army Corps and GHQ Directed Carolina Maneuvers" (Fort Benning, Ga.: HQ, Second Armored Division, 10 December 1941), 1.

25. HQ, 2AD, "Report of Operations" (10 December 1941), 6.

26. Ibid.

27. Annex No. 7, 1.

28. Ibid., 2.

29. Ibid., 2–3.

30. Ibid., 7.

31. HQ, 2AD, "Report of Operations" (10 December 1941), 7.

32. Ibid., 1–2.

33. Headquarters, Second Armored Division, "Annex No. 8 to Report of Operations—IV Army Corps and GHQ Directed Carolina Maneuvers" (Fort Benning, Ga.: HQ, Second Armored Division, 10 December 1941), 1.

34. Annex No. 8, 2.

35. Ibid., 3.

36. Ibid.

37. HQ, 2AD, "Report of Operations" (10 December 1941), 9.

38. Ibid.

39. Headquarters, Second Armored Division, "Report of Operations—First Army vs. IV, Army," 9.

40. Ibid.

41. Ibid.

CHAPTER 8

1. Public Relations Officer, "A Brief History of the Second Armored Division" (England: HQ, 2nd Armored Division, 1 March 1944), 8.

2. John G. Getsinger, letter to author, 18 May 1995.

3. Public Relations Officer, "Brief History," 6.

4. Ibid., 7–8.

5. Ibid.

6. Headquarters, 66th Armored Regiment, "General Orders Number 16" (Fort Benning, Ga.: Headquarters, 66th Armored Regiment, 12 April 1942), 1.

7. Company H, 66th Armored Regiment, "Training Schedule for Monday, February 2, 1942" (Fort Benning, Ga.: Company H, 66th Armored Regiment, February 1942).

8. George Forty, *M4 Sherman* (London: Blandford Press, 1987), 21–35.

9. Maj. Norris H. Perkins and Michael E. Rogers, *Roll Again Second Armored: The Prelude to Fame 1940–43* (Surbition, Surrey, England: Kristall Productions, 1988), 87–90.

10. Ibid.

11. Company H, 66th Armored Regiment, "Company Roster" (Dr. Norris H. Perkins, Papers, Portland, Ore.), 1.

12. Public Relations Officer, "A Brief History," 9.

13. Ibid.

14. John H. Mayo, "War Memories" (Dr. Norris H. Perkins Papers, Portland, Ore.), 8.

15. Dr. Norris H. Perkins, "Adventures in Armor Talk" (Dr. Norris H. Perkins Papers, Portland, Ore., 5 April 1986), 5.

16. Public Relations Officer, "A Brief History," 9.

17. Ibid.

18. Getsinger, Letter, 5.

19. Mayo, "Memories," 10.

20. Ibid.

21. Getsinger, letter, 7.

22. Public Relations Officer, "A Brief History," 10.

CHAPTER 9

1. Ibid., 10, 14–16.

2. Burt, James M., letter to author, 7 February 1995.

3. Public Relations Officer, "A Brief History," 14.

4. Ibid., 15.

5. James M. Burt, War Memoirs, author's files, Martinez, Ga., 5–6.

6. Public Relations Officer, "A Brief History," 15.

7. Ibid., 16–17.

8. Ibid., 17.

9. Derden, John B., letter to author, 17 April 1995.

10. William Lloyd Rape, "Memories of World War II" (Dr. Norris H. Perkins Papers, Portland, Ore.), 4–5.

11. Perkins, "Adventures," 21.

12. Ibid.

13. Rape, "Memories," 5.

14. Ibid.

15. Perkins, "Adventures," 21–22.

16. Rape, "Memories," 5.

17. W. M. Page, letter to author, 9 June 1995.

18. Rape, "Memories," 6.

19. Perkins, "Adventures," 22.

20. Public Relations Officer, "A Brief History," 18.

21. Mayo, "Memories," 12.

22. Campbell, George, telephone interview with author, 10 January 1997.

23. Sasser, Lewis S., letter to his wife, 20 February 1943.

24. Perkins, "Adventures," 17.

25. Ibid., 16.

26. Ibid., 17.

27. Ibid., 22–23.

28. W. M. Page, letter to author, 9 June 1995, 2.

29. Ibid.

30. Arden Gatzke, "WWII Diary," March 1943 (author's files, Martinez, Ga.), 1.

31. Perkins, "Adventures," 25.

32. Ibid., 25.

33. Gatzke, "Diary," 14 April 1943.

34. James M. Burt, interview by author, notes, LaGrande, Ore., 23 January 1995.

35. Headquarters, 2nd Armored Division. "Special Orders No. 38" (Rabat, French Morocco: Office of the Division Commander, 20 February 1943), 1.

36. Mayo, "Memories," 12.

37. Perkins, "Adventures," 25.

38. Public Relations Officer, "A Brief History," 19–20.

39. Sasser, Lewis S., letter to his wife, 6 March 1943.

40. Perkins, "Adventures," 26.

41. Ibid.

42. "Regimental History" (England: Headquarters, 66th Armored Regiment, 1943), 1.

43. Public Relations Officer, "A Brief History," 20.

44. "Regimental History," 1.

45. Perkins, "Adventures," 26.

46. Ibid.

47. Critchfield, 3–4.

48. Headquarters, Combat Command A, 2nd Armored Division, "The Operations of Combat Command A for the period April 21, 1943, to July 25, 1943, Inclusive" (Palermo, Sicily: HQ, CCA, 26 July 1943), 1.

49. Public Relations Officer, "A Brief History," 20–21.

50. Getsinger, 8–9.

51. Sasser, Lewis S., letter to his wife, 22 May 1943.

52. HQ, CCA, "Operations CCA April 21–July 25, 1943," 1–2.

53. Ibid., 27.

54. "History 66th Armored Regiment" (England: Headquarters, 66th Armored Regiment, 1943), 21.

55. Burt, 29–30.

56. Sasser, Lewis S., letter to his wife, 26 May 1943.

57. Public Relations Officer, "A Brief History," 21.

58. HQ, CCA, "Operations CCA April 21–July 25, 1943," 2.

59. Getsinger, 10–11.

60. Perkins, "Adventures," 9.

61. Ibid.

62. Headquarters, 66th Armored Regiment, "The Operations of the 66th Armored Regiment for the Period July 1, 1943 to July 25, 1943, Inclusive" (APO 252, Sicily: HQ, 66th Armored Regiment, 5 August 1943), 1.

CHAPTER 10

1. HQ, 66th Armored Regt., "Operations 66th Armored July 1–25, 1943," 1.

2. Perkins, "Adventures," 29.

3. Sir Basil Liddell-Hart, "History of the Second World War: Part 51 Sicily" (Hicksville, N.Y.: Marshall Cavendish USA, Ltd., 1974), 1404.

4. Rape, "Memories," 8.

5. "Notes from Debriefing Capt. Perkins after Sicily Invasion" (Dr. Norris H. Perkins Private Papers, Portland, Ore.: 1943), 1.

6. Ibid., 1–2.

7. Gatzke, "Diary," 10 July 1943.

8. Notes from Debriefing Capt. Perkins, 1–2.

9. Ibid.

10. HQ, 66th Armored Regt., "Operations 66th Armored July 1–25, 1943," 2.

11. Getsinger, 10–11.

12. HQ, 66th Armored Regt., "Operations 66th Armored July 1–25, 1943," 2.

13. Ibid., 1–2.

14. Ibid., 2–3.

15. HQ, 66th Armored Regt., "Operations 66th Armored July 1–25, 1943," 3.

16. Dr. Norris H.. Perkins, "Lessons Learned in the Attack on Canicatti," *Armor Magazine,* May–June 1987, 32–36.

17. "Notes from Debriefing...Sicily," 2–3.

18. Ibid.

19. Perkins, "Lessons Learned," 32–36.

20. "Notes from Debriefing...Sicily," 4.

21. Perkins, "Adventures," 13.

22. "Arm Broken, Officer Led Tanks to Wreck Nazi 90s and 75s," *The Armored News*, 17 April 1944, 1.

23. Ibid.

24. Headquarters, Third Battalion, 66th Armored Regiment, "Report of Action 12 July 1943" (APO 252, Sicily: HQ, 3rd Bn., 66th Ar. Regt., 13 July 1943), 1.

25. HQ, 66th Armored Regt., "Operations 66th Armored July 1–25, 1943," 2–3.

26. "Arm Broken...," 1.

27. Gatzke, "Diary," 12 July 1943.

28. Perkins, "Lessons Learned," 36.

29. Joe Young, to Dr. Norris H. Perkins, Portland, Ore., 2 August 1981 (Dr. Norris H. Perkins Papers, Portland, Ore.)

30. H Company, 66th Armored Regiment, "Tank Action 12–13 July 1943" (APO 252 Sicily: H Co., 66th Ar. Rgt., 14 July 1943), 1.

31. HQ, 66th Armored Regt., "Operations 66th Armored July 1–25, 1943," 4.

32. HQ, CCA, "Operations CCA April 21–July 25, 1943," 4.

33. Warren, "Diary," 3.

34. Ibid.

35. HQ, CCA, "Operations CCA April 21–July 25, 1943," 4.

36. Morning Reports—Record of Events, Recon Company, 66th Armored Regiment, 2d Armored Division.

37. HQ, 66th Armored Regt., "Operations 66th Armored July 1–25, 1943," 4.

38. HQ, CCA, "Operations CCA April 21–July 25, 1943," 4.

39. HQ, 66th Armored Regt., "Operations 66th Armored July 1–25, 1943," 4–5.

40. Donald Critchfield, letter to author, 16 June 1995, 4.

41. Headquarters, 66th Armored Regiment, "S-3 Journal 7–31 July 1943" (Sicily: HQ, 66th Armored Regiment, August 1943), 6.

42. James Burt, letter to author, 27 February 1995.

43. HQ, 66th Armored Regt., "Operations 66th Armored July 1–25, 1943," 6.

44. HQ, CCA, "Operations CCA April 21–July 25, 1943," 6.

45. Rape, "Memories," 9.

46. Curtis Clark, interview by author, notes, LaGrande, Ore., 8 December 1994.

47. HQ, 66th Armored Regt., "Operations 66th Armored July 1–25, 1943," 6.

48. Headquarters, 66th Armored Regiment, "The Operations of the 66th Armored Regiment for the Period 25 July 20 August 1943, Inclusive" (APO 252, Sicily: HQ, 66th Armored Regiment, 30 August 1943), 1.

49. Luke Bolin, letter to author, 11 July 1995.

50. Sasser, Lewis S., letter to his wife, 25 July 1943.

51. HQ, 66th Armored Regt., "S-3 Journal 7–31 July 1943," 8.

52. George Lincoln to Dr. Norris H. Perkins, Portland, Ore. (Dr. Norris H. Perkins Papers, Portland, Ore.), 2–3.

53. HQ, 66th Armored Regt., "Operations 66th Armored 25 July–20 August 1943," 6.

54. Burt, James M., War Memoirs, 1 May 1980.

55. Lt. Col. Amzi R. Quillian, letter to his wife, 6 August 1943.

56. Headquarters, 66th Armored Regiment, "S-3 Journal 26 July–19 August 1943" (Sicily: HQ, 66th Armored Regiment, 30 August 1943), 1–12.

57. HQ, 66th Armored Regt., "Operations 66th Armored 25 July–20 August 1943," 2.

58. W. M. Page, letter to author, 9 June 1995, 3.

59. HQ, 66th Armored. Regt., Operations 25 July–20 August 1943, 1–2.

60. Ibid., 9.

61. Ibid., 13.

62. Headquarters, 66th Armored Regiment, "The Operations of the 66th Armored Regiment for the Period 20–31 August 1943, Inclusive" (APO 252, Sicily: HQ, 66th Armored Regiment, 1 September 1943), 1.

63. Luke Bolin, letter to his wife, 3 September 1943.

64. Gatzke, "Diary," 13, 21, 22, 28 September 1943.

65. Luke Bolin, letter to his wife, 13 September 1943.

66. Gatzke, "Diary," 6–9 October 1943.

67. Sasser, Lewis S., letter to his wife, 13 October 1943.

68. Headquarters, 66th Armored Regiment, "The Operations of the 66th Armored Regiment for the Period 1–31 October 1943, Inclusive" (APO 252, Sicily: HQ, 66th Armored Regiment, 3 November 1943), 1.

69. Donald Critchfield, letter to author, 16 June 1995, 5.

70. W. M. Page, letter to author, 9 June 1995.

71. Gatzke, 11–17 November.

72. John Getsinger, letter to author, 18 May 1995, 13–14.

73. "Brief History of the 2nd Armored Division" (c. Unk: Unk, c. 1945, National Archives), 4.

74. W. M. Page, letter to author, 9 June 1995.

75. Sasser, Lewis S., letter to his wife, 3 December 1943.

76. Thomas Domarecki, interview by author, notes, LaGrande, Ore., 23 December 1994.

77. W. M. Page, letter to author, 9 June 1995.

78. Long, Herbert S., Profiles of Courage: Lt. Col. Lindsay C. Herkness, Jr.

79. "History 66th Armored Regiment 1 January–31 December 1944" (APO 252, Germany: Headquarters, 66th Armored Regiment, 20 March 1945), 1.

80. Lt. Col. Lindsay C. Herkness, Jr., interview by author, 3 February 1998.

81. "History 1944," 2.

82. Headquarters, 66th Armored Regiment, "Operations for the Period 1–30 June 1944" (APO 252, Sicily: HQ, 66th Armored Regiment, 20 March 1945), 1.

CHAPTER 11

1. Headquarters, 66th Armored Regiment, "Operations for the period 1–30 June 1944" (APO 252, France: HQ, 66th Armored Regiment, 20 August 1944), 1.

2. Lt. John G. Getsinger, Memories, April 1995, author's files, LaGrande, Ore., 16.

3. Ibid., 17.

4. "History 66th Armor 1 Jan–31 Dec 1944," 3.

5. Johnson, *A Condensed History of Hell on Wheels*, 6.

6. Getsinger, 18–19.

7. HQ, 66th Armor, "Operations 1–30 June 1944," 2.

8. Ibid.

9. "History 66th Armor 1 Jan–31 Dec 1944," 3.

10. Donald Critchfield to the author, 16 June 1995, author's files, Martinez, Ga., 6.

11. "History 66th Armor, 1 Jan–31 Dec 1944," 3.

12. Capt. Cameron J. Warren, Normandy to Miss Carol Bowman, Washington, D.C., 4 July 1944, author's files, LaGrande, Ore.

13. HQ, 66th Armor, "Operations 1–30 June 1944," 1.

14. "History 66th Armor 1 Jan–31 Dec 1944," 3.

15. HQ, 66th Armor, "Operations 1–30 June 1944," 1.

16. Mr. Curtis Clark, interview by author, notes, LaGrande, Ore., 8 December 94.

17. HQ, 66th Armor, " Operations 1–30 June 1944," 1.

18. S.Sgt. Hubert Gwinn, Normandy to Capt. Norris H. Perkins, Fort Knox, 18 June 1944 (Dr. Norris H. Perkins Papers, Portland, Ore.)

19. HQ, 66th Armor, "Operations 1–30 June 1944," 3.

20. Headquarters, 2nd Battalion, 66th Armored Regiment, "Annex 1 to Report of Operations, HQ. 2d. 66 AR " (France: HQ, 2nd Bn., 66th Armor, June 1944), 1.

21. "History 66th Armor 1 Jan–31 Dec 1944," 4.

22. The latter two types of ammunition are generally used at ranges of less than fifty feet and indicate the ferocity of the close combat.

23. "History 66th Armor 1 Jan–31 Dec 1944," 4.

24. HQ, 2nd Bn. 66th Armor, "Annex No. 1," 1.

25. HQ, 66th Armor, "Operations 1–30 June 1944," 1.

26. "History 66th Armor 1 Jan–31 Dec 1944," 4.

27. Grover Lamar Russell to the author, 26 April 1995, author's files, Martinez, Ga., 2.

28. James M. Burt to the author, 27 February 1995, author's files, La Grande, Ore.

29. Arden Gatzke, "Diary" (Dr. Norris H. Perkins, Papers, Portland, Ore., 13 June 1944).

30. Rape, "Memories," 11.

31. HQ, 66th Armor, "Operations 1–30 June 1944," 5–6.

32. Thomas Domarecki interview by author, notes, LaGrande, Ore., 23 December 1996.

33. James M. Burt, War Memoirs, author's files, Martinez, Ga., 9–10.

34. A reconnaissance in force mission is performed primarily to gather information on enemy strengths, dispositions, and reactions but has sufficient combat strength to immediately exploit any enemy weakness discovered.

35. HQ, 66th Armor, "Operations 1–30 June 1944," 5–6.

36. Ibid., 6–7.

37. "History 66th Armor 1 Jan–31 Dec 1944," 4.

38. Capt. Cameron J. Warren, Normandy to Miss Carol Bowman, Alexandria, Virginia, 21 June 1944, author's files, Martinez, Ga.

39. William Lloyd Rape, "Memories of World War II" (Dr. Norris H. Perkins Papers, Portland, Ore.), 11.

40. Lt. Lewis Sasser to his wife, 21 June 1944, author's files, Martinez, Ga.

41. Gatzke, "Diary," 18–24 June 1944.

42. Headquarters, 66th Armored Regiment, "Operations for the Period 1–31 July 1944" (APO 252, France: HQ, 66th Armored Regiment, 18 August 1944), 1.

43. Ibid.

44. Getsinger, Memories, 19–20.

45. Burt, "War Memoirs," 21–22.

46. Bolin, letter, 3 July 1944.

47. HQ, 66th Armor, "Operations 1–31 July 1944," 1a.

48. Ibid., 1a–1b.

49. Lt. Col. A.R. Quillian to his wife, 16 July 1944, author's files, Martinez, Ga.

50. HQ, 66th Armor, "Operations 1–31 July 1944," 2.

51. Ibid.

52. Chaplain Luke Bolin to his wife, 8 July 1944, author's files, LaGrande, Ore.

53. Sasser, 9 July 1944.

54. HQ, 66th Armor, "Operations 1–31 July 1944," 3–4.

55. Bolin, letter, 19 July 1944.

56. Sasser, 13 July 1944.

57. Capt. Warren J. Cameron to Parents, 22 July 1944 (Dr. Norris H. Perkins Papers, Portland, Ore.), 1.

CHAPTER 12

1. Headquarters, Combat Command A, "Operation Cobra Field Order #4" (France: HQ, CCA, 20 July 1944), 1.

2. Ibid.

3. Headquarters, 66th Armored Regiment, "Operation Cobra Field Order No. 1" (France: HQ, 66th Armored Regiment, 20 July 1944), 1.

4. David Mason, *Breakout: Drive to the Seine* (New York: Ballantine Books, 1968), 45.

5. Grover Lamar Russell to the author, 26 April 1995, author's files, Martinez, Ga., 3.

6. Capt. Cameron J. Warren, England to Miss Carol Bowman, Alexandria, Va., 9 August 1944, author's files, Martinez, Ga.

7. Unknown, Profiles of Courage: Capt. Mario T. de Felice, M.C.

8. Headquarters, 66th Armored Regiment, Regimental Profiles in Courage: Lt. Col. Lindsay C. Herkness, Jr. (2nd Armored Division Museum, Fort Hood, Tex.).

9. HQ, 66th Armor, "Operations 1–31 July 1944," 5.

10. Ibid.

11. Rape, "Memories," 12.

12. HQ, 66th Armor, "Operations 1–31 July 1944," 2.

13. "History 66th Armor 1 Jan–31 Dec 1944," 11.

14. Gatzke, "Diary," 26 June 1944.

15. HQ, 66th Armor, "Operations 1–31 July 1944," 6–7.

16. "History 66th Armor, 1 Jan–31 Dec 1944," 12–14.

17. Lt. Finnis Smith to Capt. Norris H. Perkins, Fort Knox, 16 December 1944 (Dr. Norris H. Perkins Private Papers, Portland, Ore.), 3.

18. HQ, 66th Armor, "Operations 1–31 July 1944," 6–7.

19. "History 66th Armor 1 Jan–31 Dec 1944," 12–14.

20. Gatzke, "Diary," 30 July 1944.

21. HQ, 66th Armor, "Operations 1–31 July 1944," 7–8.

22. Critchfield to the author, 6.

23. HQ, 66th Armor, "Operations 1–31 July 1944," 7–8.

24. Luke Bolin interview by author, notes, 25 May 1995, author's files, Martinez, Ga.

25. Headquarters, 66th Armored Regiment, "Report of Operations for Period 1–31 August 1944" (APO 252, France: HQ, 66th Armored Regiment, 26 September 1944), 1.

26. Smith to Perkins, 3.

27. Rape, "Memories," 13.

28. HQ, 66th Armor, "Operations 1–31 Aug. 1944," 1.

29. "History 66th Armor 1 Jan–31 Dec 1944," 17–18.

30. Ibid., 18.

31. Warren, letter, 3 August 1944.

32. HQ, 66th Armor, "Operations 1–31 August 1944," 3–4.

33. "History 66th Armor 1 Jan–31 Dec 1944," 22.

34. Ibid., 4–5.

35. HQ, 66th Armor, "Operations 1–31 August 1944," 5–6; and "History 66th Armor 1 Jan–31 Dec 1944," 23–24.

36. G. Lamar Russell to the author, 26 April 1995, author's files, LaGrande, Ore., 3–4.

37. Ralph E. Brill to Dr. Norris H. Perkins, 6 August 1985 (Dr. Norris H. Perkins Papers, Portland, Ore.).

38. Gatzke, "Diary," 8 Aug 1944.

39. HQ, 66th Armor, "Operations 1–31 August 1944," 6–7.

40. Ibid., 7.

41. Ibid., 8.

42. Sasser, 13 August 1944.

43. "History 66th Armor 1 Jan–31 Dec 1944," 26.

44. HQ, 66th Armor, "Operations 1–31 August 1944," 12.

45. Arden Gatzke, "Journal" (Dr. Norris H. Perkins Papers, Portland, Ore.), 2.

46. Domarecki, Thomas, telephone interview with author, 23 December 1994.

47. Brill to Perkins.

48. Gatzke, "Diary," 17 August 1944.

49. Sasser, 29 August 1944.

50. William B. Brener, *Death of a Nazi Army: The Falaise Pocket* (New York: Stein and Day, 1985).

51. HQ, 66th Armor, "Operations 1–31 August 1944," 11–12.

52. Ibid., 12–13.

53. "History 66th Armor 1 Jan–31 Dec 1944," 29–30.

54. Gatzke, "Diary," 24–25 August 1944.

55. Ibid., 30–31.

56. Smith to Perkins, 4.

57. "History 66th Armor 1944," 31–32.

58. Letter (Dr. Norris H. Perkins Papers, Portland, Ore.).

59. Gatzke, 27 August 1944.

60. "History 66th Armor 1944," 53.

61. Sasser, August 29, 1944.

62. HQ, 66th Armor, "Operations 1–31 August 1944," Intell. supplement.

63. Burt."War Memoirs," 15.

64. Headquarters, 66th Armored Regiment, "Report of Operations for Period 1–30 September 1944" (APO 252, France: HQ, 66th Armored Regiment, 8 October 1944), 1.

65. John Derden "Letter to author," 9–12.

66. Sgt. Kenneth Grogan to Capt. Norris H. Perkins, 29 March 1945 (Dr. Norris H. Perkins Papers, Portland, Ore.), 4.

67. Lieutenant Sasser to his wife, 3 September 1944.

68. Headquarters, 1st Battalion, 66th Armored Regiment, "Reports of Operations for July–September 1944" (France: HQ, 1st Battalion, 66th Armored Regiment, September 1944), 2.

69. "History 66th Armor 1 Jan–31 Dec 1944," 35–37.

70. HQ, 66th Armor, "Operations 1–30 September 1944," 6–8.

71. Gatzke, "Diary," 17–18 September 1944.

72. HQ, 66th Armor, "Operations 1–30 September 1944," 9–10.

73. Ibid., 10–11.

74. Ibid., 11–12.

75. "History 66th Armor 1 Jan–31 Dec 1944," 64.

76. Bolin, letter, 20 September 1944.

CHAPTER 13

1. Headquarters, 66th Armored Regiment, "Report of Operations for Period 1–31 October 1944" (APO 252, Holland: HQ, 66th Armored Regiment, 2 November 1944), 1.

2. Ibid., 3.

3. Charles Whiting, *Bloody Aachen* (New York: Stein and Day, 1976), 15–17.

4. "History 66th Armor 1 Jan–31 Dec 1944," 41–42.

5. HQ, 66th Armor, "Operations 1–31 October 1944," 4–5.

6. "History 66th Armor 1 Jan–31 Dec 1944," 42.

7. Herkness, Interview with author, 4 February 1998.

8. Patrick C. Burke to the author, 31 May 1995, author's files, Martinez, Ga., 6.

9. Bolin, "Letter," 10 Oct 1944.

10. Burke, 31 May 1995, 43–44.

11. Capt. Cameron Warren to his parents, 10 October 1944 (Dr. Norris H. Perkins Papers, Portland, Ore.)

12. "History 66th Armor 1 Jan–31 Dec 1944," 45.

13. Rape, "Memories," 14–16.

14. Burt, "War Memoirs," 2.

15. Cameron Warren interview by author, 13 May 1995, Lake Oswego, Ore., author's notes, 2.

16. Gatzke, "Diary," 15–16 October 1944.

17. Burt, "War Memoirs," 2

18. Ibid., 2, 12.

19. Ibid., 14.

20. Ibid., 17.

21. Ibid., 24–25.

22. Ibid., 25.

23. *America's Medal of Honor Recipients* (Golden Valley, Minn.: Highland Publishers, 1980), 270.

24. Captain Warren to Carol Bowman, 27 October 1944, author's files, Martinez, Ga.

25. HQ, 66th Armor, "Operations 1–31 October 1944," 11–13.

26. Ibid., Annex No. 2.

27. Gatzke, "Diary," 7–12 November 1944.

28. Sasser, 5 November 1944.

29. "History 66th Armor 1 Jan–31 Dec 1944," 49.

30. Headquarters, 66th Armored Regiment, "Unit Report No. 1 From 312400 October 1944 to 302400 November 1944" (Basweiler, Germany: HQ, 66th Armored Regiment, 1 December 1944), 4–5.

31. Long, Herbert S., Profiles of Courage: Captain John B. Roller, Jr.

32. Derden, letter to author, 30.

33. Gatzke, "Diary."

34. HQ, 66th, "Unit Report Nov.," 6.

35. "History 66th Armor 1 Jan–31 Dec 1944," 51.

36. Ibid.

37. Ibid., 84.

38. Burt, "War Memoirs," 16.

39. History 66th Armor 1944, 54–56.

40. Sasser, 1 December 1944.

41. Headquarters, 66th Armored Regiment, "Unit Report No. 1 From 302400 November 1944 to 312400 December 1944" (Scoville, Belgium: HQ, 66th Armored Regiment, 1 January 1945), 4–5.

42. "History 66th Armor 1 Jan–31 Dec 1944," 58.

CHAPTER 14

1. History 66th Armor 1944, 91.

2. Sasser, 19 December 1944.

3. "History 66th Armor 1 Jan–31 Dec 1944," 58.

4. HQ, 66th Armor, "Unit Report Dec. 1944," 2–4.

5. "History 66th Armor 1 Jan–31 Dec 1944," 59.

6. Ibid., 60.

7. Thomas Domarecki, interview by author, notes, LaGrande, Ore., 23 December 1994.

8. HQ, 66th Armor, "Unit Report Dec. 1944," 8.

9. Gatzke, "Diary," 25 December 1944.

10. HQ, 66th Armor, "Unit Report Dec. 1944," 9.

11. Ibid.

12. Thomas Domarecki, interview by author, notes, LaGrande, Ore., 23 December 1994, 2.

13. Jean Paul Pallud, *The Battle of the Bulge: Then and Now* (London: Battle of Britain Prints Ltd., 1984), 365.

14. "History 66th Armor 1 Jan–31 Dec 1944," 61.

15. Patrick C. Burke to the author, 31 May 1995, author's files, Martinez, Ga., 1–5.

16. HQ, 66th Armor, "Unit Report Dec. 1944," 11–12.

17. Burt, "War Memoirs," 26.

18. HQ, 66th Armor, "Unit Report Dec, 1944," 14.

19. Capt. Cameron J. Warren to Carol Bowman, 31 December 1944, author's files, LaGrande, Ore.

20. Domarecki Interview, 23 December 1994.

21. Headquarters, 66th Armored Regiment, "Unit Report No. 3 From 1 January 1945 to 31 January 1945" (Stinval, Belgium: HQ, 66th Armored Regiment, 1 February 1945), 4.

22. Sasser, Celeste, letter to Luke and Roberta Bolin, 15 June 1945.

23. Sasser, 29 December 1944.

24. Arden Gatzke, "My Army Life from D-Day June 6, 1944 to Sept. 11, 1945" (Dr. Norris H.. Perkins Papers, Portland, Ore.).

25. John Hoye to the author, 20 November 1996.

26. HQ, "66th Armor, Unit Report No. 3, 1–31 Jan. 1945," 4.

27. Ibid., 4–5.

28. Warren, Cameron J., interview with author, 13 May 1995.

29. HQ, "66th Armor, Unit Report No. 3, 1–31 Jan. 1945," 6.

30. Gatzke, "My Army Life," 5–6.

31. HQ, 66th Armored Regt., "Unit Report No. 3, 1–31 Jan. 1945," 7.

32. Edward Cuthbert to the author, 5 June 1995, author's files, Martinez, Ga.

33. HQ, 66th, "Unit Report No. 3," 8.

34. Ibid.

35. Burt to author, 4 February 1995, 2.

36. HQ, 66th, "Unit Report No. 3," 8–9.

37. Ibid., 10.

38. Ibid., 12–13.

39. Ibid., 13.

40. Gatzke, "Diary," 28 January 1945.

41. Ibid.

42. Headquarters, 66th Armored Regiment, "Unit Report No. 4 From 312400 January 1945 to 282400 February 1945" (Unterbruch, Germany: HQ, 66th Armored Regiment, 1 March 1945), 2.

CHAPTER 15

1. Gatzke, "Diary," 26 February 1945.

2. HQ, 66th Armor, "Unit Report No. 4, 1–28 Feb. 1945," 2–3.

3. Luke Bolin to the Author, May 1995, author's files, Martinez, Ga., 3.

4. HQ, 66th Armor, "Unit Report No. 4, 1–28 Feb. 1945," 1–7.

5. Burt, "War Memoirs," 1 May 1980, 26.

6. Headquarters, 66th Armored Regiment, "Unit Report No. 5 From 012400 March 1945 to 312400 March 1945" (Keersbreich, Germany: HQ, 66th Armored Regiment, 31 March 1945), 2–3.

7. Ibid., 4.

8. Gatzke, "Diary," 1 March 1945.

9. HQ, 66th Armor, "Unit Report No. 5, 1–31 March 1945," 3–4.

10. Ibid., 5.

11. Burt, "War Memoirs," 28–29.

12. Author's letter with his written comments of James M. Burt, 3 April 1995, 2.

13. Critchfield, 9.

14. HQ, 66th Armor, "Unit Report No. 5 , 1–31 March 1945," 6.

15. Ibid.

16. Cuthbert, 6 June 1995.

17. Critchfield, 10–11.

18. Explanatory Note: A coil is a 360½ defensive formation used by tank units when halted in a dangerous area.

19. HQ, 66th Armor, "Unit Report No. 5," 6.

20. Ibid., 7–8.

21. Ibid., 7.

22. Donald Evans, letter to the author, 7 February 1997.

23. Warren, Cameron, The Dash for the Teutoburger Wald.

24. Headquarters, 66th Armored Regiment, "Unit Report No. 6 From 012400 April 1945 to 302400 April 1945" (Braunschweig, Germany: HQ, 66th Armored Regiment, 1 May 1945), 3–4.

25. Warren, Dash.

26. HQ, 66th, Unit Report No. 6, 3–4.

27. Ibid., 4–5.

28. Ibid., 5.

29. Ibid., 6–7.

30. Gatzke, "Diary," 5 April 1945.

31. HQ, 66th, Unit Report No. 6, 7.

32. Long, Herbert S., Profiles of Courage: Captain John B. Roller, Jr.

33. Gatzke, "Diary," 7–8.

34. Ibid., 8–9.

35. Ibid., 9–10.

36. Ibid., 10–11.

37. Gatzke, "Journal," 6.

38. Warren Interview, 25 June 1995, 1.

39. "A History of the Second United States Armored Division 1940 to 1946" (Camp Hood, Tex.: HQ, Second Armored Division, 1946), 144.

40. Ibid.

41. HQ, 66th Armor, "Unit Report April 1945," 17.

42. Ibid.

43. Ibid., 2.

44. John Fabian to the author, 4 June 1995, author's files, Martinez, Ga., 1.

45. Headquarters, 66th Armored Regiment, "Unit Report No. 7 From 302400 April 1945 to 312400 May 1945" (Lebenstedt, Germany: HQ, 66th Armored Regiment, 1 June 1945), 1–3.

46. Domarecki Interview, 22 November 1994, 1.

47. Headquarters, 66th Armored Regiment, "Unit Report No. 8 From 312400 May 1945 to 302400 June 1945" (Trebnitz, Germany: HQ, 66th Armored Regiment, 30 June 1945), 1–2.

48. Burt, "War Memoirs," 7.

49. John Fabian to the author, 4 June 1995, author's files, Martinez, Ga., 2.

50. Bolin, 12 July 1945.

51. "A History of the Second United States Armored Division 1940 to 1946," 145.

52. Interview with Cameron Warren, 13 May 1995, Lake Oswego, Ore., 3.

53. Burt, "War Memoirs," 26.

54. Fabian, 2–3.

55. Bolin, 12 July 1945.

56. "History 2 AD 1940–1946," 146–47.

Bibliography

PRIMARY SOURCES

The National Archives Suitland, Maryland
Record Group 407, Entry 427

"Brief History of the 2nd Armored Division." c. Unk: Unk, c. 1945, National Archives.

Headquarters, 2nd Armored Brigade. "Training Memorandum No. 21." Fort Benning, Georgia: HQ, Office of the Brigade Commander, 24 October 1940.

Headquarters, Second Armored Division. "Annex Number 1 to Report of Operations Second Army Maneuvers." Fort Benning, Georgia: HQ, Second Armored Division, 10 July 1941.

Headquarters, Second Armored Division. "Report of Operation Second Army Maneuvers." Fort Benning, Georgia: HQ, Second Armored Division, 15 July 1941.

Headquarters, Second Armored Division. "March Table Second Army Maneuvers." Fort Benning, Georgia: HQ, Second Armored Division, June 1941.

Headquarters, Second Armored Division. "Field Order Number 3, Second Army Maneuvers." Chickamauga Park, Georgia: 15 June 1941.

Headquarters, Second Armored Division. "Annex Number 3 to Report of Operations—Second Army Maneuvers." Fort Benning, Georgia: 15 July 1941.

Headquarters, Second Armored Division. "Annex Number 4 to Report of Operations—Second Army Maneuvers." Fort Benning, Georgia: HQ, Second Armored Division, 15 July 1941.

Headquarters, Second Armored Division. "Annex Number 5 to Report of Operations—Second Army Maneuvers." Fort Benning, Georgia: HQ, Second Armored Division, 15 July 1941.

Headquarters, Second Armored Division. "Annex Number 6 to Report of Operations—Second Army Maneuvers." Fort Benning, Georgia: HQ, Second Armored Division, 15 July 1941.

Headquarters, Second Armored Division. "Train Schedule." Camp Forrest, Tennessee: HQ, Second Armored Division, 28–30 June 1941.

Headquarters, Second Armored Division, "Field Order No. 8." Decherd, Tennessee: HQ, Second Armored Division, 27 June 1941.

Headquarters, Second Armored Division. "Report of Operations, Corps Field Exercises and Army Maneuvers." Fort Benning, Georgia: HQ, Second Armored Division, 23 October 1941.

Headquarters, Second Armored Division. "Annex Number 4 to Report of Operations Corps Field Exercises and Army Maneuvers, August and September 1941." Fort Benning, Georgia: HQ, Second Armored Division, 16 October 1941.

Public Relations Bureau. "Comments by General Krueger." Camp Polk, Louisiana: Public Relations Bureau, 21 August 1941.

Headquarters, Third Army, Office of the Commanding General. "Letter to Major General George S. Patton, Jr." Camp Polk, Louisiana: HQ, 3rd Army, 23 August 1941.

Headquarters, Second Armored Division. "Annex Number 5 to Report of Operations Corps Field Exercises and Army Maneuvers, August and September 1941." Fort Benning, Georgia: HQ, Second Armored Division, 16 October 1941.

Headquarters, Second Armored Division. "Annex Number 7 to Report of Operations Corps Field Exercises and Army Maneuvers, August and September 1941." Fort Benning, Georgia: HQ, Second Armored Division, 16 October 1941.

Headquarters, Second Armored Division. "Field Order No. 17." Zwolle, Louisiana: HQ, Second Armored Division, 15 September 1941.

Headquarters, Second Armored Division. "Annex Number 9 to Report of Operations Corps Field Exercises and Army Maneuvers, August and September 1941." Fort Benning, Georgia: HQ, Second Armored Division, 16 October 1941.

Headquarters, Second Armored Division. "Report of Operations—IV Army Corps and GHQ Directed Carolina Maneuvers." Fort Benning, Georgia: HQ, Second Armored Division, 10 December 1941.

Headquarters, Second Armored Division. "Annex No. 1 to Report of Operations—IV Army Corps and GHQ Directed Carolina Maneuvers." Fort Benning, Georgia: HQ, Second Armored Division, 10 December 1941.

Headquarters, Second Armored Division. "Annex No. 2 to Report of Operations—IV Army Corps and GHQ Directed Carolina Maneuvers." Fort Benning, Georgia: HQ, Second Armored Division, 10 December 1941.

Headquarters, Second Armored Division. "Annex No. 5 to Report of Operations—IV Army Corps and GHQ Directed Carolina Maneuvers." Fort Benning, Georgia: HQ, Second Armored Division, 10 December 1941.

Headquarters, Second Armored Division. "Annex No. 6 to Report of Operations—IV Army Corps and GHQ Directed Carolina Maneuvers." Fort Benning, Georgia: HQ, Second Armored Division, 10 December 1941.

Headquarters, Second Armored Division. "Annex No. 7 to Report of Operations—IV Army Corps and GHQ Directed Carolina Maneuvers." Fort Benning, Georgia: HQ, Second Armored Division, 10 December 1941.

Headquarters, Second Armored Division. "Annex No. 8 to Report of Operations—IV Army Corps and GHQ Directed Carolina Maneuvers." Fort Benning, Georgia: HQ, Second Armored Division, 10 December 1941.

Headquarters, Second Armored Division. "Report of Operations—First Army vs. IV Army Corps Maneuvers." Monroe, North Carolina: HQ, Second Armored Division, 22 November 1941.

Headquarters, 66th Armored Regiment. "General Orders Number 16." Fort Benning, Georgia: HQ, 66th Armored Regiment, 12 April 1942.

Headquarters, Combat Command A, 2nd Armored Division. "The Operations of Combat Command A for the period April 21, 1943, to July 25, 1943, Inclusive." Palermo, Sicily: HQ, CCA, 26 July 1943.

Headquarters, 66th Armored Regiment. "The Operations of the 66th Armored Regiment for the Period July 1, 1943 to July 25, 1943, Inclusive." APO 252, Sicily: HQ, 66th Armored Regiment, 5 August 1943.

Headquarters, Third Battalion, 66th Armored Regiment. "Report of Action 12 July 1943." APO 252, Sicily: HQ 3rd Battalion 66th Armored Regiment, 13 July 1943.

Headquarters, 66th Armored Regiment. "S-3 Journal 7–31 July 1943." Sicily: HQ, 66th Armored Regiment, August 1943.

Headquarters, 66th Armored Regiment. "The Operations of the 66th Armored Regiment for the Period 25 July–20 August 1943, Inclusive." APO 252, Sicily: HQ, 66th Armored Regiment, 30 August 1943.

Headquarters, 66th Armored Regiment. "S-3 Journal 26 July–19 August 1943." Sicily: HQ, 66th Armored Regiment, 30 August 1943.

Headquarters, 66th Armored Regiment. "The Operations of the 66th Armored Regiment for the Period 20–31 August 1943, Inclusive." APO 252, Sicily: HQ, 66th Armored Regiment, 1 September 1943.

Headquarters, 66th Armored Regiment. "The Operations of the 66th Armored Regiment for the Period 1–31 October 1943, Inclusive." APO 252, Sicily: HQ, 66th Armored Regiment, 3 November 1943.

Headquarters, 66th Armored Regiment. "Operations for the Period 1–30 June 1944." APO 252, France: HQ, 66th Armored Regiment, 28 June 1944.

Headquarters, 2nd Battalion, 66th Armored Regiment. "Annex 1 to Report of Operations." HQ, Second Battalion, 66th Armored Regiment France, June 1944.

Headquarters, 66th Armored Regiment. "Operations for the Period 1–31 July 1944." APO 252, France: HQ, 66th Armored Regiment, 18 August 1944.

Headquarters, Combat Command A. "Operation Cobra Field Order #4." France: HQ, CCA, 20 July 1944.

Headquarters, 66th Armored Regiment. "Operation Cobra Field Order No. 1." France: HQ, 66th Armored Regiment, 20 July 1944.

Headquarters, 1st Battalion, 66th Armored Regiment. "Report of Operations for July–September 1944." France: HQ, 1st Battalion, 66th Armored Regiment, September 1944.

Headquarters, 66th Armored Regiment. "Unit Report No. 3 From 1 January 1945 to 31 January 1945." Stinval, Belgium: HQ, 66th Armored Regiment, 1 February 1945.

Headquarters, 66th Armored Regiment. "Unit Report No. 8 From 312400 May 1945 to 302400 June 1945." Trebnitz, Germany: HQ, 66th Armored Regiment, 30 June 1945.

H Company, 66th Armored Regiment. "Tank Action 12–13 July 1943." APO 252, Sicily: H Company 66th Armored Regiment, 14 July 1943.

"Notes for Critique by General Krueger—September 11, 1941." National Archives, Suitland, Maryland Branch.

The National Archives Washington, D.C.

Headquarters 301st Center, Tank Corps AEF. "Memorandum to Chief of Tank Corps, American E. F. France, Subject: Movement of Troops." Camp Worgret, England: 301st Center, 23 August 1918.

Headquarters 301st Center, Tank Corps AEF. "General Orders No. 47." Camp Worgret, England: 301st Center, 2 August 1918.

Headquarters First Tank Regiment. "Roster of Officers of the First Tank Regiment and Attached Units." Fort George G. Meade, Maryland: Office of the Regimental Commander, 1 September 1929.

Headquarters, 66th Infantry (Light Tanks) Regiment. "History, 66th Infantry (Light Tanks) 1933." Fort Meade, Maryland: HQ, 66th Infantry (Light Tanks) Regiment, 1934.

Headquarters, 66th Infantry (Light Tanks) Regiment. "Letter to the Adjutant General, U.S. Army, Subject: Requisition for Machine Guns." Fort Meade, Maryland: Office of the Regimental Commander, 11 March 1935.

Headquarters, 66th Infantry (Light Tanks) Regiment. "History, 66th Infantry (Light Tanks) 1935." Fort Meade, Maryland: HQ, 66th Infantry Regiment (Light Tanks), 1936.

Headquarters, 66th Infantry (Light Tanks) Regiment. "History, 66th Infantry (Light Tanks) 1936." Fort Meade, Maryland: HQ, 66th Infantry Regiment (Light Tanks), 13 January 1937.

Headquarters, 3rd Battalion, 66th Infantry (Light Tanks) Regiment. "History of the Third Battalion 66th Infantry (Light Tanks), less Company I, for the Year 1936." Fort Devens, Massachusetts: Office of the Battalion Commander, 5 January 1937.

Headquarters, 2nd Battalion, 66th Infantry (Light Tanks) Regiment. "History of the Second Battalion 66th Infantry (Light Tanks) 1936." Fort Benning, Georgia: Office of the Battalion Commander, 7 January 1937.

Headquarters, 66th Infantry (Light Tanks) Regiment. "History, 66th Infantry (Light Tanks) 1937." Fort Meade, Maryland: HQ, 66th Infantry Regiment (Light Tanks), 1938.

Headquarters, 66th Infantry (Light Tanks) Regiment. "Letter to the Adjutant General U.S. Army, Subject: Journal of March." Fort Meade, Maryland: Office of the Regimental Commander, 26 October 1937.

The Patton Museum of Armor and Cavalry
Fort Knox, Kentucky

Rosenhagen, Sgt. Carl E. "Co. 'C' 301st Heavy Tank Corps." n.d. Unpublished Memoirs, Patton Museum, Fort Knox, Kentucky, [post-1926, probably after 1945].

Sasse, Maj. R. I. "Operations of the 301st Tank Battalion—T. C. Sept. 29th to Oct. 23rd 1918."

Dr. Norris H. Perkins Papers
Portland, Oregon

Mayo, John H. "War Memories." Dr. Norris H. Perkins Private Papers, Portland, Oregon.

Perkins, Dr. Norris H. "Adventures in Armor Talk." Dr. Norris H. Perkins Private Papers, Portland, Oregon, 5 April 1986.

Rape, William Lloyd. "Memories of World War II." Dr. Norris H. Perkins Private Papers, Portland, Oregon.

Warren, Cameron J. "Diary Licata—Agrigento—Palermo, The Sicilian Campaign." Portland, Oregon: Dr. Norris H. Perkins Private Papers, 23 July 1943.

"Arm Broken, Officer Led Tanks to Wreck Nazi 90s and 75s." *The Armored News*, 17 April 1944, 2.

"Notes from Debriefing Capt. Perkins after Sicily Invasion." Portland, Oregon: Dr. Norris H. Perkins Private Papers, 1943.

Company H, 66th Armored Regiment. "Training Schedule for Monday, February 2, 1942." Fort Benning, Georgia: Company H, 66th Armored Regiment, February 1942.

Company H, 66th Armored Regiment. "Company Roster." Dr. Norris H. Perkins Private Papers, Portland, Oregon.

The Second Armored Division Museum
Fort Hood, Texas

Headquarters, 66th Armored Regiment. "History 66th Armored Regiment 1 January–31 December 1944." APO 252, Germany: HQ, 66th Armored Regiment, 20 March 1945.

Headquarters, 2nd Armored Division. "Special Orders No. 38." Rabat, French Morocco: Office of the Division Commander, 20 February 1943.

"History 66th Armored Regiment." England: Headquarters, 66th Armored Regiment, 1943.

"A History of the Second United States Armored Division 1940 to 1946." Camp Hood, Texas: HQ, Second Armored Division, 1946.

Public Relations Office. "A Brief History of the Second Armored Division." England: HQ, 2nd Armored Division, 1 March 1944.

66th Armor Regiment. "Anti-Machine Gun League, Order of the Little Red Tank, Tank Chapter No. 1 History." n.p.: 66th Armored Regiment, n.d.

The U.S. Army Armor School Library
Fort Knox, Kentucky

Headquarters, 66th Armored Regiment. "Report of Operations for Period 1–31 August 1944." APO 252, France: HQ, 66th Armored Regiment, 26 September 1944.

Headquarters, 66th Armored Regiment. "Report of Operations for Period 1–30 September 1944." APO 252, France: HQ, 66th Armored Regiment, 8 October 1944.

Headquarters, 66th Armored Regiment. "Report of Operations for Period 1–31 October 1944." APO 252, Holland: HQ, 66th Armored Regiment, 2 November 1944.

Headquarters, 66th Armored Regiment. "Unit Report No. 1 From 312400 October 1944 to 302400 November 1944." Basweiler, Germany: HQ, 66th Armored Regiment, 1 December 1944.

Headquarters, 66th Armored Regiment. "Unit Report No. 1 From 302400 November 1944 to 312400 December 1944." Scoville, Belgium: HQ, 66th Armored Regiment, 1 January 1945.

Headquarters, 66th Armored Regiment. "Unit Report No. 4 From 312400 January 1945 to 282400 February 1945." Unterbruch, Germany: HQ, 66th Armored Regiment, 1 March 1945.

Headquarters, 66th Armored Regiment. "Unit Report No. 5 From 012400 March 1945 to 312400 March 1945." Keersbreich, Germany: HQ, 66th Armored Regiment, 31 March 1945.

Headquarters, 66th Armored Regiment. "Unit Report No. 6 From 012400 April 1945 to 302400 April 1945." Braunschweig, Germany: HQ, 66th Armored Regiment, 1 May 1945.

Headquarters, 66th Armored Regiment. "Unit Report No. 7 From 302400 April 1945 to 312400 May 1945." Lebenstedt, Germany: HQ, 66th Armored Regiment, 1 June 1945.

The U.S. Army Center for Military History
Washington, D.C.

Childs, 1st Lt. Bob. "Report on Operations of First Platoon, Company 'B', First Tank Regiment from June 21, 1932 to August 4, 1932." Fort George G. Meade, Maryland: 5 August 1932.

Cootes, Col. H. N. "Report on Operations, 3rd Cavalry Regiment" n.p.: 3rd Cavalry Regiment, n.d.

The Army Adjutant General to Commanding General, III Corps, Area. Letter to entitled "Redesignation of Infantry (Tank) Units." Washington, D.C.: War Department, 13 August 1929.

The Army Adjutant General to Commandant. The Tank School letter entitled "Redesignation of Infantry (Tank) Units." Washington, D.C.: War Department, 13 August 1929.

First Tank Regiment. "History of the First Tank Regiment (Light)." n.p.: First Tank Regiment, [1930].

Headquarters, 16th Tank Battalion. Letter to Adjutant General of the Army entitled "Silk Streamers for Colors." Camp Meade, Maryland: HQ, 16th Tank Battalion, 9 February 1923.

"History of the First and Second Tank Regiments." n.p.: First Tank Regiment, [1931].

Historical Section, U.S. Army War College. "Memorandum for the Historical Section, U.S. Army War College." Washington Barracks, Washington D.C.: Army War College, 9 March 1923.

Headquarters, 66th Infantry (Light Tanks) Regiment. "History, 66th Infantry (Light Tanks) 1932." Fort Meade, Maryland: HQ, 66th Infantry Regiment (Light Tanks), 1933.

Headquarters, 66th Infantry (Light Tanks) Regiment. "66th Infantry (Light Tanks) Swimming Pool." Fort Meade, Maryland: HQ, 66th Infantry Regiment (Light Tanks), 1933.

Headquarters, 66th Infantry (Light Tanks) Regiment. "History, 66th Infantry (Light Tanks) 1934." Fort Meade, Maryland: HQ, 66th Infantry Regiment (Light Tanks), 1935.

Office of the Chief of Infantry. "Letter to The Adjutant General; Subject: Activation of Headquarters and Headquarters Company and Maintenance Company, 66th Infantry." Washington, D.C.: War Department, 29 September 1939.

Operations and Training Division. G-3, "Memorandum for the Chief of Staff; Subject: Tank Units." Washington, D.C.: War Department General Staff, 12 October 1939.

The U.S. Army Military History Institute Archives
Carlisle Barracks, Pennsylvania

Chynoweth, Bradford G. "Recollections of My Army Career, 1890–1941, Box 3," Date unknown, location unknown. Archives, U.S. Army Military History Institute, Carlisle Barracks, Pennsylvania.

Chynoweth, Lt. Col. B. G. "Letter to Colonel E. L. Gruber, Chief Control Officer." Tank Camp, Harmony Church, Georgia: 1st Battalion, 66th Infantry, 20 April 1940.

Gillem, Col. A. C. "Conference for Officers, 2nd Armored Division Lessons Drawn from a Concentration of the Provisional Tank Brigade." Fort Benning, Georgia: 66th Armored Regiment, 7 October 1940.

Gillem, Alvin C., Jr. "Division School—January 6, 1941 The March to Panama City." Fort Benning, Georgia: HQ, 66th Armored Regiment, January 1941.

Pyle, David A. "World War I Survey." Carlisle Barracks, Pennsylvania: U.S. Army Military History Institute, n.d.

Headquarters, Fort Benning. "Letter to Colonel A. C. Gillem, Jr., 66th Armored Regiment (Light Tanks). Subject: Commendation." Fort Benning, Georgia: Office of the Commanding General, 26 November 1940.

SECONDARY SOURCES

A Co. Tank, 301st Battalion Tank Corps. Philadelphia: Wright Co., 1919.

America's Medal of Honor Recipients. Golden Valley, Minnesota: Highland Publishers, 1980.

Blumenson, Martin. *The Patton Papers 1885–1940*. Boston: Houghton Mifflin Co., 1972.

Brener, William B. *Death of a Nazi Army: The Falaise Pocket*. New York: Stein and Day, 1985.

Coombs, Rose E. B. *Before Endeavors Fade: A Guide to the Battlefields of the First World War*. London: Battle of Britain Prints, 1979.

Cranston, Dr. John. "1940 Louisiana Maneuvers Lead to Birth of the Armored Force." *Armor Magazine,* May–June 1990, Volume XCIX, No. 3.

Crookenden, Napier. *Battle of the Bulge 1944*. New York: Charles Scribner's Sons, 1980.

Forty, George. *M4 Sherman*. London: Blandford Press, 1987.

Foss, Christopher F. *The Illustrated Encyclopedia of the World's Tanks and Fighting Vehicles*. London: Salamander Books, 1977.

Houston, Donald E. *Hell on Wheels: The 2d Armored Division*. Novato, California: Presidio Press, 1977.

Johnson, Maj. Gen. Briard P. *A Condensed History of Hell on Wheels 2d Armored Division*. 2nd Armored Division Association, c. 1980.

Lefevre, Eric. *Panzers in Normandy: Then and Now*. London: Battle of Britain Prints Ltd., 1983.

LeTissier, Tony. *Berlin Then and Now*. London: Battle of Britain Prints Ltd., 1992.

Liddell-Hart, Sir Basil. "History of the Second World War: Part 51 Sicily" Hicksville, New York: Marshall Cavendish USA, Ltd., 1974.

Macksey, Kenneth, ed. *Tank Facts and Feats: A Record of Armoured Fighting Vehicle Achievement*. New York: Stanley Publishing, 1980.

Mason, David. *Breakout: Drive to the Seine*. New York: Ballantine Books, 1968.

Pallud, Jean Paul. *The Battle of the Bulge: Then and Now*. London: Battle of Britain Prints Ltd., 1984.

Perkins, Dr. Norris H. "Lessons Learned in the Attack on Canicatti." *Armor Magazine,* Vol. XCVI, No. 3 (May–June 1987): 32–38.

Perkins, Maj. Norris H. and Michael E. Rogers. *Roll Again Second Armored: The Prelude to Fame 1940–43*. Surbition, Surrey, England: Kristall Productions, 1988.

Perret, Geoffrey. *America in the Twenties: A History*. New York: Simon and Schuster, 1982.

Stanton, Shelby L. *Order of Battle U.S. Army, World War II*. Novato, California: Presidio Press, 1984.

Stubbs, Mary Lee and Stanley R. Connor. *Army Lineage Series Armor—Cavalry Part 1: Regular Army and Army Reserve*. Washington, D.C.: Office of the Chief of Military History, United States Army, 1969.

Whiting, Charles. *Bloody Aachen*. New York: Stein and Day, 1976.

Wilson, Dale E. *Treat 'Em Rough!: The Birth of American Armor, 1917–20*. Novato, California: Presidio Press, 1990.

Winslow, Susan. *Brother, Can You Spare a Dime?: America from the Wall Street Crash to Pearl Harbor*. New York: Facts on File Publications, 1976.

Index

Page numbers for photos are in italics.
The following abbreviations are used: B—Belgium; FR—France; G—Germany; GB—Great Britain;
N—Netherlands/Holland

Stackpole Military History Series

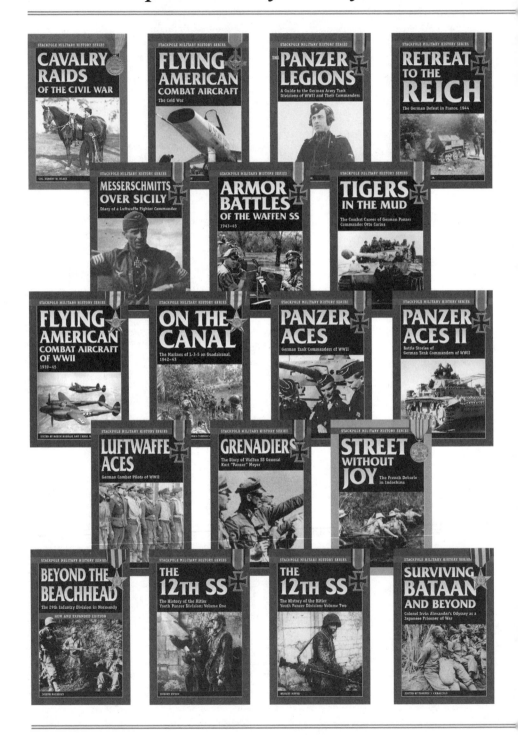

Real battles. Real soldiers. Real stories.

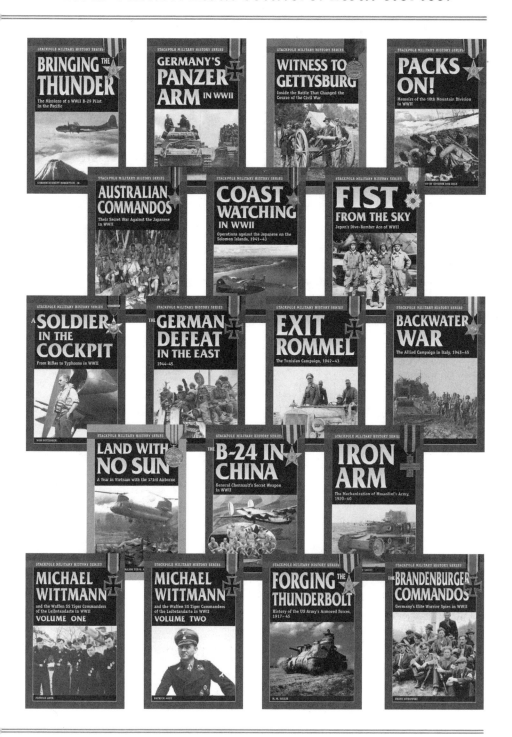

Stackpole Military History Series

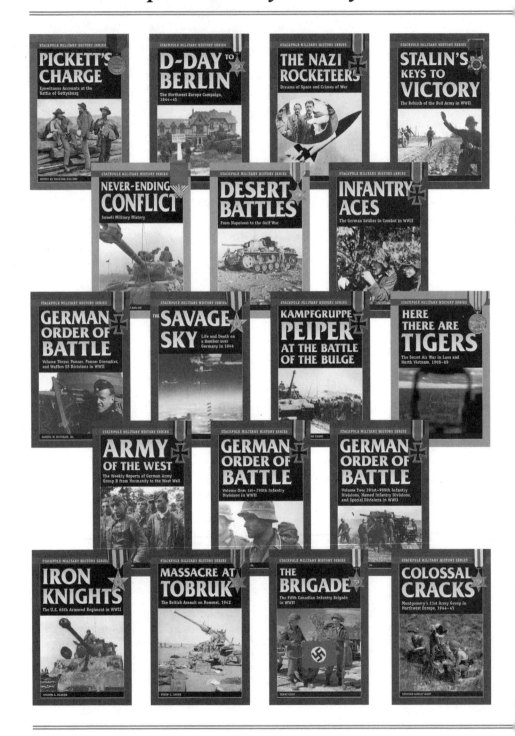

Real battles. Real soldiers. Real stories.

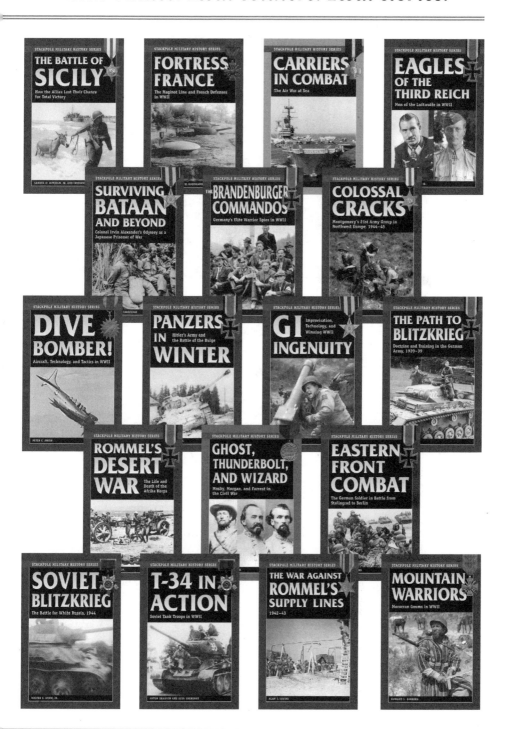

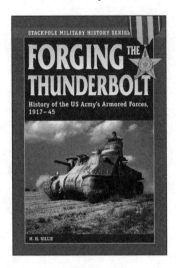

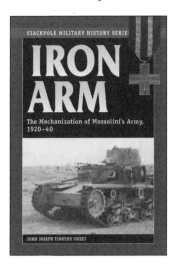

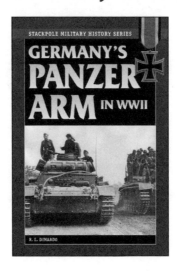

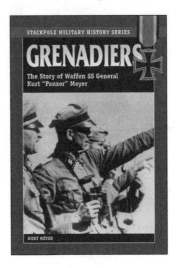

Stackpole Military History Series

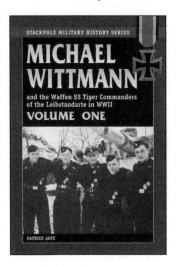

MICHAEL WITTMANN AND THE WAFFEN SS TIGER COMMANDERS OF THE LEIBSTANDARTE IN WORLD WAR II
VOLUME ONE

Patrick Agte

By far the most famous tank commander on any side in
World War II, German Tiger ace Michael Wittmann destroyed 138
enemy tanks and 132 anti-tank guns in a career that embodies the
panzer legend: meticulous in planning, lethal in execution, and
always cool under fire. Most of those kills came in the snow and mud
of the Eastern Front, where Wittmann and the Leibstandarte's
armored company spent more than a year in 1943–44 battling the
Soviets at places like Kharkov, Kursk, and the Cherkassy Pocket.

$19.95 • Paperback • 6 x 9 • 432 pages • 383 photos • 19 maps • 10 charts

WWW.STACKPOLEBOOKS.COM
1-800-732-3669

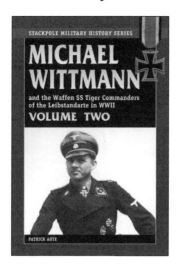

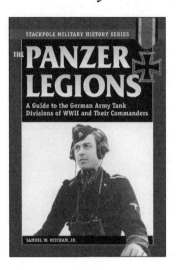

Stackpole Military History Series

ARMOR BATTLES
OF THE WAFFEN-SS
1943–45
Will Fey, translated by Henri Henschler

The Waffen-SS were considered the elite of the
German armed forces in the Second World War and
were involved in almost continuous combat. From
the sweeping tank battle of Kursk on the Russian
front to the bitter fighting among the hedgerows
of Normandy and the offensive in the Ardennes,
these men and their tanks made history.

$19.95 • Paperback • 6 x 9 • 384 pages
32 photos • 15 drawings • 4 maps

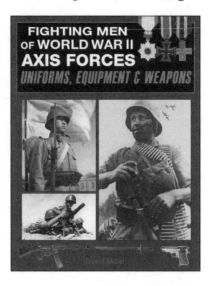